MEMOS FROM THE BESIEGED CITY

Cultural Memory

in

the

Present

Mieke Bal and Hent de Vries, Editors

MEMOS FROM THE BESIEGED CITY

Lifelines for Cultural Sustainability

Djelal Kadir

STANFORD UNIVERSITY PRESS
STANFORD, CALIFORNIA

Stanford University Press
Stanford, California

©2011 by the Board of Trustees of the Leland Stanford Junior University. All rights reserved.

No part of this book may be reproduced or transmitted in any form or by any means, electronic or mechanical, including photocopying and recording, or in any information storage or retrieval system without the prior written permission of Stanford University Press.

Printed in the United States of America on acid-free, archival-quality paper

Library of Congress Cataloging-in-Publication Data

Kadir, Djelal.
 Memos from the besieged city : lifelines for cultural sustainability / Djelal Kadir.
  p. cm. -- (Cultural memory in the present)
 Includes bibliographical references and index.
 ISBN 978-0-8047-7049-1 (cloth : alk. paper) -- ISBN 978-0-8047-7050-7 (pbk. : alk. paper)
 1. Comparative literature. 2. Literature--History and criticism. I. Title. II. Series: Cultural memory in the present. PN871.K24 2011
 809--dc22

2010015071

Typeset by Bruce Lundquist in 11/13.5 Adobe Garamond

They graciously gave me the inferior role of chronicler
I record—I don't know for whom—the history of the siege
—ZBIGNIEW HERBERT,
"REPORT FROM THE BESIEGED CITY" (1982)

Contents

Acknowledgments   xi

Introduction
Comparative Touchstones of Literature   1

1. Auerbach's Scar
    I. Ancestral Antiphony: Autolycus/Abraham   19
    II. The Comparatist Mirror   31

2. The Siege of Baghdad: Rashiduddin Fazlullah, Orhan Pamuk, and the Commissions of History
    I. History's Rhyme   41
    II. Narrative's Edge   46
    III. Vanishing Point   51
    IV. Rhyming History: The Baghdadization of America   56
    V. Frank Perspective   60

3. Of Learned Ignorance: Nicholas of Cusa and Cardinal Spaces of Culture
    I. Space-Time-Culture   64
    II. Concentric Deviations, Elliptic Orthodoxies   70
    III. Ignorance by Degrees: Identity and Equivalence   74

4. Memories of the Future: Giordano Bruno Remembers Us
    I. Remembering Mnemosyne   84
    II. Culture and Memory   89
    III. Memory, Countermemory   100

5. A Carceral Archive and the Culture of Conspiracy: Fray José Servando Teresa de Mier Noriega y Guerra, Enlightenment's Contestant
    I. Culture, Conspiracy, and the Value of X   108
    II. Divertimento: Since Time Immemorial   119
    III. Philology's Hearth, Conspiracy's Home   121

    IV. Truth Mission as Reinscription, Narrative Plot as
        Cultural Conspiracy   125
    V. Compensatory Gestures: From Imperial Monarchy to
        Republican Anarchy   127
    VI. Epistemania and the Cloak of Invisibility   130

6. **The Arts of Mitigation, the Garden in the Barbarian: Zbigniew Herbert**
    I. "Oracular Rockings"   134
    II. Unbridled Torrent   141
    III. The Poetics of Mitigation   148
    IV. The Delicate Art of Political Assuagement   152
    V. The Trials of Poetry   154

7. **The Labors of Cassandra: Arendt in Jerusalem**
    I. The Trials of Posterity   158
    II. Cassandra and the Poets: Goodness Beyond Virtue,
        Wickedness Beyond Vice   172

8. **The People's Republic and the Republic of Letters: The Alarming Gao Xingjian**
    I. The State of the National Subject   177
    II. The Fugitive Pronoun: A Peripatetic Mirror   184

9. **Memo from the Next Millennium: A Coda for Calvino**
    I. On Perseus's Shield   194
    II. Consistency   197

Epilogue
The Inventions of Comparative Literature: A Minute on Method
    I. Defining Figures   204
    II. Trivium, Tradition, Translation: Survival   209
    III. Beyond Metanarrative: Conversation   214
    IV. Memorandum of Understanding   217

Notes   221
Bibliography   249
Index   263

Acknowledgments

We are always in the middle of a conversation. And the colloquy with our *phanes* and their ghosts takes on meaning and immediacy through the ongoing dialogue with our living and enlivening interlocutors. I count myself immensely fortunate to have had the benefit of continuing exchange with colleagues from a number of institutional contexts, where the engagement of scholarly and pedagogical obligations to literature and its cultures have made my own professional calling infinitely richer and more rewarding. The present book is the fruit of these conversations, though I take sole responsibility for any of its shortcomings. I am particularly grateful to my colleagues and fellow board members at the Stockholm Collegium of World Literary History; Synapsis: The European School of Comparative Studies; the American Comparative Literature Association; the International American Studies Association; the International School of Theory in the Humanities; and to my colleagues on the Standing Committee on Literary Theory of the International Comparative Literature Association. I am especially grateful to my colleagues and students in the Department of Comparative Literature at Pennsylvania State University, and the library staffs of my own university and of numerous other institutions around the world for their diligent support of my endeavors, whose arcane nature at times amused them and troubled their routines. My coeditors on the *Longman Anthology of World Literature* have been, and continue to be, an endless source of encouragement, as are my coauthors on the ongoing multivolume *Literature: A World History* project under the aegis of the Stockholm Collegium. I have benefited greatly from the professional synergy and human solidarity between my own solitary efforts and the collective labors of these communal projects.

The hospitality of a number of colleagues and institutions gave me the opportunity to rehearse early versions, or segments, of a number of

xii   *Acknowledgments*

the chapters in this book. I am grateful in this regard to Franco Moretti and the Stanford Center for the Study of the Novel; Rita Copeland, Asma Al-Naser, and their colleagues in the Comparative Literature Program and the Kelly Writers House, University of Pennsylvania; K. David Jackson and the Yale University Council on Latin American Studies; Donald E. Pease and Silvia Spitta, Dartmouth College; Lois Parkinson Zamora, University of Houston; Linda Hutcheon and the Canadian Federation of Learned Societies; Talat Halman, Bilkent University, Ankara; Paul Giles, Rothermere Institute, University of Oxford; Stephanos Stephanides, University of Cyprus; Ayhan Bilsel and Lorraina Pinnell, Eastern Mediterranean University; Remo Ceserani, University of Bologna; Donatella Izzo, Universitá degli Studi di Napoli l'Orientale; Marianne Marroum, Kenneth Seigneurie, Vahid Behmardi, and Samira Aghacy, Lebanese American University, Beirut; Manuel Broncano, Cristina Garrigos, and María José Alvarez Maurín, University of León, Spain; Dario Villanueva and Constante González, University of Santiago de Compostela; Felix Martín and Jaime de Salas, Universidad Complutense, Madrid; Gunilla Lindberg-Wada, University of Stockholm; Eliana Avila, Universidade Federal de Santa Catarina, Brazil; As'ad Khairallah, Patrick McGreevy, Sirene Harb, and Maher Jarrar, American University of Beirut; Anders Pettersson, Umea University, Sweden; Anthony J. Tamburri, Calandra Italian American Institute, New York; Peter Caravetta, Stony Brook University, New York; Luiza Franco Moreira, Department of Comparative Literature, Binghamton University, New York; Zhang Longxi, City University of Hong Kong; Bo Utas, Uppsala University, Sweden; Susana Araujo, Helena Buescu, João Fereriga Duarte, and Angela Fernandes, University of Lisbon; Ellen Sapega and Bala Venkat Mani, Institute for Research in the Humanities, University of Wisconsin, Madison.

An itinerant in a peripatetic discipline whose métier consists in traversing boarders and disciplinary frontiers, my fellow travelers have been many and their aid immeasurable. Since there are many and each, I suspect, has a better idea than I do as to how far I might have strayed were it not for their guidance, now deliberate, at times inadvertent, I shall simply list them. I am confident they know where and how our paths crossed and can appreciate the measure of my gratitude: Hülya Adak-Cihangiroglu, Sergia

Adamo, Emily Apter, Susan Bassnette, Sandra L. Berman, Bella Brodzki, Shuang Chen, John M. Coetzee, Jonathan Culler, Theo D'haen, David Damrosch, Osman Deniztekin, Enrique Dussel, Rachid El-Daif, Nergis Ertürk, Carlos Fuentes, Talat Halman, Eric Hayot, Fred Gardaphe, Wlad Godzich, Ramón Gutierrez, Ursula Heise, Hermann Herlinghaus, Eileen Julien, Martina Kolb, Kader Konuk, Brian Lennon, Françoise Lionnet, Sophia A. McClennen, Allen Mandelbaum, Giorgio Mariani, Simona Micali, Aamir Mufti, Marta Sofia López Rodríguez, Reingard Nethersole, Julio Ortega, Orhan Pamuk, Jale Parla, Christopher Prendergast, Martin Puchner, Basem Ra'ad, Bruce Robbins, Gonzalo Rubio, Haun Saussy, Samira Sayeh, Elzbieta Sklodowska, Gayatri C. Spivak, Harish Trivedi, Jing Tsu, Dominique Vaugeois, Robert Weninger, Hayden White.

A series of graduate research assistants in my home department over the years have aided me immensely with new technologies and archival pursuits: Barbara Alfano, Sara Scott Armengot, Beyza Atmaca, Germán Campos-Muñoz, William Castro, Nesrine Chahine, Oscar Fernández, Mariano Humeniuk, Ipek Kismet, María Luján Tubio, Nicole Sparling, Kahori Tateishi, Lori Ween, Quentin Youngberg. I am grateful to each and wish them well as they successfully pursue their own academic and scholarly careers, hopefully, to discover through their own students, as I have through them, how pertinent seemingly impertinent questions can be.

On matters equine, where in the agon between life and death horsesense aligns with the former, as we see in Chapter 6, I am grateful to my anthropology colleagues Alan Walker and Pat Shipman, who read and commented on my treatment of equine biology in my Herbert chapter, and to my equestrian friends Kirsten Jepp and Anthony Warren of Halfmoon Creek Farm in central Pennsylvania for the opportunity to continue that most salutary of conversations for one engaged in scholarly activity—a conversation with a horse. I also salute the indomitable *butteri* and my fellow-academicians of the Accademia di Monta da Lavoro and their perennial labors in the rites of the centuries-old equine transhumance through the heart of the Italian peninsula.

As always, I am grateful to my most constant interlocutor Juana Celia Djelal, as well as to our daughter Aixé and her husband Matthew Proctor for their understanding, incorrigible sense of humor, and unflagging support.

My gratitude to my editor at Stanford University Press, Emily-Jane Cohen, is more than pro forma. I am grateful for her intelligent and sensitive reading of the manuscript and for her professional efficiency. The press's editorial assistant Sarah Crane Newman has been most helpful in the preparation of the final copy. The comments from the press readers, self-identified and anonymous, have helped me reframe the book most effectively. I am truly appreciative of their exemplary commitment and scholarly generosity.

MEMOS FROM THE BESIEGED CITY

Introduction

COMPARATIVE TOUCHSTONES OF LITERATURE

> To articulate the past historically . . . means to seize hold of a memory as it flashes up at a moment of danger. . . . The danger affects both the content of the tradition and its receivers. The same threat hangs over both: that of becoming a tool of the ruling classes. In every era the attempt must be made anew to wrest tradition away from a conformism that is about to overpower it.
> —Walter Benjamin, *Theses on the Philosophy of History*, VI (1940)

> This is more than an academic matter.
> —Bella Brodzki, *Can These Bones Live?*

Memory intensifies when cultures that memory made possible come under siege. Cultural memory and cultural literacy have always been coeval. Literature, an integral part of this cultural history, is a line of stories. Comparative reading and teaching draw the lines of literature into a force field. The energies of that field coalesce into a series of problems. These problems aggregate into a set of disciplinary practices called comparative literature. This book explores and illustrates a number of these practices. It does so by tracing a genealogy of the discipline through certain defining precedents that inform its current institutional protocols. Each of the interconnected chapters is devoted to a particular set of problems. Historically focused by means of a number of predecessors and their legacies, each chapter illustrates a significant facet of a multifaceted discipline: the subject (Chapter 1); world history and world literature (Chapter 2);

cultural space and identity (Chapter 3); memory, culture, and memory management (Chapter 4); orthodoxy, consensus, and conspiracy (Chapter 5); poetics and ekphrasis (Chapter 6); ethics (Chapter 7); literature, the nation, and the state (Chapter 8); metadiscourse and spectralization (Chapter 9). Each of these sets of problems at the forefront of today's concerns in the discipline of comparative literature is addressed through a memo to key figures who serve as touchstones for our literacy and as keystones for the sustainability of our cultural edifice. These figures range in time from the thirteenth century to the present period: Rashiduddin Fazlullah (1247–1318), Nicholas of Cusa (1401–64), Giordano Bruno (1548–1600), Fray Servando Teresa de Mier (1763–1827), Erich Auerbach (1892–1957), Hannah Arendt (1906–75), Zbigniew Herbert (1924–98), Italo Calvino (1923–85), Gao Xingjian (b. 1940), Orhan Pamuk (b. 1952).

The disciplinary processes described here occur regularly at certain points in time and in highly diverse spaces, where the multiple worlds of literatures, stories, and the network of their intersections converge. This convergence is the encounter of textuality (written, oral, visual, cognitive) and the world humans happen to inhabit at a given time. As maximal convergence this is called world literature. Comparative literature traces the lines of this process, thus lending the diversity of the world's literatures a dimension of mutual commensurability. This intercession gives the worlds of literature their legibility, cogency, and comprehensibility. In this process, comparative literature focuses primarily on the intersection of story lines whose conjunctions and disjunctions form the intricate web of literatures, their stories, and the memory of their genesis or their colligated histories.

Comparative literature engages particular literary traditions with an eye to discerning what texts and literatures mean beyond themselves and their individual specificity. This is to say that comparative literature is interested principally in what literatures signify in a larger arena than themselves, without neglecting the mechanics or modes of their situational signification. Thus, the explications of comparative literature are not strictly textual. They are, perforce, contextual, transhistorical, and extraterritorial. Traditional modes of exegesis, what the French call *explication de texte*, are not neglected, especially in instances of literature where language is subjected to its most intense forms of condensation, as is the case with poetry, as demonstrated in Chapter 6 of this book, devoted to the reading of poetry, particularly poetry in or on translation. Even in the context of poetic close reading, however, as the poet himself, in this case the Polish poet Zbigniew Herbert, illustrates, the focus is on the repercussions of the poem beyond itself, whether as translation of another mode of artistic representation, as literary afterlife in another language, or as political allegory.

These intersections, then, are the junctures we could call the way stations of comparative literature. Their discernment is traceable to certain practices of remembering, reading, and teaching, revisited, explored, and illustrated in the chapters that follow. This book itself is an integral part of the processes described here. As practice at one of comparative literature's way stations, the present endeavor figures as an instance of participation in, rather than as presumptively dispassionate objectification of, its subject matter. In this sense, like all comparative engagements, my task is, perforce, (self-)consciously performative. As a brief for comparative literature, this book and its memos serve as a reminder of and report to certain key predecessors, or those whom we would take as predecessors, in the history of the field and its formative genealogical lines. These, then, are memos to and on defining precursors whose legacies and their relevance continue to inform the field practices and the disciplinary culture that perpetuate their inheritance. Foremost in these legacies, and consistent with their lessons, is the necessity of alertness to history and to the historical moment in which one happens to live while carrying out this process.

Such alertness has its perils. It is no less perilous than inattentiveness to the time and place one happens to occupy. In this wakefulness to our life-world, we cannot escape the fact that *occupation*, as noun or in the infinitive *to occupy*, is now a loaded term. Recent history bedevils the word, just as it did for Walter Benjamin during a historical time he referred to as "a moment of danger."[1] And as Benjamin's sixth thesis on history, partially cited here in the epigraph, suggests, in occupying one's historical time and place one is occupied by that historical moment even more—already preoccupied and inevitably defined by it in turn. Historiography has intermittently felt the acute effects of this inevitability. And, if there is a discipline other than history that is more keenly aware of this predicament, it is likely to be that of comparative literature. This is because comparative literature is by definition the disciplinary place in between—between literatures, cultures, histories, times, places, and their memory. In a strong etymological sense, any *intelligent* reading has something of the comparative in it, with "intelligence," yet another perversely degraded term at this historical moment, rooted in the Latin etymons of *inter-legere* or "reading between." As the perennial third term between two or more comparables, then, comparative literature is constantly negotiating a viable position for itself, often between contending ideologies and contentious identities, and between the historical epochs that correspond to them. In this sense, comparative literature is inevitably local and temporal, no matter how distant its objects of reading and writing. More accurately, it is strongly locative, as grammarians of inflected languages would have it.

Thus, comparative literature, while enmeshed in the world, is distinctly marked by an extemporized status as an outsider, or as alterity to the times, the terms, or the parties it mediates. From that eccentric mobile position, it inflects, in turn, every here and now in which it operates as disciplinary discourse and analytical instrument. Comparative literature's locative position, then, traditionally referred to as a *tertium comparationis*—the third term of comparison—occupies a nomadic locus that is a translocal and itinerant articulation between or among other positions or locations. Its focus—searching, epistemic, analytical—is usually trained on a direction that mythology's two-faced Janus does not countenance. Literary masters such as the amateur philologist and polyglot Brazilian novelist João Guimarães Rosa dramatize this third dimension as "the third bank of the river."[2] Certain literary theorists such as Homi K. Bhaba telegraph it as the "Third Space."[3] As a result of this condition, the discourse of the discipline is preoccupied just as often with charting its own historical and epistemic place as a subject as it is occupied by the analytical investigation of its disciplinary objects. This is most acutely the case at critical junctures of history, which, for the critical vocation of comparative literature, would include all historical points in the chronically crisis-prone peripety of human cultures.

Though some might be inclined to view our own present as especially crisis-bound, it is unlikely that our historical moment is exceptional in this regard. Ours differs incidentally from other historical eras, hence the aleatory nature of the discipline's current self-definitions and the peculiar language of our self-characterizations as comparatists. These characterizations are just as likely to be symptoms of our contingencies as they might accurately portray the actual practices of our vocation as comparatists. Our lexicons and notional constructs about the field, then, could well speak as much of us as they speak for us. This is why our differentiations among diverse modes of praxes in the discipline are doubly articulate—they define us symptomatically by virtue of what we claim to be or claim to be doing, as much as they identify us by what we actually do. Any equivalence between these two defining modes is a contested function of a politics of identity, a cultural politics whose discernments date from the philosophical cavilations and cross-cultural labors of Nicholas of Cusa at the historic threshold between the periods we call medieval and the Renaissance, as we shall see in Chapter 3. Identity—individual, disciplinary, or cultural—then, has been recognized as a historical and social construct, rather than as being equal to any absolute reality, to what the philosophers call an apodictic truth, for much longer than our own cultural politics' felt urgency about this realization in the latter part of the last century. This is not to say that the culturally constructed or politically staged identities are not possessed of a reality—and a strongly consequential one at that. But the likelihood that this reality will actually correspond to whatever is deemed to be real outside of those constructs is problematic at best. This is the slippery ground between local and locative reality and its irrepressible universal ambitions that comparative literature has to negotiate. And this is why a quotient of self-irony and a margin of relative doubt, as opposed to absolute self-conviction, are indispensable in our own self-characterizations as comparatists.

Such epistemological decenteredness and skepticism characterize all the figures addressed by the memos in this book. Their legacy inexorably inflects our present practices, and these memos are intended as a way of informing those ancestors who continue to inform our disciplinary praxes and theoretical speculations. And while considered healthy in the abstract, such reflective self-questioning of disciplinary formations and discursive jurisdictions are more likely to be suspiciously tolerated, and even more often targeted by self-serving institutional interests, triumphalist cultural politics, and the commandeered academic cadres that sustain a status quo in a literalist public sphere that is invariably spooked by any self-reflection and its defining shadows. Self-privileging centeredness and unreflective literalism are the preferred fulcrums that institutions tend to safeguard zealously, and any self-decentering discourse is considered an opportune target and is viewed askance as a potential contaminant that threatens the privileged center and firm footing of the institutions' cultural capital—idealistic and symbolic, or materialistic and vile, or both.

It is in the problematic spirit of this sentience, this (self-)consciousness of being present in this here and now, that I offer these memos to/through a number of historical figures who continue to challenge the field of comparative literature and its practices across a wide and interlinked territory of the globe. By noting this continuity across time and geography I do not wish to imply that the field is uniform, universal, level, unhistorical, undifferentiated; or that its claims—tendentious, more often than not—are incontrovertible. Nor do I mean to set my own practice incommensurately apart from the praxes of all other comparatists.

If, as I believe to be the case, the present we occupy (pre)occupies us just as much, self-differential claims are bound to be no less a symptom of preemptive anxiety as they would be delusional if taken to be absolute. Such conviction would certainly be the greatest "moment of danger," in Benjamin's terms cited in the epigraph above, as well as in the context of Haun Saussy's cautionary diagnosis of comparative literature's parlous success in having "won its battles" and in "our conclusions hav[ing] become other people's assumptions."[4]

Because it occupies a happenstance present, then, comparative literature's "here . . . today" with all its historical contingencies, is perpetually in "a moment of danger," as Walter Benjamin never stops reminding us. These memos comprise an attempt at historical articulation of this present to a number of defining figures of the tradition of comparative literature, an articulation made perennially necessary by history, especially when danger threatens as ominously as it does at the beginning of this century. What is recalled here, like the act of recalling itself, constitutes what one scholar of memory and crisis characterizes as "a site and source of cultural disquiet."[5] We do well, then, to remember that our disquieting present is no less "under siege" than the historical epochs of the key precursors of the discipline addressed here. Their attempts to articulate historically the traditions they sought to wrest from conformity for the sake of posterity were no less a cultural self-salvaging operation than the one described by Walter Benjamin. Like Benjamin, all of these figures engaged tradition in their respective modes of disconformity. Most of them paid the ultimate price, as did Benjamin himself. Their bones live in us, to paraphrase Bella Brodzki's recent book title, and, as she notes, "this is more than an academic matter."[6] It certainly was not "merely academic" for the addressees of these memos. It is no different for us. Their practice of historical articulation was no scholastic rummaging in the archive or in humanity's ossuary, just as it is not so for us, as Brodzki's own performative intervention eloquently demonstrates.[7] It was certainly not necromancy, just as today's comparative literature is no postmortem autopsy, as Gayatri Spivak, who declares the "death of a discipline" and our obligation to resuscitate it, Lazarus-like, would have it.[8]

I take the panoply of descriptors for today's comparative literature, then, to be as predictably inevitable in their historical conditioning as the characterizations of the discipline have always been. Ours are contingent variations inflected by the locative urgency of the peculiar sort of barbarism that, in Walter Benjamin's terms, circumscribes and defines civilizations at yet another critical juncture in the leaps and lapses of human history. In this sense, there is something wholly consonant between our current array of descriptors for the present practices of comparative literature and the tradition of self-characterization in the ancestral discourses we have inherited—*distant, close, translational, worldly, planetary, republican, global, ekphrastic, identitarian, imperial, hegemonic, postcolonial, iconoclastic, emancipatory, transnational, transcultural*. What distinguishes our present self-defining lexicon might well be our limited memory, willful or otherwise, of its genealogy. Our philological neglect is matched by a certain historical amnesia that does indeed turn the present into presentism rather than a way station on a lurching line of narrative continuity. Alembicated in the crucible of romanticism's elective affinities and of our modernity's penchant for self-succeeding discontinuities, we tend toward the delusion of viewing all kinship and affiliation as voluntaristic association sanctioned by our willed consent and mutual consensus. And so, like certain historians who overlook the difference between will and vitality, we have often forgotten that we are as much the product of history as the history we produce is of our own making. Rather than this amnesiac capitulation to the present and its solipsisms, the memos gathered here are intended as an anamnesic articulation, a re-membering, or recalling and reconnecting, of historical temporality to the life-world of our intellectual labor and its (re)productive practices.

Thus, in these memorial articulations the linkages that bind the diverse figures convoked in this book do not simply comprise an associative mode of comparative literature but an inexorably filial continuity, and an urgent one at that, as has been perennially the case, according to Benjamin. These are the precarious lines of filiation referred to in the subtitle of this book as the "lifelines for cultural sustainability." They are the narrative threads that connect the often-fraught way stations of the historical moments articulated in the ligatures attempted here. These lines run through our own labors of articulation and, in the process, find their points of intersection as they converge in and pass through us. As defining primal scenes of comparative literature, these junctures may not always lie within the conventional parameters the discipline has traditionally identified as its originary sites. However, as we are discovering, and as I hope the range and scope of this book illustrate, the genealogical locations of comparative literature extend much farther in geography and further back in time than commonplace institutional accounts and more recent pedagogical claims have designated. There is something otiose in such precise self-certainty that would define comparative literature's primal scene as someone's inspired invention on a particular day, at a particular hour,[9] or as a "Greenwich Meridian" by whose compass the value of the literatures we study find their direction and worth.[10]

I am urging greater alertness and less certainty. To be alert to the lines of sustainability retraced in these memos is to be "on line" in a more complex sense than being plugged into the hyperlinks of one's circumscribed academicist network, or bound by the solipsistic links of one's vested personal calculus and self-centering global positioning system. Our connection to a broader set of lifelines, broader in time and geography as I seek to demonstrate here, is a linkage to the fraught ledger of cultural history and its defining vicissitudes beyond the immediate perimeters of our present academic commonplaces.

I pick up these threads at a key intersection—the pedagogical threshold whose daily crossing introduces us into the conversation already long underway. Our anamnesic performance—this constellation of memos—traces a roadmap for entry into and passage through what we have traditionally understood, and what we currently understand, by comparative literature. Traced here is a genealogy of the discipline as it is critically informed by such currently dominant notions, notions that Erich Auerbach had termed *Ansatzpunkte*,[11] defineable as axiomatic hypotheses and points of departure from which radiate certain interpretive modes of understanding: *decenteredness, itinerancy, subject agency, historiography, identity and cultural politics, memory, imperial revanchism, ekphrastic intertextuality, the ethics of poetic justice, statist and culturalist republicanism, and metanarrative indirection.* These are defining elements that mark our disciplinary practices today, even when we neglect their philological, which is to say, political, morphologies. They are variously taken up in these memos, with each chapter reflecting, and reflecting on, a facet of the comparatist prism defined by these concepts. The treatment of these features illustrates the multifaceted vocation of comparative literature as it reflects, refracts, and is defined by the legacy of the ancestral figures that continue to serve as disciplinary touchstones. This is not a narrative of a linear continuity, necessarily, but the record of certain intersections where the inheritance of these precursors and our current notions and practices crisscross, diverge, and transform each other en route.

What is the nature of *the subject* of comparative literature as it is understood and practiced today? This question is explored in Chapter 1. By *subject* here I mean the historic embodiments of the field as an academic subject of study and the personification of the discipline by a human subject—Erich Auerbach—whose persona and personal history we are given to identify, for a number of reasons we shall be examining, as paragon and inheritance of contemporary comparative literature. At the heart of this chapter's argument is the demonstrable history that, though Auerbach is currently the most frequently mentioned protagonist of the field's prosopopoeia, Auerbach effaces himself, directly and through the spectral indirection of Montaigne, whom he takes as mirror—for himself and for his professional vocation. In this paradoxical self-positioning—defensive, tactically self-mitigating, survivalist, historically cast out—the principal does not escape the vicissitudes of history—political, professional, academic, or philological. His paradoxical predicament might well be what inclines many comparatists to see him as posterity's emblem and inheritance for today's practitioners of comparative literature, obliged to constantly negotiate their own precarious institutional position, made even more perilous by the role envisioned for the discipline as gadfly to more institutionally grounded national literatures and their critical discourses. As one of our contemporary practitioners, Franco Moretti, aptly phrases it, "The point is that there is no other justification for the study of world literature (and for the existence of departments of comparative literature) but this: to be a thorn in the side, a permanent intellectual challenge to national literatures—especially the local literature. If comparative literature is not this, it's nothing."[12]

It is this lot, or curse, that leads us to harken to the precursors for the discipline that we identify here. Most often, this is not a role comparatists choose, unless theirs is nothing but a privileged academic elective, just as they do not elect their exilic dislocations and the vicissitudes of their displacement. And the occasional trivialization of the comparatist's historical fate as a "fetish" only speaks of a certain academic glibness that inadvertently borders on the inhumane.[13]

What might we learn from the history of the siege of a city that has been literally besieged perhaps more repeatedly than any other? As we shall see (Chapter 2), the most remarked siege of Baghdad—that of 1258—was neither unique nor the first. It would not be the last either, as most recent history tragically demonstrates. Of particular significance for comparative literature are the discursive consequences of the 1258 siege of Baghdad by the Mongol Khan Hülagü. It proved a momentous encounter between the world and textuality. What issued from that event is the text of a self-described "world history" redacted by a court chronicler not long after the siege. The author, Rashiduddin Fazlullah, was commissioned to compose this history between the years 1300 and 1311 by Ghazan Khan, Hülagü's great-grandson and successor. Like the primal work of historiography in the Hellenic Mediterranean—Herodotus's *Histories* (composed between 450–430 B.C.)—Rashiduddin Fazlullah's *Jami 'u't-tawarikh* (History of the World) offers a primal scene for a decentered comparative textuality that sets yet another precedent for the itinerant, exilic, and transcultural genealogy of what would emerge as the transdiscursive discipline of literature. In fact, there is a certain spectral echo between the situation of Herodotus—a translocated Dorian writing in Ionian Greek, who was born in Halicarnassus, a city under Persian rule, and exiled to Thurii, which is in present-day Italy but then was one of the western-most Greek colonies near the end of the earth—and Rashiduddin, a Persian chronicler at the Mongol court in Baghdad who rose to the position of vizier and would meet his untimely death at the hands of the executioner of the same dynasty he immortalized through his history. Rashiduddin wrote his history of the world invoking the Persian epic poet Fardowsi (Firdawsi, as he spells it), even as Herodotus wrote his with a keen awareness of Homer, whom he invokes at the beginning of his opus.[14]

The Baghdad of the thirteenth to fourteenth centuries radiates outward as a defining locus no less than the Baghdad of the first decade of the twenty-first century has proved, now in every sense of the term, a "radioactive" pivotal site that defines, yet again, the culture and history of its invaders. As we shall see, Baghdad inflects with historic connotations the notions of world, literature, and what we understand by "comparative." There is a direct textual line from Rashiduddin's Baghdad to Istanbul that converts the former Ottoman capital on the threshold between Asia and Europe into yet another decentered radial point of comparatism, an axis through which passes the refugee Erich Auerbach on his way to America, and passed before him, in a previous avatar of the city as Constantinopolis, Nicholas of Cusa in his diplomatic and philosophical efforts to mediate between East and West.

What precedents exist for our explorations of difference, identity, and coexisting ethno-cultural pluralities (Chapter 3)? These topics that so urgently concern the discipline of comparative literature and the study of cultures today preoccupied no less intensely the Persian Rashiduddin in Baghdad and, before him, the itinerant Herodotus from the Persian colony of the Hellenic city of Halicarnassus. These decentered identities that find their textual rehearsals as history in dialogue with identity-forming literary epics will find their belated discursive formations in disciplines such as comparative literature and in the warped politics of what the twentieth century came to call multiculturalism. The spatial trajectory of these pluralities has been as contested as their narrative formulations have been subjects of controversy through historical time. The space of culture, what latter-day critical discourse would dub "territoriality," has been particularly problematic in this trajectory. One of the first authors to deal with that spatial cartography of culture as philosophical problem, as discursive metaphor, and as ideologically saturated topography in early modernity was Nicholas of Cusa. From Cusa we learn that cultural identity and the location of culture occupy a negative space. Cusa also teaches us, as much by argument as by practical example, that space takes on substantive historical meaning as it is traversed.

Identity and culture have been perennial touchstones for comparative literature; the discipline has conventionally traced this discursive genealogy from the eighteenth century (re)birth of ethnography, modern philology, and what Herder, a key link in this genealogy, called "radical difference." However, differential questions of equivalence and identity, so crucial to the field and protocols of comparative literature, have a much earlier history than the eighteenth-century European Enlightenment. The radial lines of that history traverse the archipelago, cultural and topographic, through which Herodotus sailed in his time and Cusa navigated in his philosophical explorations and ambassadorial itinerary in his attempts to articulate, to connect to each other, what the governing ideologies of his historical moment deemed incommensurable worlds of Christianity's East and West.

From that experience, we have inherited the awareness that, like space and knowledge (the *docta ignorantia* of Cusa), identity is a negative value. It is nonequivalence, a differential compromise, a forged and adjudicated construct that evaded Cusa's own devoted efforts in shuttle diplomacy and ideological negotiation between East and West, specifically in the Council of Florence of 1439. From that experience, simultaneous with composing his best-known work, Nicholas of Cusa has given us the prototype (what Auerbach called *Ansatz*), our modernity's point of departure, for negotiating the traversal of this negative space and the comparable (though, often incompatible) convergences that contend within it. He has done so through philosophical argument and by living example in his ambassadorial shuttling between Constantinopolis and Florence, between Byzantine patriarch and Roman pope—two processes he was carrying out simultaneously, one scholarly-philosophical, the other diplomatic-political. This could be most instructive to anyone attempting a translation of the academic into the worldly and in subjecting the world to the rigors of comparative analysis. It certainly injects into such seemingly anodyne notions as "world literature" an epistemic catalyst we have yet to appreciate fully.

What critical junctures in the history of memory make our own memos and our technologies of memory possible (Chapter 4)? The first decade of the twenty-first century was under the epochal aegis (some might say, under the hegemony) of the technologies of memory. What we have forgotten, and what comparative literature needs to keep reminding us about, is that this era's obsessive engagement with memory on an industrial and global scale has its technological, philosophical, ideological, and political precedents in a long tradition. That legacy is most exemplarily embodied in the fate of Giordano Bruno, who was burned at the stake by the church of the Counter-Reformation, an act justified by its arts of divinely sanctioned memory supervision, reminiscent in uncanny ways of the arts of surveillance and technologies of official memory management in our own time. The Russian poet Mandelstam, who died a martyr's death in the era of Stalin, wants us to remember that Bruno may have not died in vain, as he says in the epigraph for Chapter 4.

Bruno's greatest gift to our poststructuralist discourse and its occluded authorial and political subjects may well be the key notion of imputability—the holding responsible of those subjects who do the signifying rather than overlooking the subject and stopping with the hermeneutics of indeterminate signification. Comparative literature gives us the analytical lens through which to scrutinize, forensically and hermeneutically, how the world is constructed and by whom—cybernetically, politically, ideologically, aesthetically, academically, virtually—through the technologies of memory, whether in museological constructions (New York, Venice, Bilbao, Abu Dhabi, or Buenos Aires) or in museological destructions (Baghdad, Jerusalem), or through gigabytes that render the world virtual and complicate the possibility of human virtue.

How does the itinerary of a figutive figure come to embody a pivotal moment that historically corresponds to the European inception of comparative literature as the modern discipline we have inherited (Chapter 5)? The trajectory of Fray Servando, the most peripatetic precursor among all the itinerant figures addressed by these memos, straddles the threshold between the epistemic regimes of the ancient and the modern, as our historiographic conventions are wont to narrate them. In his fugitive itinerancy, Fray Servando bridges not only ideological regimes ancient and modern but also the geographical Old World and New World. In doing so, he carries the thread of a cultural narrative from the topological geometry of Nicholas of Cusa and the mnemonic technologies of Giordano Bruno through the intersections of imperial politics and technologies of reading that would define themselves as comparative and correlative, rather than incommensurable and absolute.

Straddling historical absolutisms—of the Counter-Reformation and of the Enlightenment—the nomadic Fray Servando serves as our conduit in decentered discourse and shifting identities, often literally in his impersonations and disguises for evading "the law." His imposed nomadism as outlaw, literally and metaphorically, serves as the most overt paradigm for the shiftlessness that will emerge as an indispensable trait of comparatism and as an often-neglected model for geographically defined epistemologies that govern what we would eventually call international American studies. His personal vicissitudes and their textual transformations adumbrate the fate of poets and poetry discussed in this book, such as Zbigniew Herbert, the predicament of ethicists such as Hannah Arendt, and the political/geographical nomadism of contemporary writers such as Gao Xingjian and Orhan Pamuk. It might be more than fortuitous that Fray Servando occupies the central chapter of our book. Present as a fugitive "undocumented alien" and an ardent interlocutor in the Paris salons of the late eighteenth century, where the notion of comparative literature as a modern discourse had its incipient rehearsals, Fray Servando, like Rashiduddin Fazlullah in Baghdad centuries before him, has been an unrecognized precursor whose complex precedent complicates the hitherto conventional cartography of comparative literature and its genealogical way stations.

What might poetry teach us about one of the key phenomena of comparative study that is integral to comparative literature: ekphrasis (Chapter 6)? The Greek term refers to the cross-representation of one world by another and the translation of the literary, musical, and visual arts into each other. Translational in the broadest and most intense senses of the term, the poetic and essayistic vocation of Zbigniew Herbert is an exemplary instance of countenancing the siege that accosts all of the figures in this book and the translation of that besieged predicament into a textual heterocosm. His *Report from the Besieged City*—the title of which is the source of this book's title—serves as a compelling example of salvaging civilization from the barbarity of political/ideological siege and turning the vicissitudes of that experience into a poetic praxis and a product of culture. Herbert's ekphrastic labors give expanded meaning to the notion of translation that so occupies the concerns of comparative study at this time. As we shall see, Herbert's ekphrastic achievement lends a political/social dimension to literature that illustrates, in turn, the inevitable worldliness of comparative discourse and of comparative world literature as a discipline.

How might comparative literature countenance the *ethics*—the justness of governing criteria—that inexorably emerge when one world becomes translated politically, literally, topographically, or figuratively, into another (Chapter 7)? The ethical dimension of comparative literature has been implicit in the life-world of its founders and practitioners, be it in the incipient worldism of fourteenth-century historiographers such as

Rashiduddin Fazlullah in his Baghdadi dislocation, or in vernacular poets such as his contemporary Dante in his exile from Florence. Though its disciplinary academic institutionalization at the beginning of the twentieth century coincided with a more positivist, formalist, and instrumentalist era, comparative literature has always been possessed of an ethical impulse, precisely because its métier consists in the juxtaposition of differing peoples and their divergent cultural practices held in counterpoint. In this dimension, comparative literature has found resonance in contemporary ethicists such as Martha Craven Nussbaum and her contrapuntal reflections on law and literature.[15]

Chapter 7, then, explores the dimension of ethics through Hannah Arendt, one of the most uncompromising voices of ethical discourse in the twentieth century. She is a sobering inheritance for us at the beginning of the twenty-first century, especially, where her most dreaded fears have become realized on a global scale. For the discipline of comparative literature, Arendt serves as a pivot between classical tragedy and lethal postmodern farce, between the gulags of twentieth-century Europe and the gulags of the new century that extend from the Caribbean New World of Fray Servando, through the "sacred heart" or holyland of the Old World, and into the Central Asia of Rashiduddin Fazlullah. As a student of the classical European canon and of nineteenth-century literatures, Arendt bridges philosophy and literary discourse, elucidating both, often with merciless clarity. Thus Arendt shows us how ethics and literature can interface productively for social and political relevance, especially when contemporary comparative literature is confronted with worldly realities that differ little in their inhumanity from those countenanced by Arendt herself in her life and in the literatures she studied. Her observations on the besieged city evince the clarity that extends from Dante and Rashiduddin through Cusa, Bruno, Servando, and Auerbach, down to Herbert and Gao. Arendt offers us not just a narrative thread on which to string these figures diachronically with positivist literalism. Her legacy is a perpetually synchronous light beam whose illuminations some comparatists often find disconcerting, and from whose principled elucidations they would rather avert their eyes.

What is the relationship between the state and the state of literature when the latter comes under the official supervision of the former (Chapter 8)? Like literature itself, scholars of comparative literature have rarely fared well when the public sphere is dominated by the state and civil society, along with civility, are officially and unofficially curtailed. The literature of the state, whether as republic of letters or the republic's political instrument, has had a mixed career since the foundational era of the national epic. The oppositional or contestatory nature of literary discourse historically has carried over to the critical iconoclasm of comparatist discourse *on* literature. Whether in classical epic or in tragedy, in devotional *auto de fé* or in modern and postmodern theater of the absurd, the people's republic and the republic of letters have often proved inimical to each other, though the struggle has often spurred literary production as contestation. Comparative literature has inevitably found itself caught between, with the comparatist often surviving in being turned out as refugee and displaced cosmopolitan.

Thus, comparative literature's practitioners have most often acquired their worldliness as the castoffs of their life-world, no less so than the seminal literary figures they most often study, from Ovid to Dante to any one of the figures featured in this book. The twentieth century, a century of mass demographic displacements and ideologically inspired relocations, is especially notorious in this regard. Chapter 8 examines the fraught relationship between the subject of the state and the subject of literature through the example of the first and, to date, only Nobel laureate from China. The response to Gao Xingjian's 2000 Nobel Prize for literature becomes illustrative of how the People's Republic echoes the Republic of Letters in problematic ways that decenter and exacerbate the complex filiations of the nation- and nationality-based precepts of comparative literature. The topic is of some urgency, especially, at the beginning of this new century when the public sphere as defined by the liberal discourse of critics such as Jürgen Habermas in the twentieth century has now been mercilessly privatized as fulcrum for global capital, giving the "besieged city" greater immediacy and more global ubiquity than ever.[16]

Chapter 9, a coda for Italo Calvino, is a response to the Cuban-born Italian writer's envoi to our millennium. There is something productively apposite between Calvino's oeuvre and the necessary indirection that defines the narrative of comparative literature as a metanarrative. Comparative literature's tale consists of figurative constructs that discourse on literary traditions, which are already figuratively constructed. A "memo" is the reminder of this relation between the figural and the figured, especially as rehearsed by a master narrator and mnemopoetic artificer like Italo Calvino. His *Memos for the Next Millennium* enjoins our millennial era to respond. His treatment of the literary tradition figures as a convocation to tradition's literate inheritors. I partake of Italo Calvino's preference for *memo* and *memos*, as reported by Esther Calvino, his wife, in her prefatory note to his *Six Memos for the Next Millennium*.[17] "Memo" does manifold work by capturing in shorthand the dual case—the verbal/participial and the substantive/nominal—of the Latin *memorandum*. In its versatility, the term becomes triune—to remember, to remind, and mnemonic prompt, or *aide memoire*.

I use *memo* and its plural in the multiplicity of these semantic nuances. The resourcefulness of the term is not merely semantic; it is also temporal and transformational. And, in this sense, what one of tradition's most suggestive technicians of memory, Giordano Bruno, teaches us is that a memo is not only a harkening to the past or a telling again in order to take us back. It is, as the precedent of Bruno and Calvino's envoi suggest, a reminder of and for the future, a telling in anticipation and a cue aiming us in the direction of a way station we have yet to reach—hence the title of Chapter 4, "Memories of the Future." Calvino's *Six Memos* overtly intend this mnemonic transmission into the future as reminder from the past of what we are to remember in the millennium to come, a place where, willy-nilly, we recently arrived and now "occupy."

In Calvino's essays and self-conscious narratives the comparatist is ghosted into posterity, rendered a speculator whose only salvation, as in the trials of the mythical Perseus reprised by Calvino, is in the speculum of indirect reading and oblique discernment. This is the fate of reading we see performed, inexorably, by Erich Auerbach in the spectral twelfth chapter of his *Mimesis*, where he reads Montaigne reading himself and prefiguring us, as we read them both in Chapter 1 and, indirectly, throughout this book. It takes some consistency to traverse this invisible line between the figural and the figurative. And fate would have Calvino depart into otherworldly ghostliness before he could write his last "Memo," the one "On Consistency," for the Charles Eliot Norton Lectures he would have delivered at Harvard. Those undelivered lectures became his posthumous memos to our millennium.

"Consistency," the subject of the memo he sketched but did not live to write, is at the heart of the conversation to which the comparatist is most urgently enjoined to respond. Thus, while our book begins with the embodiment of comparative literature in the self-ghosting persona of Erich Auerbach, it could only arrive at a consubstantiation with the literary corpus through Calvino's spectral disembodied envoi. Our last memo, then, responds to Calvino's would-have-been-final memo. Perennially an itinerant vocation between literary specters and their conversative thresholds, comparative literature predictably bridges this next millennium addressed by Calvino to the last, during which the refugee Auerbach felt compelled to spectralize his literary persona in the mirror of Montaigne's besieged time that so hauntingly reflects our own besieged city at the beginning of the new millennium.

1

Auerbach's Scar

> Nothing now remains but to find him—to find the reader, that is. I hope that my study will reach its readers.
> —Erich Auerbach, coda to *Mimesis*

> I have not opened someone else's mail. The message in the bottle was addressed to its finder. I found it. That means I have become its secret addressee.
> —Osip Mandelstam, "On the Addressee"

I. Ancestral Antiphony: Autolycus/Abraham

A crossroads, as we shall see throughout this study, has been the perennial site of our literacies. This has certainly been the case of antiquity's trivium, as we shall see once again, in the Epilogue most overtly. A crossroads is also the intersection where comparative literature finds its ancestral legacy and future vocation. This is the junction where Erich Auerbach has often encountered and engaged his interlocutors from the past, and it is the site of a continuing conversation joined by successive generations. The coda of Auerbach's most significant contribution to this conversation, which serves as the chapter epigraph, enjoins us, his posterity, to partake of the colloquy through him. His contemporary Osip Mandelstam (1891–1938), quoted in the second epigraph, demonstrates a particular alertness to such an encounter. At this junction, the subject of their encounter, and ours, is Dante, a poet whose life and afterlife have been in transit from one world to another by way of many intersections. We begin here, then, wakeful to the summons, or *citation*, a term that in some Romance languages signifies encounter or assignation as well as reference or quotation. Alert to such crossroad encounters, coincidental or inevitable, Auerbach and Mandelstam prompt us to explore the significance of the occasion—in anxious anticipation of the reader, in the case of the Auerbach, or in celebration, in the "Eureka!" proclaimed by Mandelstam upon finding the message in a bottle. Whether anticipatory or recuperative, then, beginnings are an intricate juncture, an intersection whose complexity an heir of Auerbach and Mandelstam, Edward Said explored in one of his first books, aptly entitled *Beginnings*.[1]

The question for us at this particular juncture still remains: is a beginning anything other than a citation? And isn't an opening of quotation marks the opening of the bottle,[2] the release of the message? Each chapter of Auerbach's *Mimesis*—except, suggestively enough, the opening chapter, "Odysseus' Scar"—takes such citational beginnings quite literally. And, for his part, Osip Mandelstam instructs us, "A quotation is not an excerpt. A quotation is a cicada. It is part of its nature never to quiet down. Once having got hold of the air, it does not release it." It is this persistence, Mandelstam insists, that "is the main essence of an education. I mean to say that a composition is formed not from heaping up of particulars but in consequence of the fact that one detail after another is torn away from the object, leaves it, flutters out, is hacked away from the system, and goes off into its own functional space."[3] This "functional space" is the site of our conversation. It is a conversative locus, a point of conjunction, a crossroads, a middle of the road, though the road be crooked and long, where, to cite Dante's Mandelstam once more, "the word turns out to be far longer than we thought, and we remember that to speak means to be forever on the road."[4]

It is here, where words intersect and paths crisscross, albeit asynchronously, that we are enjoined to persist, patiently, so that we might meet Erich Auerbach meeting Dante. Ours is a long-distance trajectory, a long tradition, and this "forever" of Mandelstam's "forever on the road" is as long a yesterday as it is a long tomorrow whose serial way stations constitute our cultural history and our literary practice as comparatists. This enduring trajectory aimed toward the future, by Mandelstam's reckoning, could be the key to Dante's vocation as "antimodernist," modernism being programmatically committed to self-obsolescence, even through self-succession, while Dante's *futurum*, as enacted by Auerbach, is inexhaustibly contemporaneous, an endlessly dialectical present. In Mandelstam's terms: "It is unthinkable to read the cantos of Dante without aiming them in the direction of the present day. . . . They demand commentary in the *futurum*. Time, for Dante, is the content of history, understood as a single, synchronic act. And conversely: the content is the joint containing of time with one's associates, competitors, codiscoverers. Dante is an antimodernist. His contemporaneity is inexhaustible, measureless, and unending."[5]

Mandelstam finds this momentum most demonstrably in canto 26 of the *Inferno*, devoted to Odysseus's (Ulysses', for Dante) westward sally, an intrepid excursus not only into the geographical unknown but also a bursting into the future; Ulysses' speech (at *Inferno*, 26.112–20) "bulging like the lens of a magnifying glass, may be applied to the war of the Greeks and the Persians as well as to the discovery of America by Columbus, the bold experiments of Paracelsus, and the world empire of Charles V . . . the revelation of the structure of the future."[6] We, immediate inheritors of this legacy through Auerbach, are the "structure" and detail of that revealed future, as he makes clear in chapter 1 of *Mimesis*, which refers to book 19 of Homer's *Odyssey*, a book in which Odysseus is finally back home, albeit disguised as a homeless beggar. Hence, the notable absence of any epigraphic citation for this chapter in *Mimesis*, unlike all the other chapters of that book. This absence could well be read as Auerbach's own disguise, his cloak of invisibility. And this strategic gambit, as the conjunction of our "functional space," an overture that hides something at an incipient point of convergence, functions more as a problem than as a *nostos*, or homing.

This suggestive complex of problems at the juncture identified by Mandelstam and occupied by Auerbach as a "functional space" goes by any number of names—comparative literature as discipline, university as institutional formation, ethical sensibility as intellectual obligation, critical discourse as intervention in a "functional space." As a threshold to "modes of representation of reality," as the descriptive subtitle of *Mimesis* avers, this spatial threshold serves as a performative opening onto the representational culture of a long tradition.

Itinerants in this "functional space" prove roadworthy to the degree that they extend the conversation at junctures where paths converge. Like Dante, Mandelstam, Auerbach, and their academic progeny, the new arrivals enter the conversation with vigilant circumspection. They become conversant, foremost, knowing their place. Few, if any, know their place more than those out of place, as we learn from the emphatic lessons of Dante, the forerunner of exile for our modern times. This is the Dante invoked by Auerbach, in his own exile, in a March 1948 lecture at Pennsylvania State University, which was then Pennsylvania State College.[7] By then the administration of the college had made the decision, still unknown to him, that the newly arrived migrant had to move on, having been found physically unfit for the college's faculty:

You shall leave everything you love most dearly:
this is the arrow that the bow of exile
shoots first. You are to know the bitter taste
of others' bread, how salt it is, and know
how hard a path it is for one who goes
descending and ascending others' stairs.[8]

The particular functionality of this "functional space," the site of Auerbach's first American refuge, continues unchanged for those whom fate has destined to taste the same salt bread and go up and down these same stairs in what is still called, ironically, Pennsylvania's "Happy Valley." At what is now Pennsylvania State University, Auerbach, with characteristic circumspection, halts at the top of the stairs, as if staring silently at the valley mentioned in the next tercet from Dante's *Paradiso*:

And what will be most hard for you to bear
will be the scheming, senseless company
that is to share your fall into this valley. (ll. 61–63)

Location, or finding the place of things, Mandelstam reminds us, is not only a function of topical or spatial self-orientation, it is also decisively epistemic: "Things themselves we do not know; on the other hand, we are highly sensitive to their location."[9] And there seems to be an uncanny relationship between the degree of our sensitivity to where things do belong and the knowledge that we do not belong. Dante, Mandelstam, Auerbach, and those who, like them, have been dislocated by the caprices of history are keenly attuned to this inverse ratio of knowing and belonging, of pertinence and epistemology. As we shall see shortly, Auerbach's positioning calculus for reckoning our place could well be his most significant legacy to us, in our time of displacements, and to the dark wood of that searching vocation called literacy, ethical discernment, and comparative literature. Perhaps this explains his enduring significance to the field.[10]

By Auerbach's and by Mandelstam's reckoning, conversation and composition are complementary. For, if conversation is extensive and augmentative, composition, as Mandelstam has defined it, not unlike the "functional space" of the arts of music, poetry, and sculpture, is subtractive in its acts of distillation. Thus composed, a work finds its composure in the economy of rendering, in the optimal possibilities of understatement, in the silenced and indirect elisions of the comprehended. If conversation resides in the sensitivity to location and the knowledge of placement, *com*position, its etymons to the contrary notwithstanding, emanates from *dis*position, or subtraction, as Mandelstam would have it, and the combinatorial possibilities of display and displacement. *Mimesis*, Auerbach's most enduring bequest, has proved more compositional than conversational, although for the attentive student his rehearsals of our cultural legacy lack in neither. Together in their representations, conversation and composition perform the process captured by the lexical etymology of a Greek verb that we, following Auerbach, have often called *mimeīsthai*, a verb "in the middle voice, which means that its grammatical subject is necessarily affected by the action denoted. *Mimeīsthai* is what people do, not what things are. Thus *mimesis* originally does not denote a relation between a text (as in a finished *product* . . .) and its referent, but *between an action* (i.e., a *process*) *and its model*."[11] The first-person middle voice of the infinitive *mimeomai* ("to imitate") points to the agency of the subject and the implicated role of his or her mediation, as the Greek grammarian Bakker notes in the citation here, "*between an action* (i.e., a *process*) *and its model*." As an attentive philologist, Auerbach knows the implication of his own role in the declension of this verb and he is obviously alert to the original denotation of the nominative now synonymous with his own persona. In their philological discussion of the performative etymology of *mimesis*, classicists parse the term for us in ways that point directly to Osip Mandelstam's apothegm regarding our knowledge of things and our locative relation to them: "Things themselves we do not know, we are highly sensitive to their location." Since the time of Auerbach's exemplary demonstration and symptomatic embodiment of this project, our task remains constant in the shifting pursuit of determining how the "grammatical subject [you, we, I] is necessarily affected by the action denoted" by *mimeīsthai*, a verb "in the middle voice," as classicists put it.

Caught in the ironies of outspoken transit, always mindful to "remember that to speak means to be forever on the road," Mandelstam would be overtaken by his tragic death in a Stalinist transit camp. Auerbach's own transition in the commons of Bradford College, Yale University would be no less abrupt. In his exilic passage, Auerbach made landfall on this same university spot in central Pennsylvania from where I am now writing. From here, he was dislocated, in turn, in institutional hedging against his own mortality, almost as if everyone else at the university were immortal at the time. The university doctor, who had to certify all professors as physically fit to serve on the faculty then, weighed Auerbach's condition against the actuarial tables of the university health insurance program and found Auerbach wanting. Human societies historically cope with war's aftermath by shunting whatever could be perceived as disability, that is, by becoming "ablist," in the parlance of what now, in the midst of our new century's "perpetual war," is called disability studies.[12] Auerbach beached on the scene of American history in 1947 not only with other war refugees like himself but also with one of the largest contingents of disabled war veterans. Postwar "ablism" has invariably proved an expedient coping mechanism for societies that, in postbellum relief, would rather forget war and its "detritus," human or otherwise. Those who now retrace Auerbach's steps in the paths and stairways of this same institution, where the peripeties of their own exilic translocations find them, with names and provenance that, like Auerbach's at the time, correspond to the sanctioned xenophobia du jour, might often wonder what he thought as a marked man whose mortality was foregrounded with unalloyed actuarial punctiliousness and officially adduced as sufficient reason for his termination, or dis-appointment, from the faculty:

It is my opinion that an individual of 55 years of age with a hypertension as indicated in this examination should not be employed on the full time staff. Individuals suffering from this type of disease will sooner or later have a serious cerebral accident which will incapacitate them for work. There is no way, of course, for us to predict how soon or how far distant such accidents might occur, but such possibility will be part and parcel of this man's life. Sincerely yours, Herbert R. Glenn, M.D., Director, College Health Service, January 29, 1948.[13]

In his personnel file, now before me as I write this memorandum, except for a hand-written note Auerbach addressed to the college dean, he remains unremittingly silent. In the last document in his file, penned more than a year after the good doctor's irrevocable sentence on his permanent appointment and dated February 23, 1949, Auerbach writes: "We had a very cordial talk with Dr. Glenn, but, as I expected, he can do nothing in my case. I am extremely grateful to you that you are willing to write to your friends about a possible position for me. I want to mention, in this connection, that there might be possibilities not only in the field of Romance philology and literature, but also in Comparative Literature, or even German. Thank you! Very sincerely yours, Auerbach."

The case file is amply articulate, intentionally and otherwise, on a bureaucratic process worthy of Kafka. And the circumspect conversion, in Auerbach's final sentence, of his undeniable qualifications into hypothetical "possibilities" is not an insignificant index to his own self-effacement and dislocation within a precarious locus. As his syntax enjoins adverbial conjunction ("but also in Comparative Literature") to adversative option ("or even in German"), the shading from a sense of resignation into anxious urgency becomes unmistakable. The dean would indeed write to over a dozen institutions announcing Auerbach's availability and inquiring after "possibilities," principally in the Ivy League and in the Big Ten universities, though his efforts at solicitation would seem to contradict the somewhat parlous circumstances of his original appointment a year earlier as described to the dean by the head of the department:

"If this figure [four thousand dollars] is hardly consonant with the experience and publications of Dr. Auerbach, I believe that it would nevertheless suffice to bring him here for the twelvemonth mentioned [February 1948 to February 1949] principally because Dr. Auerbach is new to America and his availability is not generally known to the profession [department head's request to the dean for authorization of temporary appointment, December 8, 1947]."

As revealing as this might be of Auerbach's predicament, perhaps best captured in an apt phrase by Seth Lerer in a variant context as a "story of exile and dismissal,"[14] it is no less articulate on the incorrigible constancy of university governance as institutional culture of parsimony and self-impoverishing opportunism. Farinata's characterization of the damned consigned to the circle of heretics could well apply to the endemic penchant for myopic expediencies in our institutional culture—

We see, even as men who are farsighted,
those things, he said, that are remote from us;
the Highest Lord allots us that much light; (*Inferno*, 10.100–103)

—notwithstanding the motto of Yale University, "Lux et veritas." Yale was Auerbach's final exilic destination, where he arrived in 1950 after a year's stint at the Princeton Institute for Advanced Studies. His only other option in 1949, ironically, was the Chair of Romance Philology at Humboldt University, in what had then recently become East Berlin, an offer that came through the good graces and bad conscience of Ernst Bloch and of Werner Krauss, the latter having succeeded Auerbach at the University of Marburg from which he had been dismissed in 1935 "on racist grounds."[15]

Inevitably, one must countenance these historical details, and others even less felicitous and unworthy of dissemination, since Auerbach's predicament and intellectual vocation have so often been rendered as synonymous with the history of the discipline of comparative literature and its place in the modern university. Whether through recognition or misrecognition, this identification works by guarded occlusion—Auerbach's characteristic vigilance is no less wary than Odysseus's caution before Eurykleia's jubilant discovery of her master's scar in book 19 of the Homeric opus with which Auerbach begins *Mimesis*. It is an identification driven in no small measure by our professional need for embodiment and personification of disciplinary formations and their institutional histories. Auerbach has now become that prosopopoeia. The textual strategies of *Mimesis*, no less than the lexical connotations of the Greek verb from which the title of Auerbach's work is derived, focus the trained energies of highly attuned exegetes on Auerbach as subject, a focus rendered even more urgent by the tantalizing ironies in his reticence and exilic reserve—survival mechanisms, no doubt, well learned in history's vicissitudes and from literary tradition's monitory lessons.

Though the historical details tend to be kept purposefully sketchy and the textual analysis programmatically sparse, numerous critics have been drawn to Auerbach's precedent as defining disciplinary paradigm and, simultaneously, as that model's historical instance. Many admirable efforts, most recently by David Damrosch (1995), Seth Lerer (1996, 2002), Amir R. Mufti (1998), Edward Said (2004), and Emily Apter (2006), in diverse and eloquent ways have drawn parallels, suggested correspondences, invoked analogues, and intimated similarities between Auerbach the author as *faber* and his authorial persona as instance of the *fabula*.[16] "Mimesis" is no longer limited to the predicative connotations of the Greek verb in the middle voice from which the noun derives. It has become a *figura*, in Auerbach's most eloquent pedagogy on that term, where, in turn, he is now transfigured in the multiple refractions of its *speculum*.[17] That figurative transformation has rendered him and his itinerary coterminous, if not consubstantial, with the self-apperceptions of the field of comparative literature at a historical moment that, just as it did in Auerbach's time, puts the intellectual integrity and ethical timber of its practitioners on trial. And this might in fact be why Auerbach's example has emerged as a precursor for a discipline that historically and, it seems, perennially, must find its raison d'être on contested ground, where strife marks the parameters of cultures and their contending imbrications, and where the limits of the human in the face of the human's capacity for inhumanity are put to the test. As in most human societies, ancient and modern, the transfiguration of a historical figure into institutional prosopopoeia tends to occur in the safety of postmortem memorialization. Auerbach's abrupt demise at Yale, the final way station of the exilic alien, allayed many misapprehensions, opening the way toward his disciplinary canonization, a safe apotheosis in blessed memory. Exiles, refugees, immigrants tend to gain posthumously what might be begrudgingly conceded to them in life. Total, definitive displacement opens up a less threatening place, with death conferring a margin of safety on the living, a margin that cultures have perennially safeguarded by honoring the departed, as in the ambivalent rituals of the *apotropeia* of Greek antiquity, when the souls of ancestors were simultaneously honored and held at bay through incantations. As with honoring the elders in most cultures, obeisance is not always altruistic, driven as it is by the cautionary motive of having the departing and the departed do as little damage as possible on their way out.

Comparative literature has been an interstitial field devoted to negotiating an intellectual and ethical course among contested spaces. It mediates between the realm of the present and that of the departed. As a result, the discipline has found itself in agonic terrain. This is the territory that, perforce, spawns comparatists, or from where comparatists are obliged by historical necessity to flee for their survival. Little surprise, then, that a number of analysts of comparative literature should consider the discipline not merely in terms of comparable similitudes. Comparatists find themselves inexorably constrained to view the field through the violence of asymmetrical juxtapositions. They are constrained, as a result, to calibrate their diagnoses through an ethics conditioned by traumatic contiguities.[18] This has been especially so, when, as in Auerbach's exemplary case, the comparatists themselves, as investigating subjects, are subjected to the historical traumas they investigate.

Auerbach telegraphs all this in his anxious letter from Istanbul to Walter Benjamin on 3 January 1937, a letter that proved prophetic for the calamitous history that would shortly unfold in Europe. And his prognosis has proved visionary of what we, as we cycle through yet another deadly farce of "blood and soil," would come to call "globalization" and transculturation, our own embattled ground for comparative study and cultural pedagogy at the beginning of our new century. As in mid-twentieth-century civilized Europe's self-unmasking, our new century also witnesses civilization's unveiled barbarity, with its peripheries around the world turned into targets of rapacious hypocrisy. It was in such a "periphery," today still in the throes of assimilation into Europe, where Auerbach found refuge from Europe's campaign of "blood and soil" and from where he would write to Walter Benjamin:

But he [Kemal Atatürk] had to force through everything he did in the struggle against the European democracies on the one hand and the old Mohammedan Pan-Islamic sultan's economy on the other; and the result is a fantastically anti-traditional nationalism: rejection of all existing Mohammedan cultural heritage, the establishment of a fantastic relation to a primal Turkish identity, technological modernization in the European sense, in order to triumph against a hated and yet admired Europe with its own weapons: hence, the preference for European-educated emigrants as teachers, from whom one can learn without the threat of foreign propaganda. Result: nationalism in the extreme accompanied by the simultaneous destruction of the historical national character. This picture, which in other countries like Germany, Italy, and even Russia (?) is not visible for everyone to see, shows itself here in full nakedness. . . . It is becoming increasingly clear to me that the present international situation is nothing but a ruse of providence, designed to lead us along a bloody and tortuous path to an International of triviality and a culture of Esperanto. I have already suspected this in Germany and Italy in view of the dreadful inauthenticity of the "blood and soil" propaganda, but only here has the evidence of such a trend almost reached the point of certainty.[19]

Auerbach's own irrepressible European ambivalences toward the place that gave him refuge become transparent in this historically insightful diagnosis. He countenanced the mimetic rehearsals of "the dreadful inauthenticity of the 'blood and soil' propaganda" with greater certainty here than in the European trends he found so disturbing in their original setting. Those trends of "dreadful inauthenticity" reached a point of "certainty" for Auerbach in their translocated mimesis. Mimetically reiterated inauthenticity, then, became the certainty of "fantastic" nationalist mythmaking in the destruction of history and the invention of an illusionary national identity rehearsed by the newly emergent Turkish republic. Walter Benjamin's ill-fated flight "along [the] bloody and tortuous path" that Auerbach foresaw for Europe itself would reach its tragic end on the French-Spanish border three years later (in Beaux/Bou, Catalonia, 27 September 1940). A year earlier, Benjamin had noted in his *Über den Begriff der Geschichte* (On the Concept of History; translated in English as "Theses on the Philosophy of History") the ambiguities endemic to the history of humanity, symptomatic even in Auerbach's own ambivalences and in the baleful entwining of civilization and barbarity.[20] In such understanding of history, then, despite the blithe cheerfulness of those for whom comparatism is purely an elective academic pursuit rather than a fate born of the vicissitudes of historical necessity, comparative literature has indeed always been a fraught endeavor. The historic tumult that Auerbach witnessed in the rising of a "modern nation" and the mythic transformation of cultural traditions through the traumatic contiguities that make comparatism indispensable clearly demonstrate the "fraught background" and perennial difficulty of the field he willed to us in the United States.

Thus, it might be more than a mere coincidence that the term *fraught* should occur as frequently as it does in the initial chapter of *Mimesis*, whether applied to the context of Homer or to that of the Hebrew tradition, which Auerbach juxtaposes to the Greek in comparatistic counterpoint. And though he chooses to see the foregrounded tableau of the Homeric narrative and its "voluminous syntactical parenthesis" as equanimity,[21] he knows full well that such overlay in Homer is no less fraught than what "is left obscure," as "abruptness," and as the suggestively "unexpressed" in the Elohist narrative of Isaac's sacrifice, more accurately, Abraham's would-be sacrifice of Isaac.[22] For Auerbach's own exegesis that foregrounds what he terms, after Goethe's and Schiller's April 1797 correspondence on Homer, the "retarding element" (i.e., Homer's penchant for disruptive postponements),[23] clearly suggests that such would-be equanimity and composed movement in the *Odyssey* lurches no less through the leaps and lapses of human and divine interventions than the godly interruption of Isaac's slaughtering. Disruption, in fact, could well be as much the defining turn for Odysseus's fate as for Isaac's destiny, starting, of course, with the strife of opprobrium inscribed in the etymons of Odysseus's name—"child of woe"—as Autolycus, his grandfather, deliberately named him (*Odyssey* 19.407–9).

Thus, whether "fraught with background,"[24] as in the Old Testament narrative, whose inscrutable *Deus absconditus* Auerbach sees as symptom rather than cause of wary occlusion and guarded silence in biblical representation, or externalized and foregrounded, as in Homer, neither is immune to the incomprehensible peripeteia of fateful interruption, be it through the unfathomable motion of the Elohist's divinity or the retribution of the god Poseidon that set back Odysseus's homecoming for a decade. Though Auerbach sees them in counterpoint, then, the Homeric and the Hebraic render his "Odysseus's scar" doubly circumspect, since the Odysseus he rehearses relies no less on occlusion and circumspection than does the mysterious Elohist who perpetually slips away from disclosure into fraught secrecy and arcane insinuation. Looking for a contrapuntal mirror, then, Auerbach falls into double jeopardy,[25] susceptible at once to the caprices of historical fates and to the enigmatic arbitrariness of an inscrutable god, where his own predicament "indicate[s] thoughts which remain unexpressed,"[26] where "time and place are undefined and call for interpretation; thoughts and feeling remain unexpressed, are only suggested by the silence and the fragmentary speeches; the whole . . . remains mysterious and 'fraught with background.'"[27]

And, as much in resonance with the polytropic Homer as with the esoterically suggestive Elohist, Auerbach compounds allusive paratactic accretion into what he terms "voluminous syntactical parenthesis" that is "fraught with background" and begging for interpretation[28]—as when he writes:

> Let the reader think of the history which we are ourselves witnessing; anyone who, for example, evaluates the behavior of individual men and groups of men at the time of the rise of National Socialism in Germany, or the behavior of individual peoples and states before and during the last war, will feel how difficult it

is to represent historical themes in general, and how unfit they are for legend; the historical comprises a great number of contradictory motives in each individual, a hesitation and ambiguous groping on the part of groups; only seldom (as in the last war) does a more or less plain situation, comparatively simple to describe, arise, and even such a situation is subject to division below the surface, as indeed almost constantly in danger of losing its simplicity; and the motives of all interested parties are so complex that the slogans of propaganda can be composed only through the crudest simplification—with the result that friend and foe alike can often employ the same ones.[29]

Though Auerbach deems the representation of historical themes difficult and "unfit for legend," he consigns the historian's task "to the technique of legend," perhaps because in his time as in ours, legend and the illusionary so constantly preempt reality.

This overt historical grounding of Auerbach's endeavor is rare enough on his part that it obliges us to read it as a mirror, a speculum that deflects the countenance of its reader into parallax. There, in that fugitive presence, we could discern him as a historical figure visible in elliptical self-deflection. Like him, self-ghosted, we can begin to discern Auerbach's own *figura* in that mirror, though we remain mindful that invisibility does not mean absence—even, or especially, for ghostlier demarcations. Such is Auerbach's own understanding of human nature and human history. And he instructs us in this "functional space," as Mandelstam called it, of his own historical particularity through chapter 12 of *Mimesis*, which he, after Montaigne, suggestively entitles "L'Humaîne condition." There, Auerbach trains his self-reflecting philological focus on the beginning of chapter 2, book 3, of Montaigne's *Essais*.

II. The Comparatist Mirror

Reading *Mimesis*, particularly through its philological derivation we discussed earlier as action that reflects on the subject engaged in the mimetic process, should indeed allow us a glimpse of an otherwise furtive historical subject: Auerbach himself. This is especially true in this particular segment, chapter 12, of Auerbach's *Mimesis*. Why should this be so? And why is this particular chapter of Montaigne's *Essais* a lens and speculum for Auerbach's own strategy of self-mitigation, even self-effacement? Why, indeed, does he draw us into pursuit and decoding of his own tactical self-reinscription in the cultural narrative of mimesis, or "representation of reality," as the subtitle of his opus glosses the title and, by implication, his own endeavor? The refractions here are multiple. Through them, we shall attempt to glimpse the subject.

The answer to this variously stated question, as usual in Auerbach's work, is citational. It comes in the opening segment of Auerbach's quotation from Montaigne, scripted in the latter's sixteenth-century spelling: "Il faut accomoder mon histoire à l'heure; je pourray tantost changer, non de fortune seulement, mais aussi d'intention. C'est un contrerolle de divers et muables accidens, et d'imaginations irresolues, et, quand il y eschet, contraires; soit que je soys autre moy-mesmes, soit que je saisisse les subjects par autres circonstances et considerations [I must adapt my history to the moment. I may presently change, not only by chance, but also by intention. It is a record of diverse and changeable events, of undecided, and, when the occasion arises, contradictory ideas; whether it be that I am another self, or that I grasp a subject in different circumstances and see it from a different point of view]."[30]

Auerbach dilates Montaigne's pursuit into syllogistic procedure, emending his text, as he puts it, by "supply[ing] some syntactic vincula."[31] Then, he says, apropos of Montaigne, "The train of reasoning in the first paragraph can easily be rendered in the form of a syllogism. I describe myself; I am a creature which constantly changes; ergo, the description too must conform to this and constantly change."[32] In furnishing such emendations, however, aside from the exegetic clarity he achieves, Auerbach foregrounds and exacerbates the significance of the omissions, and he does so by shining a light on the "fraught background," as he earlier called the elisions of the Elohist narrative of Isaac's vicissitudes. While he admits that "the nuances which Montaigne expresses by omitting them cannot be caught in full," Auerbach's procedure speaks to an enactment of what Mandelstam called "composition"—formation / figuration by subtraction, elision, or mitigation. Since he depicts Montaigne's self-composition as a syllogism with a key omission—"As for the minor premise (I am a creature subject to constant change), Montaigne does not express it at once. He leaves the logical continuity in the lurch"[33]—the process becomes readily apparent as an exemplary instance of a particular kind of mimesis or representation: *enthymeme*, as it is known, is a syllogism that has one of its premises suppressed or omitted. The rhetorical procedure of the syllogism and its enthymematic variant (that the enthymeme here should be Montaigne himself and his circumstantial changeability)—"Il faut accomoder mon histoire à l'heure; je pourray tantost changer, non de fortune seulement, mais aussi d'intention"—point to Aristotle's *Rhetoric*. There, not only the formal but also the practical become salient, specifically, where prudence of judgment, relevance of contingency, and the ethics of apt comportment, converge in what Aristotle calls *phronesis* (*Rhetoric*, book II, and *Nichomachean Ethics* 1142a ff.). Thus, in a highly mutable contingency the formal/rhetorical becomes yoked to the ethical as historical moment.

Once again, what is the significance of this reading of Auerbach reading Montaigne at this time? Auerbach, no doubt, would expect this question to be broached, even if not wholly answered. Looking over his shoulder into Montaigne's mirror, we too see what he describes as "the play and counterplay between I and I, between Montaigne the author and Montaigne the theme."[34] Perforce, we need to add, observing the play and counterplay between Auerbach and Auerbach, and between "we" and "we," we see the other spectral dualities dueling for recognition that inexorably mutates into misrecognition, as *le particulier* of any given moment morphs through successive particularities. It is on this volatile morphology that a complex set of ironies pivots as a historical refraction, an agonic contestation, and a traumatic contiguity that renders Auerbach's own role not only as "contrerolle,"[35] in Montaigne's depiction of his own essayistically performed identity. Haunting in the background is Europe's history of war and that historical moment's contrapuntal realpolitik that seals Auerbach's own fate, even as he would disavow as "inauthentic" and dreary any determinacies that circumscribe the verve of changeability and the potential to adapt to the "contrerolle de divers et muables accidens." There are accidental ironies and there are ironies by design. Auerbach's and, alas, now ours in our own time, are by historical necessity. That is to say, they are ironies born of human designs that foundered on a catastrophic scale on the accidents of their "inauthentic" delusions, and to the detriment of innumerable, and deliberately discounted, human lives. The mutable morphologies of individual identity that form the experimental self-rehearsals, the *essais*, of Montaigne's privileged explorations in the tower of the Château Montaigne between 1571 and 1580, serve as an ironic mirror for Auerbach's reflections during the fourth decade of the twentieth century in the seam between fascist Europe and the ambivalently and complexly "fascisizing" Turkey as emergent modern nation-state. In Auerbach's spectral juxtaposition, the nationalist rehearsals of borrowed and forged national mythologies to create a new political and ethnic culture, and the elective rehearsal of identities in the Montaigne essays, do indeed serve a historic "contrerolle," as Montaigne called his essayed part(s) in the personal theater he enacted in the tower of his family château.

These contiguous and contrapuntal rehearsals of nation and of a "particulier," or private individual, are certainly the fertile ground of comparatistic analyses that lend themselves to philological pursuits of contrastive mythologies best exemplified by Auerbach's contrapuntal reading of Homer and the Hebrew Bible and his juxtaposition of European and Turkish national fantasies. The disciplinary institutionalization of those contrastive procedures as an investigative field goes by the name of comparative literature. No less apposite to such institutional and epistemic formation, however, is the historic irony of Auerbach's alterity, at the edge of these morphing historical and individual identities, as someone named "Auerbach." He sees himself through the refractions of his critical explorations as someone who is inexorably trapped within an otherwise itinerant identity of exilic Jewishness. Far from escaping as political history's refugee through the successive way stations of his flight, he knows, and he divulges as much in the ambivalences and equivocations of his own mimesis, that he is rigidly fixed in an existential vise at that historical moment. That vise is defined on the one hand by the essentialist ideology of a grand scheme of imperial millenarianism and univocal soteriology under German National Socialism's deadly messianic fantasy. And it is defined on the other hand by a no less absolute and doctrinaire orthodoxy, which Auerbach counterposes with the skepticism allowable in Homer:

> One can perfectly well entertain historical doubts on the subject of the Trojan War or of Odysseus' wanderings, and still, when reading Homer, feel precisely the effects he sought to produce; but without believing in Abraham's sacrifice, it is impossible to put the narrative of it to the use for which it was written. Indeed, we must go even further. The Bible's claim to truth is not only far more urgent than Homer's, it is tyrannical—it excludes all other claims. The world of the Scripture stories is not satisfied with claiming to be a historically true reality—it insists that it is the only real world, is destined for autocracy. All other scenes, issues, and ordinances have no right to appear independently of it, and it is promised that all of

them, the history of all mankind, will be given their due place within its frame, will be subordinated to it. The Scripture stories do not, like Homer's, court our favor, they do not flatter us that they may please us and enchant us—they seek to subject us, and if we refuse to be subjected we are rebels.[36]

Described here is the absolutist doctrine that Auerbach has identified as the "fraught background" to the Elohist's biblical narrative of Isaac's vicissitudes. In counterposing it to Homer and the allowable margin of skepticism or disbelief in the Greek epic, his comparatistic juxtaposition is not merely dualistic (Hebraic/Homeric) but triune. It is only dualistic inasmuch as Auerbach's counterpoint opposes fixity to changeableness, orthodoxy to skepticism, absolutism to mutability, tyranny to persuasion. The "tyrannical" exclusivity he imputes to the biblical credo is not merely biblical, it is also political and historical because of the realpolitik that implacably deems him an irredeemable Jew and delegitimized human, and thereby legitimately dispensable alien on ethno-racial grounds. The delusional absolutism of the regime that dismissed Auerbach from Marburg University in 1935 is founded on an ideology no less doctrinaire than the religion that brooks no disconformity and marks as "rebels," and therefore as legitimate targets, those who would dissent. Auerbach, then, is the weak middle premise in this syllogism of self-universalizing absolutes—the biblical and deviant millenarianism that underwrites German fascism. Auerbach's unforgettable legacy to us in this contrapuntal juxtaposition is a secular critical sensibility. We call this secular impulse humanism. It serves as Auerbach's and our hedge against what he calls the "tyrannical" orthodoxy of absolutism, whether biblical or political, or the even deadlier combination of both. That combination is a legacy whose significance becomes all the more apparent to us at the beginning of the new century that is in the throes of replicating the absolutisms and doctrines of intolerance, now through all three religions of the Abrahamic tradition in convergence with a no-less deluded realpolitik not much different from the convergence of ideological absolutes that hounded Auerbach's era. This is what links Auerbach to Montaigne and his humanist concerns with "l'humaine condition," as he was surrounded by France's civil war of religion in the sixteenth century. This is the middle term at the heart of Auerbach's syllogism, refracted in the syllogistic mirror that he frames for Montaigne. This, in other words, is that omitted middle premise of Auerbach's mirrored predicament in Montaigne's speculum that renders elliptical his own *mimesis* as grammatical subject of the verb in the middle voice, *mimeĩsthai*; a verb, in other words, whose action in this particular context renders his syllogistic predicament enthymematic. In this rhetorical and ideological strategy of elision Auerbach, the grammatical subject of history's mimesis and predicate object of a realpolitik, is banished, eliminated rhetorically, geographically, and historically into the ghosted representation of exile and otherness as the enthymeme of history's syllogism and of "l'humaine condition" in the middle of the twentieth century.

Thus, his meaningful descriptors, the epithetic characterizations that Auerbach employs for sketching the volatile and itinerant identity of Montaigne as *figura* of a "contrerolle de divers et muables accidens," in his own terms, echo in the mirror Auerbach countenances in order to characterize his own destiny no less than that of his subject: "Concealed behind self-irony and modesty there is a very definite attitude which serves his major purpose and to which he adheres with a charmingly elastic tenacity which is his own."[37] Obviously, not entirely Montaigne's own in his role as echoing mirror that reflects those who look into it, and not entirely Auerbach's own either, since he has us overlooking, overhearing, reflecting in the same speculum entitled *Mimesis*. "C'est une espineuse enterprinse," indeed, as Montaigne spells it in his sixteenth-century French orthography.[38] The flower complement in the thorny (*espineuse*) nature of the enterprise is "the irony he displays . . . , a mixture of several motifs: an extremely sincere disinclination to take human beings tragically . . . ; a faint note of proudly aristocratic contempt for the writer's craft . . . ; finally, and this is the most important point of all, an inclination to belittle his own particular approach."[39] Whether as thorn or as flower, irony tends to be as self-betraying as potentially misleading, a tactical situation Auerbach efficiently diagnoses, and embodies, as "reservedly ironic modesty. . . . Concealed behind self-irony and modesty there is a very definite attitude which serves his major purpose and to which he adheres with the charmingly elastic tenacity which is his own."[40] These are, of course, specular glimpses in Montaigne's mirror, which means that their reflection carries superposed upon it the visage of the scrutinist(s).[41]

The contradance of the two-step in this irony, whether as duplicity or as dialectic, is carried out between fixity and randomness, performative improvisation and essentialist decree, necessary contingency and implacable necessity. Auerbach invariably identifies with Montaigne, and Montaigne with the first of these binomial constructs in mirrored reversal. And the master irony that frames them both is indeed historical—the personal histories of the two mirrored "particuliers," Auerbach and Montaigne: Auerbach's history as self-consciously ethno-racialized progeny of what he terms a "fraught background" governed by the inscrutable God who, through "a ruse of providence," as Auerbach calls it in writing to Walter Benjamin apropos another paradoxical context, tests Abraham's conviction and subjects Isaac to divine experiment. Auerbach takes this as an inheritance whose effects he seeks to allay, albeit with a diffident contestation toward the enigmatic omnipotence of a *Deus absconditus*, whom he refers to, translating the Gnostic phrase from the Latin, as "a hidden God. . . . The concept of God held by the Jews is less a cause than a symptom of their manner of comprehending and representing things."[42] Auerbach is constrained by historical circumstance to foreground such inexorability, even as the millenarian salvationism of the Third Reich would define, just as inexorably, his professional life and exilic displacement by negating his performative impulses as free improvisational subject, rendering him into essentialized object of a lethal ideology and racist realpolitik. The danger of this "fraught background" only becomes compounded, when, as Auerbach writes to Benjamin from Istanbul in 1937, he witnesses in his exile the mimetic enactment, a mimesis of representation not of reality but an inauthentic replication and mythic reinscription of what he calls "a fantastic relation to a primal . . . identity . . . , a ruse of providence, designed to lead us along a bloody and tortuous path to an International of triviality and a culture of Esperanto."[43] Trivial and "inauthentic" as this "ruse of providence" might be, the providential self-empowerment proved no less lethal in mid-twentieth-century millenial Europe, and it is proving just as deadly today at the beginning of our new century and the beginning of a third millennium. These echoes of Auerbach's historical epoch in ours, though the actors are different and the roles reversed, could well carry some explanation for Auerbach's emergence as paradigmatic precursor of our disciplinary pursuits as comparatists.

There is little that is aleatory or contingent in these absolutist orthodoxies of "blood and soil" and in the phantasmagoric myths of primal identities—ethnic, religious, racial, national, or all together at once, whether in Auerbach's own time, or in ours. The most baleful irony here resides in the self-contradictions of the illogic and in the blindness of ideologies of death that assert their own justification in the name of preserving what is deemed worthy of life through the persecution and extermination of those expendable for a higher cause, whether this perennial constancy in "l'humaine condition" be in Auerbach's century or in ours, or for that matter in Montaigne's war-ravaged time. And Auerbach's insistence on randomness in Montaigne, and, no less so in his own "random" choice of prooftexts for treatment in *Mimesis*,[44] beg the question of irony as much in the peculiar case of Montaigne's self-rehearsals as in the randomness of textual exempla for Auerbach's treatise on *The Representation of Reality in Western Literature*, as the subtitle of his opus avers. The fact is, Auerbach is as much chosen by his texts as Montaigne was formed by his historical circumstances, unmistakably overdetermined circumstances in which Montaigne, rather than being a product of randomness, lived from birth as his father's experimental control group of one, a condition he was fated to reiterate throughout his life as an ongoing experiment conducted on the specimen and laboratory he embodied. In humanism's emerging new science, in which his father firmly believed, Montaigne himself was an experimental object subjected from birth to strict and programmatic conditions, as Auerbach well knew. His eventual decade-long self-seclusion in the tower of the Château Montaigne was no random event.

In the inhospitable world of mid-twentieth-century, racist determinacies and fantastical schemes that led as easily to the extermination of peoples as to the salvation of the chosen few, to have chosen Montaigne as exemplary locus of "l'humaine condition" does have some logic to it. As Auerbach the philologist was well aware, however, logic and irony have rarely been mutually exclusive. And finding in "Montaigne's undertaking the portrayal of his own random personal life as a whole," compounds the irony that Auerbach himself identifies as "reservedly ironic modesty."[45] Auerbach's succumbing to the impression that Montaigne's life ever constituted "a whole," even after his transfiguration into posthumous textuality with the safety valve in the form of an in-built volatility, is itself ironic. And there is no less irony in Auerbach's observation that "the obligatory basis of Montaigne's method is the random life one happens to have."[46] Auerbach precipitates a rhetorical catachresis, or strained paradox, born of the fact that in Montaigne there is no possible separation between "the obligatory method" and "the random life one happens to have," since that life is the product of its obligatory method. This makes that life far from random by virtue of being the obligatory extension of its studious pre- and postprogramming. The historical determinacies of Montaigne's morphology as subject, as the historical-biographical record suggests, compounds the inevitable nature of his method, a fact that moots any randomness in his life, despite his unrelenting destabilization of subjectivity. The only possible exception to this inevitableness might be in the degree of unpredictability by which studied intention and diligent method are bedeviled by the surprise of unexpected consequences and by the peripeties of history's caprices, as Auerbach came to understand from firsthand experience. Thus, to claim as he does that Montaigne "displays himself embedded in the random contingencies of his life and deals indiscriminately with the fluctuating movements of his consciousness, and it is precisely his random indiscriminateness that constitutes his method," might be explained by an irrepressible nostalgia in Auerbach for the possibility of "random contingencies" and for a possible freedom from the ideological determinacies that deliberately, and often brutally, condition what we take to be the spontaneity of our indiscriminateness and any method that might issue from it. In an epoch of delusional realpolitik and rabid totalitarian ideologies that proved implacably determinative of Auerbach's own itinerant "contingencies," indeterminacy and randomness clearly must have had a powerful attraction. And his conclusions on "l'humaine condition" as embodied and exemplified by Montaigne could well be as articulate on the "random contingencies" of Auerbach's exilic life as they are eloquently expressive of Montaigne's circumstances:

Among all his contemporaries he had the clearest conception of the problem of man's self-orientation; that is, the task of making oneself at home in existence without fixed points of support. In him for the first time, man's life—the random personal life as a whole—becomes problematic in the modern sense. . . . He conceives himself too calmly, despite all his probing into his own insecurity. Whether this is a weakness or a strength is a question I shall not try to answer.[47]

As to whether this "problematic in the modern sense" applies also to us, Auerbach's and Montaigne's inheritors, in our postmodern era is more than a self-indulgent question. For, like Mandelstam's Dante, Auerbach's Montaigne, whom he ventriloquizes so eloquently, speaks to us through Auerbach in perennially relevant ways. And what Mandelstam says about *The Divine Comedy* also applies to Montaigne's representation of "l'humaine condition," though the first be called *divina* and the latter *humaine*, to wit: "It is unthinkable to read the cantos of Dante without aiming them in the direction of the present day. . . . They demand commentary in the *futurum*."[48] That enduring futurity that resonates for us still can be found already in the opening words, the incipit of chapter 2, book 3, of Montaigne's *Essais*, which Auerbach cites as the epigrammatic gambit of his own chapter on Montaigne: "Les autres forment l'homme: je le recit; et en représente un particulier bien mal formé, et lequel si j'avoy à foçonner de nouveau, je ferois vrayment bien autre qu'il n'est [Others form man; I narrate him; and represent a particular, very ill-formed one, whom, if I were to fashion him anew, I would remake him quite other than he is]."[49]

Montaigne's *futurum*, to use Mandesltam's ascription to Dante, resonates dialectically, speaks to us dialogically as Bakhtinians would say, in this incipient oscillation between *formation et recit*, what our linguists and cultural diagnosticians differentiate as constitutive formation and performative narration. The two collude to construct the phenomenon (the text, the subject, the culture, the nation, the discipline, the institution) in question. And this is the oscillatory motion between defining structure and its enactments as individual performance that makes it possible for Montaigne, as it does for Mandelstam's Dante, to keep from falling into tragedy and to keep the performative act sufficiently destabilized so that it remains in motion rather than resolving into the tragic. The studied and deliberate precariousness of this "particulier," as Montaigne refers to his perpetually morphing self, constitutes what Auerbach terms "this particular equilibrium of his being [that] prevents the tragic, the possibility of which is inherent in his image of man, from coming to expression in his work."[50] And this is, of course, the uncanny equilibrium precariously achieved by the authorial gestures, what the rhetors call the deictic performatives, that define Auerbach's *Mimesis* and the mimetic signals within it, and that keep the enterprise from becoming the record of "the personal tragedy of the individual."[51] This precarious "equilibrium" could also be, as in the case of Odysseus, what betrays the sign of recognition as a scar rather than as an open wound. And this also might be among Auerbach's most significant legacies as *futurum* to us and to our scarred epoch, at the beginning of a new century that is still marked by humanity's millennial delusions.

2

The Siege of Baghdad

RASHIDUDDIN FAZLULLAH, ORHAN PAMUK,
AND THE COMMISSIONS OF HISTORY

> It is not concealed from the minds of the intelligent and perspicacious or those possessed of vision and insight that history consists of recording and arranging. . . . It is the custom of wise men and scholars to record the dates of the important events, both good and bad, of every time so that thereafter they may serve as examples to their insightful descendants and followers, so that in ages to come they may know the conditions of the past, and so that the names of renowned monarchs and successful princes may thereby remain forever on the face of the pages of time, for with the passage of days and months and through long ages and years untoward events may efface and erase them. . . . An example of the truth of this assertion is that despite the vast kingdom that Sultan Mahmud of Ghazna acquired, with its effulgence of pomp and abundant wealth, innumerable possessions, treasure troves beyond counting, paraphernalia of success and the good things of this world, today his good name and renown remain solely because of the poetry of Unsuri and Firdawsi and the writings of Utbi.
> In this world the good relics of Mahmud of
> Ghazna's career have remained bound by rhyme.
> Hence it can be known that poets and historians are the best propagandists.
> —Rashiduddin Fazlullah, *Jami 'u't-tawarikh* (History of the World,
> c 1300–11 A.D.)

I. History's Rhyme

Rashiduddin Fazlullah's life and death attest to Baghdad's history as a perennial theater of destiny's caprices. His is an instructive and timely lesson for our own era. "Bound by rhyme" and beyond reason,[1] the fate of Kwaja Rashiduddin, as he is honorifically known, is exemplary of those commissioned to execute the testaments of history, who, not infrequently, become in turn the object of historic executions. In history's rhyme and reason, his fortunes indicate, neither rhyme nor reason—much less ideological zeal—can prevail. From the emperor's vizier to abject pariah, from philanthropist to outcast, and from court chronicler to court fatality, his itinerary spans the gamut of fortune. His final hour, along with that of his son, would come in his seventy-first year: "On the 17th of Jumada I, 718 [July 17, 1318 A.D.] in the vicinity of Uma in the village of Khashgudar, the executioner first cut off Khwaja Ibrahim's head in his father's presence. Then he stepped before Khwaja Rashid, who said to him, 'Say to Alisha, "You have had me killed for no crime. It will not be long before fate will requite you of me, and the only difference between us will be that my grave will be older than yours."' Then the executioner cut the Khwaja in two at the waist."[2] Nearly seven hundred years later, in the first decade of the twenty-first century, the executioners in Baghdad were diligently persevering in their labors. The aftershocks of their awful labors define, yet again, the destiny of the besieging hordes. The blowback from the siege defines as well our understanding of the world, its history, and the transcultural yield of such violence ripples through our disciplinary practices in comparative literature and historiography. There is a direct line between the textual after-effects of the siege of 1258 and the siege of 2003, as we shall see.

Kwaja Rashiduddin Fazlullah wrote his *Jami'u't-tawarikh* (History of the World) between 1300 and 1311, commissioned by Ghazan Khan, great-grandson of Hülagü Khan and last Buddhist emperor of the Mongols, who, at the beginning of June 1295 converted to Islam, the religion of the Abbasid dynasty, whose 525-year reign was brought to an end by his great-grandfather's siege of the caliphate city of Baghdad in 1258. While he was composing his "History of the World"—binding, as he says in the chapter epigraph, history's rhyme into his own rhyming and thereby finding himself in a double bind, in a distant place—an equally universal history was being composed in tercet rhyme, known to that other world as the *Divina commedia*. Its author, an avid partisan of the White Guelph faction in the city of Florence, is known to posterity as Dante Alighieri. An exile from his city who would immortalize himself as a transient through the afterlife in his vernacular rhymes, he also understood the caprices of this world and the retributions of the next. Like his contemporary Kwaja

Rashiduddin, Dante understood the significance of poetry for history and the role attributed to poetry as propagator of cultures: "Hence it can be known that poets and historians are the best propagandists"—a vocation in which Dante also excelled.[3] Few understood this power of poetry more than Dante's mentor and guide Virgil, whose epic, the *Aeneid*, like Kwaja Rashiduddin's *Jami'u't-tawarikh*, was commissioned by his emperor and would serve as imperial propaganda. The Florentine Dante, like Kwaja Rashiduddin in his reflections on world governance in *Jami'u't-tawarikh*, also ventured into philosophical speculation on world history and world government in a work called *De monarchia* (On Monarchy).

The worlds of Dante and Kwaja Rashiduddin were *the* world; the two ran in parallel as universal realms, as did God's providential dispensation for their respective universality. Their parallel worlds would not converge for some time, as was already inevitable as early as the siege of Baghdad by the great-grandfather of Kwaja Rashiduddin's royal patron, who, as the chronicler noted in his *Jami'u't-tawarikh*, was not immune to the ideological convictions of his favorite wife:

> His chief wife was Doquz Khatun of the great "bone" of the Kerayit, the daughter of Ong Khan's son. Since she had been his father's wife, she was greater than the other wives, even though he had married some of them before. He married her after crossing the Oxus River. Toloui Khan [his father] had not yet touched her. She had influence and was extremely domineering. Since the Kerayit tribes were originally Christian, she constantly favored Christians, and during her time that group became strong. For her sake Hülagü Khan also favored them and held them in honor, so much so that they built churches throughout the realm.[4]

Baghdad, the besieged city, would become the crossroads where Hülagü Khan's Mongolian Buddhism, his wife's Nestorian Christianity, and the conquered Abbasids' Islam converged, and where the besiegers and the besieged would cross history's horizon into transformations not foreseen by either. Thus, their legacy, like the history of Kwaja Rashiduddin, would transform and be cast into new rhymes whose permutations continue still as they traverse new horizons into what we now call vanishing points in time's historical and poetic unfolding. Baghdad, the perennially besieged city, has always consumed and transformed its besiegers, no matter their spiritual zeal or material rapacity; indeed, at the beginning of the twenty-first century, it still continues to do so.

Vanishing points in history, like vanishing points in painting and architecture, function as the receding horizon of perceptual transformations. The edge of that horizon becomes the focus point, especially for imperial cultures, because empires have tended to identify that edgy expectation with their destined moment of glory. Through such vanishing points on the horizon of history, cultures that are sure of having an edge on every other culture have tended to see themselves as having reached their own apotheosis, that is, their self-deification and historical transcendence, when history is considered to have come to an end. Predictably enough, at the end of the twentieth century and the beginning of this third millennium, the most recent example of this process emerges in the latest declaration of the end of history by the neoconservative intelligentsia following the disintegration of the Soviet system in 1989.

Cultures that see themselves as posthistorical tend to feel triumphant not only over history but over having their self-perceived uniqueness corroborated. Thus, they feel confirmed in their self-vindication as incomparable to any other culture. At these moments of self-transcendence and historical apotheosis, when such cultures have stood tall in the inimitable narrative of their invincibility, certain historical contingencies have inevitably emerged along with their unanticipated consequences. At such climactic moments of what is considered an unprecedented apex from where such cultures see themselves as exceptional and incomparable, their panoptic eye has had to blink no matter its location of omnipotent impregnability, whether at the top of the city gate, at the summit of the pyramid, the tip of the ziggurat, the spiral of the cathedral, the peak of the minaret, at the acme of World Trade Towers, or on the face of the coin of the realm.

For cultures that see themselves as occupying the pinnacle of history, the virtues of the vanishing point are threefold. If they should feel that they are about to reach and surpass such a climactic point, that point automatically recedes. Thus, like the prognostications of the prophetic tradition, the cultural apotheosis becomes projected into a perpetually self-succeeding horizon that ensures its continuity and the illusion of endurance in perpetuity. Second, having moved into what is perceived as virgin territory hitherto untouched by any other history, such cultures are more prone to think of themselves as providentially unique, unprecedented, and therefore also inimitable. And, third, with the ever-receding vanishing point there vanishes as well any norm or law as grounds for assessment, valorization, or judgment outside of the standard and criteria engendered by the self-perceived transcendental culture itself.

Such illusory immunity from history has tended to translate into impunity of practices that are inevitably historical and subject to time. And despite a sense of righteous invulnerability, there lingers a certain mixture of anxiety and urgency in the life-world of such cultures. These anxieties may well be the unavoidable symptoms of the self-perceived perennial exception. If a culture considers itself exceptional, the anxiety of repeating itself is no less acute than the dreaded possibility that, in some way, it may be repeating some other culture. And the pinnacle of triumph, a rather precarious peak, is fraught not only with the vertiginous anxieties of success and self-succession but is threatened by the simple but implacable law of gravity.

Kwaja Rashiduddin's *Jami'u't-tawarikh* offers numerous instances of such inevitability. We shall adduce a few more historical examples along the way, some perhaps startling because of their remoteness, and some no less discomfiting by virtue of their proximity to us. There is a great danger in exemplifying exceptions, that is, in making exceptionalism exemplary, since by definition what considers itself exceptional does not look kindly on its being considered an example of anything else, and most certainly not a reiteration of itself. Exceptionalism, by definition unprecedented and irreproducible, would not deign to think of itself as reproduction, or as repeatable model, an example that anyone else might emulate, except as a lesser imitation under the aegis and in the shadow of the inimitable grandeur of what sees itself as the authentic, the unique, and the original at history's apogee. This is an urgent issue in the study of imperial histories, with the exceptionalism that has marked the genesis of any given empire under study all too often recapitulated in the academic disciplines devoted to it. Such disciplinary implosion turns the exceptionality into a flash point of epistemological debate and its imperial parameters become the hotly contested arena for the production and management of knowledge. The devotion to the study of exceptionality, in other words, has often convinced those so preoccupied of the exceptional nature of their own knowledge. For this reason, to allay any possible anxieties among practitioners of, say, comparative literature, history, or American studies, it should be stated that in this discussion of the vanishing points of cultures and their apotheosis any similarities between the examples adduced and the current status of empire and its global realpolitik may be purely fortuitous. Such coincidences might only be a product of the human imagination's penchant for seeing patterns in history and in poetic memory—a chronic inclination exaggerated in scholars and chroniclers as readers. This said, it is difficult not to see such patterns when reality and its literature exhort us to see them as, for example, when, at the beginning of the twenty-first century, it becomes impossible to avoid being haunted by the prophetic verses of the neoclassical Iraqi poet Mohammad Mahdi al-Jawahiri, whose life nearly spanned the whole twentieth century (1900–1997). From his Damascene exile he would write to Baghdad the verses many in the Arabic world recite from haunted memory and with a heavy heart:

I see a horizon lit with blood
And many a starless night.
A generation comes and another goes
And the fire keeps burning.[5]

Nor do the conscientious discoveries and reporting of contemporary investigators allow us to forget the persistent echoes of the past in the present. Such is the case, for example, of the diligent investigations by the Latin American scholar Fernando Baez, whose findings were reported in the *Asia Times* on Tuesday, February 17, 2005, by the Inter Press Service reporter Humberto Márquez: "CARACAS—One million books, 10 million documents and 14,000 archaeological artifacts have been lost in the US-led invasion and subsequent occupation of Iraq—the biggest cultural disaster since the descendants of Genghis Khan destroyed Baghdad in 1258, Venezuelan writer Fernando Baez told Inter Press Service (IPS)."[6]

II. Narrative's Edge

When Hülagü Khan, the grandson of Genghis Khan, besieged and devastated the Abbasid-caliphate city of Baghdad in 1258, the sense of history suddenly shifted from the timeless torpor of the Abbasid dynasty to an urgent timeliness, after 525 years of self-convinced eternity. This was a defining moment that spelled simultaneously the end of the caliphate and the cresting of the Mongol empire that destroyed it. Coincidentally enough, the year 1258 was also the year in which Osman I founded what would become the Ottoman empire. He would institute the Ottoman state one year later. This was indeed a cutting edge of history, with history's horizon plunging through yet another vanishing point. Here is how the Turkish novelist and 2006 Nobel laureate Orhan Pamuk dramatizes that moment in the history of Baghdad, in his 1998 historical novel, an ekphrastic tour de force on genre painting—miniature painting, to be exact. It is a moment in history when one cultural horizon at its instant of apotheosis broke off into the precipitous vanishing point of history to be succeeded by another, that eventually would endure the same fate. The novel's principal plot and narrative time are set at another imperial highpoint, in the last quarter of the sixteenth century, when the Ottoman empire arrived at its own greatest geographical reach shortly after the reign of Süleyman the Magnificent, after which, like the Mongol empire in 1258, it was to begin its chronic decline that would become terminally critical three hundred years later, to expire anticlimactically at the beginning of the twentieth century. Pamuk's novel is entitled *Benim Adim Kirmizi* (*My Name Is Red*).[7] Oscillating between the year of the Mongol Khan Hülagü's siege and destruction of Baghdad and the reign of the red-bearded Ottoman Sultan Murat III between 1574 and 1595, the novel narrates this monumental shift, what could be described as a passage from the timelessness of the utopic to the timeliness of the topical and the dislocation of the historical horizon beyond its own vanishing point. And while the original date of this novel's publication in Turkish is 1998, its fountainhead dates to the Turkish translation in 1425 of a section from Kwaja Rashiduddin's own *Jami'u't-tawarikh*. That section, which deals with the Qayi tribe, was translated by Yazizāde Ali, the court scribe and chronicler of Sultan Murat II. Constrained to convince the Anatolian masses of its genealogical legitimacy and noble origins, the ascendant Ottoman court, whose dynastic house was launched by Osman I, traced its lineage through Kwaja Rashiduddin's history to the Turkic Qayi people.[8] Notorious for his archival diligence, Orhan Pamuk, who had ready access to the Ottoman collections through his former wife, Aylin Turegen, a historian and specialist on early Turkish and Turkic history, may well have begun his research for his novel with these Yazizāde Ali pages from the *Jami'u't-tawarikh*. Here, then, is Orhan Pamuk's narrator on Hülagü's 1258 siege of Baghdad, as witnessed by the calligrapher-turned-painter Ibn Shakir from atop the minaret of the caliphate mosque:

> When Baghdad fell to the Mongols and was mercilessly plundered on a cold day of the month of Safar [February], Ibn Shakir was the most renowned and proficient calligrapher and scribe not only of the whole Arab world but of

all Islamdom; despite his youth, he had transcribed twenty-two volumes, most of which were Korans and could be found in the world-famous libraries of Baghdad. Ibn Shakir believed these books would last until the end of the world, and, therefore, lived with a deep and infinite notion of time. He'd toiled heroically all through the night by flickering candlelight on the last of those legendary books, which are unknown to us today because in the span of a few days, they were one by one torn up, shredded, burned, and tossed into the Tigris River by the soldiers of the Mongol Khan Hülagü. Just as the master Arab calligraphers, committed to the notion of the endless persistence of tradition and books, had for centuries been in the habit of resting their eyes as a precaution against blindness by turning their backs to the rising sun and looking toward the western horizon, Ibn Shakir ascended the minaret of the Caliphate Mosque in the coolness of morning, and from the balcony where the muezzin called the faithful to prayer, witnessed all that would end a five-centuries-long tradition of scribal art. First, he saw Hülagü's pitiless soldiers enter Baghdad, and yet he remained where he was atop the minaret. He watched the plunder and destruction of the entire city, the slaughter of hundreds of thousands of people, the killing of the last of the Caliphs of Islam who'd ruled Baghdad for half a millennium, the rape of women, the burning of libraries and the destruction of tens of thousands of volumes as they were thrown into the Tigris. Two days later, amid the stench of corpses and cries of death, he watched the flowing waters of the Tigris, turned red from the ink bleeding out of the books, and he thought about how all those volumes he'd transcribed in beautiful script, those books that were now gone, hadn't in the least served to stop this horrifying massacre and devastation, and in turn, he swore never to write again. Furthermore, he was struck by the desire to express his pain and the disaster he'd witnessed through painting, which until that day, he'd belittled and deemed an affront to Allah; and so, making use of the paper he always carried with him, he depicted what he saw from the top of the minaret. We owe the happy miracle of the three-hundred-year renaissance [this is being narrated during the reign of Sultan Murat III, which lasted between the years 1574 and 1595] in Islamic illustration following the Mongol invasion to that element which distinguished it from the artistry of pagans and Christians; that is, the truly agonizing depiction of the world from an elevated Godlike position attained by drawing none other than a horizon line. We owe this renaissance to the horizon line, and also to Ibn Shakir's going north after the massacre he witnessed—in the direction the Mongol armies had come from—carrying with him his paintings and the ambition for illustration in his heart; in brief, we owe much to his learning the painting techniques of the Chinese masters. Thereby, it is evident that the notion of endless time that had rested in the hearts of Arab calligrapher-scribes for five hundred years would finally manifest itself not in writing, but in painting.[9]

Exactly three-hundred-and-thirty-three years after Hülagü's siege and devastation of Baghdad, in a naval battle that lasted only four hours, but which proved just as defining for the history of painting and literature, the invincible navy of the Ottoman empire was vanquished by the combined naval forces of Christendom, led by Venice, at the Battle of Lepanto on October 7, 1571. The battle was immortalized in paintings by Titian, by Tintoretto, and by Veronese, and in dramatic form by one of the combatants, the Spanish novelist Miguel de Cervantes y Saavedra, in the now lost drama *La batalla naval*. Cervantes lost the use of his left hand from wounds sustained from a musket shot during the battle, a fact not unrelated to his writing the first modern European novel, *Don Quixote*. Despite the glorious victory of Lepanto, Venice was obliged to relinquish to the Ottomans one of its most prized strategic islands in the eastern Mediterranean, the island of Cyprus. And this is why, ultimately, a native of that perennially unfortunate island is writing this present memo in English, the language of another island in the northern periphery of the "Great Western Sea," rather than in Dante's Tuscan vernacular or in Venetian dialect.

Because imperial apotheoses, despite the providential design empires attribute to them, are bedeviled by improvident contingencies, events such as the siege of Baghdad of 1258 and the Battle of Lepanto of 1571 find their lasting significance through unforeseen dramatic turns in aesthetic practices. These events emerge, in other words, as historical peripeties that become illustrative watersheds in cultural history. Contingencies that issue from such unpredictable shifts often converge in equally startling ways. And so it is that despite losing the naval battle and gaining Cyprus, or precisely because of it, the Ottoman court of Sultan Murat III would become the site of a profound shift in aesthetic norms. It was there, in Istanbul, between 1574 and 1595, that the rapture in the traditions of painting perpetrated by the devastation of Baghdad in 1258 would reach a new apex, as narrated by Pamuk through the Baghdadi calligrapher Ibn Shakir's successors. These are the masters of miniature painting in Pamuk's novel in their parlous plots that define the opportune modernization of aesthetic topology. At that highpoint, this art of painting was to encounter the strains of Venetian and what they then called Frankish (European) aesthetics.

Sultan Murat would sponsor the production of the *Book of Skills*, the *Book of Festivities*, and the *Book of Victories* in his court's workshops. This is the corpus classicus of Turkish miniature painting. All three works now are in the treasury vaults of Topkapi Saray in Istanbul, as is the masterpiece of the Persian poet Firdusi, whom Kwaja Rashiduddin calls Firdawsi in his prefatory reflections on history and poetry, which I have used as the epigraph for this memo. This is Firdusi's *Shahnama*, or *Book of Kings*, which the poet himself had presented to the Ghaznavid Sultan Mahmud, his imperial patron, in the year 1010, a work that would inspire miniaturist painters, especially from their eighth (by our calendar, fourteenth) century onward. Sultan Murat's imperial court, by virtue of its concentration of talent and the cultural interpenetration with archrival Venice, was also to become the site of what was referred to as "Frankish painting," that is to say, perspectival representation of subject matter, whether of landscape or of the human form. The contamination of the empyrean panoptic that was Allah's vantage point and its line of horizon, as seen and drawn for the first time by Ibn Shakir from atop the minaret of the caliphate mosque of Baghdad in 1258, according to Pamuk's novel, would scandalize more than one orthodox Muslim and court calligrapher. As Pamuk dramatizes it through one of his ambivalent characters, a master miniaturist of maximal ambiguity who, alas, would meet his untimely death at the hands of true believers and masters of disambiguation,

nothing is pure.... In the realm of book arts, whenever a masterpiece is made, whenever a splendid picture makes my eyes water out of joy and causes a chill to run down my spine, I can be certain of the following: Two styles heretofore never brought together have come together to create something new and wondrous.... Today, if men cannot adequately praise the book-arts workshop of Akbar Khan in Hindustan, it's because he urged his miniaturists to adopt the style of the Frankish masters. To God belongs the East and the West. May He protect us from the will of the pure and unadulterated.[10]

In these unorthodox words of Pamuk's Enishte Effendi, one is bound to recognize resonances of our own time's heterodox notions of syncretism, hybridity, métissage, and transculturation, terms and processes no less controversial and no less susceptible to the zeal of what we call today, in the argot of our academic guild, identity politics and self-reifying autoethnographies. These are certainly key concepts, lexical codes that circumscribe disciplinary discourses within parameters that would be jolted no less than the miniaturists of Murat III's court, were their practitioners to make themselves conscious of and receptive to the historical events that surround, consume, and define them.

The Siege of Baghdad   51

This is to say that such startling contingencies also converge to define the beginning of our own twenty-first century: a haunting adumbration of this historical peripety emerges on the horizon through the lens of a suggestive passage from Michel de Certeau's 1980 treatise *L'invention du quotidien* (*The Practice of Everyday Life*).[11] Now, at the beginning of the third millennium, in a time no less shrill with Manichean claims at poles of orthodox professions and sanctified purity—of the axis of evil and of the nexus of good—de Certeau's passage from a quarter-century ago resonates as an ominous ghostly echo:

Seeing Manhattan from the 110th floor of the World Trade Center, beneath the haze stirred up by winds, the urban island, a sea in the middle of the sea, lifts up the skyscrapers over Wall Street, sinks down at Greenwich, then rises again to the crests of Midtown, quietly passes over Central Park and finally undulates off into the distance beyond Harlem.... The 1,370 foot high tower that serves as a prow for Manhattan continues to construct the fiction that creates readers, makes the complexity of the city readable, and immobilizes its opaque mobility in a transparent text.... The ordinary practitioners of the city live "down below," below the threshold at which visibility begins. They walk—an elementary form of this experience of the city; they are walkers, *Wandersmänner*, whose bodies follow the thicks and thins of an urban "text" they write without being able to read it.[12]

III. Vanishing Point

In the calamitous destruction of those skyscrapers on September 11, 2001, a calamity that would lead directly from the New York of that date to the latest siege of Baghdad, what de Certeau refers to as "the 1,370 foot high tower that serves as a prow for Manhattan [that] continues to construct the fiction that creates readers, makes the complexity of the city readable, and immobilizes its opaque mobility in a transparent text" has been lost irrevocably. In the absence of that elevated fulcrum and the tall-tale narratives in its imperial shadow that reached around the world, the readers it created, the legibility of the complex city it made possible, the transparency of a mobile opaqueness it projected have all vanished beyond a historical horizon whose edge, once again, has been shattered. Like Pamuk's Ibn Shakir on the balcony of the minaret of Baghdad's caliphate mosque in 1258, like Enishte Effendi in the Istanbul court of Murat III in the 1590s, we are faced with the urgency of finding a substitute set of constructions for functional legibility, for readership, for mobile opacity, for textual transparency, and for historical density. There is no irony in the fact that our labors are compelled to follow a continuous line on a horizon that extends from what de Certeau called "the 1,370 foot high tower that" served "as a prow for Manhattan" to the rubble of Kabul of 2001, the pulverized and pillaged Baghdad of 2003, and to the bombarded lighthouse and perimeters of Beirut in 2006. What has been lost is not only the 1,370-foot-high tower and its optical vigil that, in de Certeau's words, "construct[ed] the fiction that creates readers" in its complexity, but also lost with the pulverization of the skyline of Kabul, Baghdad, and parts of Beirut is the moral high ground that pointed to the heinous act of criminality that destroyed that high tower in Manhattan. What remains at either end of this line of destruction is far from a justification of the unjustifiable. And the most recent siege of Baghdad has transformed the execrable into a desecration of the spectral towers that continue to haunt the Manhattan skyline as ghosts. One unforgivable act has been compounded by many others, thereby blurring the line between the act of criminality and the acts of retribution, blending the two so that it is no longer possible to discern which is the crime and which the just reprisal.

As with Ibn Shakir at the top of the minaret, as with Enishte Effendi in the most powerful court of his time, our own ceaselessly surveyed critical predicament today consists in the unlikely possibility of seeing without being seen, of reading without being read—and read biometrically down to our genetic composition, at that. We strain to find a vantage point, no matter how minimal, even as we know ourselves to be under the scrutiny of the panoptic eye at the pyramidal peak of universal global positioning systems, perhaps the same eye that suffuses world trade and global capital, the eye that, though rendered ghostly at one particular locus on "the 1,370 foot high tower," in de Certeau's portentous depiction, now more than ever proliferates ubiquitously into every corner of the world and on every dollar bill as it blinks at the summit of a pyramid embossed on the quotidian coin of the global realm.

Mere seeing, then, much less critical insight, under the circumstances risks being subsumed into the hegemonic fury of omnipresent surveillance and blinding righteousness. Any movement beyond the triumphalism of the righteous and the apotheosis of the self-convinced at the moment, a historical moment saturated with terror and terror-obsessed global realpolitik, would seem to be futile. We hover as a spectral echo across a line in history that mirrors us in a time when Genghis Khan's Mongol grandson Hülagü Khan—son of a Nestorian Christian mother, Sorghaghtani Beki, and husband of Doquz Khatun, also a Nestorian Christian princess from Persia, of the Kerayit tribes, as Kwaja Rashiduddin points out[13]—was dispatched by his elder brother and egged on by his mother to conquer Persia. He was to hunt down and exterminate the sect of "terrorists"—"Assassins" or "Ismaelians," according to Edward Gibbon[14]—that plagued the region at the time, crush the "heretics,"[15] the Islamic Abbasid caliphate in Baghdad, and destroy the Muslim states of the Middle East, thereby remaking the map of the region. Hülagü Khan rampaged all the way to the already ill-starred Gaza on the Mediterranean, besieged still at the beginning of this twenty-first century. His expedition was referred to as the Mongol crusade because, in addition to the heretical zeal of his Nestorian mother and of his Nestorian wife, Hülagü's campaign attracted the enthusiasm and support of a number of Christian communities, with many Georgian and Alan mercenaries joining his campaign in what one might recursively describe as prototype of "a coalition of the willing."[16] The methods of such "coalition building" have changed little since they were described by Kwaja Rashiduddin:

> For one month they remained there, issuing decrees to the monarchs and sultans of Iran, saying, "We are on a campaign to eradicate the strongholds of the Heretics by command of the Qa'an. If you come yourselves and assist us with soldiers, weapons, and provisions, your territories, troops, and homes will remain yours and your efforts will be appreciated. If you allow any negligence of this command to take place, when by God's grace we are finished with them, we will head straight for you—and no excuse will be accepted—and the same thing will happen to your territories and homes that will have happened to them." Swift-traveling messengers were dispatched on this mission, and when the news of the arrival of the world-conquering banners was spread abroad, the sultans and maliks of every part of Iran set out for court.[17]

The formula has been distilled by now to the economic phrase "you are with us, or you are with the terrorists," though the subtleties of "coalition building" remain unaltered.[18] And the zeal of the sectarians of Nestor then is matched now by the zeal of the born-again believers who claim no less that their evangelical mission originates directly in God's will. Nestorius was Archbishop, between the years 428 and 431, of what was then Constantinopolis, which would become, after 1453, the Istanbul of the miniaturist successors of Ibn Shakir the calligrapher, who, by the Istanbullu Pamuk's telling, came by his new calling as a painter when he witnessed the siege and sacking of Baghdad in 1258. Having claimed that the nature of Christ is at once mortal and divine, the monophysite orthodoxy of the Christian church would defrock Patriarch Nestorius in 433 and banish him eastward into the wilderness of the orient, from where his teachings would coalesce into Nestorian Christianity, which reached all the way to China, Kwaja Rashiduddin's "Cathay." Nestor's heretical legacy would ricochet westward through Baghdad into the annals of history to foreshadow what we are given to refer to as an early modernity.

When he laid waste to the city of Baghdad in 1258, Hülagü Khan's own horizon would indeed crest into its vanishing point, an apotheosis that was at once the zenith of Genghis Khan's imperial legacy and the beginning of the end of the imperial Ilkhanid hegemony. Having fallen out of favor with the crusaders of his coalition who were holding Palestine, Hülagü pulled his armies back to the Tigris, which would serve thereafter as the westernmost frontier of the Mongol empire. Returning home to internecine strife following the death of his elder brother, Hülagü Khan withdrew to Azerbaijan and converted to Islam. He died within seven years of sacking Baghdad. Certain learned men were spared, including Orhan Pamuk's Ibn Shakir, who observed and recorded with shock and awe the mayhem and pillaging of the siege from his perch on the caliphate mosque's highest minaret, as were all the members of Baghdad's Christian community at the behest of Hülagü's Nestorian Christian mother. As chronicled by Kwaja Rashiduddin, "Fierce battle was fought for six days and nights. Hülagü Khan ordered six decrees written, saying, 'The lives of cadis, scholars, shaykhs, Alids, and Nestorian priests, and persons who do not combat against us are safe from us.' The proclamations were fastened to arrows and shot into the city from six sides."[19] Hülagü's "Mongol crusade," was not only political and economic, then, but also racial and religious in its ideological zeal. It is not known for certain how many people were put to the sword. Precedent-setting in yet another way, Hülagü Khan and the Mongol horde eschewed "doing a body count," as more recent language on the matter would have it. From the pyramid of corpses, however, observers estimate that between eighty thousand and a quarter million inhabitants of Baghdad were killed, with unnumbered bodies and the size of human pyramids ominously foreshadowing the countless human corpses of the future.

In the early twentieth century the Harvard philosopher George Santayana, in volume 1 of his work *The Life of Reason* (1905), made an observation that has now become a commonplace, namely, that those who cannot remember the past are condemned to repeat it. What is invariably overlooked in the wisdom of this apothegm is its converse, or its mirrored echo, to wit, that there may well be those who repeat the past precisely because they remember it well. Santayana, working at the end of the nineteenth century and beginning of the twentieth century, still labored under the illusion that remembering was tantamount to self-redemption and that aggregate knowledge guaranteed wisdom. At the beginning of the twenty-first century, one hundred years after Santayana's optimistic opus, we are disabused, yet again, of the illusion that any necessary correlation exists between knowledge and wisdom, memory and redemption, poetry and civility, sensibility and sense, science and civilization, or longevity and improvement.

In this regard, the persistent redundancy with which Baghdad has been subjected to siege and devastation since Kwaja Rashiduddin's chronicle may not be insignificant. The repetition of the past, in other words, may not reside in amnesia but in something more proactive than the automatic default action Santayana imputed to the loss of memory. Those of us in comparative literature and in American studies who study and teach the latest self-proclaimed imperial avatar that not only sees itself as posthistorical but is replete with ideologues who have already appropriated the new century as the "project for a new American century," are constrained to inquire how and where it is that the latest siege of Baghdad and sacking of Iraq fit in the long history of this redundancy. We have to do so, especially those of us inside the Leviathan's belly, because the exertion of power does not only affect its targets but it also defines those who exert it. Inevitably, the conquerors are defined by those they conquer and by the acts of their conquest, as the worldly history, the *Jami'u't-tawarikh* of Kwaja Rashiduddin makes abundantly clear. This may be the only consolation for those subjected by overwhelming power. They, the subjected, ultimately identify and redefine, in incalculable ways, those who have subjected them.

The identity of the conqueror passes through the conquered, as the religious conversion of Hülagü Khan and of his great-grandson Ghazan Khan to the faith of the besieged and conquered amply demonstrates. In the annals of history, the common wisdom could well be, "Tell me whom you've invaded and I'll tell you who you are." Thus it is impossible for anyone to understand the hegemon of the day in the siege of Baghdad without factoring into that understanding the ways in which Baghdad, and by extension all of Iraq, defines what and who the besieger is. This is a pivotal detail because it is here, on this fulcrum, that the imperial tall tale and the "insignificant rabble" of history are balanced. And while the tall tale may overshadow the minute, it is the latter that gives content, shape, and historical density to the former. As with Kwaja Rashiduddin's time, then, for early twenty-first-century imperial studies as a scientific discipline and field of scholarship to be meaningful, it must pass through Baghdad. And this applies not only to the investigation and pedagogy of empire as a post-2001 phenomenon, but it applies as well to the besieger's imperial history in its full chronological spectrum from the end of the fifteenth century, starting with the "discovery," conquest, settlement, and colonization of what was to become the United States of America on March 20, 2003, the day of the latest siege of Baghdad, and after.

IV. Rhyming History:
The Baghdadization of America

What, then, can we learn about America from the siege of Baghdad? Perhaps the most significant lesson for us, as comparatists, especially, and for the United States of America is that the narrative of exceptionalism and its current violent reiteration notwithstanding, America is not unique, it is not an exception, it is not sui generis, it is not unprecedented, and it is not inimitable. In fact, it has never been these things despite its own imperial mythology to this effect, often reinforced and reenacted by those who have investigated and taught this nation as a school subject called American studies. There is something even more enduring than the myth of American exceptionalism: the perennial and, one may be tempted to say, somewhat perverse, penchant of Baghdad to be subjected to siege after siege with historical regularity. One is driven to suspect that, ironically, the city's founding epithet, "the City of Peace," might have something to do with it. This latest instance, then, is a symptom of an obsessive recurrence that dates from the middle of the first millennium and extends into the present.

The siege of Baghdad is so persistent in its compulsive redundancy as symptom that it should more properly be called an imperial syndrome. It begins within a century of the city's founding, with the first invasion coming in the year 945 by the Buwayhids of Persia; and recurs a century later with the 1055 takeover by the Seljuks; to be repeated in 1258 by the Mongols led by Hülagü; in 1340 by the Jalayrs; in 1393 and again in 1401 by the Mongols, led this time by Tamerlane; in 1411 by the Turkoman Black Sheep (the Kara-Koyunlu); in 1469 by the Turkoman White Sheep (the Ak-Koyunlu); in 1508 by the Persian Safavids; in 1534 by the Ottomans under Sultan Süleyman the Magnificent; in 1623 again the Safavids; in 1638 by the Ottomans under Sultan Murat IV; in 1917 by the British; and in 1941 again the British. Alas, some people never learn, and between 1991 and 2003 the siege not only of the city but of the entire country of Iraq under a United Nations–sanctioned economic embargo and regular aerial bombardment by the American and British air forces, culminating in the March 20, 2003, Anglo-American-led invasion and still-current occupation.[20]

This litany of calamity visited upon Madinat as-Salam, the City of Peace, as its Abbasid founder Abu Jafur al-Mansur originally called it, is now an unavoidable part of the repertoire of anyone wishing to be a scholar of America with any degree of authority. In the calculus of that inexorable ledger that the American Transcendentalist Ralph Waldo Emerson called the law of compensation, the Baghdadization of America has become as undeniable as the Americanization of Baghdad. America is now, more than ever, a Middle Eastern country and the resultant status of Baghdad a synonym for Americanization. Despite the asymmetry of power, the unevenness of the playing field, the discrepancy between conqueror and vanquished, if history be a guide, there is a direct ratio in the intensity of this inexorable compensatory interchange. The more vehement, the more profound, the more protracted the siege and the more egregious its effects, proportionally greater will be the countereffects that define the besieging power. The precedent of Hülagü Khan and the fate of the Mongol empire following the siege of 1258 are certainly instructive in this regard, as is the example of the Ottoman empire that sustained its siege and occupation of Baghdad the longest. And where these two, the Mongol and the Ottoman, converge most eloquently in the annals of literature may well be in "a three-hundred-year-old Mongol inkpot,"[21] a vessel of immortality through the arts of writing and painting, but also a lethal instrument of murder, whose bronze weight and red ink find their graphic dramatization in the novel by Orhan Pamuk. This novel on the convergence of the heterodoxy of miniature painting and the orthodoxy of imperial apotheosis henceforth will also have to figure as a point of convergence of the earlier and latest sieges of Baghdad. Hence, Pamuk's novel will be indispensable in any reading list in American studies, even though America's name does not appear in the pages of that narrative.

And Kwaja Rashiduddin's munificence as precursor of Orhan Pamuk's "inkpot" is no less significant, nor is it, in Pamuk's masterful hand, any less ironic. The inkpot, that genie's lamp of literature and historiography, fountain of calligrapher and painter alike, comes to Pamuk and to us as more than personification of a mixed blessing, what the Greeks call a prosopopoeia. Kwaja Rashiduddin's *Jami'u't-tawarikh* deeds it to us in the historical personage of the volatile and rabblerousing Mujahiduddin Aybak the Dawatdar, who overreached well beyond the competency of his all-important office inside the Abbasid court of Baghdad as the *dawatdar* (inkpot holder). This, according to Kwaja Rashiduddin's history, occurred while Hülagü Khan's invading horde encircled the besieged city. It was an official overreaching on the part of the Abbasid court's official *dawatdar* who sought a natural harmony with the meteorological conditions that seemingly conspired with the curse of the besieging horde—the Mesopotamian flood that inundated the city and wreaked havoc in the imperial ranks awaiting Hülagü's onslaught. Kwaja Rashiduddin describes it thus:

Toward the end of the summer of 654 [1256 A.D.], a huge flood came and so inundated the city of Baghdad that the lower part of the inhabited section disappeared under water. For fifty days the flood increased, and then it began to subside. Half the outlying districts of Iraq were destroyed. The "Musta'simid flood" [Musta'sim being the caliph at the time] is still proverbial in the mouths of the people of Baghdad. During the catastrophe, [the] rabble took over, and every day they killed people. Mujahiduddin Aybak the Dawatdar called the rabble to himself, and in a short time he had become very powerful. When he was strong, and since he knew the Caliph Musta'sim to be indecisive and simple-hearted, he conspired with a group of his henchmen to depose the caliph and put another of the Abbasids in his place.[22]

The dramatic counterpoint that drives Pamuk's 1998 narrative is as timely for the latest siege of Baghdad as it is compelling for the siege of 1258 as seen through the aerial perspective of Ibn Shakir, the calligrapher who turned painter by virtue of that experience. The novel's dynamic counterpoint consists in the oscillation between the grand narrative of the imperial tall tale and the seemingly insignificant minutiae of history. The first, the imperial tall tale, is founded in and projected from the panoptic apex of the divine eye from atop the highest platform of the caliphate mosque's minaret. Its narrative radiates from the empyrean height of ideological conviction, girthed with the omnipotence of economic dominance, the orthodoxy of belief, and the unquestioned apotheosis of cultural self-deification. The second, the minutiae of history, emanates from the incidental and negligible detail of human contingencies rendered through the perspective of the calligrapher who witnesses the eternal grandeur of his books flowing and disintegrating into the river, an experience that turns his eye and vision toward the minutiae of the historical moment that would make him a painter and, eventually, a translator and recorder of the historical into the meticulously detailed genre of miniature painting. The way these contrapuntal narratives converge in the imperial Ottoman court in Istanbul during the reign of Sultan Murat III in the last decade of the sixteenth century—the millennial anniversary (in lunar years) of the Hegira (the flight of Muhammad from Mecca to Medina in 622 A.D. and the beginning of the Muslim era)—is most instructive. That convergence as depicted dialogically in Pamuk's ekphrastic novel brings together the eternal tradition's divine word as calligraphic art, the miniature as earthly marginal vignette, and the newly discovered perspectival centrality of blasphemous representation, achieved through ocular distortion and optical illusion. This, the novel tells us, is the hybrid legacy of Sheikh Muhammad of Isfahan:

Working in the Chinese black-ink style—brought to us by the Mongols—with skill and an elegant sense of symmetry, he was the one who introduced the terrifying demons, horned jinns, horses with large testicles, half-human monsters and giants into the devilishly subtle and sensitive Herat style of painting; he was the first to take an interest in and be influenced by the portraiture that had come by Western ships from Portugal and Flanders; he reintroduced forgotten techniques dating back to the time of Genghis Khan in decaying old volumes.... "Our book is no longer a secret," I answered. "Perhaps this isn't important. But rumors are spreading. They say we've underhandedly committed blasphemy. They say that, here, we've made a book—not as Our Sultan had commissioned and hoped for—but one meant to entertain our own whims; one that ridicules even Our Prophet and mimics infidel masters. There are those who believe it even depicts Satan as amiable. They say we've committed an unforgivable sin by daring to draw, from the perspective of a mangy dog, a horsefly and a mosque as if they were the same size—with the excuse that the mosque was in the background—thereby mocking the faithful who attend prayers. I cannot sleep for thinking about such things."[23]

What the court painters and miniaturists are discussing at the very heart of the Ottoman empire are the optical innovations in art and architecture that, because of the multiple perspectives they interject into a monolithic world, would place imperial mastery and governance in peril, eventually mining the absolute authority of sultan and emperor as well as the monologic and inviolable orthodoxy of the holy faith. In technical terms of comparative arts and literature, the traditional aesthetics of *orthomorphosis* have transmuted into the revolutionary modes of *anamorphosis*, so that for reality or its objects to be seen accurately it becomes necessary to skew or distort those objects through the optical artifice of representation. The perceived cosmos and its reality, then, become a by-product of human intervention, in this case ocular distortion, and the world, God's realm, an outcome of a reality effect. As philosophical concomitant of this transformation, pure reason yields to the volatile contingencies of rationality and rationalization, and, in the realm of the political, absolute norm and divine law are faced with the possibility of having to cede primacy to the expedient necessity of realpolitik. Thus, Ibn Shakir's abandonment of calligraphy for painting as he observes the siege and destruction of Baghdad in 1258 from a vantage point of the divine eye becomes further complicated by the discovery of perspective through the human eye and the painter's capacity to construct plausible fictions that correspond to reality, *as if* they were reality itself.

V. Frank Perspective

These transformations that the court painters and book-making miniaturists referred to as "Venetian" or as "Frankish" techniques can be dated with some precision to the publication in 1435 of a treatise in Latin, *De pictura*, by the polymath Leon Battista Alberti—a lawyer, architect, painter, mathematician, horseman, and encryptologist. Born in Genoa in 1404 and educated in Bologna, he would die in Rome in 1472, but not before he revolutionized the mathematics of architecture and the optics of painting. He dedicated the Italian edition of his treatise, which appeared a year after the Latin original, to his Florentine friend and fellow mathematician Filippo Brunelleschi (1377–1446), who might be most known as the architect of the dome of the cathedral of Florence, an architectural wonder of its time and ours. The American philosopher George Santayana, whose 1905 treatise *The Life of Reason* we invoked earlier, would be amused to know that Leon Battista Alberti might be the exception that proves the rule in the matter of being fated to repeat the past as the inevitable cost of forgetting it. Alberti turned to science and to the theory of art and architecture when as a young man he had to abandon his pursuit of law studies because of an illness that caused him to lose his memory. Here is how the conflicted miniaturist who would murder his Usta (Master) Enishte Effendi by bashing his skull with the Mongolian bronze inkpot discussed earlier depicts these scientific innovations and their insinuation into the miniature genre that we have been referring to as the contingent minutiae of history:

Your use of the science of perspective and the methods of the Venetian masters was nothing but the temptation of Satan. In the last painting, you've supposedly rendered the face of a mortal using the Frankish techniques, so the observer has the impression not of a painting but of reality; to such a degree that this image has the power to entice men to bow down before it, as with icons in churches. According to him, this is the Devil's work, not only because the art of perspective removes the painting from God's perspective and lowers it to the level of a street dog, but because your reliance on the methods of the Venetians as well as your mingling of our own established traditions with that of the infidels will strip us of our purity and reduce us to being their slaves.[24]

That unbreachable distance between "God's perspective" and "the level of a street dog" remains an abyss, or it so remained until recently, when the siege of Baghdad at the beginning of the twenty-first century witnessed another divine mission, yet another crusade, only this time from the West, rather than Hülagü's Mongol crusade from the East. The spectralization, or the mirrored imaging, of the two invasions has often been noted. It may well take some time for historians, ethicists, and scholars of

American and imperial studies to ascertain the degree to which the divine nature of the ideological mission and the vulgar means that debase the vanquished in the process of conquest are conjugated. This is the perilous juncture of "God's perspective" and "the level of a street dog," where the besieged and subjected are ravished of worldly possessions and life for a higher cause, and where they are deliberately degraded and sadistically dehumanized. Thus, in one of the photographs from the torture chambers of Abu Ghraib that may well stand as emblematic icon of the latest siege of Baghdad, the robotically instrumentalized soldier, on her divine mission, pulls the denuded vanquished on a dog's leash, blithely enacting the dramatic contrast between "God's perspective," which is the omnipotent optic of the imperial tall tale of liberation and democratization, and "the level of a street dog" that is the predicament of the besieged at the end of her leash. Ironically enough, the soldier's name is Miss England, a coincidence between name and provenance of the invading Anglo-American horde that, were it a character's name in a work of fiction, its deadly banality would strain credulity. All of this melancholy detail is minutely recorded in the mass media, reproduced through the most up-to-date technology with an accuracy that would be the nightmare of any miniaturist painter and the dread of Walter Benjamin, whose "Theses on History" would have us remember the inalienability of barbarism from civilization, and whose 1936 essay on photography and cinema, "The Work of Art in the Age Mechanical Reproduction," exposed the simultaneously auratic/religious dimension and the politically regressive possibilities of reproductive technologies as instruments of subjugation.

The path from Leon Batista Alberti's perspectival technologies in art and architecture to the latest siege of Baghdad takes a rather direct line. The pivotal articulation of these two points occurs within sixty years of Alberti's 1435 treatise, when one of the students of his mathematical sciences and arts translated the optical perspectivism of *anamorphosis* into its political possibilities, giving the world a handbook, in his treatise of 1513, that would prove just as consequential as the revolutionary work of Alberti, if not more so. The student in question is Niccolò Machiavelli (1469–1527), and his treatise is entitled *Il principe* (*The Prince*).[25] Unlike the dramatized resonance of Alberti's treatise in the Ottoman court of Sultan Murat III as narrated in the passages from Pamuk's novel cited here, there is no evidence of Machiavelli's penetration of the Ottoman imperial court, though the evidence for his percolation into global politics, or his symptomatic embodiment of those politics that surrounded that imperial center, is quite pervasive. The notion of what we refer to as realpolitik, that is, the practice of politics through pragmatic expediency rather than ethical, moral, or poetic principles, is at the core of Machiavelli's insight, as is the concomitant notion of "the reality effect," a phrase that articulates Machiavelli most efficiently to the perspectivist technologies of painting and the ocular illusion of reality that comes with the necessary distortion as a corrective for accurate perception—or the illusion of accurate perception, to be more exact. And this is what the court miniaturists of Sultan Murat III looked upon with ambivalent trepidation. Nonetheless, both the perspectival distortion and the reality effect would have, and still have, inestimable resonance in the science of optics and in the arts of politics, the latter consummated in the code term *realpolitik*. What we have in the latest siege of Baghdad is the legacy of this double inheritance, maximally deployed so that "God's perspective," so terrifically intoned as the tall tale of imperial righteousness, and the minutiae at "the level of the street dog," now imprinted on the historical retina by the melancholy video recording of Abu Ghraib prison, are expediently conjugated into synergy, to the point that it becomes impossible to discern the difference between virtual reality and actual reality, between God's providential agency and the invader's hallucinated mirror that reflects God back as anagram. James Joyce had already seen this specter in his own heretical struggle with apostasy as a Catholic Irishman who sought to awaken from the nightmare of history, where, in his ludic iconoclasm in the famous Circe episode of *Ulysses*, God could only be legible when spelled backwards. So illusionary and so brazenly deluded is the latest siege of Baghdad, its doublespeak so inverted and the perversity of control over its historical details so obsessively spun and sadistically minute, that it will not be long before some interested party seeks to disprove that the siege of 2003 ever happened as siege, the graphic evidence notwithstanding. Then, when invasion and occupation are made synonymous with liberation, democracy, and freedom, the vanishing point of an imperial apotheosis will have been completed, yet again, as much for the invader as for the besieged.

3

Of Learned Ignorance

NICHOLAS OF CUSA AND
CARDINAL SPACES OF CULTURE

> To God belongs the East and the West. May He protect us from the will of the pure and unadulterated.
> —Orhan Pamuk, *My Name Is Red*

> The relationship of our intellect to the truth is like that of a polygon to a circle; the resemblance to the circle grows with the multiplication of the angles of the polygon; but apart from its being reduced to identity with the circle, no multiplication, even if it were infinite, of its angles will make the polygon equal the circle.
> —Nicholas of Cusa, *De docta ignorantia*

I. Space-Time-Culture

At the beginning of this third millennium, when the dominant realpolitik deems itself providentially ordained and nonnegotiable, it seems inevitable that we should turn to Nicholas of Cusa, master of paradox and paragon of mediation. The last century did likewise, under historical circumstances no less ominous and at a time just as threatening, through such writers as Ernst Cassirer in his *Individuum und Kosmos in der Philosophie der Renaissance* (*The Individual and the Cosmos in Renaissance Philosophy*), for steadying the precarious predicament of human life in the world.[1]

Of Learned Ignorance 65

From Cusa comparative literature stands to learn the subtleties of transcultural traversal and of ideological negotiation. His lessons come from a time and place when true place and time were deemed otherworldly, when providential sanction trumped worldly argument for antagonists from the East and the West who felt divinely and incontrovertibly justified. Ours too is a time of confessional extremes, where competing kingdoms of God moot all counterarguments one would dare rehearse against the professions of those fully convinced that they reign with true divine dispensation. It is at such times, Cusa teaches us, that space and culture become coterminous, that real estate and enforceable culture are commensurable, and such compelled commensurability makes the land (and its subsoil deposits) vulnerable to the claims of those who can impose their demands with greater force and the illusionary impunity that comes with self-conviction.

If, under such circumstances, territorial space and culture are made to converge, time and culture, Cusa suggests, diverge and become antithetical. Time, being corrosive, renders culture vulnerable to time's depredations. It falls to culture-space, then, to compensate for what is lost to time. And memory, in all its leaps and lapses, becomes the instrument for that recovery, as we shall see in the next chapter, devoted to Giordano Bruno. The process of cultural recuperation as recompense for what is lost in time occurs in space. More specifically, that salvaging comes about in the conversion of space into place and of place into definable topography and territorial claims.[2] And within the disciplinary transformations of space into sites of institutional discourse such as comparative literature, we are rediscovering, yet again, the incongruities of identity and equivalence that Cusa teaches us with mathematical precision and prescient insight. His early modern lesson is now our commonplace. As we shall see in the following section of this chapter, so thoroughly has Cusa been assimilated to our cultural discourse that one contemporary comparatist crystallizes this critical legacy, without even the need to recall Cusa by name, as follows: "Comparison . . . involves a very particular form of incommensurability: space offers a ground of comparison, but no given basis of equivalence."[3]

Space is most fundamentally interval and distance: interval in musical composition, bent trajectory in the receding perspective of artistic and architectural constructs. As such, space invariably exerts a presence, an affirmation, even in / through what the Marxist philosopher and musicologist Theodor W. Adorno has called "negative space," as corollary to what he has referred to as "negative dialectics." With this articulation he interjects a theologizing philosophical intention into what music utilizes as contingent or instrumental "passage" through space as valuable interregnum.[4] Space, then, is chromatic (i.e., value-laden) silence in music, and it serves as ocular distortion and as perceptual corrective for the visual faculty in art and architecture, as Cusa's older contemporaries in Florence, referred to in the last chapter, Filippo Brunelleschi (1377–1446) and Leon Battista Alberti (1404–1472), taught the engineers, architects, and stonemasons of their time. It was through the calculus of Brunelleschi, the goldsmith's apprentice turned architect who opened up the possibilities of linear perspective and the vanishing point, that we came to understand the possibilities of the interval—the sound of silence in music, of optical distortion through space in architecture.

In this paradoxical dimension of music and of visual composition, our early modern art, in effect, discovered the parameters for the spatial definitions that make music music, visual art art, and architectural space substantive. In other words, space emerged as the auditory, visual, and structural dimension of a paradoxical process that defines an identity for music, art, and architecture. At Cusa's insistent prompting, I refer to identity and not equivalence, a differentiation he harped on so often, because as we have also learned from the master reenactors of the classical Arabic *makamat* (the musical *sententiae* or canonical passages of that venerable tradition), as well as from the jazz musicians of our own time, that music, like visual art, or "music in space," is never equivalent to itself or to anything else. We learn from these traditions that repetition as equivalency is impossible, though recognition of what is enacted depends on the variable differentials of what is reiterated each time within the inherited corpus of these cultures. This is a key issue for what we could refer to as citational performativity that architects, poets, choreographers, and filmmakers inevitably countenance no less so than actors or musical performers. We have since come to understand the inevitable, namely, that by virtue of its genesis in paradox, identity is also paradoxical, founded as it is in the dimension of self-difference and self-differentiation, not to say self-contradiction.

This paradox of identity, then, is not unlike the paradoxes of music and visual art, the space of silence, the interval, which makes music possible. In our modernist time, the American composer John Cage elevated this interval into virtuoso performance stretched to at least four minutes and thirty-three seconds in his now classic composition "4'33"," the title referring to the space, or interval of silence it takes to "perform" the work. And, in dramatizing the ocular distortion of perspective that makes for accurate visual perception through space, a certain Russian painter of the early twentieth century by the name of Kasimir Malyevich displayed his starkly performative act of space by representing visual plenitude on the blankness of his white canvases. The whiteness of those canvasses outruns the frame that would delineate and define their space as contained art objects.

And, so, just as the equivocal title of Cusa's memorable treatise, *De docta ignorantia* (Of Learned Ignorance; 1440),[5] teaches us, entity becomes identity by virtue of what it is not. This dialectical affirmation through the foregrounding of negativity (the wisdom of ignorance, in the case of his book's title and contents), we now understand, is the legerdemain or prestidigitation that culture, like Cusa in his philosophical speculations and diplomatic feats, has had to perform in space-time in order to make cultural existence possible. The documentary record of this maneuver, Cusa's legacy to our posterity, endures in memory, and he would say, in its inalienable concomitant, collective forgetfulness. It is culture's paradoxical fate, then, to take from time to give to space the trace of what no longer is, if indeed it ever was anything other than a mental construct dubbed memory, subsequently re-membered *as if* it had been something other than culture's artfully spaced memorial maneuver, traditionally called philosophical knowledge. Many a philosopher would seek to redeem this legacy from the genesis of its morphology in paradox and legerdemain, among them Walter Benjamin, who sought to counterpose knowledge to truth. Knowledge, he claimed, seeks to possess its object through representation; truth, for its part, foregoes representation, or translation, since it is the object's own self-revelation or self-presentation.[6]

All such admirable efforts notwithstanding, mucking around in contradiction is what makes or constitutes culture, as Cusa knew well from his peripatetic trudging among sovereign lords of righteousness and their cultured claims, as we shall see presently. There is no subject or agency called "culture" in the space prior to this messy process. Before this, space is indeed space—that is, expressive silence, expectant interval, imminently articulate interregnum, bent distance around the bend and (as yet) out of sight—what Cusa knew as virtual possibility still without a place, what we now encode as cyberillusion and as mathematical probability. Culture, then, is literally what *takes place* from space, as we, Cusa's philological and philosophical progeny, have come to understand. The French, who presume to already have it ipso facto, refer to it as *avoir lieu*; the Spanish, likewise, *tener lugar*; ditto for the Italians, *avere luogo*. The English would have it in the grasping—*to take place*. Culture and cultural space, in other words, through these lexical turns translate literally as what occurs in place, the happenings of history, and the Greeks, who have had culture long enough to know how precarious and fragile it is, encounter it as contingency: *brischō fi sunantō tuchaia*, implying a fortuitous encounter, which, prudently accounting for the law of unintended consequences in the encounter with the fortuities of fate, a literary translator may render the phrase into the colloquial English of our day as "stuff happens."

Culture's happenstance genesis is culture's greatest anxiety, as Cusa well knew, a perspicacity that his mediating and translational endeavors between East and West relentlessly pressed upon him. Reason enough, this paradoxical ontology, for every instance of culture to compensate for its genesis in paradox by deeming itself necessary, inevitable, indispensable, unique, and, more often than not, preeminent above and beyond any other culture. Hence, culture's relentless and compulsive self-cultivation, self-memorialization, and defensive-aggressive assertion of identity, all of which are aimed to serve as leaven and catalyst for cultures' self-perpetuation. Memory becomes more the yeast culture for the future, certainly more efficaciously and often more accurately anticipated in its predictable self-exertions than it is the preservation of the past. The wildcard in the process is the unforeseen peripeties and their unanticipated consequences. That self-hedging against futurity's contingencies and the fates' caprices takes on diverse guises that go by a variety of designations, key terms that define our own current disciplinary and cultural horizon—sociospace, ethnoterritory, geography, architecture, cognitive map, *polis*, *locus amoenus*, *habitus*, *hesteia*, *vesta*, *domicilium*, *nostos*, *agora*, and, in the mixed virtue of our twenty-first century's virtual spatiality and its memes, *phantasm-agora*. This, in short, is culture's tenuous morphology, its ideological locus, its *commonplace* and lapidary architecture.

It is an elaborately circumscribed architecture—graphically encircled, that is. And whether those circumscriptions are called cartography, ethnography, lexicography, or biography, the graphic self-encirclements figure as reaching after a monograph that is a culture's self-delineation in the unique space that would be exceptionally recuperated as place and its monuments. History, the twisted daughter of time, would flout, time and again, the fragility and vulnerability of those circumscriptions that have often proved little more than lines in the sand, shifting and shiftless and inevitably evanescent. And so it is that the ephemeral "line in the sand" has come to compensate for its own volatility by taking on the semantic intransigence of "firm stand" and "uncompromising ultimatum," a determined stance as risible as Caesar crossing the Rubicon in a huff and as hilariously ironic as this event's cinematic representation in Federico Fellini's *Roma* (1972). Impoverished in humor and devoid of self-irony, our epoch has eschewed the volatility of the "line in the sand" in favor of "red lines," chromatically more apt for the blood-soaked sands that mark the frontiers of our civilization and define its barbarity. And so it was in the history of circumscriptions that the earliest maps were drawn in the circular bottoms of bowls, kitchen implements whose magic should have sympathetically domesticated space into geography and brought the horizon into the encircled geometry of home for manageable ménage and containment.

Nicholas of Cusa mastered this alchemical vocation of transmuting the unknowable into the vessel of knowledge. His work remains a locus classicus of the graphic avatars of this alembication. And the volatile centrifuge of his encyclical circulates still as paradoxical geometry with a paradoxical title: *De docta ignorantia*, in English, "Of Learned Ignorance."

Cusa's fifteenth-century Byzantine, Florentine, and Venetian contemporaries, who looked to him to negotiate the treacherous terrain that divided them, called him Nicolaus Cusanus, after his native German town of Keus on the Mosel River, today's Bernkastel-Keus. Having survived the vicissitudes of time and the caprices of history, Cusa is called upon to teach us, yet again, how to forge space into traversal, into political mediation, into epistemic metaphor, into heuristic instrument, into profession of faith with reason, and into assuasive rhetoric that might bridge religious schism and the terrors it spawns. We have come to understand that Cusa did not merely discourse on space but that he spatialized discourse and orthodoxy, now through metaphor, now through syllogism, but always through ulterior space in the name of another place and an *obiter dictum*, which is to say via allegory that could otherwise be called the alibi of faith and the alias of dialogic reason. We now call Cusa's an "early modern project" that, for some, still resonates as a postmodern precursor by virtue of the fact that Cusa perfected the art of deflecting the hypostatic, the dispersion of fixity, and the translocation of conviction's Archimedeian fulcrum from its orthodoxies and self-righteous dogmas. Cusa spoke of circles and in them, circles with ubiquitous centers and unspecifiable circumferences, of "machina mundi whose centre, so to speak, is everywhere, whose circumference is nowhere."[7] Many would come to paraphrase his apothegm, notably Blaise Pascal, who speaks in his *Pensées* (327b) of Cusa's "ignorance savante,"[8] some two centuries after Cusa's death. Following Pascal, a certain Argentine by the name of Jorge Luis Borges recapitulated Cusa's geometry via Borges's American precursor, Ralph Waldo Emerson.[9] For it was Emerson's poem "Circles" and its accompanying aphoristic essay by the same title (published in 1841, exactly four hundred years after Cusa's work) that brought Cusa's concentric horizon to the New World, even as Emerson connected Cusa to the Old World with his essay's *incipit*: "The eye is the first circle; the horizon which it forms the second; and throughout nature this primary figure is repeated without end. It is the highest emblem in the cipher of the world. St. Augustine described the nature of God as a circle whose centre was everywhere and its circumference nowhere. We are all our lifetime reading the copious sense of this first of forms."[10]

II. Concentric Deviations, Elliptic Orthodoxies

We have rehearsed the facts often in our classroom recitations and in our examinations. The year was 1437. It fell to Nicholas of Cusa to survey the horizon and traverse the immensity of space, even more immense ideologically than geographically, that divided Rome and Constantinople. The stakes were high, the abyss vast, and the time, for Cusa as an eschatologist, was well nigh. In the epistle to his patron, Lord Cardinal Julian, also known as Cardinal Cesarini, that serves as coda to published editions of Cusa's treatise, he sums up the *circumstances*, that is, literally and metaphorically the contending stances and self-circumscriptions of the two Christendoms and the breach between them, the mute interruption, or space, that reshaped Christ's Church from a consonant and harmonious sphere into dissonant and schismatic hemispheres. Cusa's ambassadorial mission between Rome and Byzantium had him sailing to the Greek Orthodox see as part of the papal delegation that accompanied back to Venice the Emperor

John VIII Palaeologus, the patriarch of Constantinople, and his theologians to negotiate the reunification of the Church. Our history books are mute on the fractious deliberations, though not on the controversial outcome of the mission. We do know that in the Council of Florence of 1439 the two Churches converged but, ultimately, could not be reunited. Their paths simply intersected momentarily. The negotiated unification through Cusa's deft mediation would prove elusively contentious, chaotic, and short-lived. This would only lend another layer of complexity to his philosophical spatialization of episteme and doxa. The question would then become: which is the space (or interregnum) in the life of the Church, the schismatic breach or its brief bridging, in part through Cusa's good offices as mediator? His treatise *De docta ignorantia* would be published one year later, in 1440, the year of Cusa's ordination. He never says at what time of day he was able to compose his philosophical meditations between forays of shuttle diplomacy. Nor does Cusa indicate whether he took his meals in the refectory or in his private cell; he does not specify either the common language through which he mediated between the Greek patriarch and the Latin pope.

During the passage from Constantinople to Venice, a sea voyage that lasted from November 1437 to February 1438, Cusa may well have been anticipating these unknowns also as part of the "ignorantia" that is the circumstantial space of knowing. The philosophical insight on the nature of knowledge would come to Cusa, as he avers in his epistle, in the course of that journey. That Cusa should have predicated the epistemology of illumined rationality in the transitional space between one sacred place and another, between one topological orthodoxy and its alterity, is not insignificant, as he himself informs us. Cusa's diplomatic intercession did manage to breach the space between place and place, however tenuously. The peripatetic doxology that shuttled between the Greek East and the Latin West managed, as well, to transmute doxa into paradoxa and visionary epiphany into epistemic epiphenomenon. That insight continues unabated still, and it hovers with pertinent immediacy over our own concerns of space and culture today. It does so as the particular mode of spatial rationality that views knowledge in terms of geometric metaphor. The allegory of Cusa's philosophical discourse may have had greater significance for the realpolitik of splintered orthodoxy, and Cusa may well have intended that allegory to be preeminent for those who deliberated the fate of the universal Church on earth at the time.

What continues to resonate more significantly for us, however, is not the allegory but the metaphor of Cusa's meditation. Epistemologically speaking, the way Cusa locates knowledge in space emerges as a signal instance of culture's political life, that is, of the way culture "takes place" in, through, and as space. And, ultimately, this is what makes Cusa, his *De docta ignorantia,* and his *De pace fidei* (On the Peace of Faith; 1453) so urgently relevant to the cultural space of our own moment at the beginning of the third millennium. And the plenipotentiaries of our time, who today arrogate to themselves the role of drawing lines in the sand—lines they redden with human blood, and do so in our name and ostensibly on our behalf—if they would or could read Nicholas of Cusa, might well find some instruction that could mitigate their vengeful vehemence and deadly buffoonery. All this is merely a symptom of the baneful human comedy of our time, a comedy that would indeed be farcical if its consequences were not also lethal. And lest his legacy be dimmed by our historical amnesia, I should like to rehearse here what our cultural and textual memory still commonly holds from Cusa. I do so in the hope that this excursus into the paradoxical space of ignorance and knowledge might serve as reminder of what in Cusa's work continues to have relevance for our time.

It would be restating the obvious, but I risk redundancy for the sake of clarity, to recall that Cusa countenanced epistemology and human history at an acutely polarized moment. His conciliatory commission in diplomacy found its correlative in Cusa's philosophical mission as an instructive allegory aimed at the antagonists through rhetorical misdirection. The reconciliation of opposites, the *coincidentia oppositorum,* as Cusa termed it, and as it has circulated in binomial commonplace since, was aimed as much at the geopolitics of the Christian church, split into two since the year 1054, as it was an invocation of the *theologia negativa* that Cusa inherited from his medieval precursors Meister Eckhardt (1260–1328) and John Scotus Erigena (815–77). The *De divisione naturae* of Erigena spoke to Cusa, as it speaks to us still, of divisions and *logomachies* of a different order from the schisms of Cusa's time. What proved original, by virtue of circumstantial exigencies and his pedagogical conveyance of orthodoxies from one time-space to another, was Cusa's uncanny ability to translate and articulate the received ideas to the emergent occasions and crises of his day. Hegel, as much as Marx, learned a good deal from Cusa and his tripartite treatise about dialectical antithesis and tertiary syntheses that they have passed on to us in diverse refractions. But the crisis of Cusa's historical materiality was clearly more urgent and worldly than theirs, though the polar points of contention Cusa had to confront had otherworldly horizons and sacred teleologies. And Cusa, obviously, had to have been much more pragmatic than either Hegel or Marx, and certainly more so than the more current explorers of tertiary spaces in "the location of culture,"[11] because the critical issues that Cusa, as papal legate, had to countenance and negotiate were most immediate, pressing, and personally involving. And this is why the discursive configuration of Cusa's vision is not the vector of abstracted history or its linear progress, despite his eschatological notions and enthusiasm for last things. Instead, the space-graph of Cusa's epistemology is the circle, or the planetary sphere, earthly and transcendental, physical and metaphysical, political and universal. And so it is that Cusa hoped for little more than minimal results in his worldly mission, and the outcome of the 1438 deliberations in Ferrara and the 1439 Council of Florence would bear out his discerning pragmatism. We can only surmise the degree of Cusa's prescience with regard to the collateral significance of this encounter between East and West that he helped to bring about. But it would be difficult to overestimate the significance of Cusa's treatise to what subsequent cultural history closer to our own time would see as the threshold through which Europe transits from medieval into Renaissance space. Many historians see this transition as the incidental side effect of the 1439 Council of Florence, as much under the aegis of Cosimo de' Medici as of Pope Eugenius IV. But, though a diplomatic minimalist, Nicholas of Cusa did articulate his doxology with his allegorical coaxing of pope and patriarch in maximal terms. Cusa spoke, then, of the *maximum absolutum* and of the *maximum contractum*, ostensibly, and not necessarily, as these might synthesize in the Christological theology of the third book of his treatise. Aiming through the ostensive counterpoint at the otherworldly space above and beyond Roman papacy and Byzantine patriarchy, Cusa was fully aware of laboring still in the space of the Churches' worldly jurisdiction. There, Cusa saw the need to have the maximal mitigated by the practical, and the practical modulated by the relational. Thus, Cusa articulated a shifting space where the absolute and the contractual might engage in dialectical intermediation in the name of an unmediated *maximum* that awaits the fullness of time and the coming of the eschaton. That Second Coming was imminent for Cusa, who reckoned and prophesied at one point that the year 1734 would see the end of this world. In the meantime, Cusa insinuated, the logomachies of the polarized Church might pursue their reconciliation in the negative space of a negative theology, where enlightened ignorance might illumine the darkness of the kingdom of this world.

Paradox, as it obtains in negative theology, or in Cusa's *docta ignorantia*, is integral to the orthodox tradition and, as he demonstrates, expediently and strategically accommodated within its strictures. What has fared less well in the face of orthodoxy is the heterodox, and Cusa was always careful not to raise the issue of heterodoxy in the ecclesiastical schism. His strategy in this deflection consists in spatializing the heterodox, moving it into space, into geography and territorial claims. Thus, through his ingenious intervention, the ideologically fractured topography of the Church emerges not as heterodoxy but as heterotopia.

Heterotopia is not one of Cusa's usages, though no doubt it must have been integral to his Greco-Latin lexicon. We have come to understand only recently the space that Cusa describes by synonyms to this term. The *oppositorum*, or antithesis, of heterotopia is neither utopia nor dystopia, since such spaces were yet to be designated as places—the former, dystopia, only fairly recently, and Thomas More's treatise of 1516 on the latter still some seventy-six years in the offing. The mirror opposite of heterotopia for Cusa, he gives us reason to suspect, would have been an orthotopia, which he did not term as such, but whose description fits what he designated as the space of the *maximum absolutum*. That locus is undifferentiated identity and beyond any degree of knowability and, as such, is the absolute unknowable or maximal ignorance. Thus, its space can be no particular place; as topos, it is at once ubiquitous and utopic, the most perfect of circles, in Cusa's own terms, whose center is everywhere and whose circumference nowhere, as he elegantly diagrammed it for us.

III. Ignorance by Degrees: Identity and Equivalence

Short of this absolute, Cusa has given us to understand, all knowledge is partial and relational, which is to say it is ignorance by degrees. In other words, the space of knowledge is what we would call heterotopic space. In the first chapter of book 2, Cusa illustrates this calculus with reference to the space of astronomy, geometry, music, and arithmetic, the traditional subjects of the quadrivium. In each instance the orthotopia of the maximum is compromised because, Cusa says, "it is a fundamental principle that where degrees of difference are found it is impossible to arrive at a maximum which is actual and the greatest possible."[12] Negotiating this impossibility and forging a common ground between Western and Eastern orthodoxies in politico-theological terms was Cusa's mission on the cusp between medieval and Renaissance Europe.

This is the bugbear that bedevils confessional orthodoxies and their territorial orthotopias still at the beginning of the twenty-first century. In the last century, Michel Foucault diagnosed the threat that the heterotopic presents for the zeal of the purist and for the dogmatically self-convinced. Foucault noted: "*Heterotopias* are disturbing, probably because they secretly undermine language, because they make it impossible to name this *and* that, because they chatter or tangle common names, because they destroy 'syntax' in advance, and not only the syntax with which we construct sentences but also that less apparent syntax which causes words and things next to and also opposite one another) to 'hold together'. This is why utopias permit fables and discourse."[13] Then as now, the orthodox opted for their respective utopias and stuck to their irreconcilable fables.

Then as now, the maximalists, absolutists, and fundamentalists would spurn any "fundamental principles . . . where degrees of difference are found" that might serve for negotiated conflict resolution. Our Herculean task today, as for Cusa's time, is to persuade the plenipotentiaries of the new millennium that, as Cusa so elegantly teaches us, it is these degrees of difference that indeed make our knowledge possible, a knowledge which of necessity is predicated on the defining limits of our ignorance and not of our dogma. Thus, Cusa illustrates that in arithmetic, for example, "where there are two there is necessarily a difference; and a numerical variation involves a variation to infinity of all things: composition, combination, proportion, harmony, change and so on—a fact which explains to us why we are ignorant."[14] And in music, likewise, in harmonic concordance of instruments, Cusa says, "all are only relatively true and all differ necessarily according to place, time, natural characteristics and so on. Consequently the most perfect, faultless harmony cannot be perceived by the ear, for it exists not in things but as an ideal conceived by the mind. From this we can form some idea of the most perfect or infinite harmony, which is a relation in quality."[15] Since 1976 and the work of Richard Dawkins, some refer to this relational complex as the memeplex, or the defining linkages through memes that construct us culturally the way our genes form us genetically or biologically.[16]

Cusa projects this "relation in quality" between perception and intellect as spatial contingency onto the geometry of his favorite configuration, the ever elusive circle that remains unattainable, except as a relational quality that does make knowledge possible but also keeps it this side of the absolute. Cusa says, in chapter 3 of book 1: "The relationship of our intellect to the truth is like that of a polygon to a circle; the resemblance to the circle grows with the multiplication of the angles of the polygon; but apart from its being reduced to identity with the circle, no multiplication, even if it were infinite, of its angles will make the polygon equal the circle."[17]

It might amuse Cusa to know that all manner of streams have flowed from the relational source of this philosophical spring—Bishop Berkeley's and Schopenhauer's Idealism, Husserlian phenomenology, Sausseurian linguistics, and Derridian *différance*. I would like to reiterate the dependent clause "but apart from its being reduced to identity with the circle" (and, of course, it would be a dependent clause) in this identification of polygon with circle. I do so because the "identity," more properly a "simile," serves as descriptor for the relationship of intellect to truth. I wish to emphasize this because, in the geometry of this simile, equivalence and identity diverge, with identity devolving unto a reduction and equivalence perpetually evading apprehension.

It is not without some risk to say so in the political environment of the twenty-first century, but it must be said that by Cusa's reckoning identity emerges as a compensatory gesture or as a residual reparation for the unattainable. Identity, in other words, is what we are reduced to when desired equality or equivalence equivocates into the multiplicity of identity's relational possibilities. It is in the realm of this equivocation, and this is critical to our vocation as comparatists of cultures and of literatures, that we can identify anything as knowable, or that we can attain an identity, cultural or otherwise. Because, as Cusa concludes, identity is tantamount to what we can never know, and we can only know to the degree that we can identify with what anything is not. In Cusa's own terms and the crux of his argument: "It is clear, therefore, that all we know of the truth, such as it is, is beyond our reach. The truth, which can be neither more nor less than it is, is the most absolute necessity, while, in contrast with it, our intellect is possibility. Therefore, the quiddity of things, which is ontological truth, is unattainable in its entirety; and though it has been the objective of all philosophers, by none has it been found as it really is. The more profoundly we learn this lesson of ignorance, the closer we draw to truth itself."[18] One can only hope that Cusa is not unduly chagrined that despite the lucidity of his argumentation on the problematic perspicacity of philosophers, critical sensibilities such as the English schoolmaster Matthew Arnold would still claim in the mid-nineteenth century that critical practice resides in the knowledge of a thing "as in itself it really is."[19]

For those who would revisit Cusa's own words, in this summation of his own paradoxical construct lies the most succinct definition of what we have understood Cusa to mean by *docta ignorantia*. And this also happens to coincide with his definition of "identity." In an epoch such as ours, identity politics and self-empowerment through assertion of one's own putative identity—individual, tribal, ideological, or ethno-national—there seems to be little space for light to sift through to illumine the nature of the paradox for the self-authenticators. This leaves us identical with the ignorance of self-conviction and impervious to the possibilities of nonidentical self-reflection. This hermetic redoubt defines most aptly the impermeable space we call ideology and righteous self-conviction.

We also understand, and in the turmoil of our time we must understand this now with greater urgency than ever, that Cusa's programmatic mission at the heart of this spatial and cognitive dicing was to get pope and patriarch and their respective godmen to recognize the possibility of something other than their own maximal absolutes. While the principals and many of their theologians did indeed accede, at least ostensibly, to alternative plausibility—hence the 1439 denouement at the Council of Florence—their respective political constituencies did not, or the plenipotentiaries themselves, in their diplomatic ledger of double bookkeeping, would have had them reject what was supposedly negotiated and settled in their name. And so, the Latin pope continued to be the Antichrist for Constantinople, and Byzantium's patriarch the Schismatic Heretic for Rome. Sultan Mehmet II and Martin Luther would not be long in coming to moot the argument and cut dispensational history's Gordian knot into supernumerary bits. The first came calling at the gates of Constantinople on April 2, the day after our April Fools' Day, in 1453. Luther nailed his ninety-five Theses, a number of which Cusa had already foreshadowed, at the door of Wittenberg's castle church the night of Halloween, October 31, 1517. After 1453 and 1517, what had been a bipolar world of East-West, whose conflicts and symptoms Cusa's mediation attempted to allay, would become myriad and polymorphous. The definition of cultural identity in that primal scene of what we now call multiculturalism would move from the space of geometry to the hard place of geopolitics, and it would be circumscribed and defined not by the word and the pen but by the sword and the silk chord. Cusa's treatise *De pace fidei* in the year of Sultan Mehmet II's conquest of Constantinople would dramatize the interfaith conversation among Greek, Italian, Arab, Indian, Chaldean, Jew, Scythian, Gaul, Persian, Syrian, Spaniard, Turk, German, Tatar, Armenian, Bohemian, and Englander. As much as an interfaith congress, Cusa's dramatic enactment of a would-be "concord of religions . . . in the heaven of reason,"[20] as Cusa optimistically phrased it, stands as prototype for a league of nations, a united nations led by wise leaders in the spirit of global unity. While the world would indeed arrive at such a global institution and call it the United Nations some five hundred years after Cusa's adumbration of it, more than a half a century after its founding we still struggle toward the concord of what Cusa termed "perpetual peace," a desideratum Emmanuel Kant would reiterate at the end of the eighteenth century ("Perpetual Peace: A Philosophical Sketch"; 1795), albeit still in vain.[21] At the end of part 3 of his treatise, ironically, the locus Cusa envisioned as "the most suitable" place for "perpetual peace," Jerusalem, far from a site of concord, serves today as a cauldron of discord and as an irradiating nucleus of strife. Cusa's displacement of inter*faith* dialogue unto inter*national* colloquy, while prescient and politically visionary, did not suffice then and does not suffice now, to quell contention among peoples. It is no less an irony of history that what Cusa translocated from religion to national affiliation, today, at the beginning of the third millennium, reverts in the opposite direction, with religious fervor and ethno-racial affiliation overtaking the national membership we call, especially since the Gallic Enlightenment of the eighteenth century, secular citizenship. Thus, with the beginning of the twenty-first century, we have reverted to faith-based governance, with national governments and sectarian enthusiasts profiling their targets and pressing their claims on the basis of confession and ethno-religious sectarianisms, inside and across national borders. In his desiderata for intercommunal concord, Cusa may well have anticipated the possibility of this dialectical reversal when he convoked transnational reason to dialogue on faith, rather than invoking faith to define national reason. Even in his time, however, negotiation and civil discourse had already succumbed to discord and protracted wars. And logomachia would become alembicated into *Machtpolitik* and Kulturkampf, for while Cosimo de' Medici was the host of Cusa's Council of Florence in 1439, Lorenzo II de' Medici, soon-to-be duke of Urbino, to whom Niccolò Machiavelli dedicated his opus *The Prince* (1513), would be the cunning ruler that embodied the realpolitik that Machiavelli had to negotiate three-quarters of a century after the Council of Florence. In that transition from the faith of reason to reasons of state, theology's and faith's scruples would indeed become alienated from politics, with Machiavelli's memorable notation in *The Prince* that the closer one is to Rome and the papacy the more irreligious one is likely to be. The same could have been said about Constantinople, of course, had Sultan Mehmet II not mooted the lineage of the Roman Caesars by finalizing the parenthesis that was opened by the first Constantine and was now being closed with the abdication of the last. Sultan Mehmet II, thus, completed the fearful symmetry of Byzantium with a notable act of regime change. This sort of change, especially as faith-based initiative, would prove a constant in the history of such regimental changes perpetuated in the historical oscillation between East and West, which at the threshold of the new millennium veers from West to East.

The fractures of the bipolar world that Cusa struggled so earnestly to heal never quite mended; more often than not, Manichaeism has ruled the day well through the twentieth century. The twentieth-century version of a bipolar world has been superseded in the twenty-first by a New World Order that simultaneously has splintered and globalized the planet. Realpolitik has reached its apogee at the threshold of the new millennium in what the French call *hyperpuissance*. Our day's *Machtpolitik* has us craning our necks, like Banquo's heirs in Shakespeare's *Macbeth*, toward "th'crack of doom" (IV.i.116). The circle and the polygon, be it as pentagon or as any other bellicose configuration, have been perforce squared and transfigured into planetary global hegemony. And the options as dictated to and by the rebarbative mouthpiece of this global multinational stateism are now starkly stuttered as mechanical ventriloquy. MacWorld's Macbeth in

Hamlet's guise now mouths the ontological question with a cupidity that subsumes any semblance of intelligent "quiddity," as Cusa's Thomistic lexicon would have it, into the well-oiled ledger of the vulgar quid. In the argot of our time this is known as "free market economy," though there are those who call it capital's predatory optimization, or more pointedly, gangster maximalism, in which neoliberalism and neoconservatism converge with rapacious zeal.

The spatial philosophy Cusa willed to us was made possible by a bipolar space in which paradox oscillated between its contradictory poles. Today, the space of realpolitik brooks no such possibility because the geopolitical spectrum is neither bipolar nor multivalent; or it is bipolar only in the pathological sense of acute psychiatric instability. Nor does our realpolitik admit of ambiguity. Identity is made into equivalence with might and main that deems and enforces its acts as a *force majeure* at the barrel of a gun. The would-be lines in the sand are igneous and vulcanized as unbreachable circumscriptions, and their inflammable and explosive purchase on history and capital righteousness are now wicked by the largest oil deposits in the fields of what used to be the Babylonian gardens, now a Babylonian dystopia of putative democracy and, perforce, the entire planet's twenty-first-century Babylonian Captivity.

The dialogical space of Cusa's paradox made culture and the Renaissance not only compatible but coterminous, precisely because the world order of Cusa's day was multivalent, plural, ambiguous, and not only agonic, but also agoric. In that multifariousness, cultural memory deemed itself a rebirth, and the Renaissance re-membered the world through such ambiguous mechanisms as Brunelleschi's perspectival architectonics and mathematical topology. The *taglio* of the visual arts distended into the paradox of distortion for ocular compensation so that the eye could see through space as the world might have stood to be seen. It was seen in the reduction of identity that knew itself to be a reduction and not an equivalence or simulacrum hectored as categorical and hyperreal representation. We did learn from Cusa—or at least Cusa attempted to teach us—that ultimately it is the paradox, the ambiguity, the negative space of philosophy, architecture, and epistemology and their negotiation that make the production of knowledge and human wisdom possible. One suspects Cusa would see our own New World Order as the obstinate perversion of what he envisioned as the cultural space of his day, an inversion where the renascent now turns into the mortiferous, memory into presentist oblivion, and the future into banal and toxic residue of capital predation and ecological despair. No doubt, Cusa would agree that where there is no memory there is no future; culture can and does become fungible commodity for the fetishistic and museological possession of the most efficiently rapacious. A number of Cusa's philosophical successors—Giordano Bruno, Thomas Hobbes, Karl Marx, and Charles Darwin—would elaborate extensively and obsessively on this topic in their own time.

At the beginning of the third millennium, the space of our shrill and spectral agora is more prone to function as phantasmagora, or as virtual space, where the potential for civil society and civic participation become mooted by the marauding predatoriness of capital wedded to sectarian zeal that convert every person into a target as an individualized market niche, and where all human activity becomes the object of surveillance through the ubiquitous panopticon of *Machtpolitik* and its wardens of conformity. There was, of course, something virtual to the defining space and to the epistemic actuality of knowledge as Cusa described it. Namely, that knowledge is not a mimetic correspondence to ontology, or what Cusa termed, in his Thomistic parlance, "quiddity." Rather, Cusa discerned that knowledge is reductive depiction by the intellect that reaches for equivalence between the representation and its object, but ends, inexorably, by settling for the ambiguities of identity. For Cusa's insight, this equivocation is as much at the heart of the richness of culture and of wisdom as it is defining of the grace of humility. This could well be the most significant gift of Cusa's legacy to us, though his wise posterity has been met, more often than not, with profligacy.

History seems to demonstrate that our virtual space brooks no such grace or charity, for what we consider virtual space is, in effect, neither a space of virtue nor a space of potential, but a space that is relentlessly actualized through an imagistic network that absolves no one and leaves nothing out, *pace* the desiderata of a twentieth-century student of Cusa, Michel Serres, who claimed to have located a space "out there," or *hors-là*.[22] In the decade since Michel Serres' *Atlas*, an actual attempt at the cartography or cognitive map of virtual space, we have come to realize that the advanced information technologies of our cyberspace do not affect a delocation or displacement of the locally specific into virtuality. Rather, what we have achieved is the replacement of local content and a translocation of the particular site into the plenitude of an ubiquity whose thrust propels everything and everyone into globalized homogenization, a vulgar version of Cusa's *maximum absolutum*, a spatiality that is minutely traceable and surveilled through universal global positioning systems. The mechanism of this monitoring pervasiveness is referred to in shorthand as ubicomp, the current code term for ubiquitous computation, an instrumentality Cusa had attributed to the calculus of the divinity and the divine eye.

Just as often, this translocation of ours constitutes a displacement of any possible truth for ulterior motives that have nothing to do with the local, except as they ensnare its economic life and proscribe its possibilities for independent existence and thinking, often in the ostensible name of democracy and freedom of thought and free speech. The danger for us, then, is not that we might be left out in space, wandering *hors-là*, as Michel Serres would have it. The greater danger than being left out is our constantly being taken in, and the impossibility of our delinking ourselves or declaring our independence from the cosmic black hole of the World Wide Web and its gravitational force. The danger, in other words, is not in our virtuality but in the actuality that jams our discrete spaces with indiscrete spam and interpellates us, inextricably, into a network with no possible exit. The virtues of connectivity, as we are wont to call our communion, become vitiated by the inescapable predicaments of virtuality's actualizations in a global space that, in Cusa's terms, rams the polygon into equivalence with the circle, or the quintessential polygon of *Machtpolitik*, the pentagon, into parity with the terrestrial sphere. The global encirclement, then, becomes a circumscription that defines identity, not as libratory ambiguity and polyvocity, but as absolute conformity, disambiguation, and monologism, even more powerful and less tractable than the schismatic doxologies Cusa had to negotiate between Byzantium and Rome.

Ours, then, is a forged consensus, achieved through subtleties of propaganda, persuasion, seduction, coercion, informational strategy, manipulative informatics, loyalty oaths, or through schlock manipulation of communal affectivities such as patriotism, ethnocentrism, racial superiority, godliness, exceptionalism, and collective righteousness. In other words, to invoke Antonio Gramsci's definition of hegemony, ours is a self-interestedly manufactured consensus.

For the refined acuity of Cusa's polyglot ear, to say "monologic hegemon" is to utter a tautology. But this is precisely the pleonastic redundancy of the twenty-first century's *Amtssprache*, our banal "officialese," that imposes itself as self-equivalence, a tautological repetition that underlies the unitary and unambiguous form of cultural identity. It is an identity leveraged through the force of an ideology whose subject is guided by the conviction of being identical to oneself, without any fissures, seams, suture lines, pleats, or overlap. It is, despite what Cusa has taught us, the coterminous, commensurate, and self-commensurable coincidence of absolute equivalence. It is death. It is not the realm and prosopopoeia of a negative space, but of a plenary space of destruction, a plenum of desolation. Its paradox is not in the self-knowing multiplicity of what Cusa called *coincidentia oppositorum*, or the coexistence of contraries. Rather, it is an overweening contradiction that utters life but wreaks death; that proclaims a project of liberation but practices domination and occupation; that professes political idealism but operates as predatory materialist pragmatism; that expounds law and order but sows disorder and rejects all lawful jurisdictions. In this space, Cusa's subtleties and scruples are razed, the tolerance of Cusa's heterotopia is flattened into what believes itself to be uncontaminated orthotopia, but which in reality is a dystopia in which force reigns and the discourse of terror ensures not rational government but the persistence of anomie and antinomian rule. This is the reign of the New World Order that defines its instrumentality as equivalent to its domain, its space as equivalent to its performance. It calls itself "full spectrum dominance."

It turns out that there are no lines in the sand here, after all. They are unnecessary. The whole desert, every grain of sand, surface minerals and subsoil deposits, are all within hegemony's jurisdiction. Lines in the sand would not be only superficial but also superfluous. This is the space of "total information awareness" governed by the impunity of its superintendents. Though in its evangelical messianism it might like to conjure with the *maximum absolutum* discerned by Cusa, the domain of this space is, rather, the absolutism of the minimal, and its deadly banality the dimension and measure of virulent vacuousness. Its tautological buffoonery and historical redundancy would be a farce, were the farce not so lethal. Its baneful benightedness gives Cusa's good term ignorance a rather bad name.

4

Memories of the Future

GIORDANO BRUNO REMEMBERS US

> Images do not receive their names from the explanations of the things they signify, but rather from the condition of those things that do the signifying.
> —Giordano Bruno, *On the Composition of Images, Signs, and Ideas*

> We have forgotten how to describe the only thing which by its structure yields to poetic representation, namely the impulses, intentions, and amplitudes of oscillation. Ptolemy has returned by the back door! . . . Giordano Bruno was burned in vain!
> —Osip Mandelstam, "Conversations About Dante"

I. Remembering Mnemosyne

The future haunted Giordano Bruno's memory as much as the past. Some four centuries later, we should remember, in turn, his prescient reminder on images and signifiers. It would take our linguists, semioticians, and political analysts more than three centuries to decode the significance of his admonition on the historical materiality of human agency. Some, in fact, still count on self-exculpation through an expedient delinkage between their condition as actors and the significance of their actions. They would do so, Bruno suggests, by deflecting responsibility onto convenient explanations. Bruno's inconvenient apothegm would remind us of the actionable responsibility of the imputable subject in the process of acting, which he calls here "signifying." Neither the ravages of time nor his immolation in the Campo dei Fiori in February 1600 have canceled his memory of us in his work or the memory of his legacy to us. Nor does his art of memory fade, though its technologies might morph from theatrical topology to virtual cybernetics. Despite the Church's apology and admission of error in the matter of his case through Pope John Paul II at the beginning of the third millennium (2003), and though his case file is missing still, his last words before the officers of the Holy Inquisition gagged and stripped him naked in preparation for the stake continue to resonate: "Perhaps your fear in passing judgment on me is greater than mine in receiving it."[1] His monumental image now stands on the spot that held the scaffold and the pyre of his execution. And, more than four centuries later, we continue to struggle with significance and explanation in the conditions and acts not of signifiers but of those who, as Bruno says, do the signifying.[2] Four centuries later, there are still apologists for the Holy Office of the Inquisition who would justify his burning at the stake.[3] Thus we remember him in the verbal tense of his memorial utterance, whose continuing resonance reconfirms that the memory he augured was not a memory of the past but one of the future, the future perfect of what will have been in our time at the beginning of the twenty-first century. His words are instructive. We can only hope that his fate and the papal recantation of his sentence might also be of some benefit to those who, in our own time, exercise the privilege and power to indict, convict, sentence, and execute with impunity.

My interest in Bruno as progenitor for comparative studies does not reside in the technicalities of his mnemonic system. Nor do I have an interest in rehearsing yet again the scientific precepts of his astronomy, amply explicated by sympathetic specialists and belittled by apologists for the Church who burned him at the stake. The consensus among divergent pronouncements on a figure that continues to be as controversial four hundred years later as he was during his tumultuous time is that his trials and death sentence by the Holy Office is not based on the mechanics of his astronomy or on his theories on mnemonics. There is no certainty on the exact grounds of his accusation, indictment, trial, sentencing, and execution since his file has been conveniently misplaced. If there is any consensus on Bruno, however, it is the sense that he was prosecuted for theological heterodoxy rather than scientific heresy. That is, unlike Galileo's prosecution for Copernican heliocentrism, Bruno's trial was based on theological grounds. His arts of memory and his cosmological theories were inseparable from his notions of religion and Renaissance hermeticism. The technical minutiae are hotly debated, and I leave that contention to the specialists.[4] My interest is in the frame of mind, the heuristic scaffolding, and the epistemological implications of Bruno's pursuit of knowledge, implications that bridge the philosophical threshold occupied by the epistemic transitions in Nicholas of Cusa, discussed in the last chapter, and the iconoclasm of Fray Servando's Enlightenment "free thinking," which we shall examine in the next chapter.

Thus, key to our interest in Bruno and of relevance to our comparative discourses is his observation in one of his last works, *De triplici minimo et mensura* (On the Triple Minimum and Measure; 1591):

> He who desires to philosophise must first of all doubt all things. He must not assume a position in a debate before he has listened to the various opinions, and considered and compared the reasons for and against. He must never judge or take up a position on the evidence of what he has heard, on the opinion of the majority, the age, merits, or prestige of the speaker concerned, but he must proceed according to the persuasion of an organic doctrine which adheres to real things, and to a truth that can be understood by the light of reason.[5]

The implications of this statement for the future we now occupy are manifold, and they continue to resonate in our contemporary culture and its formative processes. These enduring aftershocks are what I wish to pursue in this memo indirectly addressed to Giordano Bruno.

Memory, Bruno teaches us, is constitutive of culture, not only as an instrument of recuperating what we might lose or what no longer is, but, even more so, in its capacity to articulate or join the members of a community, to re-member and re-collect what still persists as productive and serviceable and to discard what does not. Thus memory and culture are coeval, and they are also coterminous as remembering and forgetting. The first, memory, augments by re-collection; the latter, culture, culls and subtracts by cultivation. Remembering Bruno by way of this memorandum might serve as a modest safeguard against the ravages of time and the depredations of history, even as these continue while future history is in the making. His memory could well help us calibrate in our bewildered time the necessary ratio between indispensable remembering and equally necessary forgetting, both vital to our existence in an epoch no less convinced of its righteousness than was Bruno's own time.

We need to recall, in keeping with the lessons of Giordano Bruno, that Mnemosyne, goddess of memory and mother of the Muses, whom Bruno invokes often, most notably in his 1584 *La cena de le ceneri* (*Ash Wednesday Supper*), dwelled on the banks of Lethe, the river of forgetting. And we also need to remember that Mnemosyne has rescued everything we know as truth for us from that lethic oblivion. This is why clarity and truth are designated in the Greek lexicon through the privative letter *alpha*, an ambiguous first letter that points to what Osip Mandelstam, in the epigraph to this chapter, called "amplitudes of oscillation,"[6] of simultaneous beginnings and erasures. It is with this letter as prefix attached to *letheia* that all disclosure, truth, and remembrance begin, and this may well be why *alpha* gives our alphabet its name and is the first letter we learn. That salvaging operation is called *aletheia*, a form of cultural recuperation that so fascinated the German philosopher Martin Heidegger (1889–1976) in the last century that in his exegesis of the visionary poetry of Friedrich Hölderlin (1770–1843), whose ecstasies led him to the tower, he could not help considering the possibility of a surfeit of *aletheia* as the cause for Hölderlin's lucid madness.[7] In his own sublime luminosity, the German poet diagnosed his plight through Pindar's fragments (e.g., Fragment 194) as the possible imbalance in the ratio of *letheia* to *aletheia*, of memory's truth to the perilous clarity of truth's *forgetting*.

Mnemosyne had a penchant for shepherds, and shepherds a fondness for her charms, and this is why Zeus seduced her by taking the form of a shepherd, a seduction from which all the Muses were born, and with them all that for us defines culture and its institutional management. Thus, in many ways, culture has always been pastoral, even in the industrial age and in our own postindustrial cybernetic epoch.

In his short story "Burning Chrome" and in the 1984 novel *Neuromancer*, which that story foreshadowed, the American novelist William Gibson (b. 1948) defines culture as a consensual hallucination. Hallucination is a prosthetic extension of *aletheia*'s anamnesis, which is memory's patchy and problematic recovery. Heidegger sensed this in Hölderlin's reverie, and Friedrich Nietzsche (1844–1900) before him traced the source of such reverie as the attribute of the god Dionysius, whose immediate presence we perpetually labor to enact and represent through every stratagem that Apollo has bestowed upon us as an instrument of art and of science. And the forms of that repertoire, Nietzsche reminds us in his 1872 treatise *The Birth of Tragedy*, are also what constitute the consensus of a self-recognition whose technologies and practices come to define culture. Writing on the art of *poēsis* some fifty years after Nietzsche, the Russian philologist Mikhail Bakhtin (1895–1975) would observe that in the culture of poetry "everything that enters the work must immerse itself in Lethe, and forget its previous life in any other contexts."[8] In an essay on the classical epic and the modern novel, Bakhtin writes: "In the genre of the 'memorial,' the poet constructs his image in the future and distanced plane of his descendants.... Artistic representation here is representation *sub specie aeternitatis*."[9] This aspect of eternity under which the poet labors suspends the present, a suspension which some fifty years after Bakhtin will have rendered that present into an object of nostalgia, as Frederic Jameson's 1989 essay "Nostalgia for the Present" avers.[10] More recently, reminiscent of Filippo Brunelleschi's fifteenth-century revolutionary calculus on the optical vanishing point, Gayatri Spivak would refer to the epistemic potential of such temporal recession as "the vanishing present" in the subtitle of her 1999 treatise *A Critique of Postcolonial Reason: Toward a History of the Vanishing Present*.[11]

In our time, then, Mnemosyne would certainly appear to have a problematic present, at best, and her past is only a prospective means for a promissory future. "In ancient literature," Bakhtin reminds us, "it is memory, and not knowledge that serves as the source and power of the creative impulse.... The novel [which Bakhtin considers the genre of modernity], by contrast, is determined by experience, knowledge and practice (the future)."[12] Clearly, we live in prosodic, and prosaic, rather than epic times. Which means we are defined more by what we forget and how fast we forget it than by what we remember. And our perpetual amnesia constructs its own future and ours through a subtractive process predicated on what is suppressed, repressed, overlooked, skewed, spun, or erased. Mnemosyne was never so thirsty at the banks of the river Lethe.

This is the intricate web of memory and forgetting that entangled Giordano Bruno. It is the same tangle that snares history at the beginning of the twenty-first century. No doubt, in the last eight years of his life, spent in prisons of the Holy Office of the Inquisition and its interrogation chambers, Bruno came to understand that whenever culture and memory are crossed what inevitably comes to the fore is the ambiguous and hazardous domain of historical and political life. This is the case because culture is by definition a process of cultivation, which means, in effect, a series of adjudicatory and managerial processes that forge consensus, hallucinatory or otherwise, by clearing the ground through exclusions and inclusions, which is another way of recalling the Latin verb *colere*, "to clear the ground" for cultivation, the verb whose action once made the site of Bruno's later immolation at the stake a "campo dei fiori" (a field of flowers), as it is still called today. It is the same verb from which we derive the terms *culture* and *colonization*. Bruno's martyrdom is a cultural act in locative and predicative terms, and his topological art of memory ironically encompasses both the loci of the mnemonic technologies of his system and the locus of the ideological and agricultural cultivation of his execution. That site, once a field and then an urban agora, Rome's most ancient market and site of executions, now is the place of his memorial. His fate is as ironically expressive as his treatises on questions of memory and culture. It should not surprise Bruno, then, that at the beginning of the third millennium, when culture and memory are in crisis, this memorandum should be addressed to him and, through him, to the critical predicament of the epoch in which we live and write.

II. Culture and Memory

Memory and culture do indeed function dialectically as each other's oscillatory complement: culture determines what is memorable and how and memory determines distinct ways of enabling a culture to manage its past and negotiate its present. From Giordano Bruno and from his fate we understand most acutely that culture functions as a memorial symptom and memory as a cultural construct, with the two alternately embodying each other symptomatically, the one realizing the other as its momentous edifice. This mutual implication entails an intricate set of historical and political mediations with material consequences, often as tragic as Bruno's own fate. As we learn from him, it is through the particular specters and embodied phantoms of this spectral process that any particular epoch is defined. We could refer to the phenomena in this refracted mirror as the culturalization of memory and the memorialization of culture by which specters find their historical materiality. His own historical predicaments and philosophical meditations on the technologies of memory and epistemology are most instructive in this dialectical oscillation between memory and culture, as he well demonstrates in his seminal work *Ash Wednesday Supper*. For our purposes, this is the more telling volume, the one that reflects on his brief tenure at Oxford University and that reprises his essays on the arts of memory from the earlier three collections, *Cantus circaeus, Explicatio trigenta sigillorum*, and *Sigillus sigillorum*. His "Circean incantations," the "thirty explicatory seals," and the "seal of seals" that explicate the intricate arts of memory are fascinating for the technologists of Renaissance mnemonics, and they are compellingly significant for those who would read the technologies he explicates in the context of Renaissance science and belief. Heeding the promptings from his *Composition of Images*, which I have cited as epigraph for this memorandum—"images do not receive their names from the explanations of the things they signify, but rather from the condition of those things that do the signifying"—I would like to focus on "the condition of those things that do the signifying," rather than on Bruno's technical "explanations that do the signifying." I would like, that is, to consider the contextual, historical materiality of his predicament at that moment in the spring of 1583 and his sojourn to Oxford, as these circumstances serve, symptomatically, to signify the particular convergence of memory and culture as they intersect and become defining of a world context larger than themselves as discrete signifiers.

His passage through Oxford was sponsored, *sub rosa*, by the French King Henri III, according to his most authoritative biographer, Frances Yates.[13] She bases her information on Bruno's relationship to the French court and to Henri III on the only extant source—the archive of Bruno's Venetian inquisitors that contains the record of his interrogation.[14] In the ideological war between France and England, Bruno and the new philosophy he espoused proved tempting as stalking horse for Paris against the English intellectuals. The caveat from the English ambassador Henry Cobham in Paris to the authorities at Oxford as forewarning of his arrival betrays the caution, not to say suspicion, that should await his imminent arrival: "Doctor Jordano Bruno Nolano, a professor in philosophy, intends to pass into England, whose religion I cannot commend."[15] The syntactical ambiguity and grammatical squalor of the ambassador's dispatch notwithstanding, his qualms are not, obviously, about the religion of England but about the religion of "Doctor Jordano Bruno Nolano." Unable to discern or judge the philosophy and its arts of memory, he passes judgment, instead, on Bruno's threatening religion. Coeval with the English ambassador's admonition is Bruno's own prologue to the volume addressed, in the third person, "to the most excellent Vice Chancellor of Oxford University and to its celebrated doctors and teachers":

Philoteus Jordanus Brunus Nolanus, doctor of a more abstruse theology, professor of a purer and more innocuous wisdom, noted in the best academies of Europe, an approved and honorably received philosopher, a stranger nowhere save amongst the barbarous and ignoble, the waker of sleeping souls, tamer of presumptuous and recalcitrant ignorance, proclaimer of a general philanthropy, who does not choose out the Italian more than the Briton, the male more than the female, the mitred more than the crowned head, the man in the toga more than the armed man, the cowled man more then the man without a cowl, but him who is the more peaceable-minded, the more civilized, the more loyal, the more useful; who regards not the anointed head, the forehead signed with the cross, the washed hands, the circumcised penis, but (where the man may be known by his face) the culture of the mind and soul. Who is hated by the propagators of foolishness and hypocrites, but sought out by the honest and the studious, and whose genius the more noble applaud.[16]

Bruno's preemptive gambit left scant options for the Oxford dons. Nevertheless, his allusion to "Oxford pedants" in his *Ash Wednesday Supper* the following year would indicate that his efforts to sue for acceptance as an outsider and as a Catholic by appealing to the ecumenical tolerance of the dons serves as a prime example of an attempt at managing the parlous fate of transcultural encounters. The only documented response to his Oxford overtures comes to us in an article by Robert McNulty, who cites one George Abbot of Balliol College at the time of his visit and later archbishop of Canterbury. Given the animus between Catholics and Protestants, in this case Calvinist Puritans, Abbot's response, included in a 1604 polemic printed at Oxford, is not surprising. If anything, it betrays certain elements of the caricature stereotype of the racially tinged xenophobic parochialism with which the institution has often been depicted:

When the Italian Didapper, who intitutled himselfe *Philotheus Iordanus Brunus Nolanus, magis elaborata Theologia Doctor, &c* (margin: Praefat, in explicatio triginta sigillorum) with a name longer than his body, had . . . seen our Vniversity in the year 1583, his hart was on fire, to make himselfe by some worthy exploite, to become famous in that celebrious place. Not long after returning againe, when he had more boldly then wisely, got vp into his sleeues like some Iugler, and telling vs much of *chentrum & chirculus & circumference* (after the pronunciation of his Country language) he vndertook among very many other matters to set on foote the opinion of Copernicus, that the earth did goe around, and the heavens did stand still; wheras in truth it was his owne head which rather did run round, & his braines did not stand stil.[17]

Caught between belligerent ignorance and implacable orthodoxy, Bruno's predicament becomes exemplary of the ways by which collective memory and institutional culture define historical life and its materiality. The phobic disdain of his person and dismissive treatment of his heliocentric Copernican theories by his Protestant Oxford hosts are matched in vehemence by Bruno's persecution at the hands of the Catholic Church. The tolerance, charity, and open-mindedness he cloyingly sued for evince the symptoms of an outsider's anxious optimism. He personified the heterodoxy at the perimeter of certain cultural circumscriptions whose orthodoxy and homogeneity would have little forbearance for cultural alterity or for alternate intellectual possibilities. That juncture where the paths of memory and culture intersect is never idle. There is a perpetual oscillation between what is remembered and what might be cultivated as knowledge for a cultural domain, even if it's for the self-reinforcement of a seemingly immutable status quo. Bruno's Oxford experience, no less than his vicissitudes with the authorities of the Catholic Church and its Holy Office, serve as a clear demonstration of the force of memory for preservation and the power of culture for self-perpetuation. Though tolerance and self-transformation, the cultivation of heterogeneity, are not necessarily precluded in the productive crossing point of memory and culture, these are, more often than not, outside possibilities rather than likely first options, if history and Bruno's experience be any indication.

For this reason, the processes and potential outcomes implied in this dialectical production of memory and culture have occupied the discourse of philosophical reflection and political action since time immemorial. *Time immemorial* is a paradoxical idiom that refers to the bliss of a prehistorical era. We are wont to call it a state of ignorance, which is yet another paradoxical turn of speech, since ignorance, as Nicholas of Cusa's negative epistemology teaches us, is not at the beginning but at the end of acquiring knowledge; ignorance and its significance are the last rather than the first things we learn. As Bruno's experience at Oxford in 1583 and his fate at the hands of the Catholic Church would indicate, some may blithely live by ignorance but they do so as its symptom. As a species, we tend to become wise to ignorance only in the end. This, at least, is how we have been taught to understand our arrival at anything resembling enlightenment or wisdom, and this is what Socrates aimed, ironically, to teach his students in the dialogues of Plato. Of course, Giordano Bruno suggests this on more than one occasion in alluding to *De docta ignorantia* of his philosophical predecessor Nicholas of Cusa. In echo of his undiminished legacy, this sort of transtemporal and translocal knowledge is what contemporary ethicist philosophers, such as Alain Badiou in his treatise *Ethics: An Essay on the Understanding of Evil*, refer to as "technologies of recognition."[18]

Technologies of recognition is as resonant a phrase as the language of Bruno's mnemonic arts. He knew full well, and passed down to us, that long tradition of "mnemotechnics," or technologies of memory, which extend from Simonides of Ceos in the sixth and fifth centuries B.C, that is, the time of Pythagoras (whose presence in Bruno's hermetic writings proved so compromising before the implacable scrutiny of the Holy Office of the Inquisition), down to the cybernetics of our virtual data banks at the beginning of the twenty-first century. Much has been written about recognition since antiquity, especially in the metaphysics of reason and the rationalizations of pragmatism, as well as in the techno-speak of what we know today as cognitive psychology. But what has proved most magnetic to our belated context in this topic is the prefix *re-*, which remands us emphatically to an anteriority to be recuperated and to a knowledge that, as memory, is at once primal and residual. And though it risks oversimplification, the definition by a contemporary scholar of postcolonialism, Sara Ahmed, may be most serviceable. Ahmed defines recognition as "the cognition of that which is already known and predetermined by political economy in mostly predictable ways."[19] In the argot of our time, then, predictability is most emphatically the domain of cultural formation and its preconditions, and the cultural recuperation of memory as self-recognition, or as recognition of alterity, aims foremost at the construction and reconstruction of the memory bank, not necessarily as an end in itself but as a purposeful fulcrum and useful configuration for particular and predictable ends. In this sense, and as Bruno already discerned, memory becomes significant not for its pastness but for its futurity. Within the realm of cultural teleology, memories of the past are overtaken by cultural projects and hypervalorized as memories of the future. Much has been written about this process before and since Thomas Moore's 1516 treatise *Utopia*, which, in effect, converts the glories of the past into the desiderata of a future now dubbed "utopian." And Bruno's own embattled interventions in the vicissitudes of this itinerary have augmented our insight, perhaps as much as they exacerbated the anxieties of his contemporaries to the detriment of his own well-being and at the cost of his life.

Those ratios of conversion of past memory into memory of the future chart the route of a political economy whose way stations emerge as defining moments in the historical life of a particular culture. These are the defining junctures of the dialectic between memory and forgetting. Here then we arrive at a convergence of two sets of dialectical chiasmata: the crossing point of memory and forgetting and the crisscrossing traversal of past memory into future memory. At this compounded juncture, we encounter one of the more revealing axial way stations of our own historical moment at the beginning of this millennium. Our predicament and the vicissitudes of culture and memory at this crossroads would come as no surprise to Giordano Bruno. He, after all, not only taught but also lived and died at the crossing point of the lethic in memory and the lethal in the living of memory's portent and promise.

Perhaps the most conspicuous fate of memory at our cultural moment is its commodification on an industrial scale and its complex deployment in self-sustaining nanotechnologies. By industrialization of memory I am not referring merely to the cache of software that comes in megabytes or gigabytes that one can insert into the hard drive of one's personal computer. This too is highly significant and it would delight Bruno, as well as Simonides of Ceos (556–468 B.C.), Metrodorus of Scepsis (331–278 B.C.), the anonymous author(s) of the *Rhetoricorum ad C. Herennium libri IV*, Marcus Tullius Cicero (106–43 B.C.), Ramon Lull (1235–1315), and Giulio Camillo (1480–1544)—in other words, Bruno's memorable genealogy in the technologies of memory. And it might have even amused Themistocles (525–460 B.C.), who, according to Cicero, snubbed the artificial memory of mnemotechnics of his time, saying he "preferred the science of forgetting to that of remembering,"[20] somewhat forgetful that forgetting and remembering are not mutually exclusive but are modalities of one and the same science. While Themistocles would spurn the technologies of artificial memory in favor of forgetting, he would not be at odds with the memory industry that is dominant now, at the beginning of the twenty-first century, since the industrialization of memory depends as much, if not more, on elaborately engineered forms of forgetting as it does on the perseverance of remembering. Simultaneously, the efficacy of the memory industry rests on the transformation of past memory into fungible and politically viable memory for the future. This potential of forgetting as a more significant experience than memory and oblivion's purposeful management was accorded a certain scientific materiality in the middle of the last century by the American neurophysiologist Geoffrey Sonnabend, in his now curious three-volume treatise *Obliscence: Theories of Forgetting and the Problem of Matter*.[21] What I have already referred to as the ratios of conversion between remembrance and oblivion serve as operational mechanisms we now call informatics, or the permutation and translation of retrievable information into serviceable and marketable knowledge, or at least information, if not knowledge. Strangely enough, Themistocles, who was so ambivalent about memory and forgetting, is remembered as much as he is forgotten, his ambiguous legacy ranging from that of the heroic *strategos*, or strategist, who successfully commanded the Athenian fleet against the Persian Xerxes in 480, to the abject exile who was condemned to death in absentia by Athens. Thucydides mentions that Themistocles' demise was rumored to have been a suicide. One can only conjecture that the fact that Themistocles was born to a non-Greek mother at a time of Athenian ethno-racial supremacism may well have complicated his fate as much as his memory. But that is another story, though not altogether irrelevant to the satraps of migration and memory management who calibrate and control the movement of peoples on the basis of biometrics and racial ethnicities in today's world and its global biopolitics.

At any rate, Bruno no doubt would recall from his own fate that, as Themistocles must have known firsthand, the alchemy of transmuting informatic lode into formative knowledge is an eminently political process. The contending dynamics of this process originate, as we already noted, in the Latin verb *colere* as etymon for the cultivational processes of culling, cutting, selecting, editing, controlling, and excluding that culminate in what we know as culture. How diverse human communities negotiate these processes is what differentiates them as cultures. But what all of these cultures have in common is memory, though of course their memories are not the same. The subtractive process of cultural formation becomes more intricate than in agri-culture, obviously, for while we might know what we "weed out," or, in our time, chemicalize or irradiate into oblivion, we cannot always be sure of the accuracy of our command as subject agents, nor can our institutions be certain of their proprietary agency, in the assortment of memory that is "selected in." Amnesia, even when deliberate and purposive may well find itself enmeshed in terrain more intricate and mysterious than imaginable or knowable. Just as we only know *that* we don't know, rather than knowing *what* it is that we don't know, we can never be sure of what we might be forgetting or might have already forgotten. We are only aware of not remembering all that there might be to be remembered. Thus, the possibilities of amnesia could be infinite. The psychologists of the twentieth century elaborated this predicament of selective recollection as determined by a patient's psychohistory into the clinical syndrome they called, after Plato's terminology, *anamnesis*. The satraps of realpolitik, for their part, in the expediencies of their pragmatism, have always known full well that, unlike oblivion, memories are precisely numerable, exactly calculable and invariably calculated, culturally manageable and politically managed in ways that are efficacious and expedient for the dominant cultural economy of any given time and place. These efficacies are what determined Bruno's own fate, differentiating him from Galileo Galilei (1564–1642). While Bruno met his destiny in the Campo dei Fiori, Galileo was appointed professor of mathematics at the University of Padua—a post for which both had competed and an appointment whose academic cover would delay Galileo's own trial and conviction by some thirty-five years.

And so, while culturally effective and politically serviceable, forgetting clearly has its perils. Oblivion is a constant and innumerable threat. The origin and confluence of the lethic and the lethal form a commonplace, as Bruno well knew. Both have their source in the same river Lethe. Even more dreaded and dangerous than forgetting, however, may be the possibility of being forgotten, a dread that drove Bruno's ambition just as often as it spurred his scientific insight and visionary perspicuity. Cultures, no less so than the individuals that constitute them, hedge against the anxious possibility of being forgotten in elaborate ways, so much so that culture itself has often been taken to be synonymous with the acts and perennial productions of such uneasy hedging—memorials, monuments, commemorations, rituals of remembrance, documentary recordings, elaborate archives, communal recollection, and even book publishing, all acts of bridging oblivion through prospective envois destined for the future and suing for its memory. And it is chiefly in these compensatory gestures that we witness *the memorialization of culture* and the predictable chiasmus of this inevitability, namely, *the culturalization of memory*. Each in its own way is a Platonic *pharmakon* in the ambiguous sense of Plato's usage in the *Phaedrus* (275a–b), where, as Bruno might have remembered, Plato has the Egyptian deities Thamus and Theuth discuss the latter's invention, that is, the technology of writing as a hedge against forgetfulness. Plato's dialogue and its *pharmakeion* are a locus classicus, in more than the obvious sense, where memory and forgetting converge. Thamus warns that the instrument of writing will become a crutch as substitute for good memory, thereby leading to amnesia. Thamus's admonitions have not prevented writing from scripting culture as the product of instrumental or mechanical reproduction. Theuth's enthusiasm for his mnemonic technology has indeed proved the sacrifice of memory at the altar of writing, thereby displacing the real by forgetfulness, or amnesia, and replacing it with the sign of its representation, what Plato called *anamnesia*. Memory, then, became a form of un-forgetting, what in English we call a "re-minder" of what has been lost to the mind. What we call culture has lived ever since by this defining ambiguity. We can call this primal juncture of memory and culture the equivocal hitch of *memorialization* and *culturalism*, as the dialogue between Thamus and Theuth lives on in the counterpoint on aura and commodification between Walter Benjamin (1892–1940) and Theodor Adorno (1903–69). Two of the twentieth century's most anxious students of cultural memory, their forceful representations continue to remind us of this juncture through their unforgettable writings.[22]

It would be difficult to say which of the two faces of this same coin has been more consequential in the life of memory, *memorialization* or *culturalism*. *Memorialization* has tended to monumentalize and to recast memory into ideological structures that often border on, and just as often stray into, idolatry. *Culturalism*, for its part, has more often than not reduced memory to modes of representation and narratives that elide the contestatory and conflictive stresses of political, economic, and ethno-national struggles that go into forming and sustaining culture. Such elisions emerge as the fault lines in the baneful history of the coexistence and mutual influence of different cultures in proximity. Thus, memorialization has always found an idol to worship, even when there is none, as in the tomb of the unknown soldier, called a *cenotaph*, which, as the Greek lexicon for the container implies, is a blank monument, but no less powerful for its vacancy. Its emptiness will always have room for the victims of collective delusions and the expedient human sacrifices of political ideologues.

Culturalization, for its part, has often melded diverse human existence into homogeneous representation, or it has reified heterogeneous elements of humanity into the essentialized parataxis of multiculturalism and the pieties of parallel coexistence. The most egregious examples of this essentialist ghettoization may be the apartheids of the twentieth century and, alas, still of the twenty-first. In either case, memory has been the object of technologies of transmission, whether these be narrative, discursive, or citational, that invariably construct and represent human experience through protocols of art, language, and ideological templates. I deliberately refer to these procedures as protocols, since I believe that these technologies are a sticky wicket of proleptic transmission that is not accidental ("protocol" is literally what's affixed or stuck to the pages at the head of a book). Nor is memory recuperated through such technologies as a form of retrofitting. Rather, the thrust of these anamnesic constructions is projective toward a future anteriority best designated by the grammatical verbal case of the future perfect, an anticipatory telos *sub specie aeternitatis*, even if this projection of eternity will have been aimed to reach only to the end of time and not beyond.

One of the most chilling instances of such projection is dramatized by the Argentine writer Jorge Luis Borges (1899–1986) in a tale that is now more of a commonplace as objective correlative of realpolitik than we may wish. The narrative is called "Tlön Uqbar Orbis Tertius," a cautionary tale that dates from 1940. Its admonition is against the perils of what Borges saw as imminent apocalyptic catastrophe, product of a shared millennial delusion, or a "consensual hallucination," as William Gibson defined culture, in the process of being concocted at that time, *sub specie aeternitatis*, by the National Socialist German Workers' Party and its leader Adolf Hitler (1889–1945). Borges ends his monitory tale against totalization and totalitarianism, whose imminence and results he diagnosed in 1940, with a prescripted postscript, which he designates as "Posdata de 1947." The construction of anticipated catastrophe viewed as recursive post factum from a future memory still seven years hence (the "posdata" dated 1947 was indeed written in 1940) is historically more persuasive in its prescience than many histories about the Third Reich written after the events of World War II. Borges learned the diverse possibilities of memories of the future from Franz Kafka (1883–1924), a number of whose dystopian stories he translated from German into Spanish.[23]

When culture becomes joined to memory, then, culture is not inadvertent nor is memory a matter of chance. The first is cultivated, while the latter is calculated, rather than being merely reflective or reflexive. Whether in the private domain or in the public sphere culture and memory work together formatively, programmatically, and for specific outcomes. Their conjugation is simultaneously productive and re-productive. As mnemonic representation, this synergy is at once proleptic projection and recursive re-membering, by which I mean the articulation of somatic components into private embodiment and as public body politic. In these nodes of recognition the constitution of individual subjectivity and of the common weal as a retributive and attributive project engaged in willful retrieval of the past and determinate construction of the future are found.

This economy of political recuperation and its technologies of recognition not only transmutes the cultural grammar's preterit into the future perfect, as already noted, it translates the radical contingency of the nebulous past into the radix, or root etymon, of a determinative necessity that, once projected into the future, becomes an inexorable teleology awaiting the realization of self-fulfilling prophecies. History demonstrates that this, in fact, has been the blueprint of our revolutions. Once the future perfect—what will have been—becomes an object of contention, the stakes become very high indeed. In that projection, *prototopia*, or the primal scene, becomes a retrospective object of desire ideologically alembicated into utopia; atavism transmutes into sure-fire prolepsis; revenant into *prosopsos* (a new appearance rather than an apparition); reminiscence into *prosechi* (cautionary immediacy or monitory adumbration); and resurrection gives way to insurrection that would ensure the perfect outcome of an ardently desired future. It is within this economy of cultural alchemy and political illusion that revolution undergoes a semantic and ideological metastasis from a devolution and return of a *status quo ante* to an innovation and reformation of the future—the finally realizable future perfect. In the process, the passage from remembering the past to remembering the future crosses a cultural and historical divide. Once this threshold is breached, the antithesis and its struggle are no longer between memory and forgetting. Rather, what takes center stage in culture's dialectical arena now is memory and countermemory, where the contestatory agon between one's memory and the memory of another compete for a cultural temporality that is at once post factum and prophetic, recapitulatory and augural, recursive and precursive. This is indeed an unseasonal time of dire necessity, a necessity that, paradoxically enough, as Nietzsche reminded us, is prone to be mediated by the contingencies of history. Giordano Bruno knew this all too well. It was the incidental and contingent circumstances of this agon that led to his infernal fate, not necessarily the philosophical or scientific issues his inquisitors could not or did not care to understand.[24]

III. Memory, Countermemory

When memory would counter memory, the arbiter called upon to mediate, more often than not, has indeed been history. History itself, enmeshed in memory, has been far from immune to dispute and from the need for arbitration, as certain lucid historiographers have noted.[25] The dialectics of historical formation are captured in the old apothegm invoked by the French historiographer Pierre Nora in the first volume of his multivolume treatise *Les lieux de mémoire* (Places of Memory; published in English as *Rethinking France*). Nora reminds us that "as always, history makes the historian more than the historian makes history."[26] It would appear that Nora does not recall Oscar Wilde (1854–1900), who, through his impish Gilbert, tells us that the only obligation we have to history is to rewrite it, and, we might add, we must inevitably do so as historical writers. As tends to be the case, the common wisdom of the apothegm, Nora's and Wilde's, is somewhat right, although the end of the twentieth century was a time that pointed up the proverbial commonplace as also somewhat less than right. In the dominant discourse of the historical imaginary that would cross the centurial threshold as hegemonic principle from the last to the present century, the primacy accorded to history in Pierre Nora's invocation is challenged with a vengeance. The "end of history" would come to be declared, as we discussed in Chapter 2, following the dissolution of the Soviet Union in 1989; a certain Mr. Fukuyama and company were the bearers of this news.[27] Where, then, did this end of history leave memory and countermemory? The answer is: everywhere, including in history itself; so much so, that cultural historians now speak of a "culture of memory" and, somewhat pleonastically, of "mnemohistory."[28] Pierre Nora would speak wistfully of "les lieux de mémoire" (the discrete locations or sites of memory) as the fragmented compensation for the displaced "milieux de mémoire" (ideational environments of memory). We can track that compensatory proliferation into the myriad places of historical experience by following its resonant traces in the French homonym, namely, "les mille yeux de mémoire," where the night has its thousand eyes and memory the serial nightmares of its haunted visions. I call this plethora of memory a "compensatory proliferation" because, having been confronted with the prospect of becoming a people without a history through the declarations of history's end, cultures around the world in the late twentieth century may well have turned to memory as a compensation and hedge against their announced historical oblivion, decreed for them by those who claimed to have found their own providential apotheosis and historic vindication in history's inevitable eschatology.

The proliferation of any phenomenon automatically triggers predictable economic and political factors that convert such phenomena into commodifiable, fungible, exploitable, and manageable objects that make them subject to laws of supply and demand and to political expediency. This is a principle our time euphemistically refers to as "free market forces." Memory has not been immune to this process in the cultural life of the late twentieth and early twenty-first centuries, especially when information technologies have emerged as highly efficient instruments whose capabilities match and enhance this human impulse for expedient reification, political exploitation, militaristic hegemony, informatic spin, and commodity management. One of the most visible symptoms of this reflexive tendency and its convergence with information technologies is the institution of the museum and the fury with which musealization of material history and spiritual life has been and is still being pursued.

The introduction of digital photographic and video technologies into the most remote preindustrial cultures of central Africa and Amazonian

America has turned indigenous peoples not only into their own spectacle but also into their own immediate phantoms in revenant visitation through digital imaging. Most immediately, we encounter this self-musealization through the family video camera and the autodocumentary. And we find this in our autoethnographic fetishization, most wrenchingly apparent to immigrants, refugees, and history's displaced peoples who suddenly are confronted with the material culture of the places they were obliged to leave behind, the things they now see in ethnographic curio shops on Madison Avenue in New York, at Harrod's in London, at Gallerie Lafayette in Paris, and KaDeWe in Berlin. They must feel no less their own narrative revenant than the Machiguengas Indians, so well documented in the Peruvian Mario Vargas Llosa's novel *El hablador* (*The Storyteller*; 1987).[29] On a grander scale, at the beginning of the new millennium we are witness to an unprecedented surge in museum construction and museum attendance in the metropolitan centers of the developed and developing world. The most conspicuous, some might say egregious, example of this museological proliferation could be the Guggenheim Museum's multiple new branches around the globe—in Bilbao, Venice, Abu Dhabi, and so on.

The museum, alas, has also emerged as a locus of strategic significance when the agon of memory-countermemory literally turns into war. The looting and decimation of the Iraqi National Museum in Baghdad in March 2003, as noted in Chapter 2, pointedly accentuates the pivotal role of the museum as a critical instrument of memory and of forgetting as a strategically purposive action of war. And in a mirrored reversal of museological destruction for the revisionary eradication of historical memory, the government of Argentina has converted the former Naval School of Mechanics in Buenos Aires into a national museum. As the location of imprisonment and torture during Argentina's "dirty war" in the 1970s, during which some thirty thousand vanished people are believed to have been tortured, maimed, or killed, the museum is now contemporary with those who did survive imprisonment, interrogation, and torture at the site and in the rooms on exhibit. These survivors, in effect, have become the ghosted spectators of their own experience as museological spectacle, at once living objects of memory and history's residual subjects of traumatized remembrance.

Mnemosyne's daughters, the Muses, must be dismayed as they watch what is being perpetrated in their name. And no less intriguing in this regard may be the expectant museum on the slopes of the Acropolis under the shadow of the Parthenon in Athens, built with Olympian enthusiasm as a blank "lieu de mémoire"–in-waiting, a national cenotaph for the plundered Parthenon marbles held in the British Museum in London.

Memory-countermemory as a site of contestation where culture is forged, in more than one sense of that verb, has emerged as the center stage of our futuristic time. Confident of our abilities, like the tenants of the Tower of Babel, to forge any future we wish, whether in Las Vegas or in Babylon, we seem to have turned most determinedly to reading our past and constructing its memory. If the avant-gardes of the beginning of the twentieth century charged ahead under the banner of their self-declared Futurisms, we as postmoderns at the far end of modernity seem to be more determined in charging toward our museological pasts converted into futures. Where, then, do we find ourselves when our futurologist *post-* and our memorialist past would seem to have converged?

I believe the question brings us to a crossroads that is no less dangerous for private well-being and communal sustainability than the juncture of memory and forgetting, or remembering and oblivion explored and experienced in life and death by Giordano Bruno. This is so because our utopic self-investments in the future, which proved so inimical to human life and to environmental integrity in the last century, may not be an antithesis to but a mirror of our self-investment in our past. If we speculated on futures that proved politically and ecologically dystopic in the twentieth century, especially when the management of futurity was taken over by the power of genocidal states in more than one part of the world, our speculations on memory may not be any less perilous, no matter the number of truth and reconciliation commissions we deputize, or the number of investigative bodies we appoint to examine the integrity of our intelligence and the veracity of our intelligence services.

Like memory and countermemory, truth and intelligence ultimately can only find some equilibrium in the negotiated edge of adjudication between truth claims and countertruth maneuvers, intelligence and counterintelligence. When it comes to conciliation and reconciliation, however, the stakes are even higher and the process more precarious. Individuals and human collectivities can agree to disagree on gradations of truth; and diverse measures of intelligence can likewise occupy differing points on the spectrum of plausibility. Conciliation and reconciliation, however, have something absolute about them—people either coexist or they don't. In all its attendant perils, reconciliation must ultimately rest on the economy of memory and the political management of the past.

How memory is managed, then, becomes crucial to coexistence, communal or ecological. In some sense, again, it is easier to coexist speculatively on futures, because that cohabitation could live on hope or, at the very least, on the postponement of despair and the deferral of foreclosure on differences, until the future corroborates conciliatory hope or contradicts it. Like the realization of prophecies, imminent fulfillment can be deferred, at least until utopian expectation proves to be dystopian nightmare. Prophecies of the past, which we call memory, unlike memories of the future, are grounded on the conviction that what is believed to be indeed already exists by virtue of its pastness. Memory in these circumstances relies on the self-convinced clarity of remembrance and on the certainty of completed action. When conviction and certainty come up against counterconviction and countercertainty, gradation, measure, scale, range, modulation, and perspectival spectrum tend to be trumped by sureness and the righteous conviction of self-justification. In this sense, there may be nothing more dangerous to coexistence than a clear and unequivocal memory.

When Mnemosyne would leave the banks of the river Lethe, in other words, the result is clear and certain danger. Mnemosyne cannot live happily anywhere but on the banks of Lethe. *Alethei* would be meaningless without *letheia*. We would be left only with a privative *alpha* and the privations of oblivion, were it not for the convergence and conjugation of the two. Shepherds, sacred to Mnemosyne, know this very well. Were it not for their capacity to shrug adversity and see beyond the memory of perennial hardship, they could not survive. They are the true inheritors of one of the oldest philosophical traditions, Stoicism, which teaches one to turn catastrophe into antistrophe and to walk the road of hope and the paradox of hopeful resignation into a new season and a new life. Human history has always faired better on the elliptical path of paradox and ambiguity than on the straight-and-narrow of disambiguation. The earth and its trajectory are more elliptical than straight and, as with all life, human existence tends to be more sustainable and more harmonious the closer it is in accord with the configurations of its environment and its planetary motions.

Like all economically and ideologically fungible commodities, however, memory, especially collective memory, and I submit even the most private memories, find their significance through modes of collective validation. Memory has rarely been permitted to find its level of maximal sustainability as intrinsic value. Exchange value and political expediency have, more often than not, trumped every other value. But, as culture is the marketplace of memory, private and collective, and as the dialectical intermediation between culture and memory is what ultimately defines both, we who, because of Bruno's legacy, are fully aware of the pliable and negotiable nature of memory as determinant of future coexistence, have an unavoidable ethical responsibility in this process. In a pedagogical site such as the university, with disciplinary formations that are dedicated to the juxtaposition, correlation, and comparison of cultures, we could well cultivate and teach those institutional acts with greatest potential for translatability and negotiative enablement in the agora of intersubjective, intercommunal and intercultural mediations.

The transference of our contemplative, conjectural, investigative, and scholarly engagements to pragmatic interventions is not without some risk. Knowing as we do that memory is more than what occurred in the past, and that technologies of recognition and misrecognition can and do reconfigure fragments and figments into new structures of reconceptualized historical density, our intervention into memory, even as speculative subject matter of academic discourse, must occur with an alertness to our inadvertent complicity with "market forces" and ideological formations. These are dynamics that may well be exacerbating the violence done to the aggrieved in the remembered past and to their descendents in the present and future. Two instances might suffice by way of cautionary examples. One of the most obvious instances for our historical time is the European Holocaust of the mid-twentieth century, whose abhorrent consequences spill into the futurity of the twenty-first. The other comes from Latin America at the end of the same century.

Few historical phenomena have elicited the intensity of discourse on memory as the European Holocaust of the 1940s. The results have not always been felicitous, and much has been written about the trivialization and disrespect accorded to one of humanity's most tragic memories. These have been extensively studied and, in terms of memory, specifically, most eloquently treated in such studies as Andreas Huyssen's *Twilight Memories: Marking Time in a Culture of Amnesia* and Miriam Hansen's article "*Schindler's List* Is Not *Shoah*: The Second Commandment, Popular

Modernism, and Public Memory."[30] In addition to these forceful critiques of the Disneyfication of the memory of human tragedy, there is also an equally appropriate and indispensable interrogation of, on the one hand, those who desecrate the memory of the victims by questioning or denying their tragedy and, on the other hand, the massive and programmatic exploitation of this Holocaust. The latter, history now proves, serves as screen of immunity for the dehumanization and dispossession of another people, extending, in effect, the consequences of genocidal practices in our memory into the twenty-first century, thereby keeping doubly alive the scourge of anti-Semitism, first by giving cause to damnable racists to feel that they are being vindicated, and, second, by practicing anti-Semitism against another Semitic people as a matter of national state policy justified on ethno-racial grounds.[31]

Converting the tragic memory of a people from a legitimate shield of immunity against repetition to a cynical screen of impunity for perpetuation of inhumanity is an execrable practice no society ought to condone, much less abet and emulate. The same must be said with regard to trivialization and exploitation of the memory of human suffering through capitalization that paves over, at times literally, and dematerializes memory with the crassest human impulses of retributive mercantilism. One of the most egregious examples of this sort of denigration is to be found in the Uruguayan capital of Montevideo. Here, amnesia and the erasure of human memory through a combination of political retribution and economic exploitation have converged in the construction of the Punto Carretas shopping mall on the site of one of the most notorious prisons of Latin America's dictatorial military regimes, where political dissidents and revolutionaries were confined, tortured, and killed in the 1970s and 1980s. By way of historical citation, the thick walls of the prison were left standing on one side as architectural accents. The entrance to the mall is the old entrance to the prison, whose three-story panoply of global commerce features establishments from Banana Republic to Burger King.[32] This is indeed a strong form of mercantile trivialization that violates tragic history, where constructed amnesia glosses over collective memory and edulcorates the violence of the act itself with quotidian ordinariness.

I close this memorandum to Giordano Bruno on this guarded and somewhat cautionary note in a time no less troubled and no less subject than his was to collective professions of self-righteous banality and its lethal potential. I do so in the hope that we might be able to countermand our institutional reflexive actions such as those Bruno experienced at the University of Oxford in 1583 and those that led to his immolation at the Campo dei Fiori in 1600. Our best hope is to disprove Osip Mandelstam's observation in the second epigraph of this memorandum that Bruno was "burned in vain." And in remembering his fate through this memorandum, I would wish us to recall the key tenet of his lesson to us, namely, that memory is one of the most significant aspects of our humanity, not because of its instrumentality as signifier, or because it is a sacred object, but because memory and being human are functionally coterminous and defining of our significance. The way we treat our memory and the memory of others, in the present and for the future, ultimately defines our humanity. I take this to be the force of Bruno's admonition in our epigraph about the conditions and responsibility of imputable subjects that give names and meaning in acts "that do the signifying."[33]

5

A Carceral Archive and the Culture of Conspiracy
FRAY JOSÉ SERVANDO TERESA DE MIER NORIEGA Y GUERRA, ENLIGHTENMENT'S CONTESTANT

> Al volver del otro mundo, que casi tanto vale salir de los calabozos de la Inquisición, donde *por así conviene* me tuvo archivado tres años el Gobierno, me hallé con una gran variación en la ortografía y excluída la x del número de las letras fuertes, por más que la reclamase el origen de las palabras. . . . Esta carta se reduce a suplicar por despedida a mis paisanos anahuences recusen la supresión de la x en los nombres mexicanos o aztecas que nos quedan de los lugares, y especialmente de México, porque sería acabar de estropearlos. Y es grande lástima, porque todos son significativos, y en su significado topográficos, estadísticos o históricos.
> —Fray Servando Teresa de Mier, "Carta de despedida a los mexicanos, escrita desde el Castillo de San Juan de Ulúa" (1820)

I. Culture, Conspiracy, and the Value of X

Fray Servando's vicissitudes begin with his sermon of December 12, 1794. When the Second Constitutional Congress of Mexico, December 11–13, 1823, extended its session by one hour to hear his final admonitions on the perils of an immoderate federal system of government, his tribulations appeared to have come to a close.[1] His troubles would not end there, however. Nor would the peripeties of his fraught itinerary cease even after his "natural life" ended on December 3, 1827, at the age of sixty-four. Fray Servando's disinterred remains were put in 1842 in the ossuary of the Monastery of Santo Domingo, his first place of incarceration, or "archiving,"[2] as he was wont to call his serial imprisonments, from where, once more, he would be "sprung," this time as mummified *corpus sine pectore*, and taken across the Atlantic to Brussels for display by his new owner, the circus master Bernabé de la Barra. There, Fray Servando would reemerge nearly twenty years later, in 1861, on exhibit as *corpus delicti* of victims of the Holy Office of the Inquisition. He could well resurface at any moment to taunt history, yet again, as he continues to do through the record of his heterodox sermons and iconoclastic writings. His bones, to paraphrase Bella Brodzki's recent study *Can These Bones Live?* continue to rattle.[3] His intricate itinerary as a fugitive from ideologically overweening regimes—of the Counter-Reformation and of the Enlightenment—instructs us amply in the shifting locus of discursive formations, in the foundational shiftlessness of what we now, finally, understand as international American studies, and in the primal scene of what would become the discipline of comparative literature.

Fray Servando's jeremiad to the Constitutional Congress of 1823 was dubbed a "discurso de las profecias,"[4] and subsequent history would indeed corroborate Fray Servando's prophetic admonitions. He was already cognizant of what it would mean for the new Mexican nation to forge its own governmental system instead of adopting someone else's: Bernardo Gutiérrez de Lara, Mexico's envoy to Washington during the country's war of independence in the previous decade had already exclaimed in his journal, "Help me, Holy Mary, and free me of these people." Mexico's first ambassador to Washington was responding to the suggestion of the U.S. Secretary of State James Monroe that Mexico adopt the same federal constitution as the United States of America, which would make it easier for the American federation to annex Mexico once it attained its independence.[5] In the twenty-nine years between Fray Servando's ill-starred sermon and his foreboding prophecies, his seven imprisonments and jailbreaks on both sides of the Atlantic would transform him into a legendary figure. No less legendary are his Parisian encounters with the emblematic dramatis personae of Napoleonic Europe's mired Enlightenment, duly noted in his memoirs, as is his "wicked" etymological parsing of *Lutetia*, the original name of Paris, which comes from the word for "mud"—*lutum*.[6] His Parisian interlocutors would include the Viscount Chateaubriand, Simón Bolívar, and Bolívar's mentor Simón Rodríguez (born Simón Carreño, otherwise known as Samuel Robinson), with whom Fray Servando would translate the viscount's America-based *Atalá* into Spanish, its first translation into another language. In the twentieth century both of these Americans would resurface, not as cotranslators of fiction but as fictional characters, Rodríguez in Arturo Uslar Pietri's novel *La isla de Robinson* (Robinson's Island; 1987) and in Carlos Fuentes's *La campaña* (The Campaign; 1996), and Fray Servando as the protagonist of Reinaldo Arenas's *El mundo alucinante* (Hallucinations; or, the Ill-fated Peregrinations of Fray Servando; 1965), and in Rosa Beltrán's novel *La corte de los ilusos* (The Court of Fools; 1995) as the haunting presence in the only imperial court to have originated in the postcolonial New World,[7] the Mexican court of "Emperor" Agustín de Iturbide.[8] At the *soirées* of Madame Récamier (Jeanne Françoise Julie Adelaide Récamier, 1777–1849), a pivotal figure in the femininization of the public sphere through the salon as apposite site of political contestation and civic republicanism,[9] Fray Servando would encounter, inter alia: the Jesuit Abbot Henri Grégoire, who, in the year of Fray Servando's sermon that changed the Spanish empire's history and his fortunes, coined the term *vandalism* and proposed to the National Convention of 1794 the founding of the Conservatoire des arts et métiers; the Baron Alexander von Humboldt, who took the New World's measurements for an emergent new science, even while Fray Servando was taking the erratic pulse of Enlightenment Europe; and, not least, Madame Germaine de Staël (née Necker), who comes by her immortality, in part, through her perpetually resonant quip upon meeting Fray Servando: "You come from a place that soon will begin to exist!"[10]

Fray Servando's peripatetic way stations serve as historic markers between imperial entropy and postcolonial uncertainty, between orthodox conviction and the incomprehensible threat of heterodox insecurity. Not only the place, as Madame de Staël would have it, but also the time of his origins are emergent from the chaos of an imperious order and its underlying squalor, cloaked in imperial violence and doctrinaire rigor mortis. As much the itinerary of a translator as of a transient, his restive way stations are symptomatic of a transitional moment in human history. This is also the historical cauldron that serves as primal scene for the genesis of what we have come to theorize and practice under the rubric of comparative literature, a discipline whose genesis is often traced to a number of Fray Servando's Enlightenment interlocutors. As much as he and his time might be the historical and ideological precursors for our discipline, he is also, mutatis mutandis, very much our asynchronous contemporary, reflected in us no less than we encounter our own agitated predicament mirrored in his embattled precedent. His coping strategy, so threatening to the order of his day and its orthodoxies, was to reach for a postimperial future by looking far into the preimperial past, so far past that the mythologies he adduced as foundational justifications for his dissidence threatened to shatter an already brittle and disintegrating world order and the authoritative myths that served as its axioms. Predictable as the official responses might have been to his temerity, he never ceased to be amazed, chagrined, or energized by the reactions of church, state, and third estate to his brazen importuning of conformity with incorrigible nonconformity. Not surprisingly, the order of Fray Servando's day, like any world order on the verge of disintegration, would prove implacably vindictive, though the ledger of history continues to corroborate his vindication. Most instructive for us remains the counterpoint between his articulate historical revision and the crumbling disarticulation of what deemed itself unassailable, perpetual, and omnipotent. His predicament, as much as his eloquent logomachia, expose the intricacy of entanglements that forge legitimate order out of whole cloth and weave imperial reality with even flimsier fabric.

It is in historical moments such as Fray Servando's and ours, when the forged order frays and the bias of cultural and historical fiber becomes exposed that we can glimpse just how shabby the substance and how squalid the craft of seemingly impregnable and ostensibly invincible world orders can be. It is at such historical junctures that we understand most acutely the collusive and crafty constructedness of what would otherwise delusionally define itself as natural, necessary, and inevitable. This was Fray Servando's insight: an unforgivable perspicacity. Fray Servando's clarity of vision has taught us to recognize in our own time the symptoms and anticipate the response. How or whether we can sustain the impact of such reactions with his steadfastness, or manage to escape their literal and ideological dungeons, remains to be seen.

If logical necessity, like the rules of grammar, is unforgiving, absolute necessity is absolutely merciless toward those who would contest it. The lesson of Fray Servando's predicament is unmistakable in this regard. No less instructive in his overturning of historical orthodoxy is the paradox of historical necessity, or the inherent contradiction in the naturalization of history as preordained and inevitable. Unquestioned order derives its status through remorseless deterrent, as he would discover the day after his December 12, 1794, sermon on the feast of the Virgin of Guadalupe—a crucial date and a fundamental subject for the order of his day and for the foundations of Spain's empire in what imperial discourse called "New Spain" and Fray Servando provocatively persisted in calling by its indigenous name, Anáhuac.[11] Imperial hegemony, as he was to discover, derives its sanction and authority even more from the management of language, what our current vulgate designates as "spin," than from the realm of the real. Thus, to call any of the elements of imperial history and its divinely preordained necessity by any other name than the duly sanctioned one is to incur the wrath of the empire's god and all his worldly agents, as Fray Servando well discovered the day after his sermon and for the twenty-nine years following that decisive date. His attribution of the New World's Christian evangelization to the apostle Thomas, as avatar of Quetzalcóatl centuries before 1492 and Mexico's Spanish conquest in 1521, and his identification of the Virgin of Guadalupe with the Aztec goddess Tonantzín well before her apparition to the Indian Juan Diego at Tepeyac,[12] in effect upended the ostensible rationale and ideological justification for imperial conquest and European colonization of the New World. In a fateful moment on that December day Fray Servando mooted three centuries of the empire's historical necessity. Empires, as he would discover, are not founded on reason. Their reason is the reasons of state and their instrument is the logic of power. Imperial sanction is otherworldly, as Fray Servando's vicissitudes before holy inquisitors and in prisons of the Holy Office of the Inquisition taught him. The laws that subtend legality and its sanctions are not juridical but extrajudicial, not normal but exceptional, as with the divinely ordained privilege of kings and the righteousness of those who consider themselves God's chosen agents.

Divine dispensation translates into a covenant between God and those who consider themselves God's chosen people. Those not chosen are viewed as actual or potential enemies and legitimate targets of God's wrath. Collusion among those so privileged is called communion, the foundational act at the base of community. Among those not so privileged such acts are deemed to be conspiracy. Covenanted communion is much more rare than "conspiration," or the breathing together that etymologically and politically signifies conspiracy; God's elect commune and the rest conspire. This might explain why the first planners of independence led by Miguel Hidalgo y Costilla in Mexico, once discovered by the authorities of the Spanish crown in 1810, would be referred to as the "junta de los conjurados,"[13] literally the junta of the conjured, better translated colloquially as a "band of conspirators."

This, in his heterodox way, is what Fray Servando recognized as the underlying principle of empire and of imperial reason. The Holy Office's jurisdiction saw to Fray Servando's indictment, conviction, and serial incarceration for such perilous insight. In Fray Servando's transitional epoch, when the covenanted felt more uncommon than ever in their exceptionality, the conspirators were legion, the elect the exception. Exceptionality has since become equivocal and ambivalently shared: to be deemed an exception now means to equivocate between polar extremes; the elect are exceptionally immune and exempted from any convention or law, while the dispensable are excepted from the rights and protections of any jurisprudence, exposed to any act deemed expedient by the impunity of those who, in their own exceptionality as enforcers of what they adventitiously deem lawful, see themselves as exempt from adherence to any law.[14] As exceptionality has become two-faced, conspiracy is more multifaceted and ubiquitous than ever; those with most to gain and most to safeguard still fend off those who would unmask their privilege with the derisive and preemptive epithet of "conspiracy theorist."

When the unquestionable nature of what is deemed a natural order is questioned and subjected to contestation, the pursuit of deidentifying and delegitimating those doing the questioning becomes anxiously urgent. Fray Servando's own intervention and subsequent disguises, impersonations, and multiple self-rehearsals in this agonic arena proved singularly egregious, and so he has emerged as a defining marker for the revolutionary transformations that witnessed the transition from imperial colonialism to postcolonial imperialism. Conspiracies—as compensatory strategies and/or as explanations for anxiety-ridden historical eras—abound, and Fray Servando's own itinerary crisscrossed conspiratorial junctures on both sides of the Atlantic, from Mexico to Havana to London to Paris to Galveston to Philadelphia. Philadelphia, the first capital of the first republican nation in the New World also proved to be a preeminent juncture of conspiration at the end of the eighteenth century and the beginning of the nineteenth century, which inspired the Mexican Martín Luis Guzmán to write *Filadelfia, paraiso de conspiradores y otras historias noveladas*.[15] In this context, the Mexican historian Adolfo Arrioja Vizcaíno would refer to the "city of brotherly love" as "Philadelphia, which was the hub of activity for every type of independence-minded Creole that yearned for the freedom of all Hispanic America, from Mexico to Buenos Aires, under the self-serving protection of the United States government, whose Secretary of State and future president John Quincy Adams had devised, about a year earlier [ca. 1821], the strategy known as the rule of 'political gravity,' which in essence held that the nations emerging from the Spanish colonies in America sooner or later would fall, practically in inevitable fashion, into the political sphere of influence of the United States. Two years later, this strategy would be amply corroborated with the promulgation of the famous—not always for the best of reasons—Monroe Doctrine."[16]

Fray Servando's 1821 eight-month stint in Philadelphia as a fugitive, having escaped this time from a Havana jail while being transferred from the dungeons of the Holy Office of the Inquisition (officially abolished the previous year, on June 14) to the now secularized prison of the imperial authorities, would prove an intricate link in the chain of continuity between colonial and postcolonial delusions. This too emerges as an originary site along Fray Servando's fugitive itinerary, a discursive locus from which we can trace the subsequent lineage of a hemispheric American studies on a north-south axis, and the discourses of postcolonial studies that have ebbed and waned in the last quarter of the twentieth century and the first decade of the twenty-first.[17] He would reach Philadelphia from Havana, after fleeing from the prison hospital disguised as a businessman. He boarded the steamship *Robert Fulton* in Havana's port at 4:00 P.M. at the end of May 1821, carrying a forged passport and the assumed identity of Mariano Cosío.[18] His memorandum to Mexico following its decade-long struggle for independence, a dispatch he entitled *Memoria político-instructiva, enviada desde Filadelfia en agosto de 1821, a los gefes independientes de Anáhuac, llamado por los españoles Nueva España* (Memorandum of Political Instructions, Dispatched from Philadelphia in August 1821, to the Independent Leaders of Anáhuac, Called New Spain by the Spaniards), could be considered at once a founding document of the Mexican republic and a self-incriminating critique of the founders of independence. It would result in his last imprisonment by the incipient postimperial authorities comically rehearsing a new emperor, the self-proclaimed Agustín I, Agustín de Iturbide, whom his court attendants referred to as Varón de Dios (Man of God).[19] Our imperial leaders are no less godly at the beginning of our own evangelically riven twenty-first century.

Fray Servando's *Memoria* was not simply a response to the naïveté of the "Plan de Iguala" around which the diverse members of the Mexican struggle for independence expediently had converged on March 2, 1821. His *Memoria* preemptively disclosed that the emperor had no clothes, while the contemporary Mexican novelist Rosa Beltrán has him delivering the bad news to the emperor in person.[20] Iturbide would indeed proclaim himself Agustín I, Emperador de Mexico, at the first constitutional congress of May 24, 1822, seven months after Fray Servando's admonition. Much has been written since about the conspiratorial genesis and the intricate plot among church, state, and third estate embodied by Creole interests that engendered this paradoxical document, the Plan de Iguala, in the founding of the Mexican republic as a "transitional" monarchy.[21] Fray Servando's anticipatory unmasking of its foundational contradictions proved no less troublesome for his well-being than the previous carceral reaction of the empire's courts and ecclesiastical Holy Office had proved to his heterodox revisioning of imperial history. He wrote: "God free us from emperors or kings. They keep none of their promises, and always end up becoming despots. All men are inclined to impose their will, without challenge. And there is nothing to which man is more accustomed. . . . Iturbide! Renounce the new opinion. . . . Support independence without a new master, republican independence."[22]

Fray Servando's incorrigible hope for republicanism notwithstanding, history would prove that "republican independence" has never been any less vulnerable to the unhappy conditions he warned against in his monitory *Memoria* of August 1821 from Philadelphia. We still strain to comprehend the morphology of conspiracy both as cultural practice and as preemptory accusation employed by those who conspire with impunity and divine dispensation against those who might unmask their ulterior machinations. In the historic example of Fray Servando, the crossing point or chiasmus, where culture crosses into conspiracy and conspiracy into culture, might well help us understand these formative processes somewhat.

In his 1820 "Carta de despedida a los mexicanos, escrita desde el Castillo de San Juan de Ulúa" (Letter of Farewell to Mexicans, Written from the Fortress of San Juan de Ulúa), Fray Servando eloquently pursued the chiasmus in Mexican history and in its Anáhuac name. His valedictory prison letter from the dungeons of this carceral fortress, where he would find himself so often, is an exhortation based on the letter *x*, which in Greek is at once the sign for a chiasmus and for the Calvary cross. The curious decision by the Spanish Academy of Language to excise the letter *x* from among the consonants of the Spanish alphabet during that historical period becomes for Fray Servando an analogue to his carcelary ostracism, or "archiving," as he was wont to call it. He interpreted that alphabetic excision not simply as the banishment of the letter, its value in writing and as algebraic variable in mathematics, but as a radical imperial move. Fray Servando read the Spanish Royal Academy's action as an attempt to eradicate a virtual placeholder that frequently figures in the designation of indigenous Mexico's actual place names. More than a virtual sign, however, the *x* became for him a liberation cause that reached beyond the mathematical. He saw it as inalienable part of an antihegemonic calculus, a heterodox value in the history of Mexico, an as yet indeterminate value of the future, of the still unknown potential of emancipatory, postimperial possibility for a new nation. In his impassioned disquisition on this letter, *x* is indeed the sign that marks the site of struggle for Mexican history and cultural identity, as he reenvisioned the genesis and political significance of these, much to the chagrin of imperial authority, of inquisitional orthodoxy and its apodictic truth, and, of course, much to the detriment of his own well-being. In his embattled life, Fray Servando traversed this intersection marked by *x* again and again, while each crossing point reiterated the star-crossed fate of yet one more way station in his personal and national history.

Fray Servando's itinerary is indeed defined by a long series of such transitional and often transgressive junctures, whether as temporal nodes where eighteenth-century Enlightenment crossed over into nineteenth-century romanticism; or as ideological transit points where imperial monarchies dissolved into republican anarchies; or as devotional crossroads where the church militant as empire's handmaid dissolved into meretricious political doctrine to suffuse evolving social systems with righteous conviction and the squalor of dogmatic anachronisms. And yet, these are all highly productive and self-reproductive points of germination, so prolific, in fact, as to become epidemic, especially in interstitial historical moments such as Fray Servando's and ours, when a new order has yet to fully form in place of a bankrupt disorder. His way stations, more often than not, had to negotiate such treacherous gaps and the truculence that invariably accompanies epidemic uncertainties and epistemic doubts in critical condition. Respiration in such oppressive, airless environments becomes labored conspiration, or shared breathing, whose desperate gasps become generalized as conspiracy, an oppressive atmosphere that can only be countenanced as epidemiological quandary. This is the desperation that found Fray Servando scurrying between fetid inquisitorial dungeon and stifling Enlightenment salon, a fugitive between libratory ideals and libertine cynicism in state, church, and picaresque urbanity. Respiration and breathing in unison have changed little as life processes, and, perforce, conspiration and conspiracy still continue as vital operations of the human species even at this late date that is marked by what the Argentine writer Ricardo Piglia, in his diagnoses of paranoid regimes and unspeakable ruthlessness in America's "dirty wars" of the late twentieth century, has characterized as "artificial respiration."[23]

As the siege continues still more vehemently and more globally than ever at the beginning of this third millennium, ventriloquizing the unspeakable still remains the most urgent task of literature and of critical labor. *Regime* is among the most frequently uttered terms in our own volatile time, just as it was in Fray Servando's, when history was buffeted between regimes *ancien et moderne*. We are still groping at that intersection, the conjunction of a compelling and inevitable chiasmus where the conspiracy of culture and the culture of conspiracy cross and where the narrative and plots of human history are woven. The secret, the mystery, the unknown, the esoteric, the enigmatic, the cryptic, and the threatening still depend on the imaginative faculty as an instrument capable of compensating for the occluded convictions and furtive insecurities of historical predicaments and their volatilities. It is still imagination that serves to animate, to breathe life into the enterprise of culture's and conspiracy's common, primal, and sempiternal scene. In this process, the most elusive and most alluring element of all, not unlike the place-holding x whose shifting and heterodox value Fray Servando vehemently defended, may well be the absent, the banished, the elided, the excluded quotient. As students of mathematics, literature, and history, we know that what does not exist, or what exists as virtual integer rather than as overtly actual presence, holds the greatest potential. In the as-yet-unrealized, whether in national culture or in mathematical probability, the need to be represented as reality becomes paramount, which is to say that the necessity of representation, whether mimetic as in the discourse of Erich Auerbach, or as Fray Servando's political self-affirmation, is a perennial impulse and a most powerful enablement. The indeterminacy and virtual probabilities of such potentiality have always proved threatening, and anxious familiarity has indeed been the most zealous compensation for what persists as absence or as imminence. Familiarity, as we know from human history, labors perpetually to draw everything outside its purview into its manageable commons and communal orbit. In this respect, even the formal processes of aesthetic and theoretical estrangement end by being modes of familiarization, tried means of transforming the uncanny into canny commensurability with laws of form, genre, or sanctioned improvisation.

As Fray Servando discovered subsequent to his December 12, 1794, sermon, cultures are eminently successful conspiracies, and conspiracy theories, as his and other restive Creoles' epistemic challenges to imperial hegemony at the time were viewed, are cultures in the making. The ground between the already authoritatively ordained and the transformative intrusion in pursuit of authority and ordination is an embattled terrain whose contentions can be as destructive as they might be generative. The first, that is, the already established and prevailing cultures, have sealed their mystery and assumed their dominant, not to say hegemonic statuses and venerable niches as reigning principles, or as inviolable reverential objects of orthodox sanctity. The second, cultures in the making, which would also include established cultures in radical transformation, labor as breached births, moving backward, inexorably, into the unknown and toward what they most fear. Fray Servando's reaching back to the indigenous preconquest history of Anáhuac as threshold to a future postimperial story of Mexico is most articulate on this backward movement into futurity. This move back to what had already been in order to reach what is yet to be is, as etymology would have it, another name for "revolution." It is a rupture, simultaneously recursive and precursive, that connotes the intricate and often paradoxical processes that serve as a platform for most historical transitions. We well know this to be the case for literary translation, as we move from source language to a target language that, invariably, reconfigures the source, and no less so in history when historical sequels define past events as their inexorable typological prolepses and annunciation. In the trajectory of literary posterity, we understand this as the process by which the epigones, or latecomers, create their own precursors.[24]

II. Divertimento: Since Time Immemorial

It is a precarious position, this encountering the world double-crossed on the wracked chiasmus of questioning and assertiveness, of proleptic insecurity and presumptive augury, of peering into the past to discern the future. Both hopeful prolepsis and resolute presumption are predictable instruments for confronting uncertainty and insecurity. In this sense, culture and conspiracy have been inalienably entwined by their historically joint performance as apotropeic operations, that is, as attempts to chase away what their creators fear most at the crux of their point of genesis. By *apotropeic*, once again, I am referring to those ancient Greek rituals for placating and keeping at bay the ancestral spirits on the days especially designated for the formulaic rites of language and ceremonial practices referred to as *apotropeia*.

The syncretism of Mexican rites of death and ancestral communing are no less intricate than those of Greek antiquity, as Fray Servando well knew and as the tortuous career of his own obsequies and peripatetic remains amply demonstrates. These fears of rehearsing genealogical primal scenes often end up as self-fulfilling prophecies, and the nature of that fulfillment, thus, amounts to culture's reproductive self-perpetuation as much through death as through life and the inseparable continuity between the two. Such anxious anticipations of the past in the future tend to be preemptive reactions to actions as yet inexistent except as projective memory and prophetic apprehensions, or simultaneously, as we saw in the last chapter, as memories of the past and memories of the future. This may be why the most common term accompanying conspiracy in our contemporary lexicon is the testimonial and visionary term the Greeks applied to the witnessing of the rites and spectacles of others, namely, *theoria*,[25] and, thus, "conspiracy theory." Such primal anxiety may also be indicative of the reasons why the ancient Greeks had as many as three terms for conspiracy. The ancient Romans had two. As is usually the case with the communal and collective cultivations that produce culture, conspiracy is also philologically predicated on anxious solidarity, a drawing together invariably signaled by the prefix at the head of all of these terms, whether in Latin or Greek: *syn-* in Greek, hence, *synístamai, sympnéo, synomosía*; *con-* in Latin, hence, *conspiratio, coniuratio.*

Such togetherness also endures the wrack of a chiasmus—a double-crossing yet again—that throws solidarity into suspicion and renders it clandestine. This is the slippage that moves from breath to stealth, from common prayer to uncommon paranoia, from collusion to delusion, from consensus to dis-sensus and distrust. This, in turn, becomes the anxious dynamic, the restless energy that drives the symbiosis (literally, the parasitic mutuality of living on / off each other) between culture and conspiracy. When that chiastic energy is transubstantiated into synergy, the yield is a narrative plot—the narrative of a culture we are given to call history, or the narrative of a tale we are prone to call story. In either case, it is the telltale product of a crossing point where *breath* gives life and also blows it out, and where *oath* (*giura*, in Italian, from which the Italian language derives *congiura*, one of its terms for conspiracy) is an utterance that is at once a curse and a prayer. Conspiracy or conjuring, then, becomes realized as self-fulfilling prophecy. We call that realization culture and its telltale narrative plot is known as history.

In the endless shuttling of this chiasmus, any interpretive diagnosis of its cultural history becomes, simultaneously, a conspiratorial act as well as an engagement that is productive and constitutive of culture. At this intersection, then, we have a fusion in which diagnostic agency and the symptoms of diagnosis converge. At that convergence we end up in a discursive tautology by which the crossing point of culture and conspiracy turns out to be a self-reproducing house of mirrors. The echoic resonances that emanate from that locus take on any number of names that become the key terms of our critical discourses—*paradigm, structure of feeling, discursive formation, habitus, semiotic regime, imaginary, hyperreality.*

At the heart of this spectral crossing, then, we emerge as co-conspirators with our own reflection. Any critique of the specter of such a pleonasm is invariably a new conspiracy theory, viewed simultaneously as emancipatory and as existential threat, inasmuch as it implies a shattering of cultural tautologies and an upending of the status quo and its dominant order. The greatest threat presented by such disruption consists in what Fray Servando's valedictory prison letter of 1820 noted as a variant alternative to the imperial paradigm and its narrative tall tale through the differential value of the letter *x*. What hegemonic order and epistemic orthodoxy will not countenance, as Fray Servando's own predicament and history's iterations repeatedly demonstrate, is difference, variant reading, open-endedness, infinite continuity, honest deferral of full disclosure, impossibility of resolution, perpetual projection into uncertainty, enigmatic truth, coexistence with ambiguity. These are the processes that imperial hegemonic order cannot brook, though these be the transformational and translational processes through which culture passes in order to find its perpetuation. Continuity through indispensable change, as opposed to ossified duration in immutability, as Fray Servando's sermons and exhortations persistently demonstrated, must constantly translate the past, turning its narratives and mythologies into limitless prolepsis, an augury of a yet more momentous outcome, whose revelation is perennially interrogated at the double-crossing point of a chiasmus. Fray Servando's itinerary and history's subsequent way stations demonstrate that this pivotal point is at once the paradoxical location of culture and of conspiracy in infinitely receding mirrors, simultaneously in flight from and into their own reflection.

III. Philology's Hearth, Conspiracy's Home

Fray Servando's indulgence in and embodiment of such reflections certainly proved momentous, and no less so in their peril to his person than in their augury of our own history. Alternately "archived," as he bibliographically describes his own imprisonments, and in flight—now as interlocutor to Enlightenment's luminaries now as defendant before anachronistically medieval inquisitorial courts—he traversed the gamut of epistemic and ideological formations, straddling multiple epochs at heterogeneous junctures. Dispensable to all, Fray Servando would forge his own indispensable significance, invariably finding his necessary existence in his own dire necessity, a predicament that left him more than wary of human institutions and political agendas. As sole co-conspirator ultimately in complicity with himself, Fray Servando anticipated by more than a century the paragon of American cultural paranoia, that romantic New England poet and essayist Ralph Waldo Emerson, who would note anxiously: "Society everywhere is in conspiracy against the manhood of every one of its members."[26] The dialectical counterpoint between the individual and the collective in this Emerson Fray Servando foreshadowed augurs as well the inexorable fate of particularity. Emerson's anxiety emanates from his realization that the individual's co-optation is indeed made inevitable by one's existence in society. Fray Servando had already discerned this in conspiracy's three-letter prefix and in all the lexical and ideological variants for the imperial collusion of church and state he had to countenance in the social conspiracy of his own time.

Philologically, we perennially encounter this strong suite of conspiracy's gambit as cultural instrument of consolidation and productivity, as already noted, in the Greek prefix *syn-* and the Latin *con-*. Hence, the Greek ternary lexicon for conspiracy: *synístamai* (literally, setting out or standing together, from *synéstisa*, which translates as to associate, to band, or to concert in alliance); *synómnymi* or *sympnéo* (literally, breathing together); and *synomosía* (swearing on the law, or taking an oath together). *Sympnéo* and *synómnymi* become *conspiratio* in Latin; and *synomosía* turns into *coniuratio*. The first of these becomes *conspiracy* in English, and the second *congiura* in Italian, *conjuración* in Spanish, *to conjure with* in English.

Although its vestigial connotative sense infuses the latter two terms in Latin and their modern derivatives, the first of these three Greek terms, *synístamai*, does not carry over into Latinity, and thus it is absent from the modern vernaculars. At the heart of this disappearance could well lie the submerged nucleus of our modern understanding of conspiracy. Because this arrested, suppressed, elided, or absented lexis, *synístamai*, is founded in one of the most complex of Greek verbs, *éstis*, which in its own philological morphology as copula it signifies beginning, establishment, standing, ontological existence, and, most significantly, the root for a home's hearth, *estía*. This is the etymon and discursive foundation of the Roman *Vesta* and the *lares familiars* (the domestic deities). Clearly signaled in the copula of *éstis* and its uncanny nominal derivative *estía* is a series of ontologically intricate cultural dominants that are defining of community, solidarity, and foundational order, all of which continue, from their absence, to resonate beneath this lexical complex of togetherness and connectivity that in our vernacular lexicon are common ground for both culture and conspiracy, hearth and home and the volatile neuroses of the "homeland," the German "heimat" with all its *heimlich* ambiguities explored by the uncanny Freud, its attendant paranoia, and incurable insecurities.

Thus, the historical sublimation, or philological submergence, of this resonant lexicon for conspiracy, like the chiastic value of *x* in Fray Servando's valedictory disquisition of 1820, is very significant indeed. One could suspect that conspiracy and its attendant anxieties, which we have come to know as paranoia, are grounded in a primal apprehension of a concomitant loss, or a fear of having already lost not just an originary verb but also the intimacy it connotes, a loss that signifies exclusion from the filial and affiliative closeness articulated by this verb. We have, then, with the loss of a primal inclusiveness signified by the Greek *synístamai*, a loss that spells—politically, literally, and culturally—the sundering of ties that bound a community together in a common stand. This rupture is a fall into a chiastic reversal or a spectral inversion on a chiasmus. That spectacular contretemps carries with it all the attendant anxieties entailed in the severing of linkages. The concomitant dispersal that accompanies such exclusions is the fear of falling out from the familiar *lares* of the *estía*, the hearth of home, and the expulsion from the familiar into the threatening mysteries of the alien and ostracized. As a result of losing the *estía* and the solidarity of *synéstamai*, whatever is perceived as connected, communal, and together in others, whether actual or merely perceived to be such, is now taken to exclude us, and thus we view such togetherness that excludes us with suspicion and as an existential threat. In our radical dislocation and homelessness, we even fear whatever we deem to be esoteric and endogenous, and we take it as its mirrored opposite, as its alien alterity that is exoteric, exogenous, on whose outside we are left straining to ascertain and to decipher what might be secreted inside, a dwelling we have come to perceive as exclusionary and threatening. In the middle of the twentieth century, one of Fray Servando's Mexican progeny and also one of his best readers, the poet and Nobel laureate Octavio Paz, would explore the historical dynamics of this paradoxical homelessness at home and in the national self in his now classic treatise *El laberinto de la soledad* (*The Labyrinth of Solitude*).[27]

How do we, as a culture and as individuals, domesticate the paradox of this strangeness that is us, this alienated familiarity that we embody as contradiction; that we incorporate somatically and historically and as corporate commune, as body politic and as social compact, but which we now project outward and from which we endeavor to exclude ourselves? We deal with this predicament—and the complex of conspiracy is most articulate in this regard—not by taking the strangeness, the alterity, the exoteric into the *vesta*, or into the *estía* and the cultural repertoire and materiality of our *lares familiares*, but by generalizing that strangeness we project outward into omnipresence, into perpetual time and ubiquitous space. We estrange everything because if everything is strange then we, estranged from ourselves, may not be so alien after all. Estrangement, then, becomes the common reference point by which we are commonly defined. Our ensuing cultural and communal labors are driven by the need and relentless attempt to overcome this fate.

This experience of loss, of generalized disconnection, and this feeling of exclusion serve as an optic for conspiracy theory and our governing principle for conspiracies. The absence wrought by this sense of loss becomes our view into the conspiracy of others and the prescript for our own. This optic and this principle, in turn, become defining of our culture, of us as a culture engaged in the apotropeia, or the chasing away of all that was familiar and that has become lost, which we now fear most, namely, the ancestry, philological and genealogical, of the communal compact embedded in the verb *synístamai*, which, like Plato's Atlantis, has since been submerged but whose vestigial memory resonates in us as longing for a common place and as an anxiety of the no longer knowable.

Our narrative plots, historiographic tales, archeological obsessions, museological taxonomies (auto)ethnographic epistemologies, and the conspiracy of culture connoted by all of these endeavors, figure as implacable compensatory gestures, emblematically and philologically signified in that irremediable loss. Our culture, then, is the redemptory mythologization of a mythos gone mute, of *estía*'s prosopopoeia, the Roman goddess Vesta, who has walked out on us and whom we labor to keep at bay lest we be identified with and made part of what we now deem to be departed, excluded, exclusionary, indeterminate, and strange.

Like most compensatory gestures, these become overdetermined and productive of a saturated semiosis we commonly associate with strong readings and hyperconnectivity. As a vicarious syntactical relation to a lost world, the *ars combinatoria* of these narratives now emerges as an *ars conspiratoria*, where the most casual relation becomes a strong causal motivation (usually with ulterior motives), the incidental is deemed intentional, every accident part of a design, all contingency a suspect necessity, and even the anecdotal is taken to be a symptomatic fragment of an elaborate plot. At the level of the individual, this could be called paranoia, as psychiatric practice historically has characterized such symptoms. At the plane of collective narrative it becomes History with a capital H, in which every contingency is imputable to a theodicy and a purposive teleology.

Thus, at the collective level, if broadly enough shared as generality, what might otherwise be an individual delusion serves as a binding force, as cultural dominant, as communicative circuitry defining of cultural formations and of communal identity. As the basis of a semiotic regime or epistemic principle, this cultural dominant finds its orderly normalization in that other Greek term for conspiracy in which the Italian *congiura* and Spanish *conjuración* have their genesis—namely, *synomosía*, collective pledge, taking a vow on the law, or taking an oath together among those who consider themselves outside the law. This becomes the law of drastic, because compensatory, normalization. It is the second-degree *nomos* that underwrites the social compact among those who see themselves excluded, exempted, and excepted. Any disconformity or digression from these norms is deemed an egregious deviance, and those who deviate are anxiously brought into line through social instruments and sanctioned discipline of commensurately exceptional severity. These are the egregious gestures of an antinomian *nomos*, or exceptional law. These were the measures applied to Fray Servando as a dissident and deviant from the dogma of the Church and as a critical nonconformist in relation to the political paradigm of imperial hegemony. His carceral dislocations were the black holes of the Holy Office. Today, these are still called "black holes," if not Guantánamo, Kandahar, or Abu Ghraib. Or they could equally be called "homeland security," at a time when more than one percent of the U.S. population is incarcerated.[28]

IV. Truth Mission as Reinscription, Narrative Plot as Cultural Conspiracy

"An alternative to credulity" is how our contemporary English commentator Christopher Hitchens defines conspiracy theory in an essay entitled "On the Imagination of Conspiracy." This is part of his book *For the Sake of Argument*, which antedates Hitchens' own begging of credulity, alternative or otherwise, in his bipolar political vacillations and ideological turmoil at the beginning of the unsettling twenty-first century.[29] The search for an "alternative to credulity" echoes Coleridge's "willing suspension of disbelief," where bracketed incredulity becomes willfully operative as hermeneutical principle of literary culture. In Coleridge, as in Hitchens, we can discern a dialectical space that divides, or enjoins, the actual and the virtual, a reality and its alterity. This becomes credulity and its alternative in Hitchens; belief as willing suspension of its contrary in Coleridge.

In this antithetical duality, it is not difficult to discern a certain Manichaeism, or what Hitchens calls "a bi-polar mentality."[30] Thus, it is easy to see how everything has at least two versions: an official version and a de facto one that subtends it. The hermeneutics of conspiracy is, on the one hand, a truth mission that targets the first, the official version, as a threshold that should lead to the latter, the underlying de facto version. On the other hand, meantime, those invested in the official version of any narrative are wont to consider such hermeneutical exposition a conspiratorial act or the acting out of a conspiracy theory. And while Hitchens views this obsessive vocation of conspiracy theory as "an ailment of democracy,"[31] it might well be not merely "an ailment," but an *enablement* of democratic culture, as we might glean from the Emerson of "Self-Reliance," cited above. As Hitchens himself notes in discussing Norman Mailer's novel *Harlot's Ghost*, "there exists the danger of not being paranoid enough," at least in the American tradition of Emerson and in the context of Mailer's novel, where, his eponymous hero quips at one point, "Give me a vigorous hypothesis every time. Without it, there is nothing to do but drown in facts."[32]

A "vigorous hypothesis," as Norman Mailer's protagonist would have it, is the ideological fulcrum, the basic hermeneutical instrument or interpretative tool of surveying and detection. In the absence of valence or the hygienic eradication of facts, as is the case of hypotheses deemed to be born of paranoia, surveillance will do just as well or even better. For detection does not need substance, except as corroborative desideratum, which could well come at the end as justification for its means, if indeed an end is ever achieved in this perpetual belligerence against everything and everyone deemed "alternate." As already noted, ends tend to be expediently deferred, forever if necessary, in favor of a more interesting, or of a more self-justifying hypothetical solution whose reality might perpetually lie just ahead. In this sense, conspiracy is more a hermeneutics than a praxis; more accurately, a hermeneutics that becomes a praxis in pursuit of disclosure, decipherment, and defining quest. In the process, the obsessive compulsion to discover and expose conspiracy ends by replicating the conspiratorial modus operandi, including the suspension of resolution so that suspicion, or hypothesis born of paranoia, can continuously extend its bellicose trajectory. The terrors along that projection are guaranteed in the modus operandi of the terrific hypothesis and in the terrorist acts of its targets.

Such replication in the life of culture—literary, religious, and political culture, especially—reinscribes conspiracy itself as narrative and as narrative plot, which, perforce, scholars and critics perpetuate through acts of cultural detection, textual exegesis, and political decipherment.

V. Compensatory Gestures:
From Imperial Monarchy to Republican Anarchy

Narrative as conspiracy plot, or as conspiracy theory, serves as compensatory explanation for the absence of a universally comprehensible or comprehensive discourse—social, cultural, or historical. As such, the narrative of conspiracy as compensatory supplement often supplants the reality that it would complement. In this process, private interpretation substitutes for public meaning, or for the absence of meaningful semiosis in the public sphere. This is the dynamics of transition and, simultaneously, of replication in the eighteenth century's move from the certainties of Church orthodoxy to the self-convictions of the Enlightenment. This is the crossing point of contestation that snagged Fray Servando Teresa de Mier as ordained canon and as republican dissident. It is thus that cultural practice becomes political praxis and conspiracy theory becomes enmeshed in officialdom and governmental structures.

We detect strands of this pattern, which extends from Fray Servando's nineteenth-century epistolary disquisition on the political philology of the letter *x* to the twentieth century's *X-Files*. This is also where literary culture arrives as social allegory, where literature's plots lend narrative dramatization to meaning and meaninglessness in the collective and political sphere. Conspiracy, then, becomes not just a symptomatic object of diagnosis but a complex and a cause to be espied, discerned, and reenciphered; a metamorphosis, or a *metástasis*, in epidemiological terms, that proves generative and engendering of cultural capital, epistemic governing principles, and aesthetic processes. In this regard, taking a cue from the American novelist Don De Lillo, Christopher Hitchens characterizes conspiracy theory as "the white noise which moves in to fill the vacuity of the official version."[33] No version, however inane, is "vacuous," of course, as the historical record of the concrete juridical and carceral consequences resulting from Fray Servando's alternative rehearsal of Mexican history and its mythographies cruelly and implacably demonstrate.

Tracing the continuum that moves from philological morphology to the political arena, we could say that the loss of the third ancient Greek lexis for conspiracy, *synístamai*, along with the evanescence of the social compact the verb implied, figure as dispossession that never ceases to resonate in conspiracy theory as political praxis. Here, as with Fray Servando's epochal transitions from imperial monarchy to republican anarchy, that loss functions as symptomatic distance and disarticulation between political power and people; as delinkage between the narrative of human habitus and its interpretation; as disjunction between official, clerical, or academic discourse and cultural intercourse. Conspiracy theory, then, aims to provide cultural and political significance in a sphere whose inhabitants feel there is none. The literature of conspiracy, likewise, might well be filling a void, imaginatively, with imagination's full range spanning the marvelous to the pathetic to the pathological.

Thus, as sociopolitical intercourse, as with the hybrid creolization of imperial covenants and the secularization of Fray Servando's religious communions, conspiracy's discourse functions as a cultural imaginary that substitutes narratives of imagination for collective and communal articulation of what might have been a comprehending and comprehended narrative. That operative consensus, however it might have been forged, has become dysfunctional as social compact. In this light, whether in the Mexico City, Havana, Paris, or Philadelphia of Fray Servando's time or ours, any collaboration takes on the coloring of collusion and any connection emerges as complicity. Nothing is perceived as lying outside the intricate network of their suggestive linkages and suspected semiosis. The loss of *synístamai*, then, becomes the simultaneous loss of *syntíthemi*, its synonym that literally denotes the setting, the settling, the determining, and the placing together—all that in Latin is connoted by the verb *ponere* and its collective predicates in *componere*, agglutinative processes that compose forms of aesthetic compact and social contract, baptized into *covenant* by the theo-morphology of the three religions of the Abrahamic tradition. Our own lack of composure at this historical juncture might not be unrelated to such cultural loss.

Covenant is what ties cultural aggregates together in *synomosía* or *coniuratio*, in the name of the law and through the oath, the *congiura*, that bind. It is no accident, in this regard, that far-reaching conspiracies and conspiracy theories refer to their subject in covenantal terms. These are vestigial forms of a discourse in which the language of primal acts of cultural foundations remains. The decomposition of those primal covenantal rites, far from leading to cultural entropy, in fact, spur compensatory compositional endeavors in the form of narrative plots and historical mythoi that surface to ensure the continuity of cultural formations and political compacts.

At the far end of entropy, we have learned from the second law of thermodynamics, emerge new and startling states of combinatorial coherence. More than a few of our cultural productions and conspiracy theories might well be concurrent, and often coterminous, symptoms of this emergent state that finds coalescence following the entropy and transvaluation of expired imperial regimes, cultural dominants, and social paradigms. Literature's most constant métier, in fact, may be the recomposition and aesthetic redeployment of the animating potential in such caducity. In the "poof!" of a breath and the blink of an eye, expiration turns to inspiration and the act of disappearance transmutes into an act of emergence. Our literary modernisms have been taking this as their springboard for over a century now.

Our literary corpus, canonical and otherwise, constitutes the cultural transubstantiation of such emergencies, to the point where all forms of emplotment could be said to comprise narrative plots of cultural formation and historical collusion in what is a self-sustaining conspiracy, one that goes by other names by virtue of its ubiquity and shared generality among the co-conspirators. It is not uncommon for certain literary works, in fact, to dramatize such plotting through self-reflexive acts and metanarrative formations, some historiographic, some metafictional, and most of them decidedly ironic.

The more obvious among such authors and works from the contemporary period already form part of an international, comparatistic, albeit highly heterogeneous repertoire—for example, Milorad Pavic of what was Yugoslavia; Thomas Pynchon of the United States of America; Tahar ben Jallun of Morocco; Italo Calvino, Antonio Tabucchi, and Umberto Eco of Italy; Orhan Pamuk of Turkey; Luis Sepúlveda of Chile; Haruki Murakami of Japan; and the late Reinaldo Arenas of Cuba, who has narrated and enacted Fray Servando's own vicissitudes with uncanny insight.[34]

VI. Epistemania and the Cloak of Invisibility

The works of the authors just mentioned figure prominently and, no doubt, symptomatically in our current literary culture. Their modus operandi manifests intricate and inextricable entanglements with the cultural practices they narrate and with the modes of conspiracy they thematize. In this context, literature often resembles an "undercover operation," its aesthetic objects serving as a cloak of invisibility. As in acts of conspiracy and in practices of conspiratorial orders, these literary pursuits labor dialectically on the counterpoint between occlusion and disclosure, immediacy and mysteriously complex mediations, verging imminence and perpetual deferral, interconnectedness and isolate discrepancy. As such, they form part of a web of pervasive rootedness and radical discontinuity. In this contrapuntal process, culture and conspiracy become functionally mirrored. And, in their dialectical crosshatchings, conspiracy theory and conspiracy practice implode, no longer as a chiasmus to be passed through a common juncture point but as a *catastrophe*, in the Greek sense of the term, in which differentiation of conflated terms becomes impossible. I shall refer to this as a compulsive impulse, which we could call *epistemania*, inasmuch as the impulse is driven not only by the compulsion to know, to detect, and to decode, but also to explore the know-how of exegetic and deciphering processes. Here, then, in conclusion, is how the vicissitudes of these processes might be described.

Conspiracy, whether of those said to be its theorists or of those perceived as its practitioners—and at this point the distinction might be all but moot—aims to close in and foreclose on what is exposed, to close in on what is out in the open and open-ended. Conspiracy, in other words, seeks the mantle of secrecy and its attendant instrument, invisibility. In this sense, conspiracy seeks to be esoteric, endogenous, exclusionary, and hermetic. At the same time, however, in order for conspiracy to ensure its continuity and secure its trajectory and modus operandi, it must expand continuously beyond its self-devised closures, foreclosures, and orthodox circumscriptions. Inasmuch as these constitute procedures that form and define culture, we could easily substitute the term culture for conspiracy in describing this process. The identification between culture and conspiracy becomes all the more compelling when we consider contemporary culture's obsession with self-fashioning subjects and self-consuming artifacts that endlessly labor to achieve their own expiration, their own caducity, so that they may perpetuate their self-regeneration, either as consumer goods of a throwaway society or as political ideologies driven by the anxieties of timeliness and the obsession to remain on the edge and to be perpetually just-in-time.

Thus, conspiracy, by virtue of its occlusionary necessity, and culture by virtue of its exclusionary imperatives morphologically embedded in its root Latin verb *colere*, seek to circumscribe their horizons through ties that do indeed bind their members in formative and foundational norms. Nonetheless, even as they reach for such self-circumscription, they aspire to and succeed in forging a network of infinitely expanding connectivity. In the process, culture and conspiracy proscribe and foreclose on completion, or totalization, even as they labor to achieve their own totality. They render impossible, simultaneously, closure and disclosure, iron-clad encipherment and complete decoding. The result, then, turns everything that is deciphered and decoded into prolegomena of what remains on the other side of yet another mystery. The known, thereby, serves as prolepsis or as foreshadowing of more complete explanations of phenomena that become perpetually dislocated into the unknown. Thus, conspiracy and culture render their objects and practices into perpetual epiphenomena that promise, insinuate, subtend, augur, imply, and prefigure occluded or as yet unrealized phenomena and undisclosed structures of yet another imminent order. That promissory alterity serves as the exogenetic nucleus that drives the manic pursuit of exegesis and epistemic figuration envisaged as ever receding finality. This is most evident in dominant modes of reading in the humanities and analysis in the social sciences. This is the defining mode of the currently dominant apocalyptic verve in evangelical and messianic politics, self-defined as a politics of rapture.

Culture and conspiracy, or we could say with some justification now, culture as conspiracy and conspiracy as culture, become self-reflexive. And, as much between them as each within itself, they become self-suspecting.

At such a juncture, the theory and practice of conspiracy and of culture can no longer be differentiated. Hence, by the light and shadow of what goes by the designation of postmodern epistemologies, culture as (and like) a successful conspiracy remains unknowable. This is to say that the practitioners of this culture remain unknowable to themselves, a predicament that does not necessarily assuage the irrepressible human impulse to know. On the contrary, such circumstances aggravate anxieties in the face of the unknown and exacerbate compulsions to know what, paradoxically, one knows to be unknown. This is a condition we could call *epistemania*. What one does manage to know is that culture as (or with) conspiracy remains a project; and culture's materiality—what ethnographers refer to as material culture—is simply a symptom, or epiphenomenon, a symbolic order and behavioral repertoire for a cultural reality that remains out of reach and beyond knowability. The student, the critic, and the scholar can only know those symptoms or epiphenomena of culture and conspiracy as they become perceivable, whether as legible text, as visual display, or as spectacle in performance. In other words, what we can manage to know is limited to aesthetics. To overlook this limitation is to fall into the phenomenalism of an aesthetic ideology, that is, a delusion or misapprehension that we know the phenomena themselves rather than merely their showing, that is, their perceptibility to the senses, which is the definition of the Greek etymon for aesthetics.

There is an irony in this paradox that emerges unmistakably: what conspiracy and culture aim to circumscribe, either by occlusion into invisibility or by cultivation into cultural ostentation, can only be known by virtue of what becomes visible and perceptible to the senses, in other words, what is circumscribed by a culture's aesthetics. This is the cloak of invisibility, a cover and a cover-up, which is only operative by virtue of the visibility of what it aims to make invisible. Hence, the paradoxical "apocalyptic" obsession of conspiracy theory as unremitting task of disclosing, uncovering, exposing with the goal of making the hidden invisible in plain view, not unlike Poe's "Purloined Letter."

In this chiastic double-crossing or folding back, both culture and conspiracy attain their viability under cover, via a symbolic procedure known as anacalypsis. This is the visibility of the invisible, the cloak of disclosure, or, as poetry and translation have traditionally been defined, the deliberate presence of an absence. Literary culture, in this sense, may be the most characteristic symptom of this enigmatic process, inasmuch as it is said to simultaneously give presence to the inexistent, to transubstantiate absence and ethereality, and at the same time to desubstantiate materiality into aesthetic construct. Poetry and conspiracy, then, share with politics the vocation of occluding the visible and making the invisible perceptible to the senses through representation or enactment of an absent presence, or through the affirmation of what might not be necessarily so, except as aesthetic object or political performance. We are always on the threshold of the hyperreal.

Not unlike Fray Servando's heterodox dodging among orthodoxies and his alternately interventionist stints as condemned prisoner "archived" in the dungeons of the Holy Office and as artfully elusive fugitive, the itinerary tracked by this dialectical oscillation passes back and forth between ontological value and epistemic performance, between being and know-how, between the constitutive and the performative, between the illusions of the essential and the uncertainties of the experiential, between value and negotiated exchange, between ethical principle and political expediency. One or the other term of this bipolarity may assume precedence for a moment. Ultimately, however, the endgame comes down to a rhetoric of persuasion which infuses and contaminates all narrative discourse in the pragmatics of quotidian practice as much as in the metaphysics of the transcendental, because the pragmatic and the transcendental converge toward a mean that is constituted and constructed by a symbolic order, whether through ritual acts of conspiratorial occlusion or in graphic and iconographic gestures of cultural performance.

This is the balance that Fray Servando's iconoclasm threw off-kilter on that precarious cusp of late imperial Enlightenment and early national romanticism as the unhinged order of the eighteenth century morphed into the uncertainties of the nineteenth. Fray Servando's itinerary and its vicissitudes at that unsettled intersection of history serve as a transition to our modernity. His predicaments serve as a monitory foreshadowing of our common acts of conjuring with probability in the face of implacable orthodoxies and neoimperial convictions. Fray Servando understands well, no doubt, how irredeemably implicated we are as his asynchronous co-conspirators, actual or perceived, by the criteria of the inquisitors of his time or ours.

6

The Arts of Mitigation, the Garden in the Barbarian
ZBIGNIEW HERBERT

> Always and everywhere the politics of terror proves to be the politics of the blind.
> —Zbigniew Herbert, "The Nonheroic Subject"

> Writing . . . must teach men soberness: to be awake. . . . To make people sober. . . . I reject optimism despite all the theologians. Despair is a fruitful feeling. It is a cleanser, from desire, from hope. "Hope is the mother of the stupid" [a Polish proverb]. I don't like hope.
> —Zbigniew Herbert, "Conversation on Writing Poetry"

> So aesthetics can be helpful in life
> one should not neglect the study of beauty
>
> Before we declare our consent we must carefully
> examine
> the shape of the architecture the rhythm of the drums
> official colors the despicable ritual of funerals
>
> Our eyes and refused obedience
> the princes of our senses proudly chose exile
> —Zbigniew Herbert, "The Power of Taste"

I. "Oracular Rockings"

The poetic potential of "the power of taste" and the political inevitabilities of its chiasmus—"the taste of power"—appear destined to converge at every historical crossroads, and no less so in the embattled history of the twentieth century. Zbigniew Herbert has woven the threads of those crosshatched junctures into the fabric of essayistic rehearsals and into the skein of his poetic corpus. The conversion of history's squalor into salvaging attestation and into poetic artifact could well prove a mitigating factor when human history should find itself on the dock at some as yet indeterminate future. Whether Herbert's efforts as poet and as indefatigable advocate of humane discernment might suffice to acquit our humanity remains, and might well have to remain for a long time, an open question. Herbert's exertions are paradigmatic of humanity's defining endeavors—self-characterized, tautologically enough, as humanism. Having exercised the "power of taste" with poetic mastery, Herbert has also tasted the ruthless exercise of power with noble perseverance. Unlike "the princes of our senses" in his poem, Herbert's own eyes have not been averted, nor did he choose exile. He has sensed the toll exacted by the trials of exile, and having looked "home-brewed Mephisto[s]" in the face,[1] he has tolled the warning bell against naked tyranny and tyranny dressed in the vestments of banality. "Mephistos" are perennial, as he has amply documented. Herbert's Mephistos came "in Lenin jackets"; ours, at the beginning of the twenty-first century, come in literal and figurative cowboy hats, turbans, and yarmulkes. Herbert's has been "a garden" among barbarians and he an ironically self-proclaimed "barbarian in the garden."[2] Barbarians are as sempiternal as terrorists and cannibals are ubiquitous—until such time, we seem to be incorrigibly convinced, when our civilizing mission will have achieved its ends: we shall no longer have terrorism once we kill the last terrorist and we will have put an end to cannibalism when we have eaten the last cannibal. Will we have come to our "senses" then? Will we have attained the "soberness" that Herbert prescribes as the end of writing? And are the sobriety and wakefulness that he holds up as the purpose of writing the same thing?

While the pragmatism of his colloquy in our epigraph would seem to indicate the answers to this question to be affirmative, there is more evidence in Herbert's poetry and in his essayistic reflections to indicate that being awake and being sober are much more subtly differentiated than they are synonymous. His work teaches us to focus comparatively on the counterpoint between ideological mystification and critical alertness, on the oscillatory juncture where soberness and wakefulness might intersect, though not necessarily as congruent analogues, since wakefulness has its own forms of inebriation and sobriety is not immune to the delusions of somnambulance. I take this to be the primary lesson of the poetic vocation that Herbert versifies through the prosopopoeia of *Mr. Cogito*,[3] on the one hand, and, on the other, through the optical precision he demonstrates in his luminous pedagogy on reading painting as a function of light rather than as an object of color or of chromatic value. For scholars of comparative literature, Herbert's dual achievement as an author of poetry (invariably without punctuation) and as punctual reader of visual art constitutes an ekphrastic legacy of verbal construct and ocular perception.

Herbert's legacy to comparative literature, then, resides precisely in this translational process of reading and writing one artistic genre into another, one poetic tradition through the culture of another place, and one's historical circumstances in the larger context of humanity's incorrigible penchant for inhumanity. This pedagogy for comparative literature, properly learned, reiterates all that is redeemable in the scrutiny of one culture through another and in the translational legibility of one linguistic condensation through its intricate adaptations by another. His perspicacious bequest is far from academic, in the sneering sense of that term. It is, rather, an exemplary practice of critical, comparative acumen that finds its vocation and legitimacy as much in the aesthetic as in the political, in the inseparable intermediation and translatability between the two. Herbert's pedagogical method shows us the way to the extraordinariness of the ordinary, a subtle display of what we could term in shorthand as the arts of mitigation.

There is something paradoxical in this labor of mitigation, much as what Herbert calls "the nonheroic subject" is far from the antithesis of what is commonly understood by heroism. While his focus is on human commonality, it is not commonplace. His perspicacity emanates from what Osip Mandelstam counterposed as our problematic knowledge of things, on the one hand, and sensitivity to the cardinal coordinates for locating their knowability, on the other: "Things themselves we do not know; on the other hand we are highly sensitive to their location."[4] And though Mandelstam's syntax, or its English rendering from the Russian here, is clapping with one hand, the mitigation of knowledge in these circumstances translates into something other than diminishing apprehension. On the contrary, this is an intensified form of sensibility that sharpens the acuteness of our "apprehensions," in every sense of this term—facultative, lexical, and phobic. Knowing "the location of things," which I translate in the discussion of Erich Auerbach (Chapter 1) as the domain of acute knowledge, especially for those who develop an emphatic sense of place by virtue of displacement, Herbert imputes to an "attack of alienation," which he mitigates and, in doing so, renders even more acute. He writes: "An attack of alienation, but a gentle one that touches most people transported into a foreign place. A sense of the otherness of the world, a conviction that nothing happening around takes me into account, that I am superfluous, rejected. . . . In a state of alienation the eyes react quickly to objects and banal events that do not exist for the practical eye."[5] His then, by implication, would be an "impractical eye." It is, in fact, an "inordinate eye" that intensifies the world in mitigating it,[6] an augmentative emphatic that issues not from inflationary extension but from resolute condensation.

This is the optic of poetry and the critical optic of painting, as well as the political eye of historical assessment. As I have attempted to trace it in Chapter 5, it is the communal pursuit that conjugates culture and conspiracy as compensatory gesture for what Herbert describes here as "alienation." This optic sensibility is the eye with which Herbert demonstrates to us the art of writing poetry and the act of reading a canvas, as well as the acumen for ethical discernment and political insight. It is the penetrating eye of Mr. Cogito's reason, yet an eye, his poetry reminds us, that cannot see itself despite its acuity. And in so reminding us, he teaches us that in reading poetry we must read more than the poem on the page, that the poem's significance, pace the Anglo-American high modernists and New Critics of the early twentieth century, lies beyond itself in the referents and allusive evocations of a broad cultural history that has made the particular poem possible. Likewise, a painting inevitably overflows the plane of its surface, the hues of its colors, and the frame of its canvas, and therefore must be read by a different light than the chromatic values it displays in its own physicality, despite the claims of autonomy for the art object by late symbolists and high modernist artists and poets. Herbert has given us ample demonstration of the literacy required for this sort of reading through his analyses of painting, and also in the personification or prosopopoeia of the poetic figure he calls Mr. Cogito. Through such demonstrations we have come to know what is defining of poetry not only in Herbert but also in such road companions of his as the American poet Wallace Stevens, who enjoins us to behold "the nothing that is not there and the nothing that is,"[7] and another Mr. C (*quid vide*, Stevens's "The Comedian as the Letter C"), progenies both of a certain irrepressible cogitator by the name of "Monsieur Teste" (1896), self-ironically sent up by Paul Valéry.[8] This, perhaps, is the same author of wakeful lucidity (I say, perhaps, since in at least one of his avatars Valéry avidly adhered to the notion of the succession of personality) whose admonition against reading painting neither escaped nor dissuaded Herbert from that vocation. Writes Herbert with Valérian irony: "Valéry warned: 'We should apologize that we dare to speak about painting.' I was always aware of committing a tactless act."[9] Herbert might also recall Stevens's Crispin, then, who

> was too destitute to find
> In any commonplace the sought-for aid.
> He was a man made vivid by the sea,
> A man come out of luminous traversing,
> Much trumpeted, made desperately clear,
> Fresh from discoveries of tidal skies,
> To whom oracular rockings gave no rest.
> Into a savage color he went on.[10]

No doubt, the "savage color" that absorbs Stevens's "nonheroic" Mr. C reflects the tone of Herbert's favorite monochromes and their subtler luminosity,[11] much like the monomaniac ratiocinations of luminous reflection that swallow Monsieur Teste, Crispin, and Herbert's Mr. Cogito, all of them progenies of a certain ingenious Chevalier August Dupin, Edgar Allan Poe's incomparable master of rational detection who ends by being trapped in the cage of his implacable cogitations.[12] The wakefulness Herbert prescribes, then, is the alertness to the limits of sober reason itself, the barrenness of a landscape utterly emptied of any human illusion or solidarity, as we shall see in his poem "The Trial," with which we shall be concluding this discussion. His arts of mitigation, then, would mitigate the very faculties of mitigation itself, lest those same arts end by replicating the extreme politics of "self-conviction" in the dual sense of the phrase, that is, the atrocious delusions of self-righteousness and the inadvertent betrayal of self-incrimination. Such cautionary lessons from Herbert's century to ours have translated poorly, inasmuch as the first decade of the twenty-first century has not avoided any of the twentieth century's worst delusional convictions and violence. And though countries and cities change names and the principals switch roles, the invasions of Herbert's poem "September 17" recur with unrelenting brutality, and the perennial siege in his "Report from the Besieged City" continues unabated, *sine die*.[13] The chroniclers still struggle to find the language and the apt pitch that might translate the atrocious deeds, while those at the "top of the stairs" appear to us still "with a hushing finger always at the mouth."[14]

Emblematic of his century's baneful history, Herbert's poetry has also proved prophetic of what will have been in the future perfect of its composition, namely, our own historical present. Before elaborating further on the relationship between his poetic vision and our current predicaments, however, it might prove apposite to revisit for a moment Herbert's instructive legacy in the reading of painting. This, I believe, will make more salient the continuing relevance of his lessons in ekphrasis, or the translation of one artistic genre into another. I am referring to what was in its historical year of 1614 and its material context of Dutch society at that time an emblem, literally, one whose message was temperance and moderation, a purpose that was intricately compromised in its appropriation by an artist whose relationship to moderation and restraint was problematic at best. This is a complication whose irony Herbert clearly found too intriguing to pass up in his lucid meditations on Dutch painting of the seventeenth century. The emblem in question would become the circular canvas whose title (*Emblematic Still Life with Flagon, Glass, Jug, and Bridle*) Herbert appropriated, in turn, for the title of his book of essays. The oil painting, as Herbert titles it, is *Still Life with a Bridle*, and the artist, Jan Simon [Johannes Symoonizs] van der Beeck, as Herbert notes, renamed himself Torrentius.[15]

I wish to focus on what I have referred to as Herbert's arts of mitigation through Torrentius and his work, this being a work the poet has discussed extensively. This is the Dutch artist's only extant painting, though a small engraving has also survived the righteous flames of the Haarlem prosecutors. I opt for this focus because I sense that Herbert's fascination with this particular painter and painting speaks to us of what we find fascinating in his work, the poetry and the essays, namely, an irony of mitigation that borders on paradox. This in itself would not be extraordinary either in Torrentius or in Herbert. Artists and poets have been wont to find the generative spark for their composition in those disjunctive incongruities that verge on the incommensurable elements we call paradox, irony, and ambiguity. Artists and writers have also been known to embody such incommensurabilities in their own lives. The peculiarity beyond this topos in the case of Torrentius, and no less so in Herbert's historical context, and now ours, is the added element of courting paradox and ambiguity in a decidedly literalist, some might say Pharisaic, historical moment bent on disambiguation. Such historical times in pursuit of unproblematic transparency of conviction, and the derogation, to put it mildly, of anyone who would interject complexity into such clarity, are prone to be characterized by a rigidity like shatterproof crystal. What Torrentius has done in this painting, a good bit of which we know because of Herbert's lucid exegesis, has its analogue in Herbert's own poetic achievement. In this sense, the Polish poet compounds the value of his inheritance to us—a compounding, ironically enough, that is conveyed not through exaggeration but through mitigation, through that subtractive gesture whose yield proves to be an increase and a continuous augmentation.

I am obviously reiterating here the definition of the act of composition crystallized by Osip Mandelstam in his ongoing conversation with us about Dante, namely, that art is something "formed not from heaping up of particulars but in consequence of the fact that one detail after another is torn away from the object, leaves it, flutters out, is hacked away from the system, and goes off into its own functional space."[16] In the case of Herbert's poetry, as was the case of the poetry of Mandelstam, and in the case of the artistic achievement of Torrentius, the historical context of composition that would yield the "functional space" of its object was, by contrast, a dysfunctional social space, so much so that the historical circumstances of that dysfunctionality would be discomfiting to Herbert and would prove as fatal for Mandelstam in his conflicted era as it had been for Torrentius in his. All three, Torrentius, Mandelstam, and Herbert, dared to ignore the counsel of those at the "top of the stairs" who never fail to appear "with a hushing finger always at the mouth," to cite Herbert once more. In this, our time is different from theirs only to the degree that at the beginning of the twenty-first century everyone seems to have moved to the "top of the stairs."

Herbert remarks, not without a certain unmistakable delight, that Torrentius, starting with the paradoxes semantically embedded in his choice of *nom de guerre*, was fully aware of the ambiguities he wrought on the virtues of decent Dutch society. And he was awake as well to the self-contradictions between the emblematic morality and temperance professed in this particular canvas that posterity has vouchsafed for us, and the intemperate, some would say scandalous, comportment in the artist's life, which he turned into another genre of performative art. In this regard, the only other extant work of art attributed to him, likely produced for his patron, England's King Charles I, and also in the Rijksmuseum in Amsterdam, is a signed ("Torrentius fecit") engraving of a man and a woman in furtive copulation.[17] Perhaps, Herbert might have remarked about this other surviving work of Torrentius, were it not for the fact that the serendipitous nature of discovery in art museums Herbert cultivated so consummately made the possibility of its surprising him less than likely. At any rate, it would have merely added a graphic dimension to the incommensurability he has aptly remarked between devotional profession and actual practice: "Only simpletons and naïve moralizers demand exemplary harmony of life and work from an artist."[18] As he suggests, the contradictory verve of the artist is captured in Torrentius's adopted name, the Latin translation of his Dutch surname, "beek," or "stream," whose true semantic register Herbert found in its lexical derivatives "from the word *torrens*, which in its adjectival form means 'hot, incandescent,' and as a noun means 'a wild, rushing stream'—the two unreconciled, antagonistic elements of fire and water. If one could write one's own destiny into a pen name, Torrentius did it with prophetic intuition."[19] No less irreconcilable with the name and the destiny it boded, we might add, is the fact that posterity would come to know the turbulent Torrentius only through a "still life," a genre designation even more ironic in Spanish (*naturaleza muerta*) and in French (*nature morte*). The title in French given to Torrentius's *Still Life with a Bridle*, ironically enough, is *Nature morte à la joie*.[20] It was, of course, a certain irrepressible *joie de vivre* that complicated Torrentius's life with egregious contradictions that Dutch society at the time could not countenance. In 1614, when he painted this work, he may well have been anticipating his arrest, imprisonment, torture, and trial for blasphemy and immoral conduct in 1627, his subsequent "rescue" by England's Charles I, and his return from English exile in 1642 to imminent retrial and death two years later.

II. Unbridled Torrent

Still Life with a Bridle, as Herbert notes, must have been one of the works Torrentius took to England with him as a gift for Charles I since the back of the canvas, like his other extant work, carries the seal of the English monarch and the monogram of the painter. There is another identifying detail Herbert does not remark since he was not likely to have seen it from his viewer's position when he happened upon the painting's exhibit during his first visit to the Rijksmuseum in Amsterdam. Closer scrutiny reveals that in the middle of the top third of the painting, at a key point on what Herbert said were "the metal objects I could not at first identify,"[21] is etched "T. 1614." The letter of course is the initial for Torrentius, and 1614 is the year of the painting's composition, which also happens to be the year in which a particular emblem was in wide circulation in Haarlem for the moral edification of the populace.[22] Three salient objects that Herbert identifies in the painting are in that emblem, arrayed in the same sequence as he describes them:

On the right side a potbellied pitcher of burnt clay in a warm, saturated brown; in the middle a massive glass goblet, called a *roemer*, half filled with liquid; and on the left side a silver-gray pewter pitcher with a lid and spout. In addition, [and these are Torrentius's own additions to what was in the emblem circulating at the time], are two porcelain pipes, a piece of paper with music, and a text on the shelf where the utensils were standing. At the top, metal objects I could not at first identify.[23]

It is principally those "metal objects" that I wish to discuss here, especially because of their centrality to the painting as the emendation of Torrentius to the moralizing emblem, then in circulation. I also wish to focus on these "metal objects" because of their significance to the semantic horizon of the work, and, not least, as this work relates to Herbert's poetry and its legacy to us.

Central as it is, Herbert's eventual identification of those "metal objects" receives a rather summary comment from him, albeit a most suggestive comment and an unanswered question, because, one suspects, horsemanship did not figure among his many talents. Herbert writes:

At the top is the object I could not decipher at first, which seemed to be a piece of old armor hanging on the wall: at closer observation, it appeared to be a chain bridle used to tame exceptionally skittish horses. This metal contraption, stripped to its stable commonness, emerges from the dark background, hieratic, somber like the specter of the Great Commander. . . . How to explain, for instance, the exceedingly daring and "surrealist" juxtaposition in the picture of the bridle hanging menacingly over the trinity of vessels?[24]

It would appear that Torrentius did indeed know something about bridles and horses, certainly enough to stay on one, since, as Herbert notes early in his essay, "Torrentius . . . rode a horse."[25] Riding a horse does not necessarily make one a horseman, especially in Torrentius's time, even if Herbert's reading, correctly, I believe, of the initials "E.R.," in the musical score at the forefront of the shelf holding the objects, as "Eques Rosae Crucis" (Knight of the Red Cross, i.e., a Rosicrucian) is accurate.

The depiction of the bridle in this still life would indicate that Torrentius had some horse sense as attributable to humans, and that he knew something about horses, tack, and the allegorical or emblematic significance of horse and bridle. I am hopeful that these remarks might go some way toward allaying the suggestive perplexity Herbert has expressed before this painting—"How to explain, for instance, the exceedingly daring and 'surrealist' juxtaposition in the picture of the bridle hanging menacingly over the trinity of vessels?" What Torrentius depicts here is more properly the bit of the bridle. He paints not the whole bridle itself but its synecdoche. While the bit is crucial, it is not in itself sufficient (there are, after all, bridles without bits), though it has been identified by tradition as the emblem of restraint. The bit touches the point in the horse's anatomy where manipulation, literally, brings one of the most sensitive parts of the animal into contact with the most able instruments of the human, the hands. Getting the bit into the horse's mouth, a crucial step in putting the bridle on the horse's head, entails a delicate ritual that goes back to the beginning of the history of human domestication of a large animal, on average ten times heavier and more powerful than the human. It is an asymmetrical encounter and, hence, certain protocols have always been indispensable for negotiating the relationship between two distinctly different species, human and equine. These are the rituals signaled by this bit of metal in the painting, and their intricacy, now second nature to equestrians and to domesticated horses, carries highly emblematic significance. Torrentius was clearly sensitive to those rituals and quite adept in incorporating them into what historical evidence indicates, and Herbert accurately notes, is a highly allegorical painting.

The asymmetry of power between horse and human has often been viewed as a reflection of the ratio between humanity's own brute potential and the human ability to harness, restrain, and moderate that latent brutality. Herbert's twentieth-century fellow poet and an earnest reader of his work, Seamus Heaney,[26] elaborates on the relationship between the human's brute nature and the nature of poetry as the human's self-validating achievement through self-government by the tongue—"When I thought of 'the government of the tongue' . . . what I had in mind was this aspect of poetry as its own vindicating force. In this dispensation, the tongue (representing both a poet's personal gift of utterance and the common resource of language itself) has been granted the right to govern. . . . The poet is credited with a power to open unexpected and unedited communications between our nature and the nature of the reality we inhabit."[27] While Heaney's gloss of what we might call a poetic "glossarchia" as mediating instrument between human communicative potential and poetic reality is a metaphorical figure, those who bridle horses know that the art of negotiating and mediating the asymmetries of bulk and power between horse and human consist, in key part, in the fine touch of ensuring that the tongue of the horse remain properly comfortable under the bit of the bridle for optimal governance and productive cooperation.

The allegorical potential of this fact is poetically intuitive for Heaney as well as for Zbigniew Herbert. One suspects it was that for Torrentius also, as his painting avers, but he certainly must have had full cognizance of the literal and unadorned reality of this fact as *eques* ("knight") in the plain sense of the term and in his allegorical title "Eques Rosae Crucis." Thus, Torrentius would have known not only from his own personal character but also from his emphatic human nature of a further asymmetry that compounded the relationship between the human species and the equine: the latter is a prey animal, while the former, the human, is a predator species. This difference itself is determinative in the interspecies "protocols," an interspecies mode of ekphrasis that has some potential for comparative literature as a field that has had little attention. In this instance, then, Herbert's creative essayistic prose on painting opens up another facet for the field of comparatism to consider—interspecies communication.

The particular concern in this essay by Herbert would have us focus critical insight and poetic sensibility on the modus operandi that governs the relationship between *Equus* and *Homo sapiens*. It begins with the manner in which the human approaches the horse, that is, with an awareness of location and the capabilities of the visual faculty in both, a factor which a painter like Torrentius, who dealt in perspective and the optical medium as well as in riding horses, would have been alert to. As a predator, the human has the eyes set forward; they are binocular, that is, the clarity of focus occurs with both eyes. As a prey animal, the horse's eyes are set much farther apart for peripheral vision and alertness against potential predators. A horse's lateral vision extends 146 degrees on each side, with frontal vision spanning 65 degrees. This gives the horse maximum surveillance against predators, except for certain significant blind spots that can prove fatal and that also could prove perilous even in the nonhostile, workaday interaction between human and horse. This includes a three- to four-degree blind spot directly behind the horse, which, in effect, means that no experienced horseman would approach a horse unannounced from the rear, as well as a blind spot that extends from six inches from the head of the horse to some four feet straight ahead—hence the danger of approaching a horse head-on (the caveat obtains figuratively as well, a fact which tints this interaction with a hue of poetic protocols). And while the horse has both binocular and monocular vision for each eye independently, the transition from one kind of focus to the other is slow, an interregnum in perception that could prove startling to the animal, causing it to "spook." Furthermore, while the horse's optical range can cover a near circular perimeter, the animal cannot see its front hooves or immediately down below its head. This makes vocal communication from the human while working closely from the ground with a horse imperative, allowing the horse to orient its movements aurally, something it is equipped to do very well, like most animals of prey. Working closely with a horse from the ground, as already noted, means not doing so frontally but from the side—from the near side, to be exact, that is to say the left side of the horse, rather than the off side, or the right. Tradition has it that this is so because of the difficulty of mounting a horse when one is armed with a sword, since the scabbard would extend from the rider's waist down to the left side, thereby proving an impediment to placing one's body in the saddle if one were to attempt to mount from the right or from the off-side. In the case of sport, since polo is only played with a mallet in the right hand, the same principle of unobstructed mounting from the left, or the near side, applies.

I review these technical details on equestrian interaction and the physiology of equine vision because we are presented here with a visual medium, by a visual artist, in the context of a composition in which a key equine-related object hovers centrally in the canvas. The haunting presence of this object identifies that artistic achievement by defining what

Osip Mandelstam called the composition's "functional space." The poet's functional space here has its analogue in that of the painter, and, in turn, both are reflected in the visual parameters of a functional space defined by the survival faculties of a horse. Torrentius the horseman and painter gives us reason to surmise that he was amply aware of this, hence the shape of his canvas—in the round, 360 degrees—which, in addition to its consonance with the ocular subject of the painting, as the fortuities of history would have it, is also what proved the saving grace for the survival of the work itself. As Herbert points out, the work was discovered in a functional second life before it was returned to its original status in the museological archive as painting. That second life consisted in its use as a cover of a raisin barrel, until its chance discovery in 1913, "almost exactly three hundred years after its creation."[28]

As Torrentius clearly understood, the pivotal point of communication between a horse and a human occurs when the horse's mouth meets the human's hands. This occurs through the instrumentality of the bridle, but the bridle, lest it be the occasional bitless kind, is purely ancillary; it was designed to hold the bit in the horse's mouth. The central object in this Torrentius still life, thus, is not a "bridle" but a bit. It is, to be exact, a Dutch snaffle gag bit with eggbutt ends, those protruding ends that look at the painting's viewer like bulging eyes. In the painting these eggbutt ends of the bit become exaggerated in diameter because of the perspectival foreshortening of the span of the bit, making it look as if the eggbutt ends could not possibly fit in the horse's mouth between the front teeth and the molars (called the diastema) and across the so-called bars, the toothless space on the gum overlaying the lower jaw. Evolutionary biology endowed the horse with these spaces, not for the benefit of human bridles and bits, but as a result of the lengthening of the horse's skull for grazing purposes. This is not because the horse's head would otherwise not reach the ground but because the horse, as animal of prey, had to keep the ability for visual reconnaissance for self-defense above the tall grasses even while it grazed. This evolutionary morphology, of course, gives new meaning to the acute sensitivity of location, especially by the dislocated and the vulnerable, whether the refugees or exiles in the context of Mandelstam and Auerbach, or, as in the case of Torrentius after 1627, the persecuted, as was the case also of Fray Servando Teresa de Mier and Giordano Bruno, the latter two victims of the Holy Office of the Inquisition, on which Herbert reflects quite eloquently in his essay "Albigensians, Inquisitors, and Troubadors."[29]

There is another particular detail about this bit so central to Torrentius's still life, something in addition to the fact that Torrentius etched his initial, T, and the year of composition, 1614, across the bit and at such a point that it was not visible to Herbert and would not be within visual range from the four feet out and straight-on angle, a regimental position generally accorded to exhibited paintings by curators in museum displays. Hence, in mirrored reversal of the horse's four-foot blind range head-on, Herbert did not notice the inscription, one of the few things that escaped his binocular viewer's scrutiny. He would have had to violate museum strictures and move within six inches of the canvas and, like a horse, lift his head up for focus, in order to have seen the identifying inscription (horses raise their heads to focus simultaneously both eyes on close-up objects, and they lower their heads to achieve that bifocalization for distant ones). The other particularity of Torrentius's bit, and I qualify it thus not inadvertently, is its structural design. It is built with "D rings" where the reins are to be attached, a fairly standard design as variant of the common "O rings" for reins and cheekpiece leathers (the straps from which the bit is suspended and that go up over the horse's head to form the crownpiece behind the ears). There are no reins in the painting; they are only suggested here by their "place holder"—the rings to which they would be attached. Torrentius's bit extends below its "D rings," however, and this too is fairly common. The added rings below the "D rings" at the ends of the bit are for second reins, and the lower these rings extend, the greater the pressure on the horse's mouth from the other end of the attached reins in the rider's hands. For this reason, this second rein is usually held between the small finger, the pinky, and the next finger for optimal modulation and subtlety of pressure and, at the same time, if need be, for maximum restraint when the human hand clenches around the reins. The peculiarity of Torrentius's Dutch snaffle gag is that these lowest rings on the bit are cut out in the shape of a heart, as the "valentine" iconography of the human heart is most commonly depicted. And here too, as Herbert noted with regard to his choice for a *nom de guerre*, Torrentius is unmistakably inscribing his autobiography and his destiny in that negative space in the shape of the heart destined for the more compelling second rein. In addition to his heterodox beliefs as a Rosicrucian, or "Eques Rosae Crucis," Torrentius's vicissitudes originate in what the upright folk of Haarlem would have considered his "sins of the heart and the loins." This emblematic instrument of restraint as depicted here, then, is as much the emblematic self-portrait of a torrent as it is Torrentius's paradoxical iconography in the still life for the virtues of restraint, temperance, and moderation.

The rest of the bit is otherwise conventional, with curb chain dangling below the bit and, above it, a noseband also in single-link chain—not uncommon and, in fact, more merciful than the twisted rawhide hackamore, whose spiraled edges can be hard as blades across the animal's nose. The leather cheekpieces fade into the chromatic darkness of the canvas above and from either side of the noseband, emanating from squared strap ends just above the "D rings." The rest conforms to Herbert's apt suppositions on the mitigation of excess and to his persuasive reading of the foregrounded text on the musical score sheet, whose lyrics praise moderation and admonish the viewer against intemperance: "In ethical categories Torrentius's 'Still Life' is not at all an allegory of Vanitas if my suppositions are correct, but an allegory of one of the cardinal virtues called Moderation, Temperantia, Sophrosyne. This interpretation is suggested by the represented objects: a bridle, the reins of the passions, vessels that give shape to formless liquids, and also the tumbler only half-filled as if recalling the praiseworthy custom of the Greeks of mixing wine with water."[30] Praiseworthy indeed, but one wonders whether the Greeks' mixing was more likely to have been of water with wine, an act of Ananke, of necessity, rather than temperance or Sophrosyne, given the quality of the water. In the end, the libation might have been the same, but, we are left wondering, did the purpose for its composition alter the taste and, no less, the effect? The answer to this question we shall pursue in Herbert's own poetic compositions.

III. The Poetics of Mitigation

In the genealogy of Herbert's poetic tradition, the fate of poets seems to be to clamor for what things could, should, or might be, knowing all along that once a poem itself becomes a thing called "poem," it too assumes the potentialities of what it might or could be. It is this realization that lies at the heart of what I am referring to as a poetics of mitigation—

a peripety that at once curtails only to compound and augment the possibilities of the poem and of the poet's vocation. Here is one instance of Herbert's own clamoring for what we might call the ontological firmness of a phenomenon as concrete as a pebble, and the ironic contravention of that constancy by the very poem that issues from Herbert's desired order:

The pebble
is a perfect creature

equal to itself
mindful of its limits
filled exactly
with a pebbly meaning.[31]

To be equal to the task of being equal to itself must be a mission of quite a tall order even for "a perfect creature" as hard as a pebble. We have seen the difficulties of such a possibility in the lessons taught us by Nicholas of Cusa on equivalence and identity. We know a rose foundered on a similar assignment once it was declared, with iterative insistence, a rose. And many an element, from socks to artichokes, went astray once they were granted their elemental apotheosis in *Elemental Odes*.[32] A pebble will henceforth never be a pebble but an element in a poem about this poet's desire to have a pebble be itself, as the poem's persona deems it could, might, or should be. And in a venture no less perilous, the poem itself suffers the lot of the pebble, which thereby becomes the poem's synecdoche and the metaphor of its fate. This is to say, the pebble, rather than "equal to itself," ends by being decidedly something other than a pebble by virtue of Herbert's poem, even in his northerly land where pebbles may well be viewed as nothing more than pebbles, though the comparative adverb is clearly moot, at once redundant and obviously superfluous, by virtue of the qualities imputed to this pebble in the hand of Herbert's poetic persona—perfect, mindful, meaningful, immemorably scented, imbued with temperature and dignity, thermo-conductive, indomitable, clear-eyed. I transcribe Herbert's qualifiers stanza by stanza. In their incremental buildup, this litany of attributes for the pebble ends by mitigating the concrete object, whose ontology the poem would seek to simplify to a mathematical equivalence of a thing equal to itself. This disparity between what the poem would pretend to do and what, in fact, is done by the poem interjects an ambiguity that begs comparison between what the poem's object is purported to be and what it ends up being, and between what the poem itself claims to be and what the poem does. This *décalage*, or slippage, ironically purposeful here, is the poetics of mitigation, of which Herbert is a master.

There is yet another comparatistic calculus demanded by Herbert's poem, an evocative quotient of comparison that intervenes to compel the engagement of the practitioner of comparative literature. This is the element that Osip Mandelstam, yet again, calls the "location" of things, which is what we might know about things rather than the things themselves, even pebbles. And by that reckoning, a pebble is not only something other than just a pebble within a particular poem such as this, but it is also something else again when the poem itself is read by someone admittedly conditioned by a life devoted to literature. Thus, for other latitudes than Herbert's northerly location—for example, for certain Mediterranean islands whose ancient cultures have shaped Herbert's and our own ways of reading—a pebble is always a potential *tessera*, either for a floor or for a wall mosaic, a perfect candidate-in-waiting for just the right spot in the geometric, black and white *krokalia*, so called in Greek because the surface resembles the crocodile's back once all the pebbles are set into mosaic formation. By *mosaic formation*, as Herbert with his classicist's etymological curiosity well knew, we mean a composition, not unlike most classical poetry, "dedicated to the Muses." And, as the summer advances and the wheat fields turn gold, a pebble takes on an even sharper prospect. Once split or flaked and set beneath the threshing board, the pebble becomes the flint stone that rescues the grain from the grip of the chaff, setting the stage for the perennial rites of winnowing. The indomitable pebble that Herbert sees, then, as the calm and clear eye, for a primitive reader like this literary comparatist, that pebble-eye becomes at once an eye-stone, the inscrutable eye of the horse that takes in the world as a convex mirror, and the surrealist's lunar eye of a harvest moon traversed by the razor's edge at the hand of Luis Buñuel in his primal work of modern cinema *Un chien andalou* (An Andalusian Dog; 1929). And so the claims for a simple pebble multiply, and could go on multiplying unpredictably, as do the requirements of Herbert's poem that simultaneously teach the ambiguities of comparison and task us with the comparative readings demanded by his poetics. To read, then, and especially to read comparatively, Herbert's poetry seems to say, is to recognize the multiple claims each poem makes on us. A pebble inevitably becomes a touchstone whose radiant connections can be innumerable, limited only by the location and context of where it happens to be found, its semiotic and figural ripples circumscribable only by the cultural waters into which it happens to be dropped.

The hazardous fate of this poetic enterprise, whose fortuities invariably waylay the concreteness of its desired outcome, constitutes an adventitious contingency in itself worthy of a poem—if, that is, one could ever get a poem, like a pebble, to be itself. Here is how Herbert's contemporary Brazilian poet Carlos Drummond de Andrade versified the peripety of that lapidary coincidence, in his poem "In the Middle of the Road":

In the middle of the road there was a stone
there was a stone in the middle of the road
there was a stone
in the middle of the road there was a stone.[33]

We find ourselves, yet again, as with Herbert's "Pebble," at a juncture of innumerable translatability, definable only by the location and contextual epistemes that happen to circumscribe one's particular literacy, that, in this instance, in the case of Herbert's and Drummond de Andrade's self-conscious poetic genealogy could range from the incipit of Dante's *Inferno*—"Nel mezzo del cammin di nostra vita" (In the middle of our life's journey)—to Stephan Mallarmé's *Un coup de dés jamais n'abolira le hasard* (A Throw of the Dice Will Never Abolish Chance; 1897).[34] The contextual, locative poetics of writing and reading forge the defining parameters that mitigate randomness and chaos. It is this mitigation that enables the composition of the poem and its legibility as performative achievement. As interruptive as the chance encounter with a stone in the middle of the road might be, the disruption of the itinerary is productive and generative; as is the case in Greek tragedy where it originated, the peripety leads to unforeseen directions with unexpected consequences rather than ending in curtailment. And, while this might be a boon to those who create, it has proved anathema for those who would control. It is at this juncture that poetry encounters politics, where poetic vocations such as Herbert's have had to countenance political determinants violently averse to creative indeterminacy and deathly afraid of historical unpredictability, what Hannah Arendt has called "spontaneity as such, with its incalculability."[35] Herbert's poetic corpus also reads, then, as the chronicle of this historical confrontation that he was destined to live and record. Herbert's legacy teaches us a good deal with enduring relevance, inasmuch as such predicaments are not unique to his time.

IV. The Delicate Art of Political Assuagement

The political correlative to the poetic arts of mitigation marks Herbert's poetry as a form of condensation of emotive intensity. I take this laconic economy, not as an expedient stratagem in the face of political power and peril, but as a poetic decision that carries greater vigor and persuasive consequence. The deployment of poetic strategy to rhetorical effect may well have its origins in Herbert's early training in jurisprudence at the University of Kraków, which already made itself apparent in his arguing the six-and-a-half-century-long case in "Defence of the Templars" before the "High Jury" of his readers.[36] While his advocacy may have achieved a moral victory of "acquittal," the case still resists closure, extending into yet another century, something Herbert anticipated fully in the would-be closure of his essay: "In history nothing remains closed. The methods used against the Templars enriched the repertoire of power. That is why we cannot leave this distant affair under the pale fingers of archivists."[37] The methods remain qualitatively the same, as do the underlying motives, and the "repertoire of power" is more ample and more insidiously ubiquitous than ever. In our own time, the geographical setting, or the scene of the crime also remains a constant, extending from the shores of Gaza on the eastern Mediterranean to the banks of the Euphrates. And those whom Herbert's argument indicts most pointedly also remain unaltered: "The intellectuals, as usual, proved unreliable."[38] The intellectuals' constancy notwithstanding, history has not stood still, especially in the heart of the baleful geography of the Abrahamic traditions. But Herbert's prescience anticipates the nature of this progress as well: "Progress in our civilization, High Jury, consists mainly in the fact that simple tools for splitting heads were replaced by hatchet-words, which have the advantage of psychologically paralysing an opponent. Such words are: 'mind-debaucher', 'witch' and 'heretic'. The Templars were accused of heresy, chiefly to deprive the Pope of the possibility of intervening on their behalf. Moreover, the battle was difficult from the start. Philip the Fair had power, the Holy See just diplomacy."[39] As Herbert might have noticed in 1991, when he traveled to Jerusalem to collect the Jerusalem Prize, the template for invasion, conquest, and occupation remains the same, as do the ulterior motives, usually economic and political, dressed in the cloak of religion and galvanized by ideological zeal. Only the lexicon has morphed and the methods refined. The operative "hatchet-words" today are *crusader*, *terrorist*, *Zionist*, and *anti-Semite*. These, and many others, tend to be adjectival descriptors that corral and "neutralize" their target. As Herbert notes in his plea to the "High Jury," "abundance of adjectives is a sure sign not only of bad poetry, but also of accusations weak on fact," symptomatic of what he terms "the gurgle of rage."[40]

Power still trumps diplomacy with predictable efficiency. And while the Holy See may have fallen to the marginal (ir)relevance hoped for it by the Ghibellines of the time of Dante and Philip the Fair, we have an analogous body of "just diplomacy," as Herbert says, called the United Nations. And though we have more than one Fair Philip thumping for crusades, much in the mold of Philip's grandfather Louis IX the Crusader, we have no Frederick II, whose epithet *Stupor Mundi* (Wonder of the World) has been given new meaning by current imperial pretenders set on liberating and civilizing the barbarians. Louis IX, *Rex Christianissimus*, "Most Christian King," a legendary title for France's first king Clovis, a historically documented title in France since the fourteenth century, is the only sainted French king. His crusades in 1248 and 1270, which proved ill-starred, risible, and deadly, were the obsessed Western parenthesis of crusading fervor, the nearly contemporaneous Eastern pincer action coming from the Nestorian-Christian inspired Mongols with the 1258 siege and sacking of Baghdad by Hülagü Khan, as chronicled for us by the calligrapher and court historian Rashiduddin Fazlullah a few years later, a legacy we discussed in Chapter 2. In the second decade of the third millennium, the siege and its human and environmental depredations continue from Gaza to the Euphrates, even as I write this memo to / on Zbigniew Herbert.

I review these historical details on the way to Herbert's poetry, once again, because his legacy to the discipline of comparative literature also consists in teaching us to factor the facts, whether weak or strong, into the labors of reading and writing. And as poetry is eminently factual (poetry is made, it makes poets in turn), certainly stronger as fact than the Orwellian conjurations of political doublespeak, even if far from being as deadly, as Herbert says, "facts should not be treated in isolation, but be judged against the political and social background of their time."[41] As we read the historical facts, political realities, and poetic stratagems by the light of Herbert's admonition, the shadow of a peculiar irony falls across those comparative perspectives he would have us track with a discerning eye. Historically, his essayistic treatment of Albigensian heresies and the trials of the Templars have become meaningful as figures, whether in the "functional space" of metaphor or of allegory, trained on the "dysfunctional spaces" of his Soviet-era Poland and its political dystopias. As we read Herbert's essays and his poetry, those figures morph back into literal facticity—the quotidian reality of our historical context at the beginning of the twenty-first century. Thus, the topography, the ideologies, and the zealotries that served as distant mirror for Herbert's own embattled historical moment are once again the actual places, invoked orthodoxies, and sanctified arenas of strife and slaughter. What was his figurative mirror is now our literal reality, the world he labored to reflect and critique having vanished into the dustbin of history, leaving behind the afterimage that is our actual historical predicament. In reverting from spectral image to our factual life-world, the history of Herbert's distant mirror now reflects much more refined methods of lethality and more efficient forms of cruelty. And, once again, with all methodological and instrumental refinements factored in, the validity of Herbert's observations continues to hold true: "The real terror is to be found in the inventories of torture chambers."[42]

V. The Trials of Poetry

Though Herbert's position is unmistakable—"It is difficult, truly, to be reconciled to sky-high injustice"—the trials of poetry do not necessarily lead to poetic justice.[43] By the light of history, of his history and ours, the uncertainty and clarity in what Herbert optimistically terms "uncertain clarity" are rendered moot.[44] Uncertainty's ambiguity becomes cynically appropriated into expedient doublespeak; clarity is subjected to the petrification of doctrinaire certitude by zealous disambiguation. That was indeed the fate of Herbert's dysfunctional historical space, so diligently chronicled by his poetry, and it is the reality of our new millennium, the admonitions of Italo Calvino in his *Six Memos for the Next Millennium* notwithstanding, as we shall see in the last of our memos, destined as a response to his final and, as fate would have it, unwritten envois for our millennium. In the redoubled fervor of born-again convictions, ambiguity has no redeemable value and clarity brooks nothing but the transparency of its own immaculate infallibility. If the Marxist orthodoxy of Herbert's time and political space grounded its justification on a redemptive future and its promissory soteriology, our triumphant canon considers itself already posthistorical, postapocalyptic, and in no need of further self-justification. The reign we live under deems itself justified and incontrovertibly just. Herbert's Mr. Cogito has morphed into a current avatar of absolute certainty. His twenty-first-century apotheosis finds him beyond cogitation, indubitable, incontestable, cocksure. Ditto the transfiguration of Wallace Stevens's Crispin—beyond the comedic, fully the embodiment of self-assured melodrama, thoroughly convinced of his epic status. Triumphant over all competing ideologies of the twentieth century—beyond irony, beyond humor, and immune to contradiction—we live in a literal apotheosis of Charlie Chaplin's Great Dictator. Ours is the kingdom of hyperpuissance and hyperreality.

Thus, Herbert's poetic chronicles and "uncertain clarity" bridge twentieth-century modernism to twenty-first-century "posthistorism." His century crawled toward deliverance and redemptive rebirth, still entertaining the possibility of awakening from history's nightmare. His vigilant anticipation is now our vigil and waking into "sober" reality, as he termed it. Herbert will not be surprised to learn that it is still a historical reality, much as he prognosticated, even if it deems itself to have arrived at a time beyond history's aftermath. And the trials of poetry still have us wrestling with the angel of history, with "uncertain clarity," regardless of the outcome, whether as vanquished or as victors, as Herbert poignantly anticipated in such aptly titled poems as "The Trial" and "Babylon."[45] The accused still face the same jury before the same tribunals, and Babylon, once again, endures siege, occupation, and captivity, literally and figuratively. For now, I shall concentrate on "The Trial," leaving Babylon to the predations of the latest barbarians.

"Writing," Herbert says in the interview cited as epigraph for this memo, "must teach men soberness: to be awake." He dramatized this claim variously, particularly in "The Trial." Part of the collection *Report from the Besieged City and Other Poems*, first "published by internees in the Rakowiecka Prison in Warsaw in 1983,"[46] with most copies confiscated by the prison authorities, "The Trial" is a dramatic exhibit of an "awakening" from one nightmare (the judicial process) into another (the historical/political reality) that contains it. The difficulty lies in discerning which is more terrifying, the hypnotic or the wakeful. The predicament of the accused, the poetic persona, transits from the history of a nightmare to the nightmare of history, an awakening from a synecdoche of historical terror, "beyond the limits of time the senses and reason," into its macrocosm:

therefore when I wake I don't open my eyes
I clench my fingers don't lift my head
breathe lightly because truly I don't know
how many minutes of air I still have left[47]

Terror was the official mainstay of Herbert's historical time; it is even more so at the core of our own time in these initial years of the twenty-first century, when terror, official and otherwise, is pervasive enough to have permeated human existence on a global scale as daily practice, political performance, as reigning paradigm, and as intellectual discourse.[48]

As it unfolds, then, "The Trial" is the emergence of poetry as the paradigmatic case study of terror in what Herbert characterizes as its locus classicus: "The real terror is to be found in the inventories of torture chambers."[49] In a process worthy of Kafka, the accused is forced to internalize the accusation, assimilate and embody its guilt, whether guilty or not, and become complicit in carrying out the judgment of the court, even before a verdict:

the real trial went on in my cells
they certainly knew the verdict earlier
after a short rebellion they capitulated and started to die
one after the other
I looked in amazement at my fingers

roused to my feet by the guards
I managed only to blink and then
the room burst out in healthy laughter
my adoptive mother laughed also
the gavel banged and this really was the end[50]

Though not really "the end," except as cruel false closure, the final judgment as foregone conclusion, in fact, becomes immaterial. In this poetics of mitigation, justice, poetic or otherwise, is what is mitigated foremost. The justice system emerges as an instrument of terror, the participants—prosecutor, defender, policeman, judge, jury, witnesses, reporters, firing squad—no less uniformly instrumentalized as "the party of those without any pity," while the court chambers turn into "torture chambers" where the inventories of "the real terror [are] to be found":

During his great speech the prosecutor
kept piercing me with his yellow index finger
I'm afraid I didn't appear self-assured
unintentionally I put on a mask of fear and depravity
like a rat caught in a trap an informer a fratricide
the reporters were dancing a war dance
slowly I burned at a stake of magnesia[51]

As is the case with Herbert's poem "Pebble," here too we experience the disjunction between what the poem is and what it does. Thus, the target of Herbert's poetic trials emerges as that reflexive complicity of the human subject—the accused with his accusers—caught in that margin that we now know as "governmentality" that serves as self-regulative principle internalized by the governed. Herbert's poetics of mitigation would ensure that this regimental instrumentality that would grind down the human into its own corrosive element becomes subverted. The alembic for this depuration continues to be the contrapuntal agon between "hope," which he describes, according to the Polish proverb, as "the mother of the stupid," and "despair," which he takes to be "a cleanser, from desire, from hope."[52] Though we are not lacking for hope, at the beginning of our new century despair tends to be no less plentiful, usually of a silent variety, even among those who understand well the poetic legacy Herbert has left us, as is the case, for example, of the Nobel laureate Seamus Heaney, who keenly observes that Herbert's "true subject is survival of the valid self, of the city, of the good and the beautiful; or rather, the subject is the responsibility of each person to ensure that survival."[53] Nonetheless, Heaney and those like him, who understand Herbert's legacy well and are in positions to gainsay the silence enjoined by those at the top of the stairs "with a hushing finger always at the mouth,"[54] continue silent themselves. Our "cleansed" purity, then, appears to be assured. The "survival of the valid self, of the city" remains an open question.

7

The Labors of Cassandra

ARENDT IN JERUSALEM

> *Cassandra:* Yet I know Greek. I think I know it far too well.
> *Chorus:* And Pythian oracles are Greek, yet hard to read.
> —Aeschylus, *Agamemnon* (ll. 1254–55)

> The hostility against me is a hostility against someone who tells the truth on a factual level, and not against someone who has ideas which are in conflict with those commonly held.
> —Hannah Arendt, letter to Mary McCarthy, September 20, 1963

> The chances of factual truth surviving the onslaught of power are very slim indeed; it is always in danger of being maneuvered out of the world not only for a time but, potentially, forever. Facts and events are infinitely more fragile things than axioms, discoveries, theories—even the most wildly speculative ones—produced by the mind.
> —Hannah Arendt, "Truth and Politics"

I. The Trials of Posterity

Hannah Arendt was clear-eyed. Her writings cut close to the bone. Such insight and integrity cannot be forgiven, particularly in women, especially in patriarchal societies. Her letter of September 20, 1963, to her friend Mary McCarthy, cited as epigraph here, reveals a key distinction that should be most instructive for scholars and teachers of comparative literature. She differentiates among three elements that inevitably are at the heart of our pedagogy and scholarly practice—truth, facts, and ideas. She is chary of the truth of ideas; she is a target by virtue of adhering to the truth of facts. Facts and truth, we learn from our literary readings and we teach our students, in turn, are not always congruent, hence our constant differentiation in the teaching of poetry and fiction between what might be true and what might in fact be the case. This is a critical distinction that Arendt the philosopher understood reflexively. The hostility she confesses feeling comes from those for whom truth is absolute if it is their truth and facts are expedient grounds for their self-justification. And this is why, as she says in her essay "Truth and Politics," from which I take the second Arendt epigraph, power targets foremost factual truth, not the truth of ideas, convictions, or ideologies on which power itself is based. Her diligent laboring by the light of such distinctions is why Arendt became a target and has been as much on trial in Jerusalem and elsewhere as the Nazi defendant Eichmann on whose Jerusalem trial she reported in the work that is most associated with her name, *Eichmann in Jerusalem: A Report on the Banality of Evil* (1963).[1]

What has been deemed unforgivable is her pointing to certain facts that pertain to the thin line between retributive justice and distributive vengeance, the messy historical facts of collaboration by certain Jewish committees in Nazi atrocities, and, perhaps most egregious of all, the potential—long since realized—of the victims to turn into the victimizers. Thus, she was and, in some quarters, continues to be pilloried for divulging certain inconvenient historical truths, for reporting on the forensic and juridical facts of the moment in the Eichmann trials, and for her monitory prognoses of what might, could, and, as history amply demonstrates, is happening as the twentieth century's atrocities are carried over into the twenty-first by victims turned victimizers. Arendt understood the historical facts of her own predicament very well through her philosophical insight and her readings in classical tragedy, especially Aeschylus's trilogy the *Oresteia*, as well as her critical interest in the trials narrated by Franz Kafka. Her scrupulous negotiation of the intricacies of dramatic tragedy, narrative fiction, and tragic history, even while under siege by the hostility she was never able to overlook, as she writes to Mary McCarthy, is most instructive to the intellectual integrity of our scholarly and pedagogical endeavors. Having been turned into a Cassandra, a role she knew well from her classical readings, by "the onslaught of power,"[2] we, if no one else, must heed her testimony about the past, present, and future.

Cassandra, a barbarian who knew Greek "far too well," is forever cursed to recall what she herself did not live, and equally condemned to prophesy what would not be believed. She is excluded from the past she visibly remembers and is diminished in the future she sees all too clearly. Daughter of Troy's king, Priam, and sister of Paris, Cassandra confirmed the oracular destiny of her brother as material cause for the Trojan War and the city's destruction. She was reviled and cast into a dungeon by her own people for the clarity of her prescience on the future of her city. She would end up as war booty for Agamemnon, king of the victorious Achaeans. Neither of the past nor of the future, then, Cassandra is destined to be forever in the present. Her fate as sempiternal presence proves more immediately threatening to her perpetual contemporaries than the irredeemable content of her memory or the implacable portent of her prophetic visions. Mnemonically sentient to what was and presciently alert to what will be, Cassandra is the primal embodiment of perception, more given to elucidating the facticity of the phenomena perceived than the status of abstracted theorems and axioms ideationally conceived. In the *Agamemnon* tragedy of the *Oresteia*, Aeschylus dramatizes this distinction between seeing what is and conceiving what should be. Clytemnestra, Agamemnon's wife, and Cassandra, his war booty, stand as the dramatic embodiment of this counterpoint, with the first conceiving the plot of Agamemnon's regicide as retribution for what should not have been, while the latter recalls clearly the bloody history of the house of Atreus and sees the imminent facts of her new master's fate and of her own murder.[3]

Between seeing what is and conceiving what must be, then, the commandeering imperative of the latter overwhelms the indicative factuality of the former, just as the object of men's wooing (*Clytemnestra* means, literally, "praiseworthy wooing") exerts an infinitely greater power over men than someone who would see through their entanglements (*Cassandra* translates as "the entangler of men"). And while Aeschylus dramatized this agon and its indisputable outcome, Hannah Arendt, youthful reader of classical Greek,[4] has lived this contest under circumstances still cynically held in dispute, though the clarity of her monitory foresight continues to find its incontrovertible historical corroboration. Through Arendt, Cassandra's presence endures, as does the threat of her perennial visions, while the affairs of humans go on being governed by delusional desiderata more than by facts and factual insight. And Arendt distills the insoluble counterpoint that Aeschylus dramatized through the agon of Clytemnestra and Cassandra into the pointed questions that serve at once as Pythian apologia and as parrying ripostes against the incomprehension, perhaps genuine, but no less self-interested, that followed the publication of *Eichmann in Jerusalem*. Her questions read, in part: "Is it the very essence of truth to be impotent and for the very essence of power to be deceitful? And what kind of reality does truth possess if it is powerless in the public realm?"[5]

Arendt's questions go to the heart of our historical life, not least of our life's literary practices as writers or as scholars and teachers of literature, and they resonate not only with what Aeschylus already dramatized but also with what our contemporary writers, such as Mario Vargas Llosa, telegraph to us as "the truth of lies" (the equivocal Spanish phrase, "la verdad de las mentiras," could also be translated as "the truth about lies" and "the truth of fictions").[6] Arendt anticipates this novelist's multivalent formulation on truth, lies, and literature in the public realm by almost a half a century in her 1944 essay on Kafka, where she commemorates the twentieth anniversary of his death:

The novel-writer Franz Kafka was no novelist in the classical, the nineteenth-century, sense of the word. The basis for the classical novel was an acceptance of society as such, a submission to life as it happens, a conviction that greatness of destiny is beyond human virtues and human vice. It presupposed the decline of the citizen, who, during the days of the French Revolution, had attempted to govern the world with human laws. It pictured the growth of the bourgeois individual for whom life and the world had become a place of events and who desired more events and more happenings than the usually narrow and secure framework of his own life could offer him. Today these novels which were always in competition (even if imitating reality) with reality itself have been supplanted by the documentary novel. In our world real events, real destinies, have long surpassed the wildest imagination of novels.[7]

In supplanting the novel and its "wildest imagination," however, reality has assimilated fiction to its own truths. And if this mutual hybridization of fiction and reality had already compromised truth in Arendt's own tragic time, at the beginning of the twenty-first century our hyperreality moots the difference between the fictions of reality and the reality of truths. Vargas Llosa, as novelist and as would-be political operative,[8] partakes as much of reality's fictions as of its truths. In doing so, he corroborates Arendt's insight as well as the premonitions of Kafka, one of his unmistakable novelistic precursors:

> .... Perhaps the best way to define a closed society would be to say that in it fiction and history have ceased to be distinct and have become fused, supplanting each other and constantly exchanging their identities as in a masquerade.
>
> In a closed society power not only arrogates to itself the privilege of controlling the actions of people—what they say and what they do—; it aspires as well to govern their fantasy and their dreams and, of course, their memory. In a closed society the past is, sooner or later, an object of manipulation aimed at justifying the present. ... Organizing collective memory, turning history into an instrument of government charged with legitimating those who rule and furnishing alibis for their misdeeds is a congenital temptation of all power. Totalitarian states are capable of turning all this into reality. ... In a closed society history is impregnated with fiction, it becomes fiction, since it is invented and reinvented in the service of orthodoxy, religious and political, of the moment, or, to put it more bluntly, in conformity with the caprices of those who possess power.
>
> At the same time, a strict system of censorship tends to be instituted so that literature also fantasizes within rigid channels, so that its subjective truths divulge and illustrate, rather than contradict or cloud over official history. The difference between historical truth and literary truth disappears into a hybrid that tinges history with unreality and empties fiction of all mystery, that blanches out any initiative and nonconformity within the establishment.[9]

Vargas Llosa glosses "closed society" here to mean the society of "estados totalitarios," what Hannah Arendt analytically diagnosed as "totalitarianism" and "proto-totalitarianism" in her 1951 philosophical treatise on the morphology of this phenomenon.[10] And the "closed" nature of such societies intensifies commensurately with the degree of totality in the practices of totalitarianism, arriving at what Arendt termed "total domination," what in our time at the beginning of the twenty-first century is designated in the 2001 National Defense Strategy of the United States of America as "full spectrum dominance." Arendt's characterization of such totalitarianism reads as policy blueprint and as script for practices of twenty-first-century realpolitik, most egregiously in, but by no means limited to that baleful swath of the planet that extends from the eastern shores of the Mediterranean to the mountain passes of Hindu Kush and the Straits of Hormuz: "It is in the very nature of totalitarian regimes to demand unlimited power. Such power can only be secured if literally all men, without a single exception, are reliably dominated in every aspect of their life. In the realm of foreign affairs new neutral territories must constantly be subjugated, while at home ever-new human groups must be mastered in expanding concentration camps, or, when circumstances require, liquidated to make room for others. The question of opposition is unimportant both in foreign and domestic affairs. Any neutrality, indeed any spontaneously given friendship, is from the standpoint of totalitarian domination just as dangerous as open hostility, precisely because spontaneity as such, with its incalculability, is the greatest obstacle to total domination over man."[11] Practices of "total domination," then, seek to ensure hermetic enclosure around their targets, thereby decisively maximizing the efficacy of their strategically manufactured truths and the impunity of their tactical deployment. This is what allows them to define and control, if not supplant outright, reality's truths and reality's fictions. Arendt notes: "Just as the stability of the totalitarian regime depends on the isolation of the fictitious world of the movement from the outside world, so the experiment of total domination . . . depends on sealing off the latter against the world of others, the world of the living in general, even against the outside world of a country under totalitarian rule. This isolation explains the peculiar unreality and lack of credibility that characterizes all reports from the . . .[12] Arendt's diagnosis makes necessary the enjambment on the definite article and the opening of an ellipsis at the end of this citation, a blank that can be filled in with any number of place names around the world at the beginning of the twenty-first century. This is because the twentieth-century history she describes has emerged as a template in the twenty-first, despite the fact that Arendt deemed "the monstrosities of [her] century" to be "of a horrible novelty . . . [though] dark times . . . are no rarity in history."[13]

What was "of a horrible novelty" has proved to be an inexorable historical precedent, as Arendt well suspected it might: "It is essentially for this reason: that the unprecedented, once it has appeared, may become a precedent for the future."[14] The "concentration camps" that could fill the elliptical blank in the dark times of her description have morphed into internment centers and refugee camps of open-ended duration and their sadistically dead-end human realities. These baleful sites are called Guantánamo, Falluja, Kandahar, Baghdad, Grozny, Balata, Darfur, Kabul, Jenin, or Gaza, among an indeterminate number of "holes of oblivion,"[15] as Arendt referred to what now, in the biopolitics of our twenty-first century and its carceral regimes, proliferate as "black holes." What all these baneful places have in common, and what they share with the concentration camps of the last century is the demographic management and biopolitical maneuvering of people on the basis of ethnicity or race, merciless denigration of people's humanity, subjection of their territory and their bodies to experiments of chemical, nuclear, and nanotechnological robotic armaments.[16] These are places notorious for the political manufacture of what Arendt called "pariah peoples,"[17] who, at best, are the object of our compassion, which she deems a mixed blessing in its "mischief," and, at worst, the object of our cruelty, which she considers the opposite of compassion and defines as "a perversion, a feeling of pleasure where pain would naturally be felt."[18]

The "dark times" Arendt discerned at mid-twentieth century have metamorphosed, or more accurately have metastasized, on a global scale. And her description of what she understands by "dark times" serves as a resonant mirror for what is today the besieged city, the siege of the polis and its "public realm," which Arendt always considered central to the more benign possibilities of our humanity and its putative civilizations. Her diagnostic descriptions of "dark times" have indeed turned out to be prognostications of our present and its constructed fictions, whose political codes of doublespeak overshadow the arts of fiction and supplant the truths of reality. And, like the Bertolt Brecht poem in which the phrase originates, Arendt's visionary insight does indeed reach down to us, as the title of Brecht's work "To Posterity," clearly intended that it should. Arendt writes in her preface to the 1968 edition of *Men in Dark Times*:

> I borrow the term from Brecht's famous poem "To Posterity," which mentions the disorder and the hunger, the massacres and the slaughters, the outrage over injustice and the despair "when there was only wrong and no outrage," the legitimate hatred that makes you ugly nevertheless, the well-founded wrath that makes the voice grow hoarse. All this was real enough as it took place in public; there was nothing secret or mysterious about it. And still, it was by no means visible to all, nor was it at all easy to perceive it; for, until the very moment when catastrophe overtook everything and everybody, it was covered up not by realities but by highly efficient talk and double-talk of nearly all official representatives who, without interruption and in many ingenious variations, explained away unpleasant facts and justified concerns. . . . If it is the function of the public realm to throw light on the affairs of men by providing a space of appearances in which they can show

in deed and word, for better and worse, who they are and what they can do, the darkness has come when this light is extinguished by "credibility gaps" and "invisible government," by speech that does not disclose what is but sweeps it under the carpet, by exhortations, moral and otherwise, that under the pretext of upholding old truths, degrade all truth to meaningless triviality.

Nothing of this is new.[19]

Arendt anticipates unerringly what history constrains us, yet again, to reiterate at the beginning of the twenty-first century—"Nothing of this is new." Her prescience is corroborated by what we witness in the ongoing brutality of dislocation, mass-scale management, and brutalization of human bodies, even as the methods of domination escalate to a postindustrial biopolitics that is infinitely more efficient, remote-sensing, robotic, more hygienically dehumanized and self-perpetuating in the infliction of the technologically most advanced forms of violence on "pariah" communities (translocated or besieged *in situ*). Aiming for maximal effect and enduring carnage, the human habitations of such targets are subjected to mass ecological depredations for an indefinite future through the sawing of time-delayed cluster bombs and perpetually toxic "depleted" uranium. The only novelty, then, is a qualitative refinement in the enhanced capacity for catastrophe creation, along with a commensurate intensification of self-righteousness and stridency in the expedient bending of reality. Our communicative technologies and enhanced abilities to breach the actual and the virtual now enable "official representatives," as Arendt calls them, not only "to degrade all truth to meaningless triviality," but, often with religious sadism and exquisite righteousness, to moot the very notion of truth and to gerrymander any meaning. And here, in this commonplace, which Arendt understood as "the public realm," and which others call the public sphere, where she would have us "throw light on the affairs of men by providing a space of appearances in which they can show in deed and word, for better and worse, who they are and what they can do," now all light is strategically refracted, never "extinguished," so that neither darkness nor clarity are any longer possible. The blaring light is blinding and the decibel level deafening. Under the full-spectrum intensity of this panopticon and its media-amplified ubiquity,[20] the public sphere is rendered congruent with and inalienable from the zone of "total domination." The result for human life today, then, as when Arendt diagnosed such circumstances in 1945, essentially remains constant. Anyone who might now be reading her, *mutatis mutandis*, with any comprehension in Jerusalem, New York, Beirut, Brussels, Tel Aviv, London, Baghdad, Washington, Kandahar, Paris, Beit Hanoun, Berlin, or Gaza City could amply attest to this constancy: "The totalitarian policy, which has completely destroyed the neutral zone in which the daily life of human beings is ordinarily lived, has achieved the result of making the existence of each individual . . . depend either upon committing crimes or on complicity in crimes."[21] Universalizing responsibility has always been a tactic for cover of large-scale criminality and for the obfuscation of actionable imputability for criminal acts. Organizing guilt in this tactical fashion blurs the lines between truth and fiction by rendering credibility problematic, by turning facts into opinion, and by shouting down or browbeating all opposing "opinions" into silence. Thus, most effectively screened out in this strategy is the factual truth of the victim, as is the reality of the acts of victimization, a strategy that continues to prove effective in shifting responsibility of crimes from the perpetrators unto their victims.

Magnitude and intensity of violence are the prerogative of perpetrators, and history has taught them that the more outrageous the acts of criminality the greater the possibility of impunity. This, Arendt says, is "what the Nazis have always known," and this is the regime of impunity that serves as operative principle at the beginning of the twenty-first century in places that would hardly surprise Arendt's monitory prognoses but would certainly chagrin her incorruptible sense of ethics: "Men [and, now, we can affirmatively say, women] determined to commit crimes will find it expedient to organize them on the vastest, most improbable scale. Not only because this renders all punishments provided by the legal system inadequate and absurd; but because the very immensity of the crimes guarantee that the murderers who proclaim their innocence with all manner of lies will be more readily believed than the victims who tell the truth."[22]

Arendt's own credibility has been mooted twice over in this regard, first questioned by those whom she escaped as a Jew at mid-twentieth century and, then, derogated by those who, often refugees themselves, felt implicated, *post factum* or *a priori*, in her historical diagnoses, thereby converting her insight into self-fulfilling prophecies, which, like the prophecies of Cassandra, would be preemptively dismissed into implausibility, even as their horrors continue to be realized; even as she, herself, saw them being realized: "Because their horror at what might have been still haunts them, they often introduce into discussions of this kind that insufferable tone of self-righteousness which frequently . . . can turn into the vulgar obverse of Nazi doctrines—and in fact already has."[23]

At the beginning of the twenty-first century, the transference Arendt describes is well beyond speculation, as the daily horrors and their toll on the lives and property of the new "pariah people" now go without saying, just as the perpetrators intend that they should. Arendt's admonitions still resonate, though their derogation is no less vehement. And even when her monitory relevance is brought forth, the actual atrocities whose potential she had already foreseen are glossed over, the would-have-been victims now turned perpetrators are shielded as politically unmentionable taboo subjects, fortified with impunity behind the unspeakable criminality of their acts. Such glossing over into silence at a moment identified by Brecht, and cited by Arendt, as a moment "when there was only wrong and no outrage,"[24] has proved to be the most expedient tack even among Arendt's own students, in whom she had instilled fully the acumen of ethical insight but whom she could not fortify sufficiently in the courage of their convictions, or who are not permitted to exercise such courage, either by political pressure or by self-censorship, lest we have nothing to read by them about their former teacher if it were not for their circumspection.[25] This, as Arendt anticipated, is *a fortiori* a decisive management of fiction and reality characteristic of the first decade of the twenty-first century and its regimes of "total domination," whose repercussions are, perforce, even operative here, on this page, today, as I am obliged to look over my shoulder while I write this memo to/on Arendt. No doubt, there is something of Kafka in these trying times that demand we be circumspect in the face of demonstrable precedent in which, like factual truth, our own chances of "surviving the onslaught of power are very slim indeed," since we too, as Arendt says, are "always in danger of being maneuvered out of the world not only for a time but, potentially, forever."[26]

Hannah Arendt, anticipated this predicament and forecast its difficulty, especially for humanists and the disciplinary fields we refer to as "the humanities"—the scientific field of those who must seek to explain conditions they themselves simultaneously embody. The most pointed diagnostic moment of this predicament is in Arendt's discussion of Kafka's *The Trial*, where K, the perplexed protagonist, must countenance the dilemma of "truth" and "necessity." Confounded by the absurdity of his ordeal, in

Arendt's own expository paraphrase, K "hires an advocate, who tells him at once that the only sensible thing to do is to adapt oneself to existing conditions and not to criticize them. He turns to the prison chaplain for advice, and the chaplain preaches the hidden greatness of the system and orders him not to ask for the truth, 'for it is not necessary to accept everything as true, one must accept it as necessary.' 'A melancholy conclusion,' said K.; 'it turns lying into a universal principle.'"[27] We now have whole nations, not just national and state institutions, constructed and operating on the basis of such self-justifying necessity.

Like "the modern reader," whose "understanding of Kafka reveals more about himself than about Kafka,"[28] our critical understanding of Kafka says a good deal about our literary and philosophical discourses and about our worldly reality. Principally, it says that we are no less constrained to make a virtue of necessity than literary and philosophical practices have been obliged to do since the time of Socrates in "democratic" Athens. While we have thought to have transcended such predicaments in our emancipatory history of enlightened modernity, and even though we speak today, in what some take to be a postmodern era, philosophically, technologically, cybernetically, and biologically of "the posthuman," far from a sign of our having transcended the predicaments of the human, more often than not, the "post-" turns out to be an ideology or institutional structure we are bound to and a cross we must bear. In our institutional predicaments, though this difficulty is central to our human sciences and the place of the humanities within the university, humanists themselves are often prone to elide such thorny "complications" that circumscribe and define us. Could this be because K's last words continue to haunt us as insuperable legacy? "It was as if he meant the shame of it to outlive him." Kafka anticipates what Foucault would define as governmentality, the self-regulating strictures of the human subject. Administrative cadres and university governance, not infrequently, seize upon this impulse for reflection that turns into self-derogation, calibrating in their calculus for policy formation, resource allocation, and institutional prioritization through the prism of this self-reckoning on the part of self-questioning humanists. What in the humanist might be a self-decentering reflexive critique of the humanities is interpreted by those whom Kafka identified as functionaries of necessity as a weakness, as incoherence inimical to organizational cogency and governability. This expedient incomprehension on the part of governing subjects and administrative cadres may itself be a symptom of the human and its institutional illusions of self-transcendence into exculpatory epistemologies and organizational command posts of knowledge management. Projecting managerial strength, in other words, may be a defensive way of hiding one's own sense of vulnerability within a system that instrumentalizes its human agents. This form of institutionalized self-absolution from the human predicament and its checkered history is what Arendt's exegetic perspicacity teaches us to read and discern, even if we cannot allay its symptoms, much less ameliorate its nature that we ourselves embody.

Writing in 1945 on the heels of war and its unprecedented depredations for humanity, Arendt saw "elemental shame" as the unifying ingredient of the human. If not utterly shameless, we have by now become somewhat inured to that sentiment. The "political terms" of that common quality she discerned then have attained somewhat greater complexity, though the Hobbesian "natural law" that Arendt adduced in attempting to explain the unexplainable has not been superseded by our humanity, nor do our human acts lend themselves to human explanation or comprehensibility any more than the incomprehensible inhumanity she strained to diagnose. In January 1945 Arendt writes, as a German, as a Jew, as a human:

> For many years now we have met Germans who declare that they are ashamed of being German. I have often felt tempted to answer that I am ashamed of being human. This elemental shame, which many people of the most various nationalities share with one another today, is what finally is left of our sense of international solidarity; and it has not yet found an adequate political expression. Our fathers' enchantment with humanity was of a sort which not only light-mindedly ignored the national question; what is far worse, it did not conceive of the terror of the idea of humanity and of the Judeo-Christian faith in the unitary origin of the human race.[29]

As a universal "sense of international solidarity," shame, alas, has proved a far less than "adequate political principle" for deterring "the terror" blithely overlooked by "our fathers' enchantment with humanity," as Arendt phrases it. In fact, what she dreaded most—the overlooked potential of the national question and of the Judeo-Christian faith's idea of "the unitary origin of the human race"—has proved true to her greatest fears, with terror rather than shame serving as the operative principle that links "the international community" in a death clasp through the "national question" and Judeo-Christian axiology, now expanded to incorporate in that deadly embrace the other member of the Abrahamic tradition, Islam, and, through this Abrahamic trinity, the rest of the globe and its national redoubts, all now wrapped in defensive-aggressive postures of homelands of (in)security. The enchantment of "our fathers" that Arendt speaks of, that Enlightenment romanticism of the universal man and perpetual peace, shattered itself numerous times, starting with the French Revolution, the Napoleonic "empire," imperial-colonial Europe in its civilizing missions on dark continents, two world wars, and the still ongoing ravages of their aftermath in the geographical cradle of the Abrahamic tradition.

We too spoke, until recently, in a language of enchantment of a postnational, postcolonial, postmodern era. And our disciplinary discourses have left an ample scholarly heap in the archive on these subjects. At present, however, we too recognize the "light-minded" enchantment of this discourse in the face of the world's harsh realities, no matter how well disguised and glossed over by hegemony's doublespeak. And the severity of history proves as chastening for our discourse "posted" in illusions of postmodernism, postcolonialism, and postnationalism as the enchantment Arendt inherited proved for her as she faced the destruction of the past and moved backward, like the angel of history, into the future that is now us. If, as Walter Benjamin would have it, the angel of history would have it that our human progress be a relay through destruction,[30] Arendt has passed on the relay torch to us. We see history by its light and the future in the shadow of her admonitions, now congruent and coterminous with the shadow of our physical reality and the implacable present of our contemporary realpolitik. Hitler's observation when he finally ceased his collaboration with the Zionists and their project of selecting "suitable material" for survival in Palestine has proved to be his curse for posterity.[31] He said, according to Arendt's citation, "they could not 'jump over their own shadow.'"[32] Nor can we, as it turns out.

The torch Arendt passed to us casts its own silhouette of enchantment. She says,

> In political terms, the idea of humanity, excluding no people and assigning a monopoly of guilt to no one, is the only guarantee that one "superior race" after another may not feel obligated to follow the "natural law" of the right of the powerful, and exterminate "inferior races unworthy of survival"; so that at the end

of an "imperialistic age" we should find ourselves in a stage which would make the Nazis look like crude precursors of future political methods. To follow a non-imperialistic policy and maintain a non-racist faith becomes daily more difficult because it becomes daily clearer how great a burden mankind is for man.[33]

In our own time, the difficulty Arendt cites becomes more insurmountable than ever, and not because of how clear man's burden is for mankind, as she puts it, but chiefly because the political construct she terms "mankind" is more frayed than ever, which, in effect, splinters that congeries of humanity into tribal, racial, and ethno-nationalist fragments in contention. The "natural law" of the right of the powerful trumps every other law,[34] inexorably leading to the realization of Arendt's worst fears, namely, turning the Nazis into "crude precursors" of the new century's political methods and imperial neocolonial impulses, most vehemently, and most ironically, often by people not unfamiliar with the horrors inflicted on humanity in Arendt's own century.

Her own historical intuition has proved far from being immune to irony, however. It appears now that the perverse turns of history render Arendt's admonitions into yet another instance of wishful thinking analogous to the idealism she critiqued in the "enchantment" of our Enlightenment forefathers. Thus, while Arendt would have us practice an equitable distribution of culpability, "assigning a monopoly of guilt to no one" so as to foreclose on anyone's presumption to determine who might or might not belong to "inferior races unworthy of survival," there are indeed those who make and enforce stronger claims, who arrogate such monopolistic privilege over life and death to themselves, along with guaranteeing a supremacist role of self-exemption from any law, guilt, or equitable distribution of responsibility. Such exceptionalist dispensation comes, naturally, with a righteous self-exculpatory presumption, invariably the privilege of one or another god's self-perceived chosen people exercising decisive judgment over the life and death of others. We find ourselves, then, firmly in the grip of the terror Arendt saw as potentially implicit in that enchanted myth of "the idea of humanity and of the Judeo-Christian faith in the unitary origin of the human race."[35] Not "the element of shame," then, but terrorism, in the panoply of its practices by national states, supranational state unions, and by stateless transnational coalitions, is now the common denominator and universal measure of "international solidarity." Those with superior technical and propagandistic means who are able to dominate terror, its strategic management and tactical practice, are the most determined to exclude the laws and scrutiny of the international community and seal off their operational theater, lest "incalculability" compromise "total domination" over their human and territorial targets.[36]

II. Cassandra and the Poets: Goodness Beyond Virtue, Wickedness Beyond Vice

Hannah Arendt writes:

> If we want to know what absolute goodness would signify for the course of human affairs (as distinguished from the course of divine matters), we had better turn to the poets, and we can do it safely enough as long as we remember that "the poet but embodies in verse those exaltations of sentiment that a nature like Nelson's, the opportunity being given, vitalizes into acts" (Melville). At least we can learn from them that absolute goodness is hardly any less dangerous than absolute evil, that it does not consist of selflessness, for surely the Grand Inquisitor [Dostoyevsky] is selfless enough, and that it is beyond virtue, even the virtue of Captain Vere. Neither Rousseau nor Robespierre was capable of dreaming of a goodness beyond virtue, just as they were unable to imagine that radical evil [Kant] would "partake nothing of the sordid or of the sensual (Melville)," that there could be wickedness beyond vice.[37]

Arendt's triangulation of Immanuel Kant, Fyodor Dostoyevsky, and Herman Melville in this passage from her treatise *On Revolution* (1963), written at a time when she was redacting her reportage and subsequent book on Eichmann's 1961 trial and hanging in Jerusalem, opens a window on the complexities of truth, of good, and of evil she was able to discern. Her vicissitudes in the conveyance of that vision have proved as consequential for Arendt's posterity as Cassandra's prophecies continue to prove for hers. In this triangulation of trials—the drum-head court aboard the H.M.S. *Bellipotent* in Melville's *Billy Budd* (written 1886–91), the "Grand Inquisitor" scene from Dostoyevsky's *Brothers Karamazov* (1879–80), and the vicissitudes of censorship and royal reprimand of Kant by the Prussian emperor Friedrich Wilhelm II, who forbade any further treatment of religion by Kant following the publication of his *Religion Within the Boundaries of Human Reason* in 1793—Arendt has given us a three-dimensional prism through which to read her own trials loosed by the controversy of her *Eichmann in Jerusalem: A Report on the Banality of Evil.* That she should have us turn to the poets to understand the implications of such predicaments is not inconsistent with Arendt's wariness toward technical philosophy and its axiomatic epistemologies, or with her suspicion of political theory and its abstracted theorems. Arendt continues to be more Cassandra than Clytemnestra in her adherence to facts and in her refusal to subordinate the reality of fictions (often muscular, though invariably inconvenient) to the fictions of ideas (inevitably apposite, no matter how problematic).

Why this unholy trinity of Kant, Melville, and Dostoyevsky as frame for Arendt's most renowned and controversial work? The first paragraph of chapter 28 of Melville's *Billy Budd* may suggest the answer: "The symmetry of form attainable in pure fiction cannot so readily be achieved in a narration essentially having less to do with fable than with fact. Truth uncompromisingly told will always have its ragged edges; hence the conclusion of such a narration is apt to be less finished than an architectural finial."[38] Uncompromisingly committed to the reality of fact as much as Arendt has been, the Melville cited here shares in her suspicion of the "absolute" and the "pure" whether in fiction or in truth. In his poetic ambiguity, Melville partakes of the complexities of fact and truth as imputed to human responsibility, just as Kant's "radical evil" as self-incurred is made the responsibility of the individual, as opposed to original sin's hereditary nature, much like Dostoyevsky's Ivan, the Grand Inquisitor, and his "poem" on moral regeneration as personal responsibility would have it. The ragged edges of reality's truth, in Melville's terms, is what lies at the heart of Dostoyevsky's *Brothers Karamazov* and its patricide, with the novel having had its real-life genesis in Dostoyevsky's acquaintance with the falsely accused and condemned Ilyinsky, whom Dostoyevsky got to know while serving his own sentence of hard labor in Siberia and who was exonerated when another man finally confessed to the murder of Ilyinski's father. Melville's manuscript of *Billy Budd* would be put away in a bread box by his wife upon his death in 1891, not to be found and published until 1924; Kant's attribution of personal responsibility for moral action and the grace of salvation would border on the heresy of Palegianism (salvation on the basis of self-initiative rather than by means of God's grace); and Dostoyevsky's enactment of a Second Coming by the apocalyptically named Ivan ("John," as in John of Patmos of the Book of Revelation) would compound ambiguity by bringing forth an expressionless Messiah that comes and goes without a word, whose only communicative act is a parting kiss on the Grand Inquisitor's parched lips, the kiss of Judas anticipated by Christ (Luke 22:47–48; John 18:3–12), perhaps, finally delivered by Christ himself on the lips of an ambiguously embodied anti-Christ, the Grand Inquisitor.

Arendt assumes this ternary inheritance at a historical moment not unlike ours, eras more prone to disambiguation and the perils of absolute virtue, otherwise ambiguously dramatized as the dangers of absolutist self-righteousness by all three writers she takes as her precursors. The spirit of Aeschylus still hovers over this scene, since such absolutes resonate with Clytemnestra's incontestable conviction and implacable resentment that awaited Cassandra at Agamemnon's palace. And what Cassandra has in common with Melville's Billy Budd and the returned Christ in Dostoyevsky's Grand Inquisitor scene is speechlessness and incommunicability—Cassandra is incomprehensible despite her knowledge of Greek, the Jesus in Ivan's "poem" remains silent before the Grand Inquisitor, and Billy Budd is afflicted by a stutter that leaves him speechless in the face of false accusation, with deadly force as his only communicative response. Kant, of course, is silenced on the question of religion by royal edict, a prohibition he adheres to until the Prussian emperor's death, when he would finally express himself on questions of imposed silence and on compartmentalized inarticulateness of thought and speech in his preface to *The Conflict of the Faculties* (1798).[39] Communication, or human articulateness, by which we should understand human linkage and human eloquence, is at the heart of what Arendt recalls for us from Aristotle as the crux of political life, the life of the polis that distinguishes the human being as *zōōn logon ēkhon*, a living being capable of speech and polity (*politeia*), where being *anêa logou*, without speech, deprives one of the possibility of human coexistence, which is to say, the possibility of being human among human beings, *inter homines esse*, according to the patristic Aristotelians. In the political sense, where lexis (speech), along with praxis (action), defines life in the polis, this coexistence means being in conversation. In these cases, which Arendt takes as frame of reference, speech, or conversation, suffers a critical disruption.[40] And Arendt diagnosed this lack of articulateness and subsequent human detachment in Eichmann as key to his pathology of dehumanization that enabled inhuman acts of radical evil and "wickedness beyond vice": "He was incapable of uttering a single sentence that was not a cliché.... The longer one listened to him, the more obvious it became that his inability to speak was closely connected with an inability to *think*, namely, to think from the standpoint of somebody else."[41] This is the individual analogue to the "closed society" of totalitarianism and absolute domination, when a society closes in on itself in a collective form of exceptionalist solipsism and self-righteous unthinking. The result, as much in the inarticulate individual as in the disarticulated society, is an unwillingness to admit to the possibility of a viewpoint or historical narrative other than one's own, which makes anyone else's right to any human rights existentially threatening and unthinkable.

This, then, is the poetic context Arendt invokes for her *Eichmann in Jerusalem* with uncanny prescience of the incomprehension and controversy with which the absolutism of her time would receive her reports. The trial she reported turned out to be also a trial of reporting and a trial of truth. The subtitle of Arendt's work, *A Report on the Banality of Evil*, ends by disclosing the evil of banality no less than the banality of evil, thereby conflating the banality of the accused and the banality of the absolutist system trying him, which proved itself no more capable of exercising the faculty of thinking than was the criminal subject on trial. Herein lies the seed of vehemence driving the animus of Arendt's vilification and her own trials: banality's evil can be as radical, as evil itself can be banal. The treatment of evil as all-too-human and, therefore, sempiternal in human history—past and, potentially, future—most threatens those who cannot differentiate between understanding the phenomenon of evil and its justification, or who fear such differentiation and understanding, lest they be implicated.[42] The chiasmus that runs from convicted criminal to clamoring community and from the gallows to the gallery moves in both directions, with one absolutism (wickedness beyond vice of the tried and convicted) finding its mirrored reflection in another (in the absolute virtue and the resultant self-incrimination of those doing the trying). Kant's scene of radical evil, by which Arendt would have us understand the dehumanization of the human and the depoliticization of political life, becomes embodied and enacted, yet again, in her historic diagnoses as it was in the trinity of Melville's Billy Budd, Claggart, and Captain Vere, and in the trinity of Dostoyevsky's Ivan, Jesus, and the Grand Inquisitor. At the end of the day, the executed are dispensed with; they become the haunting specters of narrative (poetic, religious, historic, or criminal). Just as significantly, however,

Arendt and *her* trinity of assumed precursors would appear to implicate for trial those enabling criteria that legitimate the juridical action, its historical process, and, most ominously, those who sit in judgment.

By this reckoning, the tried, already convicted, sentenced, and executed, leave behind the ongoing trial of those doing the trying. Thus, the perpetual oscillation between victims and victimizers continues to propel the baneful itinerary of human history. At present, we are reading Arendt, and through Arendt her poetic and philosophical predecessors, in new trying times, when the reality of wickedness beyond vice and the possibility of goodness beyond virtue contend and implicate us inexorably in their perennial agon.

8

The People's Republic and the Republic of Letters
THE ALARMING GAO XINGJIAN

> Since it was announced that I received the Nobel Prize in Literature, the Chinese Foreign Ministry has condemned my works and criticized them harshly. All of my works are now banned from getting into China or being published in China. How many authors are there who want to return to the country that banned his or her books?
> —Gao Xingjian

I. The State of the National Subject

It took a century for the legacy of Chinese explosives technology to converge with Chinese literature in the Swedish capital. The centurial edition of the Nobel Prize in Literature, founded in the munificence of Alfred Nobel and a fortune based on dynamite, burst open the simmering perplexities on the notions of national language, national affiliation, and national literature as indices that identify literary culture and its authors. Gao Xingjian, Chevalier de l'ordre des arts et des lettres, occasioned a diplomatic incident, with State Council Premier Zhu Rongji of the People's Republic of China simultaneously condemning and commending the turn of events,[1] congratulating the minister of culture of France on Gao's being awarded the Nobel Prize for Literature for the year 2000, and at once disparaging and lauding the Swedish Nobel Committee for its choice of laureate.[2] In the intricacy of diplomatic protocols, the ambivalence and studied indirections of these official acts entail, simultaneously, disavowal and realignment.

The 2000 Nobel Prize in Literature threw into question the traditional congruence among nation, language, literature, and the writer's self-defining affiliation, an alignment we and the Nobel Committee in Stockholm have taken for granted since the eighteenth century, that is, since every literary tradition found itself consigned to a language and to a country called a nation with definable philological and political borders. In keeping with this tradition, during the course of its hundred-year history the Nobel Committee invariably has crafted its citation for the prize to include the laureate's national language, national origin, and literary culture as coextensive with these philological and political borders. In the case of Gao Xingjian, the Nobel Foundation's announcement, in which the citation is embedded, reads: "The Nobel Prize in Literature for 2000 goes to the Chinese writer Gao Xingjian 'for an œuvre of universal validity, bitter insights and linguistic ingenuity, which has opened new paths for the Chinese novel and drama.'"[3] The announcement and citation date from October 12, 2000. By December 10, 2000, the date of the presentation of the prize at the royal banquet in Stockholm's storied Concert Hall, there is a subtle but significant emendation to the provenance of "the Chinese writer." The Nobel laureate Gao is now identified as hailing from the Chinese language of which he is a native. China becomes a country he left behind. The opening of the paragraph that serves as the delicately nuanced peroration by Professor Göran Malmqvist of the Nobel Foundation, who presented the prize to Gao, reads: "Dear Gao Xingjian: You did not leave China empty-handed. You have come to look on the native language which you brought with you when you left China as your true and real country."[4] The Nobel Foundation's Web site that lists all laureates identifies the 2000 Literature Prize winner with the citation and a photo of the writer captioned as follows: "Gao Xingjian / France / b. 1940 / (in Ganzhou, China)."[5]

These evolving permutations in the Nobel Foundation's portrayal of Gao betray a compelling metamorphosis of the author's Chineseness, and point as well to certain transformations in the nature of Gao's national identity. The official response of simultaneous disavowal and reclamation of Gao as a dissident national subject by the Chinese state upon the announcement of the prize, no doubt, played a role in these subtle modulations. We can read this recalibration as the outcome of an encounter between the People's Republic and "the Republic of Letters," to echo a resonant phrase from a recent study on the life of literature in the world system of culture and its realpolitik.⁶ This raises a number of key questions with regard to the role of the state, the nation, the individual, and supranational institutions such as the Nobel Prize in the formation of culture, literary culture, especially, and identity, all enmeshed in issues that have haunted Gao as a writer and that have found their dramatic representation in the author's literary corpus and in his critical assessments.

It is not altogether irrelevant to the notion of "the Republic of Letters" that Gao has arrived at the Nobel Prize through France. In this regard, the genesis of the notional construct "the Republic of Letters" finds some vindication, and the phrase is felicitous. And attributing to Paris the status of capital and Archimedean fulcrum that leverages, defines, legitimates, and governs the letters and denizens of said Republic of Letters and its global satellites on the planetary periphery of Parisian cosmopolitan centrality might not be altogether without some historical basis. One would wish, however, that such momentous claims were being made by someone other than a French national and a resident of Paris, so as to mitigate the risk of assimilating the claimant to those she refers to as "the monopolists of universality [who] command others to submit to their law."⁷ On the "autonomization" of literature from local and national strictures and circumscriptions, a requisite emancipatory threshold for passage into the Republic of Letters, Pascale Casanova notes: "This new degree of autonomy came about as a result of the structural complementarity obtaining between the Nobel Prize and the power of consecration enjoyed by Paris. In effect, the Academy affirmed (or reaffirmed) the verdicts of the capital of literature and, as it were, grounded them in law: by making these decisions official, the Swedish Academy—with few exceptions at least through the 1960s—endorsed, ratified, and made public the judgments of Paris."⁸ In the shadow of such portentous claims lies the melancholy reminder of that alternative hexagon to Victor Hugo's and Pascale Casanova's overweening and highly localized nationalist geography. Inevitably, one thinks of that Republic of Letters characterized by the Argentine Jorge Luis Borges as "the Library of Babel," one constructed, in the words of Robert Burton's *Anatomy of Melancholy*, on "the variation of twenty-three letters" of the alphabet, "whose exact center is any hexagon and whose circumference is unattainable."⁹

The obvious question, one which Gao addresses in his writings, most notably in "Without Isms,"¹⁰ his own "declaration of independence" as a writer, is whether the epithet *Republic*, when linked to *People's* or to *Letters*, is destined inevitably to take on hegemonic, imperial entailments. Salient in this encounter between the People's Republic and the Republic of Letters is the question of what defines nation and nationality. Clearly, the criteria for nation and nationality and the official management of those criteria are not always congruent. Gao's case highlights this disjunction that we have often overlooked, persuaded by a historical presumption that a subject's nation and his or her nationality are one and the same. Equally suggestive in this case is the reminder that the culture of the nation and the culture of the state are not necessarily coterminous, even though the two cultures might inhabit the same country, defined by the same borders as a national territory.[11] Not only Gao's case at the historic moment of his being awarded the Nobel Prize but also Gao's work as a narrative of individual and national self-construction adumbrate the intricacies of the human predicament as national subject and cultural identity in any given terrain called a nation.

We know from historical precedent that state formations and their governing regimes labor mightily to render themselves identical with the nation they govern. This desideratum is referred to as sovereignty and part of the sovereign privilege exercised by the official regimes of state is to declare or trigger the declaration of certain people as stateless. The text of the presentation of the Nobel Prize to Gao by Professor Göran Malmqvist would seem to indicate, or would wish to declare, that an individual disavowed by the official governing regime of a state might indeed be stateless within the sovereign jurisdiction of that state, or even within the interstate world system, but the subject is certainly not "nationless," in the sense of the individual not belonging to, or being disposed of, any national culture.

Historical precedent and realpolitik have vested the state with the privilege of conferring legal status of affiliation called nationality or citizenship. A person declared stateless by the state, according to the United Nations (itself, clearly, a wishful nomination and, no less, a strategic one, since the organization's congeries is not an aggregate of nations but of their governing regimes or states),[12] such a person has no citizenship, no documented means of travel (no passport), no refugee status, and no ability to claim asylum in another country. As a stateless person, legally, he or she is fleeing from nowhere and nowhere is obliged to offer refuge. Such an individual, in the juridical language of the state, is "an undocumented alien," a phrase that could just as well describe a being from an unknown species or from another planet. The only hope for such persons resides in the breach of international conventions among sovereign states and the refusal of some states to adhere to the privilege of absolute sovereignty all states purportedly enjoy, at least since 1648 when the Treaty of Westphalia ended the Thirty Years War, in part by making nation, state, and sovereignty coterminous in reaction to the popes' universal claims of imperium and hegemonic exertions of Holy Roman Emperors. Absolute adherence to consensus on sovereignty would indeed leave many persons absolutely belonging nowhere, or, at best, only belonging in that legal breach where one state opts to contravene interstate conventions and confer lawful status upon such an individual. Were states willing to adhere to absolute consensus, rarely a less than ominous possibility, or should any state regime possess the ability and willfulness to exercise its administrative, coercive, and surveillance powers to enforce such global conformity, as it would appear is indeed very close to being the case in our own time, the results could prove catastrophic for stateless people, whether as individuals declared "unlawful enemy combatants," as collective ethnicities such as the Akha of Thailand's Hill Tribes, the Biharis in Bangladesh, the Roma in Europe, the Nubians in Kenya, or as whole nations of stateless people such as the Palestinians. At the beginning of the twenty-first century, the United Nations estimates that there are some eleven million stateless persons in over seventy countries around the world,[13] a number of whom have indeed been designated as "nowhere people."[14] Certain member states of the United Nations, in fact, flaunt the international consensus and its legal protocols, not for the purpose of giving refuge to those deemed stateless, but for imposing the status of statelessness on whole peoples within those peoples' own indigenous territory, under the de facto rule of the invading state's military authority and coercive occupation.

Thus, dissent from the supranational consensus among states can be, and has been, a precarious margin of safety for those besieged by states, as is the case of France, which bucked the consensus on interstate sovereignty and conferred French citizenship upon Gao, who had been declared persona non grata by the Beijing government in 1989. Flaunting of interstate conventions and international laws, however, can also cut the other way, thus spelling an ominous fate for those rendered stateless in their own besieged and occupied country and settled with client governing regimes. As current historical developments well illustrate in the case of Iraq, Afghanistan, Palestine, for example, these are regimes that ostensibly function as state formations, but, in reality, operate as surrogate command structures that derive their legitimacy through selective and expediently conditional authorization and recognition, not from their own people, but from the occupiers and from other states that have a vested interest in the dispossession of the nation these regimes purportedly "represent."

Statelessness, then, is a high-risk proposition, to the point that some people tragically succumb to the illogic and dehumanizing pressures of those risks and, in doing so, inflict the violence of their besieged predicament through suicidal acts, not only against themselves, but also against those who keep them in that dehumanized condition of stateless nonpersons as "no-man" in a no-man's-land waiting to be occupied. The only hope for such stateless people, then, most notably in the twentieth and twenty-first centuries, is the lack of absolute consensus among states on their privilege of sovereignty to render people nonpersons before any law and enforce that decision through state-legitimated violence, when state apparatuses deem it necessary. In the case of cultures, especially literary culture, the people's republic of state and the people's republic of letters, fortunately, have often diverged. In the course of its history, the Nobel Prize, as a supranational institution, has played a key role on more than one occasion in this regard. Thus, while statelessness cuts the human subject legally adrift from humanity, in that ensuing itinerancy, nationality as defined not by the state but by marks of identity that pertain to traditions of language, art, and cultural production, Professor Malmqvist's presentation of Gao suggests, becomes equally itinerant, mobile, and transportable by the subject that embodies that identity: "You have come to look on the native language which you brought with you when you left China as your true and real country."

In another disciplinary realm, that of ethnography, the Malaysian-Chinese anthropologist Aihwa Ong speaks of "flexible citizenship" and of its "cultural logics of transnationality." "Flexible citizenship," she says, "refers to the cultural logics of capitalist accumulation, travel, and displacement that induce subjects to respond fluidly and opportunistically to changing political-economic conditions."[15] Beyond Professor Ong's American-inflected Marxisant idiom, specifically focused on the 1980s and early 1990s "tiger economies" of the Pacific as driven by the entrepreneurial initiative of diasporic Chinese communities, one can discern, *mutatis mutandis*, a certain relevance of her formulation to writers and artists who, perforce, find themselves *extramuros*, outside the national walls of state-sanctioned national territory, including Chinese territory. The chief corrective one would need to make in the transposition of Ong's formulation would be in the nature of the capital in question (cultural, not purely economic), and in the circumstances of human agency—less discretionary "hedging," or volitional opportunism, and more flight in response to political siege, often life-threatening, from state regimes, certainly so in the case of Gao Xingjian, who felt obliged to flee, first into Chinese "insile," and then into European exile: "Fleeing, I think, is the most reliable strategy for the protection of the self."[16]

We also know from the exemplary history of twentieth-century China that the state not only endeavors to make itself identical with the nation by arrogating to itself the definition of, and legal purview for, nationality, but it also makes every effort to bring a country's culture into alignment with the state's official jurisdiction. This is a strategic power that states have conferred upon themselves, as signaled by the common reference to transborder relations and exchanges as "international," rather than the less common adjective *interstate*, which, in fact, more accurately defines transborder governmental relations. The actual exchange of what is more broadly national, once subsumed by the interests of the state, becomes purely instrumental and ancillary in the tactical deployment of state propaganda, euphemistically designated as "public diplomacy." As scholars and teachers of national cultures and their traditions, especially as comparatists working across languages, national literatures, and national borders, we have witnessed this time and again, and we continue to experience the exertions of official regimes as they press their global hegemonic ambition through targeted programmatic funding and selective authorization of individual and institutional research and pedagogy, including inside our own universities. In his Nobel lecture, Gao remarks this historical fact as an observation on the previous century, an observation that, given the evolution of our university structures and institutional underwriting, could well serve as a relevant caveat for us in the present, well beyond the context of the People's Republic of China:

> Once literature is contrived as the hymn of a nation, the flag of a race, the mouthpiece of a political party or the voice of a class or a group, it can be employed

as a mighty and all-engulfing tool of propaganda. Such literature loses what is inherent in literature, ceases to be literature, and becomes a substitute for power and profit. In the century just ended, literature confronted precisely this misfortune, and was more deeply scarred by politics and power than in any previous period. The writer too was subjected to an unprecedented degree of oppression.[17]

China's government-sanctioned Cultural Revolution (1966–76), whose exertions in bringing the state and the nation, as well as the national state and national culture into absolute correspondence, proved determinative in the individual and national identity and artistic career of Gao Xingjian, a career that found its métier in reaction to the state siege imposed on the nation and its culture by the state's regime. Ironically, what Gao's case makes abundantly clear is that despite the political devotion of the Chinese state to the ideological precept of dialectical materialism, it has been blind to the fact that there is a dialectical materiality to culture in which those who would define culture become dialectically subsumed by the very culture they define. Thus, their acts of definition emerge, symptomatically, as manifest traits of culture—the one they define and the one that defines them as they labor to define it. Gao's oeuvre is a dramatic narrative of this compounded dialectical implication, which makes Gao more of a dialectical materialist than the state apparatus and its regime apparatchiks, who would live by that ideological orthodoxy, at least during the Cultural Revolution, as their guiding light.

II. The Fugitive Pronoun: A Peripatetic Mirror

> Human awareness of language begins with the emergence of pronouns.
> —Gao Xingjian, "Literature and Metaphysics: About *Soul Mountain*"

> And I myself
> alone prepared to undergo the battle
> both of the journeying and of the pity,
> which memory, mistaking not, shall show.
> —Dante Alighieri, *Inferno*, 2.3–6[18]

At the threshold of the twenty-first century, we are obliged by the case of Gao Xingjian and the Nobel Prize in Literature to reconsider the commonplaces of postmodernism with regard to the place of the writer in his or her culture and its national history, as well as the problematic connection between the nation and the state. By the end of the twentieth century, political and cultural theory had trained a good deal of attention on the constructedness, rather than the universal necessity, or naturalness, of the writing subject, of national formations, and the role of the state in achieving that construct. By the end of the century, discussion of delinking nation from state was not an uncommon occurrence, especially in the context of globalization, which for some has meant the attenuation of the role of the individual state and the dwindling of the nation as defining framework for collective life in a transbordered world of globalization. The formulation "nation-state," by this reckoning, appeared to a number of analysts to be diminishing in its viability.[19]

The case of Gao, however, as well as the global realpolitik that has emerged in the first years of the new century, militate against that delinkage between state and nation. Historic developments are certainly chastening any thought of underestimating the role of the state—as coercive agency with self-legitimating violence within and, as is currently the case, outside the borders of its own national jurisdiction, or as instrumental agent for transnational interests of corporate capital, of zealous ideologies, or of expedient political entailments. These functions, we have come to realize more harshly than ever, continue to reinforce the state's own exclusive privilege as ultimate arbiter of legitimacy and its role as enforcer of what the state itself deems to be licit or "legal." Comparative literature, predicated as it is on transnational encounters among literary cultures, can ill afford to neglect the determinative role of the state and of national state formations in defining the production of literature and in determining the significance of these productions in the interrelated life of cultures, through institutions such as universities, within national borders, and across international frontiers.

Gao's literary trajectory has traversed both the national and the trans- or supranational arenas and, as such, his case becomes instructive, not only as an accomplished and embattled literary corpus to be studied and understood, but also as an exemplary case with definite explanatory power that illuminates the perennial problem of the place of literature and those who create and disseminate it in the world. In this regard, Gao's Nobel lecture is instructive on the nature of "explanation," on his own literary practice, and on how those who devote themselves to the study and teaching of literature might deal with the writer's and with their own experience of literature. He notes:

> People are human by virtue of their ability to express themselves in language and thus become aware of their own existence, not by virtue of their ability to formulate definitions and concepts that explain their existence. People were people initially without isms; isms were imposed to standardise them. Literary isms, in the same way, force literature into a theoretical framework so that it can easily be embedded in specific ideological and moral teachings that conform with the social and political order.[20]

Though the incorrigible penchant to formulate "isms" may not be any less human than linguistic self-expression, Gao's observations bear parsing. In addition to allowing us a glimpse into his own modus operandi as a writer, his remarks shed a certain light on our own endeavors as students, scholars, and teachers of literature. The experiential dimension of literature has traditionally been consigned to the realm of the writer's practice, with those who study and teach literature placed at an objective remove that might facilitate observation, reflection, interpretation, and scholarly treatment of the literary experience and the literary corpus in the larger context of tradition and cultural history in which the literature was created. As comparatists, furthermore, we are given to exploring the relationship of the particular context of literary production to other contexts and traditions. Gao's "explanatory" rehearsals, or essayistic statements, in his Nobel lecture and elsewhere, as well as what he calls his "expressions" as a writer, as opposed to "explanations," trouble these traditional, now thoroughly institutionalized, relationships. He questions discursive theories about literature as emphatically as he rejects ideological reductions of literary expression. He sees both as susceptible to political agendas, to self-justifying systems, and as inimical to life, to its freedom and creativity. He voices such concerns most emphatically in his 1995 author's preface to his collection of essays *Without Isms*:

> Without isms involves a choice: between doing something and not doing something. . . . If the choice is to do it, then it is best to go ahead and do it to the extent that one can. But there is no need to persist to the point of dying for it, either by letting oneself be killed or by committing suicide.
>
> Therefore without isms is neither nihilism nor eclecticism; nor is it egotism or solipsism. It opposes totalitarian dictatorship but also opposes the inflation of

the self to the status of God or Superman. It also hates seeing other people trampled on like dog shit.

Without isms detests politics and does not take part in politics, but is not opposed to other people who take part in politics. If people want to get involved in politics, let them go right ahead. What without isms opposes is the foisting of a particular brand of politics onto the individual by means of abstract collective names such as "the people", "the race" or "the nation."[21]

Gao's "private," literal itinerary is just as emphatic. In his actual life-world experience he has traversed the way stations of a rite of passage, some might say, a prototypical odyssey or pilgrimage, of self-loss and self-recuperation, to emerge, like the Dante of our epigraph, as a literary figure, as a character that creates its own author. In a sense, Gao emerges as a classical *figura* common to both the Chinese and to the Western traditions: he is a posthumous protagonist, twice-born, or *digenis*, as the ancient Greeks would have it, as author and as persona. His oeuvre is the best expression and documentary record of this itinerary and its intricate way stations.

The most explicit and most succinct chronicle of Gao's vicissitudes is in his short essay "Wilted Chrysanthemums," already cited. A key moment in his personal life and literary career came in the spring of 1983, when fate delivered a double life sentence—one medical, the other political. He would surmount both through peripeteia's double reversal, with the first resulting in his major oeuvre, the autobiographical novel *Soul Mountain*,[22] and the second in his permanent exile in 1987, first to Germany and, later that year, to France, where he has been a resident and French citizen ever since.[23] The first life sentence, the medical, was his misdiagnosis for lung cancer, a condition from which his father had died three months before his own diagnosis.[24] The second life sentence, the political, was the pronouncement orchestrated by He Jingzhi, the commissar in charge of literature at the Ministry of Propaganda of the Chinese Communist Party Central Committee, to the effect that "the sort of person who would write such a play [*Bus Stop*] should be sent to Qinghai for training."[25] Based on historical precedent, Gao knew that this was a euphemism that spelled a nine-in-ten death sentence, since only one out of ten of those "trainees" ever returned from Qinghai alive. Most compelling for us is the aftermath of the medical misdiagnosis and the *vita nuova* as a "life-after-life" that issued from the rectification of the medical diagnosis and fleeing from a political death sentence. This was Gao's five-month, fifteen-thousand-kilometer peregrination through the primal woods of southwest China's Sichuan province. It spells the genesis of his best-known work, *Soul Mountain*, as a "posthumous" achievement.

"It can be said that talking to oneself is the starting point of literature and that using language to communicate is secondary," Gao says in his Nobel lecture. He continues, "I began writing my novel *Soul Mountain* to dispel my inner loneliness at the very time when works I had written with rigorous self-censorship had been banned. *Soul Mountain* was written for myself, without the hope that it would ever be published."[26] At the root of this confession is an understanding of literature as something that is prior to communication, a "talking to oneself" that is literature's "starting point" and that precedes the thought of publishing and dispenses with the anticipation of publication, or literally making that "talking to oneself" public. Thus, in what could be the world's most public literary forum, the site and occasion of the Nobel Prize in Literature, Gao asserts the claim that literature is foremost a private matter, literally, *avant la lettre* as a "talking to oneself." On this score, Gao reiterates his 1993 essay "Without Isms," where he affirms, "Literature is essentially an affair for the individual. . . . Literature requires the need to affirm the existence of the self before art can arise from it."[27] And yet, and Gao's constancy on this point notwithstanding, he does not see this originary point of literature of "talking to oneself" either as soliloquy or as solipsism. In this regard, he resonates sharply with Dante in his essayistic statements, or "expressions" as he calls them, in contradistinction to "explanations." Among those explanations are the statements of Gao on the composition of his most famous novel, a composition in which, between the singularity of the collective (we, our) and the plurality of the individual self (I, you, she, he), he opts for the latter, unlike Dante, whose itinerary would mark an oscillation between the two. Gao avers:

> When I started writing this novel I knew that it was predestined not to be a bestseller. The reason it took me seven years to complete was that I wanted it to achieve a great deal. In order to write it, I made three trips to the Yangtze River during 1983 and 1984, the longest of which was a journey of fifteen thousand kilometers. I had succeeded in working out the primary structure of the book, involving the first-person pronoun "I" and the second-person pronoun "you", in which the former is travelling in the real world while the latter, born of the former, is making a magical journey of the imagination. Later, "she" is born of "you", and later still the disintegration of "she" leads to the emergence of "he", who is the

transformation of "I". This is the overall structure of the novel. It allowed me to observe the psychological levels of human language, which are in fact well suited to this type of structure, because human awareness of language begins with the emergence of pronouns. Chapters 51 and 52 discuss the structure and meaning of language in the novel.[28]

He echoes Dante most clearly in the writing of, and in the writings within his seminal novel, whose compositional self-reflection and the author's "talking to [him]self" are most evocative of the Florentine exiled poet and his *Divine Comedy*, though certainly not of the "isms" of its strong doctrinal and political ideologies. Like Dante and his opus, Gao's itinerary as author of *Soul Mountain*, and the life narrated within that text, are the record of a new life, a posthumous life in a multiple sense, as I have already noted. Within this transit, the relationship of the new life to the old remains complex and incandescent, just as the problematic relationship between the private and the public, the self and the state, the writing and the writs of language and tradition persists as open questions, often left to the reader to adjudicate, if not to explain or resolve.

The triple subject pronoun for the self deployed in the morphing voice of *Soul Mountain* is articulated by Gao as follows:

So all three pronouns (you, me, he or she) can be used to refer to one person, and if I use the first person (I or me) then it's quite clear who I'm referring to. But if I use "he" or "she," then that creates some distance. It creates some distance and it gives a different perspective and allows me to create an artifice. It's an artifice of myself, a different perspective of looking at myself. . . . The second you bring in "you," the second person, it becomes a dialogue, and it becomes a trading of thoughts between people. The use of "you" creates a dialogue.[29]

These pronominal delineations are not capricious or parthenogenic novelties that issue spontaneously from Gao's talking to himself. They are identified, in fact, by Gilbert Fong as dramatic conventions that originate in the tradition of Chinese classical theater.[30] At the base of these conventions lies the ternary construct recognized by Fong in Gao's plays and traced to his essays in Chinese: *jingguan*, or "peaceful observation,"[31] *juchangxing*, what Gao calls "theatricality,"[32] and *liangxiang*, literally "to reveal oneself," a convention operative in Peking opera, where the actor deliberately focuses the audience's attention to that differential interstice between the acting subject, the role being acted, and the character portrayed—a self-conscious performance that, notes Fong, unmasks and deconstructs "the Stanislavsky method of realistic acting, that is, total identification and immersion in the character being portrayed."[33] While these protocols might appear as little more than the spectral refractions of a detached formalism, Gao, like Dante, complicates that formality through a trenchant politicization that juxtaposes the individual and tradition, the private and the public, the singular and the social. In the case of Dante, the triple self in the third verse of the *Inferno*'s second canto—"io, sol, uno"—which one of Dante's most poetic translators into English, Allen Mandelbaum, considers "the first triple repetition of an 'I' that we have in Western literature,"[34] the trebled singular subject, rather than extricated as detached individual, is made all the more emphatically enmeshed in and continuous with the long literary tradition and the wrought political history out of which Dante himself emerges, as the essay "Dante and the Classical Poets" by Kevin Brownlee documents for us.[35] If the incipit of *Inferno*, canto 1, as Mandelbaum intimates, binds the self into collective solidarity through the plural possessive—"Nel mezzo del cammin de nostra vita," In the middle of *our* life's journey—this triply singular subject at the beginning of the second canto, in fact, sets the stage for a poetic and political genealogy that is even more binding than the plural possessive of the opening canto. Gao Xingjian, likewise, compounds the individuality of the singular self, not only through the first-, but also through the second- and third-person pronouns. He does so not for the sake of an individuated subject or a linguistic formalism, but as an emphatic strategy of engagement through language and literature, with the preposition *through* understood as a traversal whose longer itinerary tracks the author's pilgrimage and its narrative. Like the transmigration of the soul through the triple way stations of Dante's pilgrimage, sung in his vernacular's rhymed tercets, Gao's is the narrative of the tripled singular subject's (I, you, she) journey through Chinese geography and history, the space-time of tradition that constitutes the novel *Soul Mountain*, the record of an excursus that, as I have already suggested, is triply posthumous—medical-physiological, political, and metaphorical.

Nowhere in *Soul Mountain* is Gao's encounter, traversal, and transgression of the Chinese traditions his own itinerary retraces more present than in chapters 70 through 72, toward the end of his pilgrimage and of the novel, where Gao's narrative becomes most self-reflective, most intensely metadiscursive, and most acutely spectral. At the heart of this crossing and its rites of passage through ancestral legacies of painting, philosophy, and poetry, lies "the small city" of Shaoxing.[36] This city, not surprisingly, also happens to be the native place of Gao's maternal ancestry. Most salient for the novel's narrator, however, is the haunting memory of two ancestral figures, also native of Shaoxing, whose precedents are defining in Gao's own painting, plays, prose, and exilic peripeties—the poet-painter Xu Wei, and "that literary giant of the age, Lu Xun, [who] was a fugitive on the run all the time . . . [who,] afterwards, luckily moved into the foreign concessions, otherwise he would have been killed long before he died of illness."[37] While Gao's own fugitive itinerary has followed the example of the latter, it is not the refugee Lu Xun, but the more recalcitrant, and more anxiously original, Xu Wei who defines Gao's poetic and political trajectory in dealing with the regimes of state. Hence, the narrator's sense of urgency in fleeing Shaoxing, lest the fate of madness of his haunting precursors prove to be his own. Here is how Gao sets up the counterpoint between the madness and demise of Lu Xun and the madness and demise of Xu Wei:

> There is a line in one of Lu Xun's poems, "I will spill my blood for the Yellow Emperor", which I used to recite as a student, but which now I can't help having doubts about. The Yellow Emperor was, according to legend, the first emperor of this land and can also mean one's homeland, the race, or one's ancestors. But why is it necessary to use blood to promote the spirit of one's ancestors? Can one achieve greatness by spilling one's hot blood? One's head is one's own, why does it have to be chopped off for the Yellow Emperor?
>
> Xu Wei's couplet, "The world is a false illusion created by others, what is original and authentic is what I propose", seems to be more penetrating. However, if it is a false illusion why is it created by others? And whether or not it is false is irrelevant, but is it necessary to allow others to create it? Also, as for what is original and authentic, at issue is not its authenticity but whether or not it can be proposed.[38]

Gao's juxtaposition of these two defining precursors of his own writing echoes his earlier essayistic statements, what he called "expressions," in *Without Isms*. Those statements, clearly reflective of a nonpartisan, someone wary of the "blood-and-soil" "isms" that devastated many parts of the world in the twentieth century, including Europe and China, and that continue their ravages globally in the twenty-first, are no less dubious for

Gao than the "illusions created by others" in Xu Wei, or, for that matter, the claims to originality and authenticity when such illusions are engendered by one's self. What matters for Gao is the mere existence of the possibility for proposing one's illusions. Thus, in continuing the passage from *Soul Mountain* cited above, the admonition to those in pursuit of self-authenticating originality resides in the fate of madness and the death of Xu Wei, a fate no different in the end from that of Lu Xun and his devotional allegiance to the Yellow Emperor: "In seeking to survive and yet to retain the authenticity existing at parturition one will either be killed or go mad, if not one will constantly be on the run." Gao's narrative persona, like Gao himself, chooses the latter, conditional option: "I can't stay long in this small town and flee."[39]

However, flight, exilic or otherwise, where Gao is concerned, is neither a mode of escapism nor a mechanism for quietist self-contemplation or a conduit to self-redemption. He reiterates as much in his personal manifesto, "Without Isms"—"nor is it egotism or solipsism."[40] And while the fourteenth-century Dante, the paradigmatic fugitive and exile of Europe's "republic of letters," sought redemption in the way stations of medieval Christianity's doctrinal cosmogony, Gao, like many of his twentieth-century contemporary writers in a doctrinally besieged "secular" world, seeks and finds deliverance in language, specifically, the language of literature, though with an awareness that the formalisms of language are not sufficient either for life or for literature, much less for a *global* "republic of letters," as any such domain would have to be at the end of the twentieth century and the beginning of the twenty-first. At a time in which, like Gao himself, "writers had no choice but to flee into exile,"[41] flight "served to escalate globalization of trends in modern Western literary thinking. Released from nation-state consciousness, the writer confronted the world as an individual with responsibility only to the language he used for writing. In this way, the art of language assumed a position of primacy, and how something was said gradually became more important than what was said."[42] And though Gao imputes this sort of "globalisation" to "Western literary thinking," his own "globalisation" through libratory exile that obliges one to confront the world as an individual beyond "nation-state consciousness, . . . with responsibility only to the language he use[s] in writing." As his Nobel Prize citation clearly avers, and as he has frequently characterized himself, Gao is part of "Chinese literature—or to be more precise, Chinese-language literature,"⁴³ and one among those writers whom he identifies as able to "transcend political and ideological restrictions" as "Chinese writers, or to be more precise Chinese-language writers."⁴⁴ Nonetheless, Gao cautions, "I do not by any means consider the art of language to be literature. It was only after obtaining my freedom of expression that I turned my attention to language. Sometimes I even play games with language, but this is not the ultimate objective of my writing. And playing with language is often a trap for the writer."⁴⁵

What, then, is "the ultimate objective of [one's] writing"? Gao's answer to this perennial question could have well been intoned by Dante, the exilic pilgrim through the dark wood and a sinuous path: "For me," writes Gao, "literary creation is a means to salvation; it could also be said that it is a means to life."⁴⁶ Though Gao's is a "posthumous" career, following his diagnosis with terminal cancer and the official threat of an ominous death sentence in the training camps with a one-in-ten possibility of survival and return, his "salvation" in transit through a life after life is obviously far from the soteriology of Dante's destination of a "soul mountain" at the end of his pilgrimage through the way stations of Christian eschatology. What Gao does share with Dante, beyond the language of transmigration and salvation, however, is the crucial role of the writer as challenger of the state and, even more importantly, as embodiment of a self that serves as speculum, as spectral corpus of language in which the world becomes ethically perceptible and historically comprehensible: "It is through the mirror of the self that the world is reflected."⁴⁷

9

Memo from the Next Millennium

A CODA FOR CALVINO

> Thus Perseus comes to my aid even at this moment, just as I too am about to be caught in a vise of stone.
> —Italo Calvino, *Six Memos for the Next Millennium*

I. On Perseus's Shield

The "next millennium" Calvino "memoed" on the eve of his untimely demise (September 19, 1985) has now entered its second decade.[1] An accidental American (he was born in Cuba, where his Italian botanist parents were on a scientific mission at the time), death would overtake him on the eve of his departure for America, where he was to deliver his memos at Harvard as the Charles Eliot Norton Lectures of 1985–86. These memos, which the caprices of time have deemed should be Calvino's final directives to us, still prove serviceable as an instruction manual. The ancient Greeks called such instructions an *enchiridion*, etymologically as handy as a "manual," and no less informative on method than memos are admonitory for what we are to remember from the past and in the future. A memo, as Calvino teaches us, is as informing in its pedagogy aimed into the future as a manual is instructive in its methodic directions for managing the present. A memo in his hands is a reminder of the past and, as he intended, an advertence for a time to come. My own recourse to the genre is merely for reporting certain facts of the present. So, this memo, as with the preceding memos in this volume, is a mere report, a modest account refracted through the lenses Calvino and tradition willed to us as spectacles for reading and as texts to be read and heeded.

Perhaps this admission has something incongruous in it. But incongruity never fazed Calvino. On the contrary, as with ambiguity and optical indirection, the incongruous invariably served as challenge for him, and this in itself might be one of Calvino's more significant legacies to us. We are not meant to simply look through the lenses of tradition as transparency, a fact he illustrates by refocusing how we read and how we see the past and the future. In his first memo alone, Calvino's purview in this visual recalibration moves adroitly from the eyes of the Gorgon Medusa on the reflective shield of Perseus to the novelistic vision and camera shutter of novelist and film scriptwriter Milan Kundera.[2] The title of Calvino's first memo, "Lightness," captures in its portmanteau simultaneously the opposite of heaviness and the reverse of darkness, a lexical felicity that eludes the original Italian, "Leggerezza," though the nimbleness he counsels, and demonstrates, extends phonemically to the labors of reading as well as to those of writing, in this noun's verbal homonym, *leggere*, "to read." Calvino is clearly alert to the double voicing of the English as he plays masterfully on the ambiguity of lightened heaviness and of optical luminosity in the first of his "six" premonitory reminders. And, just as "Perseus comes to [his] aid,"[3] Calvino's memo continues to deliver us from the dismal gravity and ominous darkness that defines our menacing time, a time when lightness itself is under siege in the vise of the double threat of brutality's petrifying bulk and the insubstantiality of "lite" that attends it. Calvino continues the rescue by teaching us how to rescue ourselves just as we too are "about to be caught in a vise of stone." And, as in his chthonic city of Argia, where earth has replaced air, here, too, in the beginning of the new millennium "at night, putting your ear to the ground, you can sometimes hear a door slam."[4] At the threshold between the sixth and seventh years of the twenty-first century from where I address this memo, this could well be the dropping trap door of a hangman's gallows in Baghdad, or the shutting door of a torture chamber in any number of black holes around the planet Earth.

To perceive that sound one indeed must keep one's "ear to the ground," just as any light of truth and any lightness counter to the petrifying panopticon of the perennial Gorgon might only be perceptible, and survivable, on a reflective surface not unlike the surface of Perseus's shield.

As Calvino's memos to our millennium teach us, indirection's subtlety continues to be the prudent course, albeit incongruous with a time more given to the unmediated war scream and to blunt literalism. And, as history appears to be turning his admonitions into prophetic augury, Calvino's urging Perseus on us is proving more apt than he might have wished: "Perseus's strength always lies in a refusal to look directly, but not in a refusal of the reality in which he is fated to live; he carries the reality with him and accepts it as his particular burden."[5] Deliberately focused on what he is fated to countenance and, simultaneously, symptom of that hazardous predicament he is destined to live, Perseus became for Calvino the symbol of our literary labors. He saw the indirection of his perilous scrutiny as a lesson in method for the writer, who, like Perseus, "fixes his gaze upon what can be revealed only by indirect vision, an image caught in a mirror. I am immediately tempted to see this myth as an allegory on the poet's relationship to the world, a lesson in method to follow when writing."[6]

Mirror imaging as an expedient mode of indirection has a long tradition in literature, as Calvino well knew, perhaps as long as the history of the human imagination and the myth of Perseus and Medusa. This tradition reaches down to us through a number of designations—shadow-casting, reflection, mimesis, speculum, representation, simulation, hyperreality—that range from the illusory imitations derogated by Plato as shadows of archetypal forms to the sanctified speculum of the world as mirror of divine effluence to the simulacra of our postmodern hyperreality without referents that displace the mirror of nature and the holy ghost. In this regard, our new millennium has "unburdened" Perseus from what Calvino diagnosed as "his particular burden," namely, "the reality in which he is fated to live," a reality he does not refuse but he inexorably carries with him. Our incipient millennium, like Calvino's in its waning years, already strips away the paradox of Perseus's burdened lightness. In our era of simulacra and hyperreality the speculum becomes spectral, not merely reflective. Unlike the figural mimesis of Erich Auerbach discussed in our first memo, the representation of reality in our millennium crosses over from speculum into spectralization. The danger of directly encountering the Gorgon's gaze is no longer solely petrification. Just as ominous now, in our new millennium, is the threat of dematerialization.

Lightness clearly takes on a new set of meanings. The salvaging potential of spectral indirection, for which Perseus's achievement serves as primal example, takes on portentous possibilities as it passes from specular vision to spectral visitation, or the ghosting of reality unburdened of any substance. Hegemonic discourse and political doublespeak have taken those possibilities to new heights and to infernal lows. Our dominant materiality in a cybernetic age of nanotechnologies and the seemingly infinite possibilities of informatics management, then, consists in the virtual materialization of specters. Here, reality is defined by its own revenants and adventitious henchmen. As deadly as they could be benign, these specters can fade out just as expediently into evanescence with the slightest twitch of a muscle, which, forgetful of the Latin etymology, we blithely call the click of a mouse. The Latin diminutive *muscle* ("small mouse") is now as much a verb ("to muscle," transitive or otherwise, usually accompanied by an expedient preposition such as in, out, off) as it is a noun in its global English avatar. It denotes the hyperpuissance of our millennial realpolitik that can enforce all such management decisions of language and "ghostings" of reality. Indeed, as in the city of Argia, one can "hear a door slam," night and day, with persistent regularity.

II. Consistency

"Consistency" is the sixth memo, which the fates decreed Calvino should not write. A would-have-been coda, it hovers as the ghost of his *Six Memos for the New Millennium*, beckoning us, like Hekate of the ancient Greeks at crossroads and at thresholds between this world and other worlds. In the mysterious logic of their caprices, the fates that curtailed Calvino's planned sixth memo left us the symmetry of a spectral coda, the echoing closure of a parenthesis he opened with "Lightness" and the reflective shield of Perseus. In this now haunted speculum Calvino had already called "Consistency" that closes that parenthesis, I take it we are to continue reading through spectral indirection the methodical directives his memos continue to teach us. Unlike the substantive nomination of his five written memos—Lightness, Quickness, Exactitude, Visibility, Multiplicity—the unscripted "Consistency" denotes a modal attitude, a human disposition, a character trait, and a frame of mind measurable only in the performative acts of our endeavors, rather than computed by scales or photo sensors, timers, rulers, optical implements, or calculators, instruments potentially corresponding, respectively, to the phenomena designated by each of the other five memos.

Not being susceptible to computational reckoning, then, consistency, as applicable to human constancy rather than to the viscosity of pulp, can only be assessed as speculative value, that is, as reflected in the cultural and historical speculum that mirrors our performance. Mirror imaging is at once transformative and salvaging, certainly consistent with the primal scene of such speculation in which Perseus achieves the difficult task of beheading Medusa and, furthermore, freeing Andromeda by demolishing a sea monster that held her captive, a primal scene of transformation that Ovid dramatizes in his *Metamorphoses* (4.740–52), a passage which Calvino cites in "Lightness" with particular delight:

> On the relationship between Perseus and Medusa, we can learn something more from Ovid's *Metamorphoses*. Perseus wins another battle, he hacks a sea-monster to pieces with his sword and sets Andromeda free. Now he prepares to do what any of us would do after such an awful chore—he wants to wash his hands. But another problem arises: where to put Medusa's head. And here Ovid has some lines (4.740–752) that seem to me extraordinary in showing how much delicacy of spirit a man must have to be a Perseus, killer of monsters: "So that the rough sand should not harm the snake-haired head (*anquiferimque caput dura ne laedat hareno*), he makes the ground soft with a bed of leaves, and on top of that he strews little branches of plants born under water, and on this he places Medusa's head, face down." I think that the lightness, of which Perseus is the hero, could not be better represented than by this gesture of refreshing courtesy toward a being so monstrous and terrifying yet at the same time fragile and perishable. But the most unexpected thing is the miracle that follows: when they touch Medusa, the little marine plants turn into coral and the nymphs, in order to have coral for adornments, rush to bring sprigs and seaweed to the terrible head.[7]

I take the special pleasure Calvino displays in discussing this passage from Ovid to be consistent with the aptness he discovers in a poet whom he cites some ten pages later as apposite to "a lightening of language whereby meaning is conveyed through a verbal texture that seems weightless."[8] This is a poetic achievement that transmutes density into lightness, not unlike Ovid's metamorphosis of Medusa's lapidary horror into the buoyancy of coral, or flower of stone, through Perseus's "gesture of refreshing courtesy," as Calvino refers to it here. It is indeed, as he says, "extraordinary in showing how much delicacy of spirit a man must have to be a Perseus," but I submit that the poet who demonstrates such delicacy of spirit, and whose poem Calvino cites as exemplary, is not a man but a woman, who, he says, "can supply as many [such examples] as we might wish."[9] This poet is Emily Dickinson. The verses Calvino adduces as exemplum are from a poem in which the lapidary elements of a flower converge in airy nimbleness to configure "a Rose," a "rarefied consistency,"[10] as he suggestively calls it, that will be burdened with incantatory density during the early part of the twentieth century in the thumping iterations of Gertrude Stein and her modernist chorus intoning a redundant rose ("Sacred Emily," 1913), as noted in our discussion of Zbigniew Herbert's poetry in our sixth chapter. In countradistinction to Stein's "rose," Calvino invokes the "rarefied consistency" of the accidental rose wrought by "A flask of Dew—A Bee or two— / A Breeze—A caper in the trees.[11]

The connection between the "rarefied consistency" Calvino attributes to Emily Dickinson and the perpetually rarefied essay "Consistency" he was destined not to write can only be speculative, though we could never be arbitrary in such speculating, inasmuch as Calvino already furnishes the speculum and its frame for that process. Thus, we are constrained by the reflection of Perseus's shield, the stone flower of Ovid's *Metamorphoses*, and, of course, the "rarefied consistency" of the Emily Dickinson he holds up as exemplar. Marked as Calvino's pedagogical method is by a strong form of periphrastic turn in reflection and recapitulation, it is safe to say that the parenthesis he opened with "Lightness" entails the proleptic elements for the closing memo of the parenthesis the fates deemed should remain open, promissory, and prospective in perpetuity. This augural potential as temper of mind and poetic timber could well be the most consistent element in the lesson he foresees with the memo on "Consistency." In this sense, what Calvino had intended to teach us will always remain speculative as pedagogical value and as a perpetually substantial cultural patrimony.

Thus, in the spirit of this speculation, I should like to rehearse one of the most extraordinary instances of what Calvino praised in Perseus as "the delicacy of spirit" and "gesture of refreshing courtesy" that constitutes a poetic lesson on speculative value, which, as I already noted, is the yardstick by which we can assess consistency. The exemplum originates, as Calvino already suggests in his habitual mode of misdirection, in the poet he deems the inexhaustible source of examples—Emily Dickinson. In her poetic corpus, this particular instance occurs in what is indicated as poem 709 from 1863, "Publication—is the Auction / Of the Mind of Man—." As indicated in this poem, Emily Dickinson is not simply an instance of consistency but its embodiment. From her prosodic habits, to her habitual white vestments ("We—would rather / From Our Garret go / White— Unto the White Creator—"),[12] to the self-imposed rigors of her sociality, Dickinson's consistency is as steady as Perseus—like him she was capable of making flowers of stone, as Ovid would have it. Possessed no less of a "delicacy of spirit," like Perseus the slayer of monsters and the decapitator of the Gorgon Medusa, Dickinson is unyieldingly steadfast in the consistency of her poetic vocation, which she identifies as a franchise of "Heavenly Grace," a principle which Calvino calls a "gesture of courtesy." The images of her poetry may indeed attain a "rarefied consistency," but her own consistency, though slant and somewhat rare in its uncompromising economy, is neither meek nor shrinking.

In poem 709, consistency attains to speculative value in dramatic fashion as poetic practice, cultural attribute, and social value. The poem is a mirror imaging of a poem in the making, a specular enactment of consistency as performative act, an act in which the poem itself is born, topically and prosodically. In his memo "Exactitude," Calvino calls this process "icastic," which he defines as follows: "an evocation of clear, incisive, memorable visual images; in Italian we have an adjective that doesn't exist in English, "icastico," from the Greek *eikastikos*."[13] The history of the English language, as Calvino notes, does not accommodate the Greek adjective, which, for the ancient Greeks, is more than figurative and memorable visual imaging. The stem of the lexis, *eikasia*, is tied to the processes of conjecture and to comparison, as well as to likeness. Thus, an *eikastes* is one who conjectures, a diviner, that is, a speculator. *Eikastos* is to be compared, as in "like," that is, as in a simile. As a student of comparative literature, one cannot be immune to the comparatistic intricacies of these lexical resonances.

I rehearse his adjective's etymologies and their philological registers because their Greek semiosis reframes the "visual images" of Calvino's Italian within the larger economy of visualization, figural mimesis, and cultural representation. It does so through the misdirection of simile and speculation, of mirror imaging, as in the myth of Perseus which, for us, eventuate in the spectralization that marks the simulacra and simulations of our twenty-first-century hyperreality—that is, a signifying reality of ghosted and ghostly referents. This is the "icastic" lens of our comparatism and divining conjectures through which we read the "rarefied consistency" that Calvino discerns in Emily Dickinson. And this too is the haunted literacy that allows us to read the admonition of his spectral, unwritten memo, "Consistency," that continues to instruct us in our new millennium as constant textual visitation, a specter made legible by the instructions in literacy that Calvino's other five memos have given us. If Ovid had the ghastly blood of Medusa for the alchemy of his poetic metamorphoses that made flowers of stone, we have the legacy of Calvino's ghostly pedagogy whose alembic is a temper of mind he calls "consistency," a legacy he willed to us in the phantom of a memo he intended to write but was destined not to, the fates having decreed that his mere forethought should constitute Calvino's envois and final instruction. Our vocation finds strength in his example and in the specific precedents he adduces in his first memo, "Lightness," for such consistency, particularly the illustrative instances of Emily Dickinson.

I train the focus of this memo in response to Calvino's on Emily Dickinson, especially, because among all his exemplary choices she could well be one of the most attuned to indirection as salvaging operation for poetics and for society in general. Dickinson had already articulated the method Calvino praises in Perseus most explicitly in what the archivists designate as poem 1129 in her corpus. There, she enjoins us to

Tell all the Truth but tell it slant—
Success in Circuit lies . . .
. . .
A Lightening to the children eased . . .
. . .
The Truth must dazzle gradually
Or every man be blind.[14]

In reiterating the saving grace of indirection and "Lightening," Dickinson's poem delivers a double caveat that Calvino's own grace was perfectly attuned to. His unwritten memo, I surmise from the memos that precede it, wished to alert us to its cautionary note. The first part of this double admonition is a consistency with truth, the second is a certain truth about consistency, both of which, at the beginning of this new millennium, are apparently being neglected, certainly in our public life. Most frequently overlooked is the fact that indirection, or mis-direction, does not absolve us from truth. As in the refracted image in Perseus's mirror, "telling the truth slant" does not mean slanting truth itself. Consistency with truth, Dickinson tells us, requires that we "Tell all the Truth." Telling it slant rescues us from blindness, just as seeing Medusa's face through the reflection on his shield saves Perseus from turning to stone. And while un-decidability or indeterminacy might be integral to truth, willfully determining that indeterminateness, or expediently disambiguating its un-decidability, is yet another way of slanting truth rather than telling it slant. Consistency in this regard also pertains to the stamina and steadfastness implicit in the protracted experience required by Dickinson's adverb *gradually*, a social courtesy and political fortitude required of us for living with indeterminacy and coexisting in ambiguity. Consistency in this sense shades into the realm of ethics, and the characters of prosodic composition or mythmaking mirror the strength of our character. This conflation of the poetic and the ethical is especially critical in a time like ours, when "the gradual" and its measured modulations must countenance the unmodulated regimes of shrill instantaneity devoid of any measure.

The second monitory exhortation to be had in Dickinson's poem and in Calvino's unwritten memo deals with the misapprehension of consistency as dogmatic obduracy or immutable ideological orthodoxy.[15] Consistency in this sense, far from reflecting on staying power, means a petrification. Such pharisaic reading of resilience becomes tantamount to beholding the Gorgon's gaze directly and becoming beholden to it, forgetful of Perseus's example. Such mistaking of consistency happens to be the dominant principle governing contemporary realpolitik. Calvino's admonition, then, emerges as more critical than ever to our sociality and political life. In his first and second memos, "Lightness" and "Visibility," Calvino's warning is quite explicit in this regard. In the first instance, Calvino speaks to us of Perseus whose "strength always lies in a refusal to look directly" at the Gorgon's gaze, and he suggestively adds, "but not in a refusal of the reality in which he is fated to live; he carries the reality with him and accepts it as his particular burden."[16] In a socially powerful sense this acceptance of one's particular reality and the management of its burden defines the value of consistency Calvino's spectral memo urges on us.

In "Visibility," consistency takes on a dual role, a double exigency—first, as the fortitude to make the invisible visible, to "shoot the gap" or traverse the haunted emptiness we must somehow negotiate, and, second, as that very space of emptiness left to us by the absence of Calvino's intended memo "Consistency" as a potential we are enjoined by his legacy to realize. Our task, then, is to exercise the first—the necessary consistency—in order to realize the second—conjuring the substance that fills the blank his sudden departure left us. Calvino's guiding light in this tasking is the memorable Giordano Bruno of the fourth memo in this volume, for whom, as is the case with Calvino, memory concerns not only the past but also the future. Calvino writes: "According to Bruno, the *spiritus phantasticus* is 'mundus quidem et sinus inexplebilis formarum et specierum,' that is, a world or a gulf, never saturable, of forms and images. So, then, I believe that to draw on this gulf of potential multiplicity is indispensable to any form of knowledge. The poet's mind, and at a few decisive moments the mind of the scientist, works according to a process of association of images that is the quickest way to link and to choose between the infinite forms of the possible and the impossible."[17] A more common name for this operation is *ars combinatoria*, and the economy of cultural consistency sees to it that the art is not arbitrary, nor are the combinatorial possibilities fortuitous. Both, arbitrariness and fortuity are circumscribed by the very pertinence of culture to who we are, what we do, and how we do it. Our performative repertoire comes already largely defined, as do our possible deviations and combinatorial improvisations. This is not to say that we should capitulate to the tyranny of the peculiar determinisms that identify our particular culture. It is only to say that refusal to capitulate might itself be inalienable from and integral to the possibilities we embody. In this sense, consistency itself serves as the inevitable instrument or template for responding to Calvino's unscripted memo "Consistency." Calvino has furnished, to use his own terms, its "icastic" figures, given us the model at hand for the implementation of its purpose. Our performance will have substantiated what he entrusts in absence. Consistency in action, as with Perseus's "gesture of refreshing courtesy," might well be, then, an inevitable requirement for our survival. Calvino's *Memos*, as he intended, continue to serve as our prospectus for fulfilling that requirement.

Epilogue

THE INVENTIONS OF COMPARATIVE LITERATURE:
A MINUTE ON METHOD

> It is, in fact, a collection of memoranda.
> —Walt Whitman, *Democratic Vistas* (1871)

> Perennial suffering has as much right to expression as a tortured man has to scream; hence it may have been wrong to say that after Auschwitz you could no longer write poems.
> —Theodor W. Adorno (1961)

I. Defining Figures

A comparatist tends to write for the unexpected reader. To expect the unexpected is not a contradiction but an expectation to be contradicted. It signals openness to ambiguity, self-assurance at a swinging door or overture whose threshold is traversable in both directions, what best defines an opening to a conversation. This is the position from which I have sought to address, simultaneously, the reader and the historical figures assembled in this volume. This is the context of the discipline of comparative literature. As I have attempted to illustrate, the field of comparative literature is a locus of encounters defined by intersections, by the contrapuntal, by the crossover, by historical articulation of disciplinary continuities, as well as by the contiguities and productive surprise of what a fellow comparatist and long-distance interlocutor from the other side of the planet has called "unexpected affinities."[1]

In the larger cultural and historical context in which comparative literature is embedded, the figures convoked in this book reach us as lifelines that extend the conversation in which we endeavor to be articulate and through which we are articulated as a cultural continuity linked across spaces and times in diverse languages and multiple modes of human expression. Reaching across such spaces and times is not a risk-proof endeavor at this historical moment. In a time immediately preceding ours and not entirely unlike our precarious epoch, a number of scholars felt compelled to engage the cultural history of Europe as a hedge against barbarity and the derogation of civil society that plagued their own era. Their work would, in fact, form the defining protocols for what we practice today within the disciplinary complex called comparative literature. I am referring to such different works as Erich Auerbach's *Mimesis: The Representation of Reality in Western Literature* (1946) and Ernst Robert Curtius's *European Literature and the Latin Middle Ages* (1948).[2] My decision to devote the first chapter of this book to a memorandum on / to the first of these precursors has not been accidental or random, as I hope to have made clear.

Among the numerous defining counterpoints in the conversation that is the discipline of comparative literature, perhaps the most common is the labor of identifying sufficient common ground among uncommon and differential elements that make them comparable enough to yield a conversation. No less crucial to the discipline is detecting the uncommon and discrepant within what is common enough to go without saying, what considers itself sufficiently commonsensical to deem conversation unnecessary. Comparative literature's mission, then, as I hope to have demonstrated, is contrapuntally dual—at once integrative and analytical. The discipline draws its vigor and focus from contending pluralities of difference and commonality, its raison d'être grounded in highly self-aware tasks of discovery, detection, recognition, differentiation, classification, and juxtaposition. In his 1993 study *Culture and Imperialism*, the comparatist Edward Said distilled this disciplinary practice as reading "contrapuntally": "As we look back at the cultural archive, we begin to read it not univocally but *contrapuntally*, with simultaneous awareness both of the metropolitan history that is narrated and of those other histories against which (and together with which) the dominating discourse acts."[3] In their own respective ways the figures gathered in the preceding pages are defining for the enterprise of comparative literature and its manifold mission. Distant and present mirrors in which we can discern our historical moment, they share a strong commonality in being uncommon, among themselves and in their own cultural context—some so uncommon to their own historical time as to have been consigned to intermediate roles that left them belonging nowhere, some ostracized to the status of pariah, some imprisoned, some exiled, others put to the sword or burned at the stake. These memos should also serve as a way of commemorating those individual fates.

Memos from the Besieged City, then, has essayed a series of reflections on the "dispatches" we continue to receive in and through the writings these figures have willed to us and to posterity. Intended as memos to each of these heterodox predecessors, these reflections, perhaps no less heterodox in turn, are focused through disciplinary and cultural issues that define our current period and our collective conversation, which is, whether we are aware of it or not, in ongoing dialogue with this inheritance and its perennial consistency. Thus, as a performative instance of what we call comparative literature, this endeavor is itself comparative in the sense that it partakes of a contrapuntal position between the legacy of these authors and current practices in the field of comparative literature.

In traditional parlance, then, all the figures gathered in these pages are heterogeneous, though bound in their common role as agents of change and in their shared predicament of disconformity or dissidence from the dominant orthodoxy of their time and place. As such, their often oblique and elliptical vantage point provides a privileged glimpse into the society and institutions that otherwise would be occluded or screened out by the norms and conventions in which human communities cloak themselves through intricate cultural constructs that they deem natural and beyond question. The problematic nature of their respective predicaments is the strongest point that all these figures share. As exceptions that prove the rule, these forerunners of our critical endeavors question quite consciously, and just as often reflect symptomatically, the unquestionable in their respective human contexts. As a critical vocation that takes the questioning of what goes without saying as its object of inquiry and teaching, comparative literature finds, simultaneously, its object lessons and the objects for its pedagogy and scholarly pursuits in these troubled and troubling figures and their fraught predicaments. This book takes Erich Auerbach as the subject of its first chapter precisely because Auerbach's legacy, especially his 1946 opus *Mimesis*, is widely considered a precedent that shapes and continues to inform our discipline and our field practices as comparatists. Beginning with Auerbach, in fact, has certain inevitability for me, since I am writing, sixty years later, from the very geographical spot and the same university department where Auerbach landed as a refugee in 1947 to assume his first institutional post as a teacher of philology in America. Time has proved his legacy, begun here, auspiciously determinative for the field. As we have seen, his professional circumstances and personal vicissitudes at this point of entry into this continent as a refugee were less fortunate.

The contestatory character of the figures in this book as agents of change who proved defining of our cultural history dovetails with the contrapuntal calling of comparative literature as a discipline of transformations. Contestation, if we could use this term as shorthand for the call and response that in music is referred to as antiphony, is the threshold to conversation. Like antiphony in music, the result of this contestatory give-and-take is harmony, which is by no means a blending or assimilation that erases the diversity of elements that go into the convergence or intersection of such elements; instead, it makes for a concert. Nicholas of Cusa, Rashiduddin Fazlullah, and Fray Servando Teresa de Mier—like all their cohabitants between the covers of this book—provide powerful lessons on the intricate and treacherous negotiation of difference, equivalence, and identity-as-process that defines the human, our humane possibilities and inhumane capabilities. This is the fraught terrain of differential counterpoints inhabited by the scholarly pursuits and, not infrequently, melancholy professions of comparative literature. Difference, a manic desideratum of our intellectual and life practices at the end of the twentieth century and beginning of the twenty-first century, is an element that all the figures gathered here knew well. What they teach us about this engrossing *koine* of our own dealings is that difference is invariably adversarial, not just contestatory.

Each of these figures has had to cope with adversity and the adversarial, whether as aesthetic category, as philosophical position, as dogma or credo, or as scientific axiology. Just as we learn from these precursors that the contestatory is best negotiated in conversation, they also teach us that there is a direct line between adversarial confrontation and the development of capabilities to frame, articulate, and manage the seemingly intractable incommensurables without succumbing to them. They themselves have had varying success in this delicate, often high-risk business. A number of them, in fact, paid with their life for the temerity of thinking that nothing is beyond the pale of mediation and negotiation. The lesson to be gleaned from their fates is captured in the principle of indirection and deflective figuration, recalled for us by Italo Calvino as Perseus's shield on which to see the eyes of the Gorgon Medusa, revisited in the "Coda" as memo from our new millennium in response to Calvino's *Six Memos for the Next Millennium*.

There is a direct line between what is adversity and adversarial in human affairs and what we refer to as *adversative* in the technical figures and formalities of grammar, rhetoric, prosody, and poetics with which we are destined to deal and negotiate as comparatists. The adversative elements (among which figure adverbial terms such as *but, yet, however, nonetheless, notwithstanding, alternatively, still, even so, then again*, etc.) interject a differential quotient into what otherwise might be considered settled, imperturbable, or unquestionable. The American university as setting for the vicissitudes of Erich Auerbach (Chapter 1) at a foundational moment of our discipline; the Baghdad of late thirteenth-century, where Mongolian Buddhism, Nestorian Christianity, and Abbasid Islam converged; as well as the Istanbul of late sixteenth century where Persian and Islamic aesthetics encountered Florentine and Venetian technologies of painting in Orhan Pamuk's ekphrastic novel *My Name Is Red* (Chapter 2); and Oxford University and Rome where Copernican astronomy and Giordano Bruno ran into Calvinist and Catholic cosmology (Chapter 4); or Jerusalem and New York, where the judgment of one human atrocity stands as threshold to the next, as diagnosed and anticipated by Hannah Arendt in her triangulation of Herman Melville's *Billy Budd*, Fyodor Dostoyevsky's Grand Inquisitor, and the trial of Adolf Eichmann (Chapter 7)—these are all sites of adversarial life-worlds and adversative discourses that anticipate, inform, and define us and what we do today. Comparative literature, one could justifiably venture, is the discipline of the adversative, and this turn of language and thought is not a penchant; it is, rather, as with the labors of Perseus, an unavoidable necessity. How well we perform in negotiating and conversing the contrapuntal contestation in and through the adversative cultural and historical elements of discourse not only determines the outcome but it defines the nature of the success and sustainability of our comparatistic endeavors—pedagogical, investigative, scholarly, and institutional.

It could also determine our fate and well-being, personal and professional, especially in what Hannah Arendt called "dark times," after Bertolt Brecht's poem "To Posterity." We, as the "posterity" addressed by Brecht and by Arendt, live in times no less dark. And this is why the lessons of Arendt and of the other figures gathered here are critical to what we do, how we do it, and what it all might mean. Having anticipated the possibility, now corroborated by history, that we might need the experiential benefit of their own vicissitudes with which to face ours, these predecessors have willed to us, deliberately or by illustrative example, a mirror in which to see them and ourselves in palimpsest, and a lamp by whose light to negotiate our way in dark times that they saw not as unique to their own moment but as an inexorable commonality of human histories. One of the most exemplary instances of this specular superpositioning of destinies occurs, as we discussed, in chapter 12 of Auerbach's *Mimesis*. No less significant in the legacy of spectralization is the monitory memo of Italo Calvino on Perseus's mirror that safeguarded the hero against the peril of turning to stone. As the term *memo* suggests, we recall their lessons as "memoed" to us, their "posterity," through their monitory writings, and we report to them, in turn, in our reckoning on how their legacy has fared. In the process, we also extend the tracks in the relay that passes through the Brechtian "posterity" that is ours to the "posterity" still to come, which Brecht also anticipates. He, no less than Arendt, would be loath to see that legacy come to a dead end in us.

II. Trivium, Tradition, Translation: Survival

The *trivium* defined as preparatory curriculum in the verbal arts (grammar, logic, rhetoric) is a rather late gloss of the term. As we have seen with certain consistency in the preceding pages, once we move beyond etymology and into philological inquiry, *trivium* in one of its earlier lexical way stations emerges as a triple intersection. As a locus where three rooflines converged, the Romans had an architectural designation for *trivium*—*canalis*, or *deliquia*, meaning "gutter." As a point of confluence, this channel of conveyance and clearing translates by association into the first three verbal arts, the *artes liberales*, made to converge as a conduit for turning out well-refined pupils destined for conveyance into social, cultural, and political worthiness. Even earlier than architecture and the edification of educational subjects, a *trivium* was the site of temples at a crossroads, temples especially sacred in pre-Latinate times to Hekate, the Greek deity of Samothrace, Aegina, Caria, Argos, and Athens, or wherever roads formed intersections, strategic junctures of forking paths and overlapping worlds of earth, sea, and sky, and meeting point of imbricated life forms—infernal shades and supernal bodies.[4] Most significant for our pedagogical tradition, Hekate was often summoned as disciplinary admonition to potentially wayward children, for whom crossroads are the most threatening and for whom every juncture is a triple omen—in space, in time, and in affiliation. Not unlike the multidimensional iterations of the shuttling chiasmus, the intersection of *trivium* is, as the term dictates, invariably three-dimensional. The Greek denotation of the trivium's conjuncture, *akme*, constitutes, in addition to the triple intersection, the highest point in space, not unlike the roofline intersection for Roman architects. *Akme*'s heightened connotations also comprise the critical moment in time, as well as the razor's edge in perspicuity. In Latin, this Greek lexis echoes back as *acies*, the highest and sharpest point of the three-dimensional apex of convergence and vantage point, hence, the literal meaning of *acies*—the pupil of the eye.

A trivium, then, while traditionally identified as verbal, is also possessed of a nonverbal dimension no less defining and formative than the figural sciences grouped in contradistinction to the trivium under the rubric of *quadrivium*—the sciences of number, or arithmetic; of space, or geometry; of motion, or astronomy; and of time, or music. Thus, even in its most ancient figuration, the trivium is far from a purely verbal, static or flat, or merely two-dimensional intersection. Most significantly it is an architectonic conduit and, as channel and means of conveyance, its mediate role is most decidedly cultural, especially in its *bildungs* connotations of pedagogic edification. The shorthand term for this conveyance is *traditio*, a delivery system that records, accounts, reckons, transmits, and chronicles the substance and itinerary of all that is conveyed. Our somewhat frayed term for all this is *tradition*, a word whose semantic and conceptual connotations have lost the acme and acuity of their peak, not to say the awe-inspiring dread of Hekate's potential for spiriting us away to paths and parts unknown.

Our trivium is faring no better in the trivialization of its edifying potential, especially as the *artes liberales*, whose domain is converted into an ideological arena in which the productive ambiguities and potential plurality of what we call the liberal arts become degraded into academic wards, intellectual halfway houses, or ideological bunkers of ardent convictions and their orthodoxies.[5] Imposed displacement and often compulsory and chaotic translocation have, in fact, become a babelic commonplace, a predicament of refugee peoples and fugitive cultures that complicates communication and cultural commensurability. More than ever before, compensatory means of linguistic transmission and epistemic transference from one life-world to another becomes indispensable for the maintenance of any semblance of negotiated cogency and shared comprehensibility. This is a complication, simultaneously, of the itinerant process and the morphing content of what is conveyed by *traditio*, a complexity that tradition itself has anticipated through a procedure it called *translatio*.

Most fundamentally, *translatio* refers to the act of getting from here to there, no matter the problematic nature of the itinerary or its way stations, and no matter whether there might or might not be a there there. *Translatio* reassures us that there will be a there and ensures that there is. In our own vernacular *translatio* has morphed from Quintilian's Latin (*Institutio oratoria*, book 8, chapter 6) to English by taking the letter *n* as appendage, not insignificantly, the mathematical integer for indefiniteness and the extreme in our quotidian calculus (as in "the nth degree"), even if it comes by that appendix through the automaticity of a morphological linguistic protocol. Thus *translatio* becomes *translation* in relocating from imperial Roman Latin to imperious global English. Our shared dwelling place, or *habitus*, in the beginning of this new century is, more than ever before, what an incisive cohabitant has aptly termed "the translation zone."[6]

Translation is clearly more than the transference of one tradition's content, or its deliberate transformation, from one vulgate idiom to another. Divulgation, in fact, could well be an incidental achievement of translation. Translation's more urgent and perhaps primary goal is more likely to be survival, a harkening to Hekate and the triple-path intersections that simultaneously promise and threaten a new life, or another life than one's original habitation. I am loath to call it "a second life," since each survival is yet another first life each time and in each place the fates and peripeties of translocation displace us. Such a predicament is not unique to us or to our time, of course, as we have seen clearly in the case of the tactical and strategically selective translation of Rashiduddin Fazlullah's *Jami'u't-tawarikh* from the Persian into Ottoman Turkish in 1425 by Yazicizāde Ali, the court scribe of Sultan Murat II, at a critical time in the Ottoman empire's history; in the tactical abjuration of this textual legacy in reform-minded republican Turkey in the 1930s by one of Erich Auerbach's colleagues at the university in Istanbul;[7] and in the retranslation of that textual mythology into historical fiction by Orhan Pamuk at the end of the twentieth century, yet another critical moment in morphing national history and collective identity.

Thus, translation is no longer, perhaps has never been, simply the transference of textual and cultural content from one vernacular locus to another. And I use the term *vernacular* here advisedly in this translocation process since the domesticity, indigenousness, nativity, and spring-birth resonant in the etymon *verna* (the slave woman born in the master's household) become problematically salient when turned out and translocated from one hearth and home to another. We have seen the implications of these displacements (in Chapter 5, on the Enlightenment's contestations) in the context of conspiracy as symptom of the experience of vernal and vestal homelessness. Along with those literal displacements, which invariably imply serial deracinations and, just as often, translate into the extending of a crucial lifeline, go cultures and their human embodiment—people—for whom the change of venue could well be nothing less than a passage to human survival. The memos in this volume, as "memos of understanding," aim to reach and extend such lifelines through historical circumstances that are as precarious for their sustainability now as they have been throughout human history. Continuous reconnection to these lifelines is vital for the sustainability of human culture and for the survival of what makes survival possible.

This is crucially so at the beginning of the twenty-first century, when the triune intersection configures a new form of trivium, one that manifests all the symptoms of analytical differentials and integrative convergences. I am referring to a dialogical process which circles through epistemic, scientific, and cultural points of human historical life, a process that requires from us a maximal alertness to its simultaneous promise for redemptive actions and its threat for irredeemable inhumanity. The traditional role of disciplines such as comparative literature that serve as a mediating third term at triple intersections can be critical to negotiating between the affirmative/productive possibilities and the nefarious/destructive potential of this crossroads. The new trivium to be negotiated today, whether by Hekate's torch or by laser beam, is defined by its prosthetic prefix, the stem always resting on technology—"nano-," "bio-," and "info-" technologies. Once analytically parsed to its subatomic minutiae and genomic codes, the life-world reveals that at the endpoint of analysis there is integrative convergence, *convergence* being the key term of the foremost contemporary scientific formulations and their trailing philosophical discourses.

True to historical precedent, convergence becomes the threshold to certain modes of equilibrium that can be equally life-enhancing and catastrophic. Perhaps the most salient examples of such threshold traversals are the fifteenth- and sixteenth-century European Renaissance that defined the global measure of the habitable world in a flowering of science and technology, even as it spelled the extermination of whole sectors of humanity and the decimation of human cultures till then unknown. Analogously, the atomic age of the twentieth century, in whose scientific wake human knowledge and technology now operate, began with a nuclear conflagration in Hiroshima and Nagasaki. The wonders of nano-, bio-, and info-technologies at the beginning of the twenty-first century are already witnessing their first experimental applications in warfare, with unmanned, remote-sensing and self-programming instruments based on nanotechnologically-derived chemical and biological agents deployed in human and geographic wastelands such as Afghanistan, Iraq, Pakistan, and Palestine in "controlled" experiments on dehumanized human subjects and ecosystems. This, in tandem with info-technologies that drive the most advanced forms of global communication systems in spinning language and information into the most egregious forms of Orwellian disinformation, even while giving us the residual benefits of digitalized archives of libraries and genetic codes, global positioning systems, and instant connectivity. Most significantly, in the semiotic revolution that all of these technologies imply, we are rediscovering that the world of science, engineering, and technology is once again "a universe" in its atomic, genetic, and cosmic interconnection, a "uni-verse" whose "di-verse" elements can be epistemologically integrated into nodes of convergence, most symptomatically—and most ominously—exemplified by the transition from analytical to synthetic biology, along with the privatization of life forms and their autonomous self-mutating potential.⁸ Hence the renewed urgency of the university as institutional point of such universal convergence, an urgency patently seized upon and, just as often, matched by the institutional propensity to circumscribe the human sciences and the *artes liberales* of the humanities within the confines of an administrative *cordon sanitaire*, thus, containing, usually through impecunious constrictions and managerial condescension, their penchant for raising critical questions and uncomfortable truths. It falls to humane disciplines such as comparative literature, nonetheless, and perhaps more critically than ever, to seek to maintain an open conversation on the potential repercussions of convergence and integration. Such openness is more imperative than ever, lest the analytic and differential capability that guards against institutionalized self-interest, dogmatic homogeneity, and single-minded conviction morph into unquestionable convergence, or consensus, that goes without saying and, unsaid, where the unspoken becomes the laboratory and site of rehearsal for the unspeakable.

III. Beyond Metanarrative: Conversation

Critical reflection on the study of nature—physics—yielded the philosophical field of metaphysics. And the narrative of our critical scrutiny of narratives has been analogously characterized as metanarrative. Modernity has defined itself as a process of reiterative reflection, critique, and succession. Eschewing the pile-up of aggregate iterations of *meta-*, certain pioneering wits of modernism have booted the lexicon to a level of critical supersession that leaves *meta-meta-* . . . behind, jumping, instead, to the code prefix *pata-*, as in Alfred Jarry's 'Pataphysics, and the Collège de 'pataphysique, that usher in the twentieth century with iconoclastic irony.⁹

Comparative literature begins its disciplinary discourse as metanarrative, *iam pridem*, inasmuch as its vocation is that of a third term in/as the trivium, a *tertium quid comparationis*, that examines and assesses comparable and correlative terms from a third position beyond the convergent or intersecting loci occupied by its objects of comparison. Any critical self-reflection that believes it transcends that third position at a triple juncture, a veritable trivium, as defined above, inevitably elevates comparative literature somewhat beyond the reach of iconoclastic hilarity and self-indulgent irony of *'Pataphysics*. I have proposed and sought to demonstrate, then, that rather than falling off the planetary sphere into the transcendental beyond, our self-succeeding inquiries take us back to *conversation*. I say "back to conversation" since, in the pursuit of analytical, critical, and theoretical vantage points, we seem to have spun out somewhat from the art of conversation that is by definition the basis of our comparatistic interventions and through which our mediation brings cultural phenomena such as literatures and literary traditions into a conversative relation at productive and reproductive intersections.[10]

The threshold of entry, or reentry, into the conversation is usually signaled by the literary, theoretical, critical, and philological works we read—works that historically inform our scholarly and investigative pursuits and continue to serve as the bases of our pedagogy. Thus, in illustrating this conversative engagement as comparatistic performance, I have taken as the threshold for my own entry into the conversation Erich Auerbach's beckoning at the point where his *Mimesis* ends by searching for us, his readers. I have heeded his summons, along with that of the Russian poet and student of Dante Osip Mandelstam, who accompanies Auerbach in the epigrammatic entryway of our initial chapter, and whose "Conversations About Dante" inform my conversation with him, with Auerbach, and with you, reader. A philological treatise such as Auerbach's, while exceptional in its achievement and in its significance for our disciplinary formation, is not unique in this regard. In fact, Auerbach's accomplishment rests, in good part, on his exemplary performative engagement with the tradition and protocols he is tracing for us. He thus becomes, in the best traditions of our pedagogies, an instance of what he illustrates in the process of carrying out his exegetic and philological demonstration. The historical circumstances of that defining precedent resonate, whether we like it or not, in a compelling fashion in the current conditions—institutional, political, ideological—in which we are fated to carry on that legacy. Hence, the inevitability of Auerbach as threshold to any consideration of and to any reflection on what we do, especially for those such as myself, who occupy the same space, literally, as Auerbach at his point of entry into the American academy and its questionable animadversions toward the exogenous—a phobic wariness of "the alien" no less pronounced now than at the time of Auerbach's arrival, and by no means exclusive to any one institutional setting, then or now. Only the mannerisms and the particularity of sanctioned targets for those xenophobias have changed. To wish to cordon off such historical moments in order to "keep them in their place," calling the procedure neohistoricism, would amount to little more than casting such antecedents into unique or anomalous historical context, a convenient screening out of the ever-renewed phobic symptoms and their perennial wariness.

In this sense, our textual legacies offer their own convocation no less so than literary works themselves, whether through what Greek comedy referred to as *parabasis*, the actors' removal of their hypokritic masks at front-center stage following, or as part of, their performance in an interactive moment with the audience; or in modern poetry's implicit or explicit apostrophe to the reader, as in the case of the Polish poet Zbigniew Herbert; or in the epistolary, chronicle, and reportage genres' direct and misdirected envois to the addressee, as in the case of the Persian chronicler Rashiduddin Fazlullah, the Mexican Fray Servando, and the diasporic Hannah Arendt. Such forms of implicating us become most recognizably characteristic of our contemporary postmodern narratives, whose defining vocation consists in compromising the reader in their transgressive "mischief" across narrative borders and through shattered narrative frames, as in the cases of Orhan Pamuk and Italo Calvino.

We are wont to take refuge behind or seek an alibi in the distant and often placid third-person omniscient perspective and voice of our scholarly/critical discourses. This is a cultural convention rather than a natural necessity, of course, something we inherited from the empyrean, and imperial, third-person self-positioning of Julius Caesar when narrating the exploits of his own Gallic campaign. Or, perhaps, we have recourse to the third-person voice no less so as compensatory gesture and hedge against the first-person confessional voice and the redundant perils of self-reflexive self-portraiture. Contemporary writers such as J. M. Coetzee variously dramatize and demonstrate this reticence, in his case undramatically, as is his wont, but certainly symptomatically and eloquently, in such essays as "Confessions and Double Thoughts: Tolstoy, Rousseau, Dostoyevsky."[11]

Self-consciously wary of the first-person voice, and chary of the ponderousness of the empyrean third-person declamation, perhaps as literary scholars highly attuned to grammatical voice we might find our most serviceable option in the second-person enunciation. Thus, our conversative mediation as comparatists might come more "naturally" by its task of negotiating between and among signs, discourses, and cultural formations. Our vocation, and vocalization, then, might redound more productively to conversational intercourse rather than institutionalized discourse, to interlocution and dialogue rather than assertion, that is to say, *colloquy* rather than proclamation or dictating. We know that in the history of our pedagogies the second person extends back to Plato, the Athenian Academy, and the Socratic dialogues. And, closer to our time, poets and polymaths such as Goethe opted for the conversational mode, even when complicated in the vacillations of being reported in the third person, in exploring issues of literatures and cultures that defined his own and that set a paradigm of a construct called "world literature" for us. Italo Calvino would push the notion to its furthest frontiers by setting up a conversation between Marco Polo and Kublai Khan, in which an invisible world of literature and its cities come to light in the interchange.[12] Goethe's *Conversations with Eckermann*, in fact, continues still as interlocution that oscillates between Eckermann and Goethe in the *translatio*, or displacement and transformation in language and venue, as the text moves between German and English, with Eckermann's original authorship and the work's title—*Gerspräche mit Goethe*—becoming *Conversations with Eckermann*, switching authorship between the interlocutors by attributing the book to Goethe, rather than Eckermann, in the English.[13]

IV. Memorandum of Understanding

A memo, in hard copy, electronic voice, or text-message, could well be our swift epoch's conversational genre par excellence, all of the attendant circumstantial infelicities notwithstanding. And though we often speak figuratively of communing with our ghosts—often those we read, research, reflect on and teach—we rarely do so directly or transformatively. In adhering to the safety of a metaphoric tack, we end by ghosting those antecedents even further by speaking about them in their ubiquitous presence as if they were not there, or by turning, not unlike Hamlet or Richard III, to the soliloquy and the innumerable peril of our haunted first person.

Memo, in this spectral sense, takes on a double life, either as ephemera of performative technologies or as inert materiality of archival load.[14] I am not interested in the archive as memorial, either as ghosted spectacle or as haunting authoritative "magnavox." I take the "memo" as a vital communicative instrument in an ongoing conversation that reaches us through what I refer to in the subtitle of this book as lifelines for cultural sustainability. Those lines run through and connect all of the figures and pivotal intersections invoked in this book. These are the lines that, as we have seen, run from fourteenth-century to twenty-first-century Baghdad, and from Baghdad to Istanbul-Constantinopolis and Florence, from there to the New World, whether the Philadelphia, Cuba, and Mexico of Fray Servando, or the New York of de Certeau's Twin Towers, or of Hannah Arendt. In the skein of those lines that span the globe, reaching from Arendt's Jerusalem to Gao's Beijing, and from there to the carceral ensnarements of Bruno's Venice and Rome to Herbert's Warsaw and Fray Servando's ubiquitous prisons of the Holy Office of the Inquisition, the lifelines traced in this book trump every manner of ideological prisonhouse to reach us. They call for a response from us—a transformative response, as defined by Jorge Luis Borges in his 1951 essay "Kafka and His Precursors,"[15] and a contrapuntal dialogue as urged by Edward Said in his treatise *Culture and Imperialism*.[16] The "memo," as I have sought to demonstrate, might be the most fitting medium for this communication.

America's poet-prophet Walt Whitman, whose declaration resonates as an epigraph at the head of this concluding "minute on method," intones an analogous "memo" that echoes from past to future. He self-reflexively characterizes his 1871 hortatory proclamation *Democratic Vistas* as being "in fact, a collection of memoranda," and his exhortations have had their effect in the poetic tradition, the political life, and in the scholarly discourse of American history. The conjugation of this epigraphic inevitability with the palinode of Theodor Adorno on his famous 1949 declaration on poetry after Auschwitz,[17] and with the Polish poet Zbigniew Herbert's cautionary verses, the epigraph for this volume, might, perhaps, mitigate the perpetual and now globally ubiquitous echo of the stentorian "yawp," as Whitman himself termed his prophetic clamoring. And if Adorno's self-correction could indeed be allowed to reach far enough to include the Iraqi poet Mohammed Mahdi al-Jawahiri and the Palestinian Mahmud Darvish, we might indeed be mitigating self-centeredness and cultural solipsism. This is the indispensable mitigation explored in our Chapter 6, a mitigation that might prove serviceable in modulating the pitch and tenor of voice to the level of conversation and understanding. That conversation, it is hoped, might serve, in turn, as necessary cover for the "chronicler" to record the "history" of the besieged city and to ensure that

if the City falls but a single man escapes
he will carry the City within himself on the roads of exile
he will be the City.[18]

Often written on Perseus's shield, these memos, then, as much as an act of accountability to the past, are intended as "passports," or as letters of introduction, suing for safe passage, *urbi et orbi*, along the way stations of this itinerary toward a possible future.

Notes

INTRODUCTION

1. Walter Benjamin, "Theses on the Philosophy of History," in *Illuminations*, edited by Hannah Arendt (New York: Schocken Books, 1969), 255.
2. João Guimarães Rosa, "A terceira margem do rio," *Primeiras estórias* (1962; repr., Rio de Janeiro: Editora Nova Fronteira, 2007); *The Third Bank of the River and Other Stories*, translated by Barbara Sehlby (New York: Alfred A. Knopf, 1968).
3. Homi K. Bhabha, *The Location of Culture* (London: Routledge, 1994), 37. Bhabha is condensing the diagnoses of culture by Franz Fanon and Benedict Anderson, reprising both through the specialized lexicon of Lacanian psychology. His object is culture in general. The characterization applies just as well to the disciplinary culture of comparative literature: "The Third Space, though unrepresentable in itself, which constitutes the discursive conditions of enunciation that ensure that the meaning and symbols of culture have no primordial unity or fixity; that even the same signs can be appropriated, translated, rhetoricized and read anew."
4. Haun Saussy, "Exquisite Cadavers Stitched from Fresh Nightmares: Of Memes, Hives, and Selfish Genes," *Comparative Literature in an Age of Globalization*, edited by Haun Saussy (Baltimore: Johns Hopkins University Press, 2006), 3. Saussy's remarks are part of his introduction to the ten-year report of the American Comparative Literature Association on the state of the discipline.
5. Richard Terdiman, *Present Past: Modernity and the Memory Crisis* (Ithaca, N.Y.: Cornell University Press, 1993), vii.
6. Bella Brodzki, *Can These Bones Live? Translation, Survival, and Cultural Memory* (Stanford, Calif.: Stanford University Press, 2007), 11.
7. Roberto González Echevarría, *Myth and Archive* (Cambridge: Cambridge University Press, 1990). For a contrast to González Echevarría's reading of the archive as perennially reinscribed mythology, see Edward Said's discussion of reading the archive contrapuntally. Edward Said, *Culture and Imperialism* (New York: Alfred A. Knopf, 1993), 51.
8. Gayatri Chakravorty Spivak, *Death of a Discipline* (New York: Columbia University Press, 2003).

222 *Notes to Inrtroduction and Chapter 1*

9. See, for example, Emily Apter, "Global *Translatio*: The Invention of Comparative Literature, Istanbul, 1933," in *The Translation Zone: A New Comparative Literature* (Princeton, N.J.: Princeton University Press, 2006), chap. 3, pp. 41–64.

10. See the attribution of this axial role to Paris in Pascale Casanova, *La république mondiale des lettres* (Paris: Editions du Seuil, 1999); *The World Republic of Letters*, trans. M. B. DeBevoise (Cambridge, Mass.: Harvard University Press, 2004).

11. Erich Auerbach, "Philology and *Weltliteratur*," translated by Maire Said and Edward Said, *The Centennial Review* 13.1 (Winter 1969): 3 and 14.

12. Franco Moretti, "Conjectures on World Literature," *New Left Review* (January–February 2000): 68.

13. Apropos "the fetish of 'exile,'" with "exile" not only deemed a fetish, but abstracted from real life experience into the figurative realm between scare quotes, see Apter, *The Translation Zone*, 59. For a corrective, see Kader Konuk, "Erich Auerbach and the Humanist Reform to the Turkish Education System," *Comparative Literature Studies* 45.1 (2008): 74–89; and Konuk's *East West Mimesis: Auerbach in Turkey* (Stanford, Calif.: Stanford University Press, 2010).

14. C. Darbo-Peschanski, *Le discours du Particulier: Essai sur l' enquete herodoteenne.* (Paris: Editions du Seuil, 1987), 252.

15. Martha Craven Nussbaum, *Poetic Justice: The Literary Imagination and Public Life* (Boston: Beacon Press, 1995).

16. On the relentless privatization of the commonweal and its public sphere on a global scale see Naomi Klein, *The Shock Doctrine: The Rise of Disaster Capitalism* (New York: Picador, 2008).

17. Esther Calvino, "A Note on the Text," in Italo Calvino, *Six Memos for the Next Millennium*, translated by Patrick Creagh (Cambridge, Mass.: Harvard University Press, 1988), no page number. Esther Calvino had to gather the text of her husband's lectures intended for delivery as the 1985–86 Charles Eliot Norton Lectures at Harvard University. He died on the eve of his departure for Harvard.

CHAPTER 1: AUERBACH'S SCAR

1. Edward Said, *Beginnings: Intention and Method* (1975; repr., New York: Columbia University Press, 1985).

2. Osip Mandelstam, "On the Addressee," in *Modern Russian Poets on Poetry*, edited by Carl R. Proffer, translated by Jane Gary Harris (Ann Arbor, MI: Ardis, 1976), 52–59.

3. Osip Mandelstam, "Conversation About Dante," translated by Clarence Brown and Robert Hughes, in *Selected Essays*, edited by Sidney Monas (Austin: University of Texas Press, 1977), 8–9.

4. Ibid., 13.

5. Ibid., 24.

6. Ibid., 24–25.

7. "Erich Auerbach: The Three Traits of Dante's Poetry," in *Erich Auerbach: Geschichte und Aktualität eines europäischen Philologen*, edited by Karlheinz Barck and Martin Treml (Berlin: Kulturverlag Kadmos, 2007), 414–25; 420. The volume, as the title page indicates, is accompanied by a CD of Auerbach's lecture "Und einer CD mit der einzigen erhaltenen Aufnahme eines Vortrages von Erich Auerbach, gehalten im März 1948 am Pennsylvania State College" (And with a CD of the only existing recording of a lecture by Erich Auerbach delivered in March 1948 at the Pennsylvania State College). I use the textual version of Dante's work cited by Auerbach, as the editors indicate in the first footnote. The title of the lecture was furnished by one of the editors. I am grateful to my colleague Professor Gonzalo Rubio for calling the recording to my attention, and to one of the contributing editors of this volume, Professor Kader Konuk of Michigan University, for making the text of Auerbach's lecture available to me.

8. Dante Alighieri, *Paradiso*, 17.55–60; translations from Dante are taken from *The Divine Comedy of Dante Alighieri*, translated by Allen Mandelbaum (New York: Bantam Classic Edition, 1982, 1986).

9. Osip Mandelstam, "Conversation About Dante," 8.

10. There is something otiose to the antithetical counterposing of Auerbach and his contemporary refugee in Istanbul, Leo Spitzer, as alternative "founders" of contemporary comparative literature, a questionable exercise engaged in by Emily Apter, "Global *Translatio*: The Invention of Comparative Literature, Istanbul, 1933," in *The Translation Zone: A New Comparative Literature* (Princeton, N.J.: Princeton University Press, 2006), chap. 3, pp. 41–64. Apter bases her argument for attributing to Spitzer "the invention of comparative literature in Istanbul" (64) in 1933 on Spitzer's confessions in his article "Learning Turkish," which she reads as devotional commitment to what she calls "transnational humanism." Though Apter sees through Spitzer's facile enthusiasm, she overlooks the unmistakable neo-orientalist frisson in Spitzer's linguistic pursuit of easy philological prey and the condescension implicit in that presumption: "Despite the fact that he is no expert in Turcology, and despite his rudimentary grasp of the language, the intrepid philologist throws himself willy-nilly into analyzing the word for 'veil'—*Kaçgöç* (meaning 'the flight of women when a man enters the house,' 'the necessity for women to hide and escape from men'" (63). A more apt figure for the vicissitudes of the *translatio studii* Apter seeks to elucidate and yoke to the conception of comparative literature can be found in the culminating chapter of Auerbach's *Mimesis*. That is Virginia Woolf, who did learn more than enough classical Greek to confess "it is vain and foolish to talk of Knowing Greek," and to conclude from her comparison of Sophocles' and Euripides' original lines that "the meaning is just on the far side of language" (32). And in comparing the 1,663 Greek lines of Aeschylus's *Agamemnon* and the 2,600 lines of

Shakespeare's *Lear*, Woolf arrives at the conclusion that "to understand [Aeschylus] it is not so necessary to understand Greek as to understand poetry" (31). In the counterpoint between Leo Spitzer's "Learning Turkish" and Virginia Woolf's "On Not Knowing Greek," there is something more persuasive in the subtle understatement of the latter. The difference between Auerbach and Spitzer resides in their respective distance from the philological implications of Woolf's insight on language and poetry, which Apter would appear to have overlooked. See, Virginia Woolf, "On Not Knowing Greek," in her *The Common Reader* (New York: Harcourt Brace and World, 1925), 24–39.

11. Egbert J. Bakker, "Mimesis as Performance: Rereading Auerbach's First Chapter," *Poetics Today* 20.1 (Spring 1999): 16. See also Jean-Pierre Vernant, "The Birth of Images," in *Mortals and Immortals: Collected Essays of Jean-Pierre Vernant*, edited by Froma Zeitlin (Princeton, N.J.: Princeton University Press, 1991), 165–66, re. Plato's *Republic*, bk. 3, 393b–d. On Homer, *Odyssey* 8.43, see Gregory Nagy, *Poetry as Performance: Homer and Beyond* (Cambridge: Cambridge University Press, 1996), 59–86.

12. See Leonard Davis, ed., *The Disabilities Studies Reader* (New York: Routledge, 1996).

13. Here and in the next two instances, I am citing from the then college dean's personnel files on Erich Auerbach, now archived in the Pennsylvania State University Library's Special Collections. I am grateful to the Special Collections librarian for access to the Auerbach file.

14. Seth Lerer. *Error and the Academic Self: The Scholarly Imagination, Medieval to Modern* (New York: Columbia University Press, 2002), 255.

15. Karlheinz Barck and Anthony Reynolds, "Walter Benjamin and Erich Auerbach: Fragments of a Correspondence," *Diacritics* 22.3–4 (Autumn–Winter 1992): editors' note, 81. I am grateful to Professor Kader Konuk of the University of Michigan for calling this reference to my attention. See her "Jewish-German Philologists in Turkish Exile: Leo Spitzer and Erich Auerbach," in *Exile and Otherness: New Approaches to the Experience of the Nazi Refugees*, edited by Alexander Stephan (Bern: Peter Lang, 2005), 31–47.

16. David Damrosch, "Auerbach in Exile," *Comparative Literature* 47.2 (Spring 1995): 97–117; Seth Lerer, ed. *Literary History and the Challenge of Philology: The Legacy of Erich Auerbach* (Stanford, Calif.: Stanford University Press, 1996). This is the most complete compendium on Auerbach's legacy to date; Aamir R. Mufti, "Auerbach in Istanbul: Edward Said, Secular Criticism, and the Question of Minority Culture," *Critical Inquiry* 25.1 (Autumn 1998): 95–125; Edward W. Said, "Introduction to Erich Auerbach's *Mimesis*," in *Humanism and Democratic Criticism* (New York: Columbia University Press, 2004), chap. 4, pp. 85–118; Apter, "Global *Translatio*."

17. Erich Auerbach, "Figura," in *Neue Dantestudien: Dante Hakkinda Yeni*

Arastirmalar, edited by Robert Anhegger, Walter Ruben, and Andreas Tietze (Istanbul: Ibrahim Horoz Basimevi, 1944), 11–71. Also in *Scenes from the Drama of European Literature* (Minneapolis: University of Minnesota Press, 1984), 11–76.

18. Djelal Kadir, "Comparative Literature in an Age of Terrorism," in *Comparative Literature in an Age of Globalization*, edited by Haun Saussy (Baltimore: Johns Hopkins University Press, 2006), 68–77; Djelal Kadir, "Comparative Literature in a World Become Tlön," in *Comparative Critical Studies: The Journal of the British Comparative Literature Association* 3.1–2 (2006): 125–38. See Apter, *Translation Zone*, 247, note 10.

19. Barck and Reynolds, "Walter Benjamin and Erich Auerbach," 82. The original of this letter from Auerbach to Benjamin dated January 3, 1937, is held by the Walter Benjamin Archive, Akademie der Künste Berlin, Archive 13/4–13/5. A more recent English translation appeared in Erich Auerbach, "Scholarship in Times of Extremes: Letters of Erich Auerbach (1933–46), on the Fiftieth Anniversary of His Death," introduction and translation by Martin Elsky, Martin Vialon, and Robert Stein. *PMLA* 122.3 (May 2007): 750–51.

20. Walter Benjamin, "Theses on the Philosophy of History," in *Illuminations*, edited by Hannah Arendt (New York: Schocken Books, 1969), 253–64.

21. Erich Auerbach, *Mimesis: The Representation of Reality in Western Literature*, translated by Willard R. Trask (Princeton, N.J.: Princeton University Press, 1953), 7. I cite from this translation of *Mimesis: Dargestellte Wirklichkeit in der Abendländischen Literatur* (Bern, Switzerland: A. Francke AG Verlag, 1946).

22. Erich Auerbach, *Mimesis*, 23.

23. Ibid., 5.

24. Ibid., 12, 13, 17, 18, and passim.

25. On this double jeopardy, embodied by Auerbach as authorial persona that complicates the facile dichotomy between the Hellenic and the Hebraic cultures, see, among others, Geoffrey Green, "Erich Auerbach and the 'Inner Dream' of Transcendence," in *Literary History and the Challenge of Philology: The Legacy of Erich Auerbach*, edited by Seth Lerer (Stanford, Calif.: Stanford University Press, 1996), 214–39. Green speaks of Auerbach's "affinity for doubling, self-contradiction, and self-cancellation" (212), and identifies this in Auerbach as an "inherent *postmodernist* strategy: the simultaneous engagement and detachment of self within the text." Green sees this especially in the final chapter of *Mimesis* and in Auerbach's discussion of fragmentation as modernist technique in Virginia Woolf. We shall see Auerbach engaged, yet again, in a strategy akin to this presently, as we examine chapter 12 of *Mimesis* and the enthymematic strategies of Montaigne, in whom Auerbach implicitly sees himself reflected as authoring historical / critical subject.

26. Erich Auerbach, *Mimesis*, 11.

27. Ibid., 11–12.
28. Ibid., 7.
29. Ibid., 19–20.
30. Ibid., 285–87.
31. Ibid., 289.
32. Ibid., 288.
33. Ibid., 289.
34. Ibid., 289.
35. Auerbach and his English translator, Willard Trask, are clearly putting into play the homonymic resonances of Montaigne's French *rolle* ("roll," "record"), the German *die Rolle* ("theatrical role"), and the English *role* personification. In the contexts of Montaigne's French "essay" as role rehearsal and Auerbach's pursuit of the mirrored possibilities of the refracted self in essayistic self-reflection, the aural and semantic connotations resonate wildly here. Auerbach cites Montaigne's original French and translates the passage into German at the beginning of chapter 12, whose title he leaves in the French "L'humaine condition," *Mimesis: Dargestellte Wirklichkeit in der Abendländischen Literatur*, 271–73. Trask, from whose translation of *Mimesis* I am citing in this study, leaves the title of the chapter and the chapter's epigraph in Montaigne's French and gives the English rendering of the passage into English from *The Essays of Montaigne*, E. J. Trechmann, translated by (Oxford: Oxford University Press, 1927), in Auerbach, *Mimesis*, 285–88.
36. Auerbach, *Mimesis*, 14–15.
37. Ibid., 293.
38. Ibid., 292–93.
39. Ibid., 291.
40. Ibid., 296, 293.
41. On Auerbach's "composure" in the face of such parlous historical contingencies see Hans Ulrich Gumbrecht, "'Pathos of the Earthly Progress': Erich Auerbach's Everydays," in *Literary History and the Challenge of Philology*, ed. Lerer, 17 ff.
42. Auerbach, *Mimesis*, 15, 8.
43. See notes 11 and 16.
44. Ibid., 556.
45. Ibid., 309, 296.
46. Ibid., 298.
47. Ibid., 311.
48. Mandelstam, "Conversation About Dante," 24.
49. Auerbach, *Mimesis*, 285–86. I modify slightly the Trechmann translation into English that Willard Trask cites here.
50. Ibid., 311.
51. Ibid.

CHAPTER 2: THE SIEGE OF BAGHDAD

An early, abbreviated version of this chapter was delivered as the 2005 Makdissi Lecture at the American University of Beirut and published as "The Seige of Baghdad: Imperial Talltales and History in Miniature," in *Al-Abhath* 55–56 (2007–8): 53–68.

1. Rashiduddin Fazlullah, *Jami'u't-tawarikh: Compendium of Chronicles; A History of the Mongols*, translated by W. M. Thackston (Cambridge, Mass.: Harvard University Press, 1998), pt. 1, 17–18.

2. Ibid., "Translator's Preface," xiv, citing the early sixteenth-century historian Khwandamir.

3. Ibid., pt. 1, 17–18.

4. Ibid., pt. 2, 471–72.

5. Cited in Sinan Antoon, "Of Bridges and Birds: Sinan Antoon Sifts Through the Rubble of His Native Baghdad," *Al Ahram Weekly Online*, no. 634 (April 17–23, 2003), http://weekly.ahram.org.eg/2003/634/bo1.htm (accessed February 12, 2010). This issue of *Al Ahram* is devoted to the latest siege of Baghdad.

6. See Humberto Marquez, "The Plunder of Iraq's Treasures," *Asia Times on Line*, February 17, 2005, www.atimes.com/atimes/Middle_East/GB17Ak01.html (accessed February 12, 2010).

7. Orhan Pamuk, *Benim Adim Kirmizi* (Istanbul: Iletisim, 1998); *My Name Is Red*, translated by Erdag M. Göknar (New York: Alfred A. Knopf, 2001).

8. Yazicizâde Ali's translation from Rashiduddin Fazlullah's *Jami'u't-tawarikh* on the Qayi tribe was placed as preface to his general history of the Seljuks, the *Oghuznâme*, currently archived in Istanbul in the liberary of Topkapi Place under the title *Tarikh-I Al-i Selchuq* (Topkapi Sarayi, Revan 1390).

9. Pamuk, *My Name Is Red*, 69–70.

10. Ibid., 160–61.

11. Michel De Certeau, *The Practice of Everyday Life*, translated by Steven Rendall (Berkeley: University of California Press, 1984).

12. De Certeau, *Practice of Everyday Life*, "Part III: Spatial Practices," 91.

13. Fazlullah, *Jami'u't-tawarikh*, pt. 2, 471–72. See also *Women in World History Curriculum: Biographies*, "Sorghaghatani Beki: Mother of Great Khans," www.womeninworldhistory.com/heroine8.html (accessed February 15, 2010).

14. Edward Gibbon, *The Decline and Fall of the Roman Empire* (New York: Alfred A. Knopf, 1993), vol. 2, chap. 64.

15. Fazlullah, *Jami'u't-tawarikh*, pt. 2, 478.

16. Ibid., 480.

17. Ibid.

18. See "Bush Threatened to Bomb Pakistan, Says Musharraf," Suzanne Goldenberg, reporting, Washington, September 22, 2006: "The Bush administration threatened to bomb Pakistan 'back to the stone age' after the September 11 [2001]

attacks if the country did not cooperate with America's war on Afghanistan, it emerged yesterday. . . . 'The intelligence director told me that (Mr. Armitage [Richard Armitage, Assistant Secretary, U.S. State Department]) said, "Be prepared to be bombed. Be prepared to go back to the stone age,"' Gen Musharraf was quoted as saying." *Guardian* (London), www.guardian.co.uk/pakistan/Story/0,,1878619,00.html (accessed January 10, 2008).

19. Fazlullah, *Jami'u't-tawarikh*, pt. 2, 496. See also, www.deremilitari.org/resources/sources/baghdad.htm (accessed January 10 2008).

20. The original version of this enumeration, which I slightly modify here, is by Amina Elbendary, "Its Famous Names," *Al-Ahram*, issue 634, April 17–23, 2003, http://weekly.ahram.org.eg/2003/634/baghdad.htm (accessed February 12, 2010).

21. Pamuk, *My Name Is Red*, 164–65.
22. Fazlullah, *Jami'u't-tawarikh*, pt. 2, 487.
23. Pamuk, *My Name Is Red*, 157–58.
24. Ibid., 160.

25. The most overt linkage of Machiavelli to perspectival anamorphism is found in his admiring reference to Brunelleschi as a sculptor whose sculptures he finds so lifelike, see, Niccolò Machiavelli, *History of Florence*, in *Opere*, 8 vols., edited by S. Bertelli and F. Gaeta (Milan: Feltrinelli, 1960–65), 7: 303–4. In his tactically self-effacing dedication of *The Prince* to Lorenzo II de Medici, Machiavelli uses the anamorphic perspectivalism as part of his *captatio benevolentia*: ". . . for in the same way that painters station themselves in the valleys in order to draw mountains or high ground . . ." See, "Niccolò Machiavelli to Lorenzo the Magnificent, Son of Piero di Medici," in *The Prince and Discourses*, edited by Max Lerner (New York: Random House Modern Library, 1940, 1950), 4.

CHAPTER 3: OF LEARNED IGNORANCE

1. Ernst Cassirer, *The Individual and the Cosmos in Renaissance Philosophy*, translated by Marion Domandi (New York: Dover Publications, 2000), 10. See also, Jasper Hopkins, "Nicholas of Cusa (1401–1464): First Modern Philosopher?" *Midwest Studies in Philosophy*, special issue of *Renaissance and Early Modern Philosophy* 26 (2002): 13–29. See http://jasper-hopkins.info/CUSAmidwestStudies.pdf (accessed February 15, 2010). In anticipation of what Theodor Adorno would designate as "negative dialectics" (see note 4, below), Antonio Gramsci had noted a clear historical demonstration of this phenomenon in the case of Cusa: "There is no doubt that Cusa was a reformer of medieval thought and one of the initiators of modern thought. Proof of this is the fact that the church forgot him, and his thought was studied by secular philosophers, who rediscovered him as one of the precursors of modern classical philosophy. . . . It is fair to say that the Lutheran Reformation broke out because Cusa's reform activity failed: that is, because the

church was unable to reform itself from within. His religious tolerance, etc." Antonio Gramsci, *Prison Notebooks*, translated and edited by Joseph Buttigieg (New York: Columbia University Press, 1996), fifth notebook, note 53, 310–11.

2. For a late twentieth-century treatment of space and culture that juxtaposes the ethnographic language of "localization" in modern anthropology and the dialogical discourse of "chronotope" articulated in the 1930s by Mikhail Bakhtin, see the seminal essay by James Clifford, "Traveling Cultures," in his *Routes: Travel and Translation in the Late Twentieth Century* (Cambridge, Mass.: Harvard University Press, 1997), 17–46.

3. See Natalie Melas, *All the Difference in the World: Postcoloniality and the Ends of Comparison* (Stanford, Calif.: Stanford University Press, 2007), xii.

4. Theodor W. Adorno, *Negative Dialectics*, translated by E. B. Ashton (New York: Continuum, 1973). See also, Theodor W. Adorno, *Quasi una Fantasia: Essays on Modern Music*, translated by Rodney Livingstone (London: Verso, 1992), 2–3: "The language of music is quite different from the language of intentionality. It contains a theological dimension. What it has to say is simultaneously revealed and concealed. . . . Music points to true language in the sense that content is apparent in it, but it does so at the cost of unambiguous meaning, which has migrated to the languages of intentionality."

5. Nicholas of Cusa, *De docta ignorantia*, translated by Jasper Hopkins (Minneapolis: Arthur J. Banning Press, 2001). I refer to this translation. There is also a mid-twentieth-century translation of *De docta ignorantia* by Germain Heron (New Haven, Conn.: Yale University Press, 1954).

6. Walter Benjamin, *The Origin of German Tragic Drama*, translated by John Osborne (London: New Left Books, 1977), 29–30.

7. Nicholas of Cusa, *De docta*, 93 (bk.2, chap. 12).

8. Blaise Pascale, *Pensées* (1670), translated by W. F. Trotter (Corvalis: Oregon State University, http://oregonstate.edu/instruct/phl302/texts/pascal/pensees-b.html#SECTION%20VI) (accessed January 12, 2010):
The world is a good judge of things, for it is in natural ignorance, which is man's true state. The sciences have two extremes which meet. The first is the pure natural ignorance in which all men find themselves at birth. The other extreme is that reached by great intellects, who, having run through all that men can know, find they know nothing, and come back again to that same ignorance from which they set out; but this is a learned ignorance which is conscious of itself. Those between the two, who have departed from natural ignorance and not been able to reach the other, have some smattering of this vain knowledge and pretend to be wise. These trouble the world and are bad judges of everything. The people and the wise constitute the world; these despise it, and are despised. They judge badly of everything, and the world judges rightly of them.

9. Jorge Luis Borges, "La esfera de Pascal," in *Otras inquisiciones* (Buenos Aires: Sur, 1952), collected in *Obras completas* (Barcelona: Emecé Editores, 1999), vol. 2, 14–16. For a discussion of the geometric and mathematical subtleties of

"the infinite" in "that remote German Cardinal—Nicholas de Kerbs, Nicholas de Cusa—who saw a polygon with an infinite number of angles in the circumference and wrote that an infinite line would be a straight line, would be a triangle, would be a circle and a sphere (*De docta ignorantia*, I, 13)," as Borges phrases it, see also Borges' "Avatars of the Tortoise," in *Other Inquisitions, 1937–1952*, translated by Ruth L. C. Simms (Austin: University of Texas Press, 1964), 109–15. Original publication, "Avatares de la tortuga," *Sur* 63 (December 1939): 18–23.

10. Ralph Waldo Emerson, *Essays and English Traits*, vol. 5 (New York: P. F. Collier, 1909–14); in bartleby.com (2000), www.bartleby.com/5/ (accessed August 28, 2006).

11. E.g., Homi K. Bhabha, *The Location of Culture* (London: Routledge, 1994), 37: "It is that Third Space, though unrepresentable in itself, which constitutes the discursive conditions of enunciation that ensure that the meaning and symbols of culture have no primordial unity or fixity; that even the same signs can be appropriated, translated, rehistoricized and read anew."

12. Nicholas of Cusa, *De docta ignorantia*, 67.

13. Michel Foucault, preface to *The Order of Things: The Archeology of the Human Sciences*, (New York: Vintage Books, 1973; translation of *Les mots et les choses*, Paris: Editions Gallimard, 1966; no translator indicated), xviii.

14. Nicholas of Cusa, *De docta ignorantia*, 69.

15. Ibid., 68.

16. See Richard Dawkins, *The Selfish Gene* (Oxford: Oxford University Press, 1976).

17. Nicholas of Cusa, *De docta ignorantia*, 11.

18. Ibid., 12.

19. Matthew Arnold, "The Function of Criticism at the Present Time" (October 29, 1864). This Oxford University lecture by Arnold, now a touchstone and often a straw man, has been widely anthologized, most recently in *The Norton Anthology of Theory and Criticism*, edited by Vincent B. Leitch et al. (New York: W. W. Norton, 2001), 806–25. Arnold's definition of the "critical effort" and the "endeavor, in all branches of knowledge, theology, philosophy, history, art, science, *to see the object as in itself it really is* [my italics]," occurs in the first paragraph of Arnold's ex-cathedra Oxford lecture, as self-citation, in fact, that refers remarks on his earlier lecture "On Translating Homer."

20. See Nicholas of Cusa, "On the Peace of Faith" (De pace fidei), translated by William F. Wertz, Schiller Institute, www.schillerinstitute.org/transl/cusa_p_of_f.html (accessed February 15, 2010).

21. In H. Reiss, *Kant: Political Writings*, 2nd ed. (Cambridge: Cambridge University Press, 1991), 93–130.

22. Michel Serres, *Atlas* (Paris: Bourrin, 1995).

CHAPTER 4: MEMORIES OF THE FUTURE

An early abbreviated version of this chapter was delivered as the keynote address to the February 20–22, 2004, European Union–sponsored conference of the European Thematic Network: Approaches to Cultural Memory (ACUME), in Nicosia, Cyprus, and published in the conference proceedings, *Cultures of Memory/Memories of Culture*, edited by Stephanos Stephanides (Nicosia: University of Nicosia Press, 2007), 50–66. I am grateful to Professor Stephanides and the organizers of the conference.

   1. See Angelo Mercati, *Il sommario del processo di Giordano Bruno* (Rome: Città del Vaticano, 1942).
   2. Giordano Bruno, *On the Composition of Images, Signs, and Ideas*, translated by Charles Doria, edited and annotated by Dick Higgins (New York: Willis, Locker and Owens, 1991), 31.
   3. See Robert Lockwood, "History and Myth: The Inquisition," Catholic League Web site (August 2000), www.catholicleague.org/research/inquisition.html (accessed January 12, 2010).
   4. The range of the debate on Bruno is immense. Among the numerous specialized treatments of Bruno's multifaceted work I have found most useful are Sidney Greenberg, *The Infinite in Giordano Bruno, with a Translation of His Dialogue Concerning the Cause, Principle, and One* (New York: King's Crown Press, 1950); Jack Lindsay, *Cause, Principle, and Unity: Five Dialogues* (New York: International Publishers, 1964); Dorothea Waley Singer, *Giordano Bruno, His Life and Thought; With Annotated Translation of His Work, On the Infinite Universe and Worlds* (New York: Schuman, 1950); Frances Yates, *Giordano Bruno and the Hermetic Tradition* (Chicago: University of Chicago Press, 1964), and the chapters devoted to Bruno in Frances Yates's *The Art of Memory* (Chicago: University of Chicago Press, 1966); Walter Pagel, "Giordano Bruno: The Philosophy of Circles and the Circular Movement of the Blood," *Journal of the History of Medicine and Allied Sciences* 6 (1951): 116–25; Angus Armitage, "The Cosmology of Giordano Bruno," *Annals of Science* 6 (1948): 24–31.
   5. *De triplici minimo et mensura*, by Giordano Bruno, as quoted in Hilary Gatti, *Giordano Bruno and Renaissance Science* (Ithaca, N.Y.: Cornell University Press, 1999), 4.
   6. Osip Mandelstam, "Conversation About Dante," translated by Clarence Brown and Robert Hughes, in *Selected Essays*, edited by Sidney Monas (Austin: University of Texas Press, 1977), 37.
   7. Martin Heidegger, "Hölderlin and the Essence of Poetry" (1936), in *Elucidation of Hölderlin's Poetry*, translated by Keith Hoeller (New York: Prometheus Books, 2000).
   8. Mikhail Bakhtin, "Discourse in the Novel" (1934–35), in *The Dialogical*

Imagination: Four Essays, edited by Michael Holquist, translated by Caryl Emerson and Michael Holquist (Austin: University of Texas Press, 1981), 297.

9. Mikhail Bakhtin, "Epic and Novel: Toward a Methodology for the Study of the Novel" (1941), in *Dialogical Imagination*, 18.

10. Frederic Jameson, "Nostalgia for the Present," *South Atlantic Quarterly* 88.2 (Spring 1989): 517–39.

11. Gayatri Spivak, *A Critique of Postcolonial Reason: Toward a History of the Vanishing Present* (Cambridge, Mass.: Harvard University Press, 1999).

12. Mikhail Bakhtin, "Epic and Novel," 15.

13. Yates, *Art of Memory*, esp. chap. 12, "Giordano Bruno in England: The Hermetic Reform," 205–34.

14. See ibid., 203–4.

15. Cited in ibid., 204.

16. Cited in ibid., 206. Latin original in Giordano Bruno, *Opere latine*, edited by F. Florentino, V. Imbriani, C. M. Tallarigo, F. Tocco, H. Vitelli (Stuttgardt-Bad Cannstatt: Friedrich Fromman Verlag Gunther Holzboog, 1962; facsimile repr. of 1879–91 edition).

17. Robert McNulty, "Bruno at Oxford," *Renaissance News* 13 (1960):300–305. Cited Yates, *Art of Memory*, 208.

18. Alain Badiou, *Ethics: An Essay on the Understanding of Evil*, translated by Peter Hallward (London: Verso, 2002). On the recuperation by current philosophical discourse of the Hegelian notion of "recognition" in issues of identity, difference, and social justice, see *Redistribution or Recognition: A Political-Philosophical Exchange*, Nancy Fraser and Alex Honneth, eds. (London: Verso, 2003). For an application of the notion of recognition to subalternity and social justice, see Boaventura de Sousa Santos, "*Nuestra América*: Reinventing a Subaltern Paradigm of Recognition and Redistribution," *Theory, Culture, and Society* 18.2–3 (2001): 185–217.

19. Sara Ahmed, *Strange Encounters: Embodied Others in Postcoloniality* (London: Routledge, 2000), 3.

20. See Yates, *Art of Memory*, 17. The Argentine writer Jorge Luis Borges, in his story "Funes el memorioso," *La Nación*, June 7, 1942, sec. 2, p. 3, reminds us of the twenty-fourth chapter of Pliny's *Historia naturalis*, which is devoted to memory and in whose first paragraph Pliny recalls the prodigious mnemonic deeds of "Cyrus, the king of Persia, who could call all the soldiers in his armies by name; Mithridates Eupator, who meted out justice in the twenty-two languages of the kingdom over which he ruled; Simonides, the inventor of the art of memory; Metrodorus, who was able faithfully to repeat what he had heard, though it be but once. With obvious sincerity, Ireneo said he was amazed that such cases were thought to be amazing." "Funes, His Memory," in *Jorge Luis Borges: Collected Fictions*, translated by Andrew Hurley (New York: Viking/Penguin, 1998), 134.

21. Geoffrey Sonnabend, *Obliscence: Theories of Forgetting and the Problem of Matter* (Evanston, Ill.: Northwestern University Press, 1946).

22. See Theodor W. Adorno and Max Horkheimer, "The Culture Industry: Enlightenment as Mass Deception," in *Dialectic of Enlightenment* (1944), translated by John Cumming (1944; repr., London: Verso, 1986).

23. Djelal Kadir, "Totalization, Totalitarianism, and Tlön: Borges' Cautionary Tale," in *Reescrituras*, edited by Luz Rodriguez-Carranza and Marilene Nagle (Amsterdam: Editions Rodopi, 2004), 155–65.

24. See Yates, *Giordano Bruno*, 355.

25. See, for example, Hayden White, *Metahistory: The Historical Imagination of Nineteenth-Century Europe* (Baltimore: Johns Hopkins University Press, 1973), and *Figural Realism: Studies in the Mimesis Effect* (Baltimore: Johns Hopkins University Press, 1999).

26. Pierre Nora, *Rethinking France*, translated by Mary Trouille (Chicago: University of Chicago Press, 2001), vol. 1, x.

27. Francis Fukuyama, *The End of History and the Last Man* (New York: Avon Books, 1992).

28. See Andreas Huyssen, "Present Past: Media, Politics, Amnesia," *Public Culture* 12.1 (2000): 21–38.

29. Mario Vargas Llosa, *El hablador* (Barcelona: Seix Barral, 1987); *The Storyteller*, translated by Helen R. Lane (New York: Farrar, Straus and Giroux, 1989).

30. Andreas Huyssen's *Twilight Memories: Marking Time in a Culture of Amnesia* (London: Routledge, 1995); Miriam Hansen, "*Schindler's List* Is Not *Shoah*: The Second Commandment, Popular Modernism, and Public Memory," *Critical Inquiry* 22 (1996): 292–312.

31. See *The Politics of Anti-Semitism*, edited by Alexander Cockburn and Jeffrey St. Clair (Petrolia, Calif.: CounterPunch and AK Press, 2003).

32. For a lucid discussion of this site of memory and its violations see Jean Franco, *The Decline and Fall of the Lettered City* (Cambridge, Mass.: Harvard University Press, 2002), 238–41.

33. Bruno, *On the Composition of Images*, 31.

CHAPTER 5: CARCERAL ARCHIVE

1. On the subtleties of Fray Servando's delineation of a federalism appropriate to Mexico, as opposed to a centralist form of government with which his arguments are mistakenly identified, as well as on the historical corroboration of his prophetic admonitions in Mexico's national life since then, see Adolfo Arrioja Vizcaíno, *Fray Servando Teresa de Mier: Confesiones de un guadalupano federalista* (Mexico City: Editorial Grijalbo, 2003), 187–90.

2. Servando Teresa de Mier Noriega y Guerra, "Carta de despedidad a los mexicanos escrita desde el Castillo de San Juan de Ulua," in *Escritos y memorias*, edited

234   Notes to Chapter 5

by Edmundo O'Gorman (Mexico City: Ediciones de la Universidad Nacional Autónoma, 1945), 35. Abridged English-language edition: *The Memoirs of Fray Servando Teresa de Mier*, translated by Helen R. Lane, edited with an introduction by Susana Rotker (New York: Oxford University Press, 1998).

3. Bella Brodzki, *Can These Bones Live? Translation, Survival, and Cultural Memory* (Stanford, Calif.: Stanford University Press, 2007).

4. Edmundo O'Groman, prologue to *Escritos y memorias*, xxxvi. See also Arrioja Vizcaíno, *Fray Servando*, 188.

5. See Enrique González Pedrero, *País de un solo hombre: El México de Santa Anna*, vol. 1, *La ronda de los contrarios* (Mexico City: Fondo de Cultura Económica, 1993), 32.

6. *Escritos y memorias*, 84; *Memoirs*, 38.

7. I am not unaware of Brazil's contemporaneous imperial rule through the succession of the Portuguese Dom Pedro I to his own court in the New World with the September 7, 1822, declaration of independence, called "O Grito do Ypiringa" (The Shout of the Ipiringa). That imperial gesture was the shout of freedom from European royal fatherhood and an emancipatory rupture with the paternal metropolitan court in Lisbon, now reborn in Rio de Janeiro. For its part, Agustín de Iturbide's Mexican imperial gesture was an "autochthonous," some might say parthenogenic conception and delivery, hence the nomination of "the new emperor" by the Mexican faithful as the "Varón de Dios," the son of God. Not too distant in time and even nearer in New World geography, these imperial gestures are not alien as precedents to what is referred to as the "imperial presidency" at the beginning of the twenty-first century. The virility (*varón*) of the born-again now comes garbed in the "right stuff" of the bomber's jacket and bombardier's leather cod-piece, and its self-divining sanctity eschews natural paternity for supernatural fatherhood. The actors change; the comic farce unfolds to the same script, oblivious to any irony or historical antecedent.

8. Reinaldo Arenas, *El mundo alucinante* (1965; Mexico City: Editorial Diogenes, 1978); Arturo Uslar Pietri, *La isla de Robinson* (Barcelona: Seix Barral, 1987); Carlos Fuentes, *La campaña* (Mexico City: Fondo de Cultura Económica, 1990); Rosa Beltrán, *La corte de los ilusos* (Mexico City: Grupo Editorial Planeta, 1995). On the heterodoxy of Simón Rodríguez see Susana Rotker, "Nation and Mockery: The Oppositional Writings of Simón Rodríguez," *Modern Language Quarterly* 57.2 (June 1996): 253–67.

9. Dena Goodman, *The Republic of Letters: A Cultural History of the French Enlightenment* (Ithaca, N.Y.: Cornell University Press, 1994), 90–135.

10. *Escritos y memorias*, 55–90; *Memoirs*, 18–41.

11. Mier, "Carta de despedida," 39 and passim.

12. Rotker, introduction to *Memoirs*, xlviii–xlix.

13. González Pedrero, *País de un solo hombre*, xxv, xxviii.

14. On the notion of law and the exception see Carl Schmitt, *The Concept of the Political*, translated by George D. Schwab (Chicago: University of Chicago Press, 1996). See also Giorgio Agamben, *State of Exception*, translated by Kevin Attell (Chicago: University of Chicago Press, 2005).

15. Martín Luis Guzmán, *Filadelfia, paraiso de conspiradores y otras historias noveladas* (Mexico City: Compañia General de Ediciones, S.A., 1960).

16. Arrioja Vizcaíno, *Fray Servando*, 142–43.

17. I have dealt with the issues of shifting epistemologies in American studies and postcoloniality in my presidential address to the founding congress of the International American Studies Association, "Defending America Against Its Devotees," in *How Far Is America From Here? Selected Proceedings of the First World Congress of the International American Studies Association 22–24 May 2003*, edited by Theo D'Haen et al (Amsterdam: Editions Rodopi, 2005), 13–34, and in my guest editor's introduction to a special issue of *PMLA: America: The Idea, the Literature*. See "Introduction: America and Its Studies," *PMLA*, 118.1 (2003): 9–24.

18. Arrioja Vizcaíno, *Fray Servando*, 142.

19. Ibid., 149.

20. Beltrán, *La corte*, 131.

21. See Timothy E. Anna, *El imperio de Iturbide* (Mexico City: Consejo Nacional para la Cultura y las Artes / Alianza Editorial, 1991).

22. Cited in Rotker, editor's introduction to *Memoirs*, liv.

23. Ricardo Piglia, *Respiración artificial* (Buenos Aires: Editorial Sudamericana, 1980).

24. The essayistic locus classicus of this process is found in Jorge Luis Borges, "Kafka and His Precursors," in *Other Inquisitions, 1937–1952*, translated by Ruth L. C. Simms (Austin: University of Texas Press, 1964), 106–8. Walter Benjamin, for his part, would diagnose this movement as the progress of "the angel of history." See Walter Benjamin, "Theses on the Philosophy of History, IX," in *Illuminations*, edited by Hannah Arendt (New York: Schocken Books, 1969), 257–58.

25. I discuss this aspect of *theoria* at greater length elsewhere. See Kadir, "Surviving Theory," in my *The Other Writing: Postcolonial Essays in Latin America's Writing Cultures* (West Lafayette, Ind.: Purdue University Press, 1993), chap. 2, 31–44.

26. Ralph Waldo Emerson, "Self Reliance" in *The Complete Works of Ralph Waldo Emerson, Volume II, Essays I (1841)* (Cambridge: Belknap Press of Harvard University Press, 1979), digital text: Ralph Waldo Emerson Institute, www.rwe.org/comm/index.php?option=com_content&task=view&id=125&Itemid=42 (accessed February 15, 2010).

27. Octavio Paz, *The Labyrinth of Solitude: Life and Thought in Mexico*, translated by Lysander Kemp (New York: Grove Press, 1961).

28. Adam Liptak, "U.S. Imprisons One in 100 Adults, Report Finds," *New York Times* (February 29, 2008), www.nytimes.com/2008/02/29/us/29prison.html?_r=1&oref=slogin (accessed January 12, 2010). The text of the report on which the article is based, "One in 100: Behind Bars in America 2008," by the Pew Charitable Trust, www.pewcenteronthestates.org/uploadedFiles/One%20in%20100.pdf (accessed February 15, 2010).

29. Christopher Hitchens, *For the Sake of Argument* (London: Verso, 1993), 12–24.

30. Ibid., 18.

31. Ibid., 14.

32. Cited in ibid., 19.

33. Ibid., 14.

34. Reinaldo Arenas, *Hallucinations; or, The Ill-fated Peregrinations of Fray Servando*, translated by Andrew Hurley (Harmondsworth, England: Penguin Books, 2002). The trials of Arenas's novel itself resonate with the "peregrinations" of Fray Servando it narrates. Banned by the Cuban government in 1966, the novel's first publication, unbeknownst to the author, was in French, *Le monde hallucinant* (Paris: Editions du Seuil, 1968).

CHAPTER 6: THE ARTS OF MITIGATION

1. Zbigniew Herbert, "The Power of Taste," in *Report from the Besieged City and Other Poems*, translated by John Carpenter and Bogdana Carpenter (New York: Ecco Press, 1985), 69.

2. Zbigniew Herbert, *The Barbarian in the Garden*, translated by Michael March and Jaroslow Anders (San Diego: Harcourt Brace Jovanovich, 1985).

3. Zbigniew Herbert, *Mr. Cogito*, translated by John Carpenter and Bogdana Carpenter (Hopewell, N.J.: Ecco Press, 1993).

4. Osip Mandelstam, "Conversation About Dante," translated by Clarence Brown and Robert Hughes, in *Selected Essays*, edited by Sidney Monas (Austin: University of Texas Press, 1977), 8.

5. Zbigniew Herbert, "Delta," in *Still Life with a Bridle: Essays and Apocryphas*, translated by John Carpenter and Bogdana Carpenter (Hopewell, N.J.: Ecco Press, 1991), 6–7.

6. I take the phrase from the American critic and art historian Lois Parkinson Zamora, *The Inordinate Eye: New World Baroque and Latin American Fiction* (Chicago: University of Chicago Press, 2006).

7. Wallace Stevens, "The Snow Man" (*Harmonium*, 1923), in *The Palm at the End of the Mind*, edited by Holly Stevens (New York: Alfred A. Knopf, 1971), 54.

8. Paul Valéry, *La soirée avec Monsieur Teste*, vol. 2 of *Oeuvres* (Paris: Gallimard, Editions de Pléiade, 1960), 10–75.

9. Zbigniew Herbert, "Still Life with a Bridle," in *Still Life with a Bridle*, 97.

10. Wallace Stevens, "The Comedian as the Letter C" (*Harmonium*, 1923), in *Palm at the End of the Mind*, ed. Holly Stevens, 61.

11. On Herbert's fascination with monochromatic painting, see, for example, his discussion of one of his favorite Dutch painters, Jan van Goyen in Zbigniew Herbert, "Delta," esp. 14–17.

12. I am referring, of course, to Edgar Allan Poe's "Murders in the Rue Morgue," and his intrepid detective, master of ratiocination, who makes his debut there and ends by being the paradigm of the type. See, "Murders in the Rue Morgue" (1841), in *The Complete Poems and Stories of Edgar Allan Poe*, edited by Arthur Hobson Quinn and Edward H. O'Neill (New York: Alfred A. Knopf, 1967), 315–41.

13. Zbigniew Herbert, "September 17," in *Report from the Besieged City and Other Poems*, translated by John Carpenter and Bogdana Carpenter (New York: Ecco Press, 1985), 63; Zbigniew Herbert, "Report from the Besieged City," in *Report from the Besieged City*, 76–78.

14. Zbigniew Herbert, "From the Top of the Stairs," in *Report from the Besieged City*, 14.

15. Torrentius, *Emblematic Still Life with Flagon, Glass, Jug and Bridle* (1614), Rijksmeum, Amsterdam, www.rijksmuseum.nl/aria/aria_assets/SK-A-2813?id=SK-A-2813&page=1&lang=en&context_space=aria_catalogs&context_id=Term_000 26417_en (accessed January 13, 2010).

16. Mandelstam, "Conversation About Dante," 8–9.

17. See, Torrentius, *Temptation: Couple Making Love*, n.d., Rijksmuseum, Amsterdam, www.rijksmuseum.nl/aria/aria_assets/SK-A-2813?page=1&lang=en&context_space=aria_catalogs&context_id=Term_00026417_en (accessed January 13, 2010).

18. Herbert, "Still Life with a Bridle," 106.

19. Ibid., 79.

20. See *L'art e l'ecriture*, François Almaleh Web site, www.almaleh.com/ecriture/inscriptions/torrentius.html (accessed January 13, 2010).

21. Zbigniew Herbert, "Still Life with a Bridle," 79.

22. See book emblem at Rijksmuseum, Amsterdam, www.rijksmuseum.nl/aria/aria_assets/SK-A-2813?page=3&lang=en&context_space=aria_catalogs&context_id=Term_00026417_en (accessed January 13, 2010).

23. Herbert, "Still Life with a Bridle," 79.

24. Ibid., 99, 100.

25. Ibid., 80.

26. See Seamus Heaney, "Atlas of Civilization," in *The Government of the Tongue: Selected Prose, 1978–1987* (New York: Noonday / Farrar, Straus and Giroux, 1989), 54–70, for commentary on *Barbarian in the Garden*, *Selected Poems* (1986), and *Report from the Besieged City*.

27. Seamus Heaney, "The Government of the Tongue," in *Government of the Tongue*, 92–93.

28. Herbert, "Still Life with a Bridle," 97.

29. Zbigniew Herbert, "Albigensians, Inquisitors, and Troubadors," in *Barbarian in the Garden*, 101–30.

30. Herbert, "Still Life with a Bridle," 101.

31. Zbigniew Herbert, "Pebble," in *Selected Poems*, Czeslaw Milosz and Peter Dale Scott, trans, (New York: Ecco Press, 1986), 108.

32. I am referring, of course, to Gertrude Stein's 1913 poem "Sacred Emily," collected in her 1922 book *Geography and Plays*, and to Pablo Neruda's *Odas elementales* (1954–57).

33. Carlos Drummond de Andrade, "In the Middle of the Road," translated by Elizabeth Bishop, in *The Longman Anthology of World Literature: The Twentieth Century*, vol. F, 2nd ed., edited by Djelal Kadir and Ursula Heise (New York: Pearson Education, 2008), 247.

34. I am referring to the opening verse of Dante's *Inferno*—"Nel mezzo del cammin di nostra vita" (In the middle of the journey of our life . . .)—and to the posthumously published, seminal poem of Stéphane Mallarmé, *Un coup de dés jamais n'abolira le hasard* (A Throw of the Dice Will Never Abolish Chance) (1914).

35. Hannah Arendt, "Total Domination," from the *Origins of Totalitarianism* (1951), in *The Portable Hannah Arendt*, edited by Peter Baehr (London: Penguin Books / Putnam, 2000), 137.

36. Zbigniew Herbert, "Defence of the Templars," in *Barbarian in the Garden*, 131–47.

37. Ibid., 147.

38. Ibid., 144.

39. Ibid., 141. Herbert, no doubt, was aware that the "division of labor" between monarch and pope might have been for political cover. King Philip and Pope Clement V, both Frenchman, may have shared certain aims. It was not, and still is not clear when they colluded for common ends, or when they cooperated for the sake of their respective agendas.

40. Ibid.

41. Ibid., 135.

42. Herbert, "Albigensians, Inquisitors, and Troubadors," 122.

43. Zbigniew Herbert, "Atlas," in *The King of the Ants*, translated by John Carpenter and Bogdana Carpenter (Hopewell, N.J.: Ecco Press, 1999), 27.

44. Zbigniew Herbert, "Mr. Cogito and the Imagination," in *Report from the Besieged City*, 19.

45. Zbigniew Herbert, "The Trial," in *Report from the Besieged City*, 58–59; Herbert, "Babylon," in *Report from the Besieged City*, 35.

46. Translators'-editor's introduction, vii.

47. Herbert, "The Trial," 59.

48. The bibliography at the beginning of the new century is so immense as to

constitute a terror in itself. For the question of terrorism in comparative literature, see Djelal Kadir, "Comparative Literature in an Age of Terrorism," in *Comparative Literature in An Age of Globalization*, edited by Haun Saussy (Baltimore: Johns Hopkins University Press, 2006), 68–77.

49. Herbert, "Albigensians, Inquisitors, and Troubadors," 122.
50. Herbert, "The Trial," 58–59.
51. Ibid., 58.
52. See note 2.
53. Heaney, "Atlas of Civilization," 69.
54. Herbert, "From the Top of the Stairs," 14.

CHAPTER 7: THE LABORS OF CASSANDRA

This chapter is for Richard J. Bernstein: it might not be "a chitter-chatter of a transcendental matter," after all.

1. Hannah Arendt, *Eichmann in Jerusalem: A Report on the Banality of Evil* (New York: Viking Press, 1963. Based on "A Reporter at Large: Eichmann in Jerusalem," a five-art reportage originally published in the *New Yorker*, February 16, 23, and March 2, 9, 16, 1963.
2. Hannah Arendt, "Truth and Politics," in *The Portable Hannah Arendt*, edited by Peter Baehr (New York: Penguin Books/Putnam, 2000. Originally published in the *New Yorker*, February 25, 1967, and reprinted in Hannah Arendt, *Between Past and Future* (New York: Viking Press, 1967), 548.
3. Aeschylus, *Agamemnon*, translated by Richard Lattimore, in *The Complete Greek Tragedies*, edited by David Grene and Richard Lattimore (Chicago: University of Chicago Press, 1992), vol. 1, 68–69, ll. 1078–1104.
4. See Elisabeth Young-Bruehl, *Hannah Arendt: For Love of the World* (New Haven, Conn.: Yale University Press, 1982), 33.
5. Arendt, "Truth and Politics," 545.
6. Mario Vargas Llosa, *La verdad de las mentiras: Ensayos sobre literatura* (Barcelona: Seix Barral, 1990; expanded edition Madrid: Alfaguara, 2002).
7. Hannah Arendt, "Franz Kafka: A Revaluation," in *Essays in Understanding, 1930–1954*, edited by Jerome Kohn (New York: Schocken Books, 1994), 69–80; originally published in *Partisan Review* 11.4 (1944): 78–79.
8. Recall his failed presidential bid in 1990, which he lost to Alberto Fujimori, his subsequent becoming a Spanish citizen, and his appointment to Spain's national academy, the Real academia española.
9. Mario Vargas Llosa, *La verdad de las mentiras* (2002), 26–28. The translation here is my own.
10. Hannah Arendt, *The Origins of Totalitarianism* (1951; repr., New York: Schocken Books, 2004). This revised edition gathers prefaces and emendations from the 1958, 1968, 1972 editions.

11. Hannah Arendt, "Total Domination," from *The Origins of Totalitarianism*, in *Portable Hannah Arendt*, 136–37.
12. Arendt, "Total Domination," 120.
13. Hannah Arendt, preface to *Men in Dark Times* (1955; repr., New York: Harcourt, Brace, 1968), ix.
14. Arendt, *Eichmann in Jerusalem*, 273.
15. Arendt, "Total Domination," 140.
16. See Pete Warren, "Launching a New Kind of Warfare," *Guardian* (October 26, 2006), http://technology.guardian.co.uk/weekly/story/0,,1930960,00.html (accessed January 13, 2010); BBC News, "Israel Admits Phosphorus Bombing" (October 26, 2006), http://news.bbc.co.uk/2/hi/middle_east/6075408.stm (accessed January 13, 2010); ABC Newsonline, "US Defends Use of Phosphorus Bombs in Fallujah" (November 17, 2005), www.abc.net.au/news/newsitems/200511/s1508598.htm (accessed January 13, 2010); UNICEF Press Centre, "Statement on Gaza by United Nations Humanitarian Agencies Working in the Occupied Palestinian Territory" (August 3, 2006), www.unicef.org/media/media_35226.html (accessed January 13, 2010).
17. Arendt, "On Humanity in Dark Times: Thoughts About Lessing," in *Men in Dark Times*, 13.
18. Ibid., 14–15.
19. Arendt, preface to *Men in Dark Times*, viii.
20. On the role of "megaphones," human and electronic propaganda instruments, see Stewart Purvis, "Israel Ups the Stakes in the Propaganda War," *Guardian* (November 20, 2006), www.guardian.co.uk/print/0,,329636899-103552,00.html (accessed January 13, 2010).
21. Hannah Arendt, "Organized Guilt and Universal Responsibility," in *Essays in Understanding*, 124.
22. Arendt, "Total Domination," 120.
23. Arendt, "Organized Guilt," 126–27, note.
24. See note 11.
25. See, for example, Elisabeth Young-Bruehl, *Why Arendt Matters* (New Haven, Conn.: Yale University Press, 2006).
26. Arendt, "Truth and Politics," 548.
27. Arendt, "Franz Kafka," 70.
28. Ibid., 72.
29. Arendt, "Organized Guilt," 131.
30. Walter Benjamin, "Theses on the Philosophy of History, IX" in *Illuminations*, edited by Hannah Arendt (New York: Schocken Books, 1969), 257–58. See also Arendt, "Walter Benjamin, 1892–1940," in *Men in Dark Times*, 153–206.
31. Arendt, *Eichmann in Jerusalem*, 61.
32. Quoted in ibid., 63.

33. Arendt, "Organized Guilt," 131.

34. See Philippe Sands, *Lawless World* (New York: Viking Press, 2005), especially chapter 3, "A New International Court." See, also, Reuters News Service, "Chertoff [Homeland Security Secretary Michael Chertoff] Says U.S. Threatened by International Law," November 17, 2006, www.reuters.com/article/idUSN1744571420061117 (accessed February 15, 2010).

35. Arendt, "Organized Guilt," 131.

36. See United Nations Office for the Coordination of Humanitarian Affairs, "The Agreement of Movement and Access One Year On" (November 2006), www.ochaopt.org/documents/AMA_One_Year_On_Nov06_final.pdf (accessed January 13, 2010). See also Ahda Soueif, "A Project of Dispossession Can Never Be a Noble Cause," *Guardian* (November 17, 2006), http://ahdafsoueif.com/Articles/Project_of_Dispossession.pdf (accessed February 15, 2010):

Before Donald Rumsfeld departed from the Pentagon, the "Transformation Group" he headed worked with an Israeli army team to develop ideas for controlling the Palestinians after Israel withdraws from the occupied territories. Eyal Weizman, an Israeli academic who has written about this cooperation, tells us that they decided to do this through an invisible occupation: Israel would "seal the hard envelopes" around Palestinian towns and generate "effects" directed against the "human elements of resistance". We saw this concept being implemented in Beit Hanoun last week when the Israeli army killed 19 sleeping people with a missile attack. . . . To make its own denial stick, Israel has to deny and suppress Palestinian history. To impose its design on Palestine, it has to somehow make the Palestinians disappear. "Things bad begun make strong themselves by ill"; and so the ethnicide continues. The new deputy prime minister, Avigdor Lieberman, plots against the Palestinians within Israel. The Israeli army kills and terrorises the Palestinians in the West Bank and Gaza. Zionists and their friends are desperate to silence the voices of and for Palestine.

37. Hannah Arendt, "The Social Question," in *Portable Hannah Arendt*, 262. Originally published in Arendt, *On Revolution* (New York: Viking Press, 1963).

38. Herman Melville, *Billy Budd, Sailor (an Inside Narrative)*, edited by Harrison Hayford and Merton M. Sealts, Jr. (Chicago: University of Chicago Press, 1962), 128.

39. For a concise discussion of the controversy, see Immanuel Kant, *Religion and Rational Theology*, translated and edited by Allen W. Wood and George Di Giovanni (Cambridge: Cambridge University Press, 1996), xi–xxiv and 3–6.

40. I am paraphrasing from Hannah Arendt, "The Public and the Private Realm," in *Portable Hannah Arendt*, 182–205. Originally published in Arendt, *The Human Condition: The Vita Activa* (Chicago: University of Chicago Press, 1958).

41. Arendt, *Eichmann in Jerusalem*, 48–49; italics in the original.

42. Richard J. Bernstein, one of Arendt's most astute students, and my unforgettable Yale philosophy teacher to whom this chapter is dedicated, has thoroughly understood the chiastic potential of this false binarism of evil and banality and its pragmatic perils. See Richard J. Bernstein, *Radical Evil: A Philosophical*

Interrogation (Cambridge: Polity Press, 2002); and *Hannah Arendt and the Jewish Question* (Cambridge, Mass.: MIT Press, 1996). A number of historians, on the other hand, remain in denial about the potential of banality for radical evil, though they do acknowledge the continued relevance of Arendt for today's politics, especially for twenty-first-century neo-Zionism. See, for example, Russell Jacoby, "Hannah Arendt's Fame Rests on the Wrong Foundation," *Chronicle of Higher Education* 53.16 (December 8, 2006), B13. See also Susan Neiman, *Evil in Modern Thought* (Princeton, N.J.: Princeton University Press, 2002), especially the section of chapter 4, 271–304, devoted to Arendt.

CHAPTER 8: THE PEOPLE'S REPUBLIC

1. "The Chinese government and the official literary organizations on the mainland, such as the Chinese Writers' Association . . . dismissed Gao as an unknown writer in China and denounced the Swedish Academy for awarding the Prize to Gao with a political intent." Kwok-Kan Tam, "Gao Xingjian, the Nobel Prize and the Politics of Recognition," introduction to *Soul of Chaos: Critical Perspectives on Gao Xingjian*, edited by Kwok-Kan Tam (Hong Kong: Chinese University of Hong Kong Press, 2001), 3. See also Julia Lovell, "Gao Xingjian, the Nobel Prize, and Chinese Intellectuals. Notes on the Aftermath of the Nobel Prize 2000," *Modern Chinese Literature and Culture* 14.2 (2002): 1–50. Gao's own response to the official reaction to his Nobel prize, cited as epigraph for this chapter, is found in an interview with him, as reported in Asia Society, New York (February 26, 2001), see www.asiasociety.org/arts-culture/literature/a-conversation-gao-xingjian (accessed February 15, 2010).

2. "Beijing Attacks Literature Award," BBC News (October 13, 2000), http://news.bbc.co.uk/2/hi/europe/970184.stm (accessed January 13, 2010); "China in Denial over Nobel Laureate," BBC News (December 10, 2000), http://news.bbc.co.uk/2/hi/asia-pacific/1064016.stm (accessed January 13, 2010). See also David S. G. Goodman, "Regional and Global China: Culture, Society and the State," *Inter-Cultural Studies: A Forum on Social Change and Cultural Diversity* (Newcastle, Australia) 3.2 (Spring 2003): 12–13.

3. Nobelprize.org, "Nobel Prize for Literature," press release (October 12, 2000), http://nobelprize.org/nobel_prizes/literature/laureates/2000/press.html (accessed January 13, 2010).

4. Presentation speech by Professor Göran Malmqvist of the Swedish Academy (December 10, 2000), http://nobelprize.org/nobel_prizes/literature/laureates/2000/presentation-speech.html (accessed January 13, 2010).

5. Nobelprize.org, picture of Gao Xingjian and citation of his Nobel award, http://nobelprize.org/nobel_prizes/literature/laureates/2000/ (accessed January 13, 2010).

6. See, Pascale Casanova, *La république mondiale des lettres* (Paris: Editions

du Seuil, 1999; *The World Republic of Letters*, translated by M. B. DeBevoise (Cambridge, Mass.: Harvard University Press, 2004). The phrase "république des lettres" originates in Guillaume Budé, appointed to the Collège de France when Francis I instituted it in 1532.

7. Casanova, *World Republic*, 154.

8. Ibid., 153.

9. Jorge Luis Borges, "The Library of Babel," in *The Collected Fictions*, translated and edited by Andrew Hurley (New York: Viking/Penguin, 1998), 113. The quotation from *Anatomy of Melancholy* comes from pt.2, sec. 2, mem. 4.

10. Gao Xingjian, "Meiyou zhuyi" (1993), in *Meiyou zhuyi* (Hong Kong: Tiandi youxian gongsi,1996), 8–17, translated by Winnie Lau, Deorah Sauviat, and Martin Williams as "Without Isms," *Journal of the Oriental Society of Australia* 27–28 (1995–96); I am citing from "Without Isms," in *The Case for Literature*, translated by Mabel Lee (New Haven, Conn.: Yale University Press, 2007), 64–77. I shall be referring to Lee's translation. The original version of this key essay was Gao's paper presented at a November 15, 1993, conference in Paris whose subject was the previous forty years of Chinese literature.

11. The relationship between state and nation is an intricate one, which has sustained ample theoretical scrutiny. Most helpful and most on point, I have found, are Isaiah Berlin, *Vico and Herder* (London: Hogarth Press, 1976); Alfred Cobban, *Rousseau and the Modern State*, 2nd ed. (London: Allen and Unwin, 1964); John Edwards, *Language Society and Identity* (Oxford: Basil Blackwell, 1985); Eric Hobsbawm, *Nations and Nationalism Since 1870* (Cambridge: Cambridge University Press, 1990); Anthony D. Smith, *Nations and Nationalism in a Global Era* (Cambridge: Polity Press/Blackwell Publishers, 1995).

12. See Smith, *Nations and Nationalism*, 104: "As of now, the national state remains the only internationally recognized structure of political association. Today, only duly constituted 'national states' are admitted to the United Nations and other international bodies, though aspirant ethnic nations may be admitted as observers."

13. See Al Jazeera Web site (September 5, 2007), http://english.aljazeera.net/NR/exeres/790225F4-CD7E-4CBF-B30A-7EAE12CD5339.htm (accessed January 13, 2010).

14. See the documentary *Documenting "Nowhere People,"* by photojournalist Greg Constantine (August 12, 2007), http://youtube.com/watch?v=zBb9uMtIwS0 (accessed January 13, 2010).

15. Aihwa Ong, *Flexible Citizenship: The Cultural Logics of Transnationality* (Durham, N.C.: Duke University Press, 1999), 6. Ong first rehearses this concept some six years earlier in her essay "On the Edge of Empires: Flexible Citizenship among Chinese in Diaspora," *positions* 1.3 (Winter 1993): 745–78. The Chinese diaspora she refers to is that of the Pacific Rim and archipelago.

16. Gao Xinjian, "Wilted Chrysanthemums," in *Case for Literature*, 150.

17. Gao Xinjian, "The Case for Literature," in *Case for Literature*, 32–33.

18. *The Divine Comedy of Dante Alighieri: Inferno*, translated by Allen Mandelbaum (New York: Bantam Books, 1982), 15.

19. See, for example, Smith, *Nations and Nationalism*, especially chapter 4, "The Crisis of the National State," 85 ff. For a more nuanced treatment of the topic see, Ellen Meiksins Wood, "Labor, the State, and Class Struggle," *Monthly Review* 49.3 (1997): 1–18, e.g., "Behind every transnational corporation is a national base, which depends on its local state to sustain its viability" (12). See, also, Frans J. Shuurman, "The Nation-State, Emancipatory Spaces, and Development Studies in the Global Era," in *Globalization and Development Studies: Challenges for the 21st Century*, edited by Frans J. Shuurman (London: Sage Publications, 2001), 61–76.

20. Gao, "The Case for Literature," 61.

21. Gao, "Author's Preface to *Without Isms*," in *Case for Literature*, 28.

23. Gao Xingjian, *Soul Mountain*, translated by Mabel Lee (New York: HarperCollins, 2000); Chinese original, *Lingshan* (Taipei, Taiwan: Lianjing Chubanshe, 1990).

24. For a useful historical background on Gao's biography and career, see Mabel Lee, "Contextualizing 2000 Nobel Laureate Gao Xingjian," introduction to her translation of Gao's *Case for Literature*. See note 10.

25. "Two X-rays on two separate days at two separate hospitals had confirmed that he had lung cancer. His father who died a couple of years [sic] earlier of the disease also had the final X-ray. However, it turned out that the final X-ray indicated a wrong diagnosis had been made. . . . It would seem that the psychological experience of what seemed to be an interminable period of confrontation with death caused him to review the whole of his life. In his novel *Soul Mountain* dislodged fragments of memories are woven into his reflections on his personal history, the history of the people who constitute his cultural matrix, and the history of human society and its impact on the environment. The novel also constitutes an unarticulated commitment to literary creation of which he is the sole author." Mabel Lee, "Gao Xingjian on the Issue of Literary Creation for the Modern Writer," *Journal of Asian Pacific Communication* 9.1–2 (1999): 83–96.

26. Gao, "Wilted Chrysanthemums," 149.

27. Gao, "The Case for Literature," 34–35.

28. Gao, "Without Isms," 67.

29. Gao, "Literature and Metaphysics: About *Soul Mountain*," in *Case for Literature*, 96.

30. Gao Xingjian interview, Asia Society, New York.

31. Gilbert Fong, "Gao Xingjian and the Idea of the Theatre," in *Soul of Chaos*, ed. Kwok-Kan Tam, 147–55.

32. Discussed by Gao in a 1996 essay translated into English as "Cold Literature," in *Case for Literature*, 78–81.
33. In Gao's essay, the title of which Fong translates as "Playwriting and the Neutral Actor," and which appeared in the author's volume *Meiyou zhuyi* (*Without Isms*) (Hong Kong: Tiandi tushu yushian gongsi, 1996), 253–66.
34. Fong, "Gao Xingjian and the Idea of the Theatre," 153. Gao discusses this convention in his essay "My Drama and My Key," whose title is transcribed and translated by Fong, with the original having appeared in Gao, *Meiyou zhuyi*, 235–52.
35. Mandelbaum, introduction to the *Inferno*, xi.
36. Kevin Brownlee, "Dante and the Classical Poets," in *The Cambridge Companion to Dante*, edited by Rachel Jacoff (Cambridge: Cambridge University Press, 1993), 100–119.
37. Gao, *Soul Mountain*, 447.
38. Ibid., 447.
39. Ibid., 447–48.
40. Ibid., 448.
41. Gao, "Author's Preface to *Without Isms*, 28.
42. Gao, "Without Isms," 67.
43. Ibid., 67–68.
44. Ibid., 72.
45. Ibid., 73.
46. Ibid., 68.
47. Ibid., 76.
48. Ibid., 75.

CHAPTER 9: MEMO FROM THE NEXT MILLENNIUM

1. Italo Calvino, *Six Memos for the Next Millennium*, translated by Patrick Creagh (Cambridge, Mass.: Harvard University Press, 1988).
2. Calvino, "Lightness," in *Six Memos*, 3–29.
3. Ibid., 4.
4. Italo Calvino, *Invisible Cities*, translated by William Weaver (San Diego: Harcourt, Brace, 1974), 126.
5. Calvino, "Lightness," 5.
6. Ibid., 4.
7. Ibid., 5–6.
8. Ibid., 16.
9. Ibid.
10. Ibid.
11. Cited in ibid. Calvino is citing poem 93 from Dickinson's *The Complete Poems of Emily Dickinson* (Boston: Little, Brown, 1924); bartleby.com (2000), www.bartleby.com/113/ (accessed January 13, 2010).

12. *Final Harvest: Emily Dickinson's Poems*, edited by Thomas H. Johnson (Boston: Little, Brown, 1961), 176–77. Also accessible at American Poems Web site, www.americanpoems.com/poets/emilydickinson/10661 (accessed January 13, 2010).

13. Calvino, "Exactitude," in *Six Memos*, 55.

14. Dickinson, *Final Harvest*, 248–49.

15. Edgar Allan Poe, another American precursor of Calvino on the subject, lampoons this type of consistency in his 1849 futuristic send-up of scientific conviction, "Mellonta Tauta," in *The Complete Poems and Stories of Edgar Allan Poe*, vol. 2, edited by Arthur Hobson Quinn and Edward H. O'Neill (New York: Alfred A. Knopf, 1967), 688–89.

16. Calvino, "Lightness," 4.

17. Calvino, "Visibility," in *Six Memos*, 91.

EPILOGUE

1. Zhang Longxi, *Unexpected Affinities: Reading Across Cultures* (Toronto: University of Toronto Press, 2007).

2. Erich Auerbach, *Mimesis: The Representation of Reality in Western Literature*, translated by Willard R. Trask (Princeton, N.J.: Princeton University Press, 1953); Ernst Robert Curtius, *European Literature and the Latin Middle Ages*, translated by Willard R. Trask (Princeton, N.J.: Princeton University Press, 1953).

3. Edward W. Said, *Culture and Imperialism* (New York: Alfred A. Knopf, 1993), 51; italics in the original.

4. One of the most complex ancient deities, our knowledge of Hekate's roles is based on two original sources, the "Hymn to Demeter," translated in *The Homeric Hymns*, edited by Susan C. Shelmerdine (Newburyport, Mass.: Focus Publishing/R. Pullins, 1995), 35–37, ll. 24–59; and on Hesiod's *Theogony*, in Hesiod, *Theogony, Works and Days, Shield*, translated and edited by Apostolos N. Athanassakis (Baltimore: Johns Hopkins University Press, 1983), 23–24, ll. 409–51.

5. For a discussion of the perils in the instrumentalization of the trivium's verbal arts set against themselves and each other, see Paul de Man's 1982 essay "The Resistance to Theory," in *Resistance to Theory* (Minneapolis: University of Minnesota Press, 1986), 3–20. Discussion of the trivium in this context, especially, occurs between pages 13 and 19.

6. Emily Apter, *The Translation Zone: A New Comparative Literature* (Princeton, N.J.: Princeton University Press, 2006).

7. On the recasting of Turkish ethno-racial origins and the historical revisionism of this period that consigned foundational texts such as Rashiduddin's to the authorship of "racially questionable" precursors such as this Jewish-born Persian historian, see chapter 3, "Mimicry in Modern Turkey: The Place of German and

Turkish Jews," of Kader Konuk's *East West Mimesis: Auerbach in Turkey* (Stanford, Calif.: Stanford University Press, 2010).

8. ETC Group, "Extreme Genetic Engineering: An Introduction to Synthetic Biology" (January 16, 2007), www.etcgroup.org/en/materials/publications. html?id=602 (accessed January 12, 2010). See also, Stephen Leahy, "Synthetic Biology: Group Seeks Ban on 'Living Machines,'" Inter Press Service (January 21, 2007), www.commondreams.org/headlines07/0121-01.htm.

9. For one of the latest avatars of the Collège credo see Christian Ferrer et al., *'Patafisica, junto con especulaciones de Alfred Jarry* (Logroño, La Rioja, Spain: Edición Pepitas de calabaza, 2002); and the special issue of the Argentine journal *Artefacto: Pensamientos sobre la técnica*, no. 3 (Buenos Aires, 1999).

10. Wlad Godzich lucidly diagnosed the processes of this cultural conversation in his now classic treatise *The Culture of Literacy* (Cambridge, Mass.: Harvard University Press, 1994).

11. J. M. Coetzee, "Confessions and Double Thoughts: Tolstoy, Rousseau, Dostoyevsky," in *Doubling the Point: J. M. Coetzee, Essays and Interviews*, edited by David Attwell (Cambridge, Mass.: Harvard University Press, 1992), 251–93. See also Derek Attridge, *J. M. Coetzee and the Ethics of Reading* (Chicago: University of Chicago Press, 2004), especially chapter 6, "Confessing in the Third Person," 138–61.

12. Italo Calvino, *Invisible Cities*, translated by William Weaver (San Diego: Harcourt, Brace, 1974).

13. David Damrosch lucidly tracks this interlocution and its translational itinerary in his eminently conversational book *What Is World Literature?* (Princeton, N.J.: Princeton University Press, 2003). See especially the introduction, 1–36. For complete references to Eckermann and Goethe see his bibliography, 308–9.

14. The ephemerality of the archival repertoire as spectacle and performance is tracked and enacted by Diana Taylor in *The Archive and the Repertoire: Performing Cultural Memory in the Americas* (Durham, N.C.: Duke University Press, 2003). The archive as mythological overdeterminacy is explored by Roberto González Echevarría, *Myth and Archive* (Cambridge: Cambridge University Press. 1990).

15. Jorge Luis Borges, "Kafka and His Precursors," in *Other Inquisitions, 1937–1952*, edited and translated by Ruth L. C. Simms (Austin: University of Texas Press, 1964), 106–8.

16. Said, *Culture and Imperialism*.

17. Adorno's original statement on poetry after Auschwitz as being barbaric occurs in his 1949 "Essay on Cultural Criticism and Society," first published in 1951 and collected in *Prisms*, translated by Samuel and Shierry Weber (Cambridge, Mass.: MIT Press, 1967), 19–34. The palinode to that statement is published in a 1961 essay translated as "Commitment" and collected in Adorno's *Aesthetics and*

Politics, translated by Ronald Taylor (London: New Left Books, 1977); and also in *Negative Dialectics*, translated by E. B. Ashton (New York: Continuum, 1973), 362.

18. Zbigniew Herbert, "Report from the Besieged City," in *Report from the Besieged City and Other Poems*, translated by John Carpenter and Bogdana Carpenter (New York: Ecco Press, 1985), 76–78.

Bibliography

Adorno, Theodor W. *Aesthetics and Politics.* Translated by Ronald Taylor. London: New Left Books, 1977.

———. "Essay on Cultural Criticism and Society." *Prisms.* Translated by Samuel and Shierry Weber. Cambridge, Mass.: MIT Press, 1967.

———. *Negative Dialectics.* Translated by E. B. Ashton. New York: Continuum, 1973.

———. *Quasi una Fantasia: Essays on Modern Music.* Translated by Rodney Livingstone. London: Verso, 1992.

Adorno, Theodor W., and Max Horkheimer. *Dialectic of Enlightenment.* Translated by John Cumming. 1944; repr., London: Verso, 1986.

Aeschylus. *The Complete Greek Tragedies.* Translated and edited by David Grene and Richard Lattimore. Chicago: University of Chicago Press, 1992.

Agamben, Giorgio. *State of Exception.* Translated by Kevin Attell. Chicago: University of Chicago Press, 2005.

Ahmed, Sara. *Strange Encounters: Embodied Others in Postcoloniality.* London: Routledge, 2000.

Alberti, Leon Battista. *On Painting.* Translated by Cercil Grayson. New York: Penguin Books, 1991.

Anna, Timothy E. *El imperio de Iturbide.* Mexico City: Consejo Nacional Para la Cultura y las Artes / Alianza Editorial, 1991.

Antoon, Sinan. "Of Bridges and Birds: Sinan Antoon Sifts Through the Rubble of His Native Baghdad." *Al Ahram Weekly Online,* no. 634 (April 17–23, 2003), http://weekly.ahram.org.eg/2003/634/bo1.htm. (accessed February 15, 2010).

Apter, Emily. *The Translation Zone: A New Comparative Literature.* Princeton, N.J.: Princeton University Press, 2006.

Arenas, Reinaldo. *Hallucinations; or, The Ill-fated Peregrinations of Fray Servando.* Translated by Andrew Hurley. Harmondsworth, England: Penguin Books, 2002.

Arendt, Hannah. *Between Past and Future.* New York: Viking Press, 1967.

———. *Eichmann in Jerusalem: A Report on the Banality of Evil.* New York: Viking Press, 1963.

———. *Essays in Understanding, 1930–1954*. Edited by Jerome Kohn. New York: Schocken Books, 1994.

———. "Franz Kafka: A Revaluation." In *Essays in Understanding, 1930–1954*, edited by Jerome Kohn, 69–80. New York: Schocken Books, 1994. Originally published in *Partisan Review* 11.4 (1944): 78–79.

———. *The Human Condition: The Vita Activa*. Chicago: University of Chicago Press, 1958.

———. *Men in Dark Times*. 1955; repr., New York: Harcourt, Brace, 1968.

———. *On Revolution*. New York: Viking Press, 1963.

———. *The Origins of Totalitarianism*. 1951; repr., New York: Schocken Books, 2004.

———. *The Portable Hannah Arendt*. Edited by Peter Baehr. London: Penguin Books / Putnam, 2000.

Aristotle. *The Basic Works of Aristotle*. Edited by Richard McKeon. New York: Random House, 1941.

Armitage, Angus. "The Cosmology of Giordano Bruno." *Annals of Science* 6 (1948): 24–31.

Arnold, Matthew. "The Function of Criticism at the Present Time" (October 29, 1864). In *The Norton Anthology of Theory and Criticism*, edited by Vincent B. Leitch et al., 806–25. New York: W. W. Norton, 2001.

Arriojo Vizcaíno, Adolfo. *Fray Servando Teresa de Mier: Confesiones de un guadalupano federalista*. Mexico City: Editorial Grijalbo, 2003.

Artefacto: Pensamientos sobre la técnica (journal). Issue no. 3. Buenos Aires, 1999.

Attridge, Derek. *J. M. Coetzee and the Ethics of Reading*. Chicago: University of Chicago Press, 2004.

Auerbach, Erich. "Erich Auerbach: The Three Traits of Dante's Poetry." In *Erich Auerbach: Geschichte und Aktualität eines europäischen Philologen*, edited by Karlheinz Barck and Martin Treml, 414–25. Berlin: Kadmos, 2007.

———. "Figura." In *Neue Dantestudien: Dante Hakkinda Yeni Arastirmalar*, edited by Robert Anhegger, Walter Ruben, and Andreas Tietze, 11–71. Istanbul: Ibrahim Horoz Basimevi, 1944.

———. *Mimesis: Dargestellte Wirklichkeit in der Abendländischen Literatur*. Bern: A. Francke AG Verlag, 1946.

———. *Mimesis: The Representation of Reality in Western Literature*. Translated by Willard R. Trask. Princeton, N.J.: Princeton University Press, 1953.

———. "Philology and *Weltliteratur*." Translated by Maire Said and Edward Said. *Centennial Review* 13.1 (Winter 1969): 1–17.

———. *Scenes from the Drama of European Literature*. Translated by Erich Auerbach, Catherine Garvin, and Ralph Manheim. Foreword by Paolo Valesio. Minneapolis: University of Minnesota Press, 1984.

———. "Scholarship in Times of Extremes: Letters of Erich Auerbach (1933–46), on the Fiftieth Anniversary of His Death." Introduction and translation by Martin Elsky, Martin Vialon, and Robert Stein. *PMLA* 122.3 (May 2007): 750–51.
Badiou, Alain. *Ethics: An Essay on the Understanding of Evil.* Translated by Peter Hallward. London: Verso, 2002.
Bakhtin, Mikhail. *The Dialogical Imagination: Four Essays.* Edited by Michael Holquist. Translated by Caryl Emerson and Michael Holquist. Austin: University of Texas Press, 1981.
Bakker, Egbert J. "Mimesis as Performance: Rereading Auerbach's First Chapter." *Poetics Today* 20.1 (Spring 1999): 16.
Barck, Karlheinz, and Anthony Reynolds, eds. "Walter Benjamin and Erich Auerbach: Fragments of a Correspondence." *Diacritics* 22.3–4 (Autumn–Winter 1992): 81–83.
Barck, Karlheinz, and Martin Treml, eds. *Erich Auerbach: Geschichte und Aktualität eines europäischen Philologen.* Berlin: Kulturverlag Kadmos, 2007.
Beltrán, Rosa. *La corte de los ilusos.* Mexico City: Grupo Editorial Planeta, 1995.
Benjamin, Walter. *The Origin of German Tragic Drama.* Translated by John Osborne. London: New Left Books, 1977.
———. "Theses on the Philosophy of History." In *Illuminations*, translated by Harry Zohn, edited by Hannah Arendt, 253–64. New York: Schocken Books, 1969.
———. "The Work of Art in the Age Mechanical Reproduction." In *Illuminations*, translated by Harry Zohn, edited by Hannah Arendt, 217–51. New York: Schocken Books, 1969.
Berlin, Isaiah. *Vico and Herder.* London: Hogarth Press, 1976.
Bernstein, Richard J. *Hannah Arendt and the Jewish Question.* Cambridge, Mass.: MIT Press, 1996.
———. *Radical Evil: A Philosophical Interrogation.* Cambridge: Polity Press, 2002.
Bhabha, Homi K. *The Location of Culture.* London: Routledge, 1994.
Borges, Jorge Luis. "Avatars of the Tortoise." In *Other Inquisitions, 1937–1952*, translated by Ruth L. C. Simms, 106–8. Austin: University of Texas Press, 1964.
———. "La esfera de Pascal." In *Otras inquisiciones.* Buenos Aires: Sur, 1952.
———. *Jorge Luis Borges: Collected Fictions.* Translated and edited by Andrew Hurley. New York: Viking/Penguin, 1998.
———. *Obras completas.* Barcelona: Emecé Editores, 1999.
Brodzki, Bella. *Can These Bones Live? Translation, Survival, and Cultural Memory.* Stanford, Calif.: Stanford University Press, 2007.
Brownlee, Kevin. "Dante and the Classical Poets." In *The Cambridge Companion to Dante*, edited by Rachel Jacoff, 100–119. Cambridge: Cambridge University Press, 1993.

Bruno, Giordano. *The Ash Wednesday Supper.* Translated and edited by Edward A. Gosselin and Lawrence S. Lerner. Toronto: University of Toronto Press, 1995.

———. *On the Composition of Images, Signs, and Ideas.* Translated by Charles Doria. Edited and annotated by Dick Higgins. New York: Willis, Locker and Owens, 1991.

———. *Opere latine.* Edited by F. Florentino, V. Imbriani, C. M. Tallarigo, F. Tocco, H. Vitelli. Facsimile repr. of 1879–91 edition. Stuttgardt-Bad Cannstatt: Friederich Fromman Verlag Gunther Holzboog, 1962.

Calvino, Esther. "A Note on the Text." In Italo Calvino, *Six Memos for the Next Millennium,* translated by Patrick Creagh, i–ii. Cambridge, Mass.: Harvard University Press, 1988.

Calvino, Italo. *Invisible Cities.* Translated by William Weaver. San Diego: Harcourt Brace, 1974.

———. *Six Memos for the Next Millennium.* Translated by Patrick Creagh. Cambridge, Mass.: Harvard University Press, 1988.

Casanova, Pascale. *La république mondiale des lettres.* Paris: Editions du Seuil, 1999.

———. *The World Republic of Letters.* Translated by M. B. DeBevoise. Cambridge, Mass.: Harvard University Press, 2004.

Cassirer, Ernst. *The Individual and the Cosmos in Renaissance Philosophy.* Translated by Marion Domandi. New York: Dover Publications, 2000.

Clifford, James. "Traveling Cultures." In *Routes: Travel and Translation in the Late Twentieth Century,* 17–46. Cambridge, Mass.: Harvard University Press, 1997.

Cobban, Alfred. *Rousseau and the Modern State.* 2nd ed. London: Allen and Unwin, 1964.

Cockburn, Alexander, and Jeffrey St. Clair, eds. *The Politics of Anti-Semitism.* Petrolia, Calif.: CounterPunch and AK Press, 2003.

Coetzee, J. M. "Confessions and Double Thoughts: Tolstoy, Rousseau, Dostoyevsky." In *Doubling the Point: J. M. Coetzee, Essays and Interviews,* edited by David Attwell, 251–93. Cambridge, Mass.: Harvard University Press, 1992.

Curtius, Ernst Robert. *European Literature and the Latin Middle Ages.* Translated by Willard R. Trask. Princeton, N.J.: Princeton University Press, 1953.

Cusa, Nicholas of. *De docta ignorantia.* Translated by Jasper Hopkins. Minneapolis: Arthur J. Banning Press, 2001.

Damrosch, David. "Auerbach in Exile." *Comparative Literature* 47.2 (Spring 1995): 97–117.

———. *What Is World Literature?* Princeton, N.J.: Princeton University Press, 2003.

Dante Alighieri. *The Divine Comedy of Dante Alighieri: Inferno.* Translated by Allen Mandelbaum. New York: Bantam Classic Edition, 1982.

———. *The Divine Comedy of Dante Alighieri: Paradiso*. Translated by Allen Mandelbaum. New York: Bantam Classic Edition, 1986.
Darbo-Peschanski, C. *Le discours du particulier: Essai sur l'enquete herodoteenne*. Paris: Editions du Seuil, 1987.
Davis, Leonard, ed. *The Disabilities Studies Reader*. New York: Routledge, 1996.
Dawkins, Richard. *The Selfish Gene*. Oxford: Oxford University Press, 1976.
De Certeau, Michel. *The Practice of Everyday Life*. Translated by Steven Rendall. Berkeley: University of California Press, 1984.
De Man, Paul. *Resistance to Theory*. Minneapolis: University of Minnesota Press, 1986.
Dickinson, Emily. *The Complete Poems of Emily Dickinson*. 1924; repr., Boston: Little, Brown, 1960.
———. *Final Harvest: Emily Dickinson's Poems*. Edited by Thomas H. Johnson. Boston: Little, Brown, 1961.
Drummond de Andrade, Carlos. "In the Middle of the Road." Translated by Elizabeth Bishop. In *The Longman Anthology of World Literature: The Twentieth Century*, vol. F, 2nd ed., edited by Djelal Kadir and Ursula Heise, 243. New York: Pearson Education, 2008.
Edwards, John. *Language Society and Identity*. Oxford: Basil Blackwell, 1985.
Elbendary, Amina. "They Came to Baghdad: Its Famous Names" *Al-Ahram*, no. 634 (April 17–23, 2003), http://weekly.ahram.org.eg/2003/634/baghdad.htm (accessed January 12, 2010).
Emerson, Ralph Waldo. *Essays and English Traits*. New York: P. F. Collier, 1909–14.
———. "Self Reliance." In *The Complete Works of Ralph Waldo Emerson, Volume II, Essays I (1841)*. Cambridge: Belknap Press of Harvard University Press, 1979.
ETC Group. "Extreme Genetic Engineering: An Introduction to Synthetic Biology" (January 16, 2007), www.etcgroup.org/en/materials/publications.html?id=602(accessed January 12, 2010).
Fazlullah, Rashiduddin. *Jami'u't-tawarikh: Compendium of Chronicles; A History of the Mongols*. Translated by W. M. Thackston. Cambridge, Mass.: Harvard University Press, 1998.
Ferrer, Christian, et al. *'Patafísica, junto con especulaciones de Alfred Jarry*. Logroño, La Rioja, Spain: Edición Pepitas de Calabaza, 2002.
Firdusi. *The Shahnama of Firdusi*. Translated by Arthur George Warner and Edmund Warner. London: Taylor and Francis, 2001.
Fong, Gilbert. "Gao Xingjian and the Idea of the Theatre." In *Soul of Chaos: Critical Perspectives on Gao Xingjian*, edited by Kwok-Kan Tam. Hong Kong: Chinese University of Hong Kong Press, 2001.
Foucault, Michel. *The Order of Things: The Archeology of the Human Sciences*. New York: Vintage Books, 1973.

Franco, Jean. *The Decline and Fall of the Lettered City*. Cambridge, Mass.: Harvard University Press, 2002.
Fraser, Nancy, and Alex Honneth, eds. *Redistribution or Recognition: A Political-Philosophical Exchange*. London: Verso, 2003.
Fuentes, Carlos. *La campaña*. Mexico City: Fondo de Cultura Económica, 1990.
Fukuyama, Francis. *The End of History and the Last Man*. New York: Avon Books, 1992.
Gao, Xingjian. *The Case for Literature*. Translated by Mabel Lee. New Haven, Conn.: Yale University Press, 2007.
———. *Soul Mountain*. Translated by Mabel Lee. New York: HarperCollins, 2000.
———. "Without Isms." Translated by Winnie Lau, Deborah Sauviat, and Martin Williams. In *The Case for Literature*, translated by Mabel Lee, 64–77. New Haven, Conn.: Yale University Press, 2007. Translation of "Meiyou zhuyi," original publication in *Meiyou zhuyi*, 8–17. Hong Kong: Tiandi youxian gongsi, 1996.
Gass, William H. *Reading Rilke: Reflections on the Problems of Translation*. New York: Alfred A. Knopf, 2000.
Gatti, Hilary. *Giordano Bruno and Renaissance Science*. Ithaca, N.Y.: Cornell University Press, 1999.
Gibbon, Edward. *The Decline and Fall of the Roman Empire*. New York: Alfred A. Knopf, 1993.
Godzich, Wlad. *The Culture of Literacy*. Cambridge, Mass.: Harvard University Press, 1994.
González Echevarría, Roberto. *Myth and Archive*. Cambridge: Cambridge University Press, 1990.
González Pedrero, Enrique. *País de un solo hombre: El México de Santa Anna*. Vol. 1. Mexico City: Fondo de Cultura Económica, 1993.
Goodman, David S. G. "Regional and Global China: Culture, Society and the State." *Inter-Cultural Studies: A Forum on Social Change and Cultural Diversity* (Newcastle, Australia) 3.2 (Spring 2003): 12–13.
Goodman, Dena. *The Republic of Letters: A Cultural History of the French Enlightenment*. Ithaca, N.Y.: Cornell University Press, 1994.
Gramsci, Antonio. *Prison Notebooks*. Translated and edited by Joseph Buttigieg. New York: Columbia University Press, 1996.
Green, Geoffrey. "Erich Auerbach and the 'Inner Dream' of Transcendence." In *Literary History and the Challenge of Philology: The Legacy of Erich Auerbach*, edited by Seth Lerer, 214–39. Stanford, Calif.: Stanford University Press, 1996.
Greenberg, Sidney. *The Infinite in Giordano Bruno, with a Translation of His Dialogue Concerning the Cause, Principle, and One*. New York: King's Crown Press, 1950.

Guimarães Rosa, João. "A terceira margem do rio." *Primeiras estórias.* 1962; repr., Rio de Janeiro: Editora Nova Fronteira, 2007.
———. *The Third Bank of the River and Other Stories.* Translated by Barbara Sehlby. New York: Alfred A. Knopf, 1968.
Gumbrecht, Hans Ulrich. "'Pathos of the Earthly Progress': Erich Auerbach's Everydays." In *Literary History and the Challenge of Philology: The Legacy of Erich Auerbach,* edited by Seth Lerer, 13–35. Stanford, Calif.: Stanford University Press, 1996.
Guzmán, Martín Luis. *Filadelfia, paraiso de conspiradores y otras historias noveladas.* Mexico City: Compañia General de Ediciones, S.A., 1960.
Hansen, Miriam. "*Schindler's List* Is Not *Shoah*: The Second Commandment, Popular Modernism, and Public Memory." *Critical Inquiry* 22 (1996): 292–312.
Heaney, Seamus. *The Government of the Tongue: Selected Prose, 1978–1987.* New York: Noonday / Farrar, Straus and Giroux, 1989.
Heidegger, Martin. *Elucidation of Hölderlin's Poetry.* Translated by Keith Hoeller. New York: Prometheus Books, 2000.
Herbert, Zbigniew. *The Barbarian in the Garden.* Translated by Michael March and Jaroslow Anders. San Diego: Harcourt Brace Jovanovich, 1985.
———. *Mr. Cogito.* Translated by John Carpenter and Bogdana Carpenter. Hopewell, NJ: Ecco Press, 1993.
———. *The King of the Ants.* Translated by John Carpenter and Bogdana Carpenter. Hopewell, N.J.: Ecco Press, 1999.
———. *Report from the Besieged City and Other Poems.* Translated by John Carpenter and Bogdana Carpenter. New York: Ecco Press, 1985.
———. *Selected Poems.* Translated by Czeslaw Milosz and Peter Dale Scott. New York: Ecco Press, 1986.
———. *Still Life with a Bridle: Essays and Apocryphas.* Translated by John and Bogdana Carpenter. Hopewell, N.J.: Ecco Press, 1991.
Herodotus. *The Histories.* Translated by Aubrey de Sélincourt. Revised and introduced, with notes by John Marincola. London: Penguin Books, 1996.
Hesiod. *Theogony, Works and Days, Shield.* Translated and edited by Apostolos N. Athanassakis. Baltimore: Johns Hopkins University Press, 1983.
Hitchens, Christopher. *For the Sake of Argument.* London: Verso, 1993.
Hobsbawm, Eric. *Nations and Nationalism Since 1870.* Cambridge: Cambridge University Press, 1990.
Homer. *The Odyssey.* Translated by Richard Lattimore. New York: HarperCollins, 1965.
The Homeric Hymns. Edited by Susan C. Shelmerdine. Newburyport, Mass.: Focus Publishing / R. Pullins, 1995.
Hopkins, Jasper. "Nicholas of Cusa (1401–1464): First Modern Philosopher?"

Midwest Studies in Philosophy. Special issue of *Renaissance and Early Modern Philosophy* 26 (2002): 13–29.

Huyssen, Andreas. "Present Past: Media, Politics, Amnesia." *Public Culture* 12.1 (2000): 21–38.

———. *Twilight Memories: Marking Time in a Culture of Amnesia*. London: Routledge, 1995.

Jacoby, Russell. "Hannah Arendt's Fame Rests on the Wrong Foundation." *Chronicle of Higher Education* 53.16 (December 8, 2006), B13.

Jacoff, Rachel, ed. *The Cambridge Companion to Dante*. Cambridge: Cambridge University Press, 1993.

Jameson, Frederic. "Nostalgia for the Present." *South Atlantic Quarterly* 88.2 (Spring 1989): 517–39.

Joyce, James. *Ulysses*. Edited by Claus Melchior et al. New York: Alfred A. Knopf, 1986.

Kadir, Djelal. "Comparative Literature in an Age of Terrorism." In *Comparative Literature in an Age of Globalization*, edited by Haun Saussy, 68–77. Baltimore: Johns Hopkins University Press, 2006.

———. "Comparative Literature in a World Become Tlön." In *Comparative Critical Studies: The Journal of the British Comparative Literature Association* 3.1–2 (2006): 125–38.

———. "Defending America Against Its Devotees." In *How Far Is America from Here? Selected Proceedings of the First World Congress of the International American Studies Association 22–24 May 2003*, edited by Theo D'Haen et al., 13–34. Amsterdam: Editions Rodopi, 2005.

———. "Introduction: America and Its Studies." *PMLA* special issue, *America: The Idea, the Literature*, 118.1 (2003): 9–24.

———. "Memories of the Future." Keynote address to the February 20–22, 2004, European Union–sponsored conference of the European Thematic Network: Approaches to Cultural Memory (ACUME), in Nicosia, Cyprus. In *Cultures of Memory/Memories of Culture*, edited by Stephanos Stephanides, 50–66. Nicosia: University of Nicosia Press, 2007.

———. *The Other Writing: Postcolonial Essays in Latin America's Writing Cultures*. West Lafayette, Ind.: Purdue University Press, 1993.

———. "Totalization, Totalitarianism, and Tlön: Borges' Cautionary Tale." In *Reescrituras*, edited by Luz Rodriguez-Carranza and Marilene Nagle, 155–65. Amsterdam: Editions Rodopi, 2004.

Kant, Immanuel. *Religion and Rational Theology*. Translated and edited by Allen W. Wood and George Di Giovanni. Cambridge: Cambridge University Press, 1996.

Klein, Naomi. *The Shock Doctrine: The Rise of Disaster Capitalism*. New York: Picador, 2008.

Konuk, Kader. *East West Mimesis: Auerbach in Turkey.* Stanford, Calif.: Stanford University Press, 2010.

———. "Erich Auerbach and the Humanist Reform to the Turkish Education System." *Comparative Literature Studies* 45.1 (2008): 74–89.

———. "Jewish-German Philologists in Turkish Exile: Leo Spitzer and Erich Auerbach." In *Exile and Otherness: New Approaches to the Experience of the Nazi Refugees*, edited by Alexander Stephan. Bern: Peter Lang, 2005.

Leahy, Stephen. "Synthetic Biology: Group Seeks Ban on 'Living Machines.'" Inter Press Service (January 21, 2007), www.commondreams.org/headlines07/0121-01.htm (accessed January 12, 2010).

Lee, Mabel. "Contextualizing 2000 Nobel Laureate Gao Xingjian." Introduction to *The Case for Literature*, translated by Mabel Lee, 1–22. New Haven, Conn.: Yale University Press, 2007.

———. "Gao Xingjian on the Issue of Literary Creation for the Modern Writer." *Journal of Asian Pacific Communication 9.1–2 (1999): 83–96.*

Lerer, Seth. *Error and the Academic Self: The Scholarly Imagination, Medieval to Modern.* New York: Columbia University Press, 2002.

———, ed. *Literary History and the Challenge of Philology: The Legacy of Erich Auerbach.* Stanford, Calif.: Stanford University Press, 1996.

Lindsay, Jack. *Cause, Principle, and Unity: Five Dialogues.* New York: International Publishers, 1964.

Liptak, Adam. "U.S. Imprisons One in 100 Adults, Report Finds." *New York Times* (February 29, 2008), www.nytimes.com/2008/02/29/us/29prison.html?_r=1&oref=slogin (accessed January 12, 2010).

Lockwood, Robert P. "History and Myth: The Inquisition." Catholic League Web site (August 2000), www.catholicleague.org/research/inquisition.html (accessed January 12, 2010).

Lovell, Julia. "Gao Xingjian, the Nobel Prize, and Chinese Intellectuals: Notes on the Aftermath of the Nobel Prize 2000." *Modern Chinese Literature and Culture* 14.2 (2002): 1–50.

Machiavelli, Niccolò. *Opere.* 8 vols. Edited by S. Bertelli and F. Gaeta. Milan: Feltrinelli, 1960–65.

———. *The Prince and Discourses.* Edited by Max Lerner. New York: Random House Modern Library, 1940, 1950.

Mallarmé, Stéphane. *Collected Poems and Prose.* Oxford: Oxford University Press, 2006.

Mandelstam, Osip. "Conversation About Dante." Translated by Clarence Brown and Robert Hughes. In *Selected Essays*, edited by Sidney Monas, 3–37. Austin: University of Texas Press, 1977.

———. "On the Addressee." In *Modern Russian Poets on Poetry*, edited by Carl R. Proffer, translated by Jane Gary Harris, 52–59. Ann Arbor, Mich.: Ardis, 1976.

McNulty, Robert. "Bruno at Oxford." *Renaissance News* 13 (1960): 300–305.

Melas, Natalie. *All the Difference in the World: Postcoloniality and the Ends of Comparison*. Stanford, Calif.: Stanford University Press, 2007.

Melville, Herman. *Billy Budd, Sailor (an Inside Narrative)*. Edited by Harrison Hayford and Merton M. Sealts, Jr. Chicago: University of Chicago Press, 1962.

Mercati, Angelo. *Il sommario del processo di Giordano Bruno*. Rome: Città del Vaticano, 1942.

Mier Noriega y Guerra, José Servando Teresa de. *Escritos y memorias*. Edited by Edmundo O'Gorman. Mexico City: Ediciones de la Universidad Nacional Autónoma, 1945.

———. *The Memoirs of Fray Servando Teresa de Mier*. Translated by Helen R. Lane. Edited with an introduction by Susana Rotker. New York: Oxford University Press, 1998.

Montaigne, Michel Eyquem de. *The Complete Essays of Montaigne*. Translated by Donald M. Frame. Stanford, Calif.: Stanford University Press, 1958.

Moretti, Franco. "Conjectures on World Literature." *New Left Review* (January–February 2000): 55–67.

Mufti, Aamir R. "Auerbach in Istanbul: Edward Said, Secular Criticism, and the Question of Minority Culture." *Critical Inquiry* 25.1 (Autumn 1998): 95–125.

Nagy, Gregory. *Poetry as Performance: Homer and Beyond*. Cambridge: Cambridge University Press, 1996.

Neiman, Susan. *Evil in Modern Thought*. Princeton, N.J.: Princeton University Press, 2002.

Neruda, Pablo. *Odas elementales*. 1954–57; repr., Madrid: Editorial Planeta, 2004.

Nora, Pierre. *Rethinking France*. Translated by Mary Trouille. Chicago: University of Chicago Press, 2001.

Nussbaum, Martha Craven. *Poetic Justice: The Literary Imagination and Public Life*. Boston: Beacon Press, 1995.

Ong, Aihwa. *Flexible Citizenship: The Cultural Logics of Transnationality*. Durham, N.C.: Duke University Press, 1999.

———. "On the Edge of Empires: Flexible Citizenship Among Chinese in Diaspora." *positions* 1.3 (Winter 1993): 745–78.

Ovid. *The Metamorphoses of Ovid*. Translated by Allen Mandelbaum. New York: Harcourt, Brace, 1993.

Pagel, Walter. "Giordano Bruno: The Philosophy of Circles and the Circular Movement of the Blood." *Journal of the History of Medicine and Allied Sciences* 6 (1951): 116–25.

Pamuk, Orhan. *Benim Adim Kirmizi*. Istanbul: Iletisim, 1998.

———. *My Name Is Red.* Translated by Erdag M. Göknar. New York: Alfred A. Knopf, 2001.
Pascale, Blaise. *Pensées.* Translated by W. F. Trotter. Corvalis: Oregon State University, http://oregonstate.edu/instruct/phl302/texts/pascal/pensees-b.html#SECTION%20VI (accessed January 12, 2010).
Paz, Octavio. *The Labyrinth of Solitude: Life and Thought in Mexico.* Translated by Lysander Kemp. New York: Grove Press, 1961.
Pew Charitable Trust. "One in 100: Behind Bars in America 2008," www.pewcenteronthestates.org/uploadedFiles/One%20in%20100.pdf (accessed January 12, 2010).
Piglia, Ricardo. *Respiración artificial.* Buenos Aires: Editorial Sudamericana, 1980.
Poe, Edgar Allan. *The Complete Poems and Stories of Edgar Allan Poe.* Edited by Arthur Hobson Quinn and Edward H. O'Neill. New York: Alfred A. Knopf, 1967.
Reiss, H. *Kant: Political Writings.* 2nd ed. Cambridge: Cambridge University Press, 1991.
Reynolds, David S. *Walt Whitman's America: A Cultural Biography.* New York: Alfred A. Knopf, 1995.
Rotker, Susana. "Nation and Mockery: The Oppositional Writings of Simón Rodríguez." *Modern Language Quarterly* 57.2 (June 1996): 253–67.
Said, Edward W. *Beginnings: Intention and Method.* 1975; repr., New York: Columbia University Press, 1985.
———. *Culture and Imperialism.* New York: Alfred A. Knopf, 1993.
———. *Humanism and Democratic Criticism.* New York: Columbia University Press, 2004.
Sands, Philippe. *Lawless World.* New York: Viking Press, 2005.
Santayana, George. *The Life of Reason; or, The Phases of Human Progress.* 1905; repr., New York: Dover Publications, 1980.
Santos, Boaventura de Sousa. "*Nuestra América*: Reinventing a Subaltern Paradigm of Recognition and Redistribution." *Theory, Culture, and Society* 18.2–3 (2001): 185–217.
Saussy, Haun. "Exquisite Cadavers Stitched from Fresh Nightmares: Of Memes, Hives, and Selfish Genes." In *Comparative Literature in an Age of Globalization,* edited by Haun Saussy, 3–42. Baltimore: Johns Hopkins University Press, 2006.
Schmitt, Carl. *The Concept of the Political.* Translated by George D. Schwab. Chicago: University of Chicago Press, 1996.
Serres, Michel. *Atlas.* Paris: Bourrin, 1995.
Shuurman, Frans J. "The Nation-State, Emancipatory Spaces, and Development Studies in the Global Era." In *Globalization and Development Studies: Challenges for the 21st Century,* edited by Frans J. Shuurman, 61–76. London: Sage Publications, 2001.

Singer, Dorothea Waley. *Giordano Bruno, His Life and Thought; With Annotated Translation of His Work, On the Infinite Universe and Worlds.* New York: Schuman, 1950.
Smith, Anthony D. *Nations and Nationalism in a Global Era.* Cambridge: Polity Press / Blackwell Publishers, 1995.
Sonnenbend, Geoffrey. *Obliscence: Theories of Forgetting and the Problem of Matter.* Evanston, Ill.: Northwestern University Press, 1946.
Spivak, Gayatri. *A Critique of Postcolonial Reason: Toward a History of the Vanishing Present.* Cambridge, Mass.: Harvard University Press, 1999.
Stein, Gertrude. *Geography and Plays.* 1922; repr., Madison: University of Wisconsin Press, 1993.
Stephan, Alexander, ed. *Exile and Otherness: New Approaches to the Experience of the Nazi Refugees.* Bern: Peter Lang, 2005.
Stevens, Wallace. *The Palm at the End of the Mind.* Edited by Holly Stevens. New York: Alfred A. Knopf, 1971.
Tam, Kwok-Kan, ed. *Soul of Chaos: Critical Perspectives on Gao Xingjian.* Hong Kong: Chinese University of Hong Kong Press, 2001.
Taylor, Diana. *The Archive and the Repertoire: Performing Cultural Memory in the Americas.* Durham, N.C.: Duke University Press, 2003.
Terdiman, Richard. *Present Past: Modernity and the Memory Crisis.* Ithaca, N.Y.: Cornell University Press, 1993.
Uslar Pietri, Arturo. *La isla de Robinson.* Barcelona: Seix Barral, 1987.
Valéry, Paul. *La soirée avec Monsieur Teste.* Vol. 2 of *Oeuvres.* Paris: Gallimard, Editions de Pléiade, 1960.
Vargas Llosa, Mario. *El hablador.* Barcelona: Seix Barral, 1987.
———. *The Storyteller.* Translated by Helen R. Lane. New York: Farrar, Straus and Giroux, 1989.
———. *La verdad de las mentiras: Ensayos sobre literature.* Barcelona: Seix Barral, 1990; expanded edition, Madrid: Alfaguara, 2002.
Vernant, Jean-Pierre. "The Birth of Images." In *Mortals and Immortals: Collected Essays of Jean-Pierre Vernant,* edited by Froma Zeitlin, 164–85. Princeton, N.J.: Princeton University Press, 1991.
White, Hayden. *Figural Realism: Studies in the Mimesis Effect.* Baltimore: Johns Hopkins University Press, 1999.
———. *Metahistory: The Historical Imagination of Nineteenth-Century Europe.* Baltimore: Johns Hopkins University Press, 1973.
Whitman, Walt. "Democratic Vistas." In *Whitman: Complete Poetry and Collected Prose,* edited by Justin Kaplan 229–94. New York: Viking Press, Library of America, 1982.

Wood, Meiksins. "Labor, the State, and Class Struggle." *Monthly Review* 49.3 (1997): 1–18.
Woolf, Virginia. "On Not Knowing Greek." In *The Common Reader*, 24–39. New York: Harcourt Brace and World, 1925.
Yates, Frances. *The Art of Memory*. Chicago: University of Chicago Press, 1966.
———. *Giordano Bruno and the Hermetic Tradition*. Chicago: University of Chicago Press, 1964.
Young-Bruehl, Elisabeth. *Hannah Arendt: For Love of the World*. New Haven, Conn.: Yale University Press, 1982.
———. *Why Arendt Matters*. New Haven, Conn.: Yale University Press, 2006.
Zamora, Lois Parkinson. *The Inordinate Eye: New World Baroque and Latin American Fiction*. Chicago: University of Chicago Press, 2006.
Zhang, Longxi. *Unexpected Affinities: Reading Across Cultures*. Toronto: University of Toronto Press, 2007.

Index

Abbasid dynasty, 46
Abbot, George, 91–92
Ablism, 24
Abraham and Isaac, 29–30, 34–35, 37
Absolutism: cultural, 68–69, 83; Cusa and, 73; of imperial cultures, 59, 62–63; moral, 172–76; questioning of, 70, 75–76; religious, 65; of truth, 76–77; twentieth-century, 34–35, 37, 39; twenty-first century, 52. *See also* Totalitarianism
Abu Ghraib prison, 62, 63, 125
Adams, John Quincy, 114
Adorno, Theodor W., 65, 97, 204, 218
Adversative, the, 208
Aeschylus, 158; *Agamemnon*, 160; *Oresteia*, 159
Aesthetics, 132
Afghanistan, 182. *See also* Kabul, Afghanistan
Ahmed, Sara, 93
Akha, 181
Alberti, Leon Battista, 66; *De pictura*, 60–62
Aletheia, 87, 104
Ali, Yazicizāde, 47, 212
American studies, 56, 58, 109, 114
Anacalypsis, 132
Anáhuac, 112, 116
Anamnesis, 96
Anamorphosis, 60, 62, 228*n*25
Anderson, Benedict, 221*n*3
Ansatzpunkte (points of departure), 8, 12
Anti-Semitism, 106
Apotropeia, 119, 124

Apter, Emily, 26, 223*n*10
Arenas, Reinaldo, 130; *El mundo alucinante* (*Hallucinations*), 110, 236*n*34
Arendt, Hannah, 2, 14, 15, 151, 158–76, 209, 216; *Eichmann in Jerusalem*, 159, 160, 172–75
Argentina, 102
Aristotle, 174; *Rhetoric*, 33
Arnold, Matthew, 77
Arrioja Vizcaíno, Adolfo, 114
Ars combinatoria, 203
Artes liberales, 209, 211, 214
Assassins, 53
Atatürk, Kemal, 28
Atlantis, 124
Auerbach, Erich, 2, 8, 9, 11, 12, 17–40, 118, 196, 206–7, 212, 215, 225*n*25; *Mimesis*, 17, 20–21, 23, 26, 29, 31, 38, 40, 205, 207, 209, 215
Aybak the Dawatdar, 58

Badiou, Alain, 93
Baez, Fernando, 46
Baghdad, Iraq, 10–11, 41–43, 46; as besieged city, 43, 55–63; looting of museums in, 46, 102; other names of, 57; religions converging in, 43; 1258 siege of, 47–48, 54–55, 153; U.S.-led invasion and occupation of, 46, 52, 55–57, 61–63
Bakhtin, Mikhail, 87–88
Bakker, Egbert J., 23
Banality, evil of, 175
Barra, Bernabé de la, 109

264   Index

Beirut, Lebanon, 52
Beki, Sorghaghtani, 53
Beltrán, Rosa, *La corte de los ilusos* (*The Court of Fools*), 110, 115
Benjamin, Walter, 1, 3, 6–8, 28–29, 37, 67, 97, 170; *Über den Begriff der Geschichte* (*On the Concept of History*), 29, 62; "The Work of Art in the Age of Mechanical Reproduction," 62
Berkeley, George, 76
Bhabha, Homi K., 4, 221n3
Bhiaris, 181
Bible. *See* Hebrew Bible
Bio-technologies, 213
Bipolarity, 79–80, 126
Bit of horse's bridle, 142–48
Bloch, Ernst, 26
Bolívar, Simón, 109
Book of Festivities, 49–50
Book of Skills, 49–50
Book of Victories, 49–50
Borges, Jorge Luis, 70, 179; "Funes el memorioso," 232n20; "Kafka and His Precursors," 218; "Tlön Uqbar Orbis Tertius," 98–99
Brazil, 234n7
Brecht, Bertolt, 164, 167; "To Posterity," 164, 209
Britain, 57
Brodzki, Bella, 1, 6–7, 109
Brownlee, Kevin, 190
Brunelleschi, Filippo, 66, 80, 88, 228n25
Bruno, Giordano, 2, 12–13, 17, 65, 81, 84–107, 203; *La cena de la ceneri* (*Ash Wednesday Supper*), 87, 90–91; *De Triplici minimo et mensura*, 86
Buddhism, 43
Buñuel, Luis, *Un chien andalou*, 150
Burton, Robert, 179
Buwayhids, 57
Byzantium, 70, 79. *See also* Constantinople

Caesar, Julius, 216

Cage, John, 66–67
Calligraphy, 47–48, 59–60
Calvino, Esther, 17
Calvino, Italo, 2, 16–18, 130, 194–203, 208, 216, 217; Perseus, 209; *Six Memos for the Next Millennium*, 17, 155
Camillo, Giulio, 94
Capitalism, 81, 106, 182–83
Casanova, Pascale, 179
Cassirer, Ernst, *Individuum und Kosmos in der Philosophie der Renaissance* (*The Individual and the Cosmos in Renaissance Philosophy*), 64
Catastrophe, 130
Certeau, Michel de, *L'invention du quotidien* (*The Practice of Everyday Life*), 51
Cervantes y Saavedra, Miguel de: *Don Quixote*, 49; *La batalla naval*, 49
Cesarini, Cardinal (Lord Cardinal Julian), 70
Chaplin, Charlie, 155
Charles I, King of England, 141–42
Chateaubriand, François-Auguste-René de, Viscount, 109–10; *Atalá*, 110
Chiasmus, 115–17, 119–20, 123, 132, 175, 210
China, 177–93
Christianity: and concept of humanity's origin, 169–71; Cusa and Eastern vs. Western, 70–75, 77; and Mongol Crusade, 43, 53; Nestorian, 43, 54
Cicero, Marcus Tullius, 94
Circles, 70, 73, 74, 76
Citation, 20
Citizenship, flexible, 182
Civil society, 16
Closed society. *See* Totalitarianism
Clovis, King of France, 153
Coalition building, 53
Cobham, Henry, 90
Coetzee, J. M., 216
Coincidentia oppositorum (reconciliation of opposites), 72, 83

Coleridge, Samuel Taylor, 126
Communion, 112–13
Community: alienation from, 123–24; construction of coherence in, 123–33
Comparative literature: Auerbach's place in, 9, 22–23, 26–27, 37, 206–7, 215; conflict endemic to, 27–29, 206–8; contemporary status of, 4–5, 28; critique of, 186–87; ethics of, 14–15; Fray Servando and, 109–11; function of, 2, 9–10, 212–13, 214; genealogy of, 7–8; Herbert and, 136; and history, 3–4, 7; institutional role of, 26; local character of, 4–7; methods of, 2–3, 34; nature of, 3–6, 204–6; outsider status of, 206; precursors of, 3, 5–7, 205–9; problems that animate, 1–2, 8–9, 206; self-reflective character of, 4–5, 7, 216–17; as third term of comparison, 4, 212–14
Composition, 20, 23, 32, 140
Concentration camps, 164
Conciliation, 103–4
Consensus, manufactured, 82
Consistency, 197–203
Conspiracy, 112–33
Conspiracy theory, 113, 118–20, 124–33
Constantinople, 70–71, 77–78
Contingency: absolutism vs., 37; comparative literature discipline and, 4–6; of culture, 68; historical, 33, 39, 44, 49, 51
Convergence, 213
Conversation, 19–23, 174–75, 204–5, 207, 215–19
Council of Florence (1439), 12, 71, 73, 77, 79
Countermemory, 100–107
Counter-Reformation, 12, 109
Covenant, 129
Credulity, 125–26
Crossroads, 19–20, 43, 94, 103, 116, 134, 197, 213
Culturalism, 97
Culturalization, 98

Culturalization of memory, 89, 97
Cultural Revolution (China), 184
Culture: absolutism in, 68–69, 83; ambiguities in, 81; boundaries of, 92; as compensation, 124; conspiracy and, 115, 117–33; contemporary, 76–78, 82–83, 93–95, 101–3, 157, 162, 164–76, 181, 234n7; contingency of, 68–69; and cultivation, 89, 96; established vs. emergent, 118; forgetting and, 86–88; memory and, 65, 86–100, 105; negativity and, 67; posthistorical, 44–45, 55, 155; self-perceptions of, 52, 63, 68–69; space and, 2, 11, 65, 67–68; time and, 65
Curtius, Ernst Robert, *European Literature and the Latin Middle Ages*, 205
Cusa, Nicholas of, 2, 5, 11–12, 64–83, 86, 92, 149, 207, 228n1; *De docta ignorantia* (*Of Learned Ignorance*), 67, 69, 71–72, 77; *De pace fidei* (*On the Peace of Faith*), 72, 78
Cyprus, 49

Damrosch, David, 26
Dante Alighieri, 15, 19–22, 39, 42–43, 184, 188–90, 192; *De monarchia*, 43; *Divina commedia*, 42; *Inferno*, 21, 151
Dark times, 164–65, 209
Darvish, Mahmud, 218
Darwin, Charles, 81
Dawkins, Richard, 76
Death, honoring of individuals after, 27
De Lillo, Don, 128
Dickenson, Emily, 199–202
Difference, 11–12; knowledge dependent on, 75; orthodox resistance to, 121
Digenis (twice-born), 187
Diplomacy, Cusa and, 70–75
Domination. *See* Totalitarianism
Dom Pedro I, Emperor of Brazil, 234n7
Dostoyevsky, Fyodor, *Brothers Karamazov*, 172–75
Doubt: methodological, 86

Drummond de Andrade, Carlos, 151
Dystopia, 74

Eckhardt, Meister, 72
Eco, Umberto, 130
Effendi, Enishte, 51
Eichmann, Adolf, 174–75
Ekphrasis, 14, 139, 144
Elohist narrative, 29–30
Emerson, Ralph Waldo, 57, 121–22; "Circles," 70; "Self-Reliance,"126
Enlightenment, 109, 110, 116
Enthymemes, 32–33
Entropy, 129
Epistemania, 130, 132
Epistemology, 22. *See also* Knowledge
Equivalence, 66, 76, 149
Erigena, John Scotus, 72
Estrangement, 118, 123–24
Ethics, 14–15, 33
Eugenius IV, Pope, 73
Europe, Auerbach on, 30–31, 33–34
European Holocaust, 105–6
Evil, banality of, 175
Exactitude, 200
Exceptionalism, 45, 56, 113, 171
Exile: Auerbach and, 22, 24–27, 36; comparatists and, 10; Dante and, 22, 42; Gao Xingjian and, 183, 191–92

Facts, 159
Familiarity, 118, 123–24
Fanon, Frantz, 221*n*3
Farce, 15, 28, 83, 234*n*7
Fardowsi (Firdawsi, Firdusi), 10; *Shahnama* (*Book of Kings*), 50
Fazlullah, Rashiduddin, 2, 10–11, 15, 41–43, 45, 50, 53–54, 58, 153, 207; *Jami 'u't-tawarikh*, 10, 42–43, 45, 58, 212
Federalism, 108–9
Fellini, Federico, *Roma*, 69
Figura, 27, 31, 36
Figural, 16–17
Firdawsi. *See* Fardowsi
Firdusi. *See* Fardowsi

Flexible citizenship, 182
Fong, Gilbert, 189–90
Forgetting: contemporary mnemotechnics and, 95; culture and, 86–88, 96–97; dangers of, 96; memory and, 86–87, 94–95; modernity and, 88
Foucault, Michel, 75, 168
France, 177–79, 181, 187
Frankish painting, 49, 50, 60–61
Fray Servando. *See* Mier, Servando Teresa de
Frederick II, Holy Roman Emperor, 153
Free market forces, 80, 101
Freud, Sigmund, 123
Fuentes, Carlos, *La campaña* (*The Campaign*), 110
Fukuyama, Francis, 101
Functional space, 20–23, 31, 140, 146
Future, the: Dante and, 20–21, 40; memory and, 93–94, 104; Montaigne and, 40; twentieth-century investments in, 103

Galileo Galilei, 86, 96
Gao Xingjian, 2, 14, 16, 177–93; *Bus Stop*, 187; *Soul Mountain*, 187–91, 244*n*25; "Wilted Chrysanthemums," 187; "Without Isms," 179, 188, 192; *Without Isms*, 186–87, 191
Genghis Khan, 46
Ghazan Khan, 10, 42, 56
Ghibellines, 153
Gibbon, Edward, 53
Gibson, William, 98; "Burning Chrome," 87; *Neuromancer*, 87
Glenn, Herbert R., 24–25
Globalization, 185, 192
God: hidden, 37; perspective of, 61–63
Goethe, Johann Wolfgang von, 29; *Conversations with Eckermann*, 217
Governmentality, 157, 168–69
Gramsci, Antonio, 228*n*1
Green, Geoffrey, 225*n*25
Guantánamo detention center, 125

Guggenheim Museums, 102
Guimarães Rosa, João, 4
Gutiérrez de Lara, Bernardo, 109
Guzmán, Martín Luis, *Filadelfia, paraiso de conspiradores y otras historias noveladas*, 114

Habermas, Jürgen, 16
Hansen, Miriam, "*Schindler's List* Is Not *Shoah*," 105
Heaney, Seamus, 144, 157
Hebrew Bible, 29–30, 34–35, 37
Hegel, G.W.F., 72–73
Hegemony, 82–83
Heidegger, Martin, 87
He Jingzhi, 187
Hekate, 197, 210, 213
Henri Grégoire, Abbot, 110
Henri III, King of France, 90
Herbert, Zbigniew, vii, 2, 3, 14, 134–57, 216; "Albigensians, Inquisitors, and Troubadors," 147; "Defence of the Templars," 152; *Elemental Odes*, 149; *Mr. Cogito*, 136; "Pebble," 149; "Report from the Besieged City," 139; *Report from the Besieged City*, 14, 155; "The Trial," 155–56
Herder, Johann Gottfried von, 12
Herodotus, 11; *Histories*, 10
Heterodoxy, 74
Heterotopia, 74–75
Hidalgo y Costilla, Miguel, 113
Hiroshima, Japan, 213
Historiography, 10; Auerbach on, 30–31; construction of history through, 100; Fazlullah on, 41; Montaigne on, 32; poetry and, 43
History: ambiguities of, 29, 31–32; Auerbach and, 28–31, 36–38; comparative literature and, 3–4, 7; conspiracy and, 120, 124–25; contingency in, 33, 39, 44, 49, 51; end of, 44, 101, 155; memory and, 100; particular circumstances of, 22, 26, 31, 33–34, 37–39; patterns in, 45–46. *See also* Historiography

Hitchens, Christopher, 125–26, 128
Hitler, Adolf, 98, 170
Hobbes, Thomas, 81
Hölderlin, Friedrich, 87
Holocaust, 105–6
Holy Office of the Inquisition, 85, 88, 93, 109, 112–15, 125, 146
Holy Roman Emperors, 181
Homeland security, 125
Homer, 10; *Odyssey*, 21, 29–30, 34–35
Homogenization, 81–82, 98
Horses and horsemanship, 142–48
Hugo, Victor, 179
Hülagü Khan, 10, 42, 43, 46–48, 53–54, 56–58, 61, 153
Humanism, 35, 38, 135, 168
Humanity, 107, 169–71, 174, 186
Humboldt, Alexander von, 110
Humboldt University, 26
Husserl, Edmund, 76
Huyssen, Andreas, *Twilight Memories*, 105
Hybridity, 50
Hyperreality, 161, 196

Ideas, 159
Identity, 11–12, 149; equivalence vs., 74, 76; as historical/social construct, 5; as negative value, 12; as paradoxical, 66–67; self-reflection and, 31–40; as unknowable, 74, 76–77; U.S., 83
Imperial cultures: characteristics of, 44–45; and conspiracy, 121–33; Fray Servando's challenge to, 108–21; and historical contingencies, 49; U.S. occupation of Baghdad, 62–63; the vanquished as definers of, 55–56
Imperial presidency, 234n7
Impunity, 166–67
Imputability, 13
Incongruity, 195
Indirection, 195–97, 201–2, 208
Informatics, 95
Info-technologies, 213

Inquisition. *See* Holy Office of the Inquisition
Institutions, self-serving character of, 5–6, 24–26
Intelligence, 4
Interment centers, 164
Interspecies communication, 144–46
Invisibility, 130, 132–33
Iraq, 182. *See also* Baghdad, Iraq
Iraqi National Museum, Baghdad, 102
Irony, 5, 33–34, 36, 37–38
Islam, 43, 170
Israel, 241*n*36
Iturbide, Agustín de, 110, 115, 234*n*7

Jalayrs, 57
Jallun, Tahar ben, 130
Jameson, Fredric, "Nostalgia for the Present," 88
Jarry, Alfred, 214
Jawahiri, Mohammad Mahdi al-, 46, 218
Jerusalem, 78
John Paul II, Pope, 85
John VIII Palaeologus, Emperor, 71
Joyce, James, *Ulysses*, 63
Judaism, 169–71
Julian, Lord Cardinal (Cardinal Cesarini), 70

Kabul, Afghanistan, 52
Kafka, Franz, 159, 161–62, 167–68; *The Trial*, 167–68
Kandahar, 125
Kant, Immanuel, 78, 172–75; *The Conflict of the Faculties*, 174; *Religion Within the Boundaries of Human Reason*, 172
Khatun, Doquz, 43, 53
Knowledge: conspiracy and, 130–33; Cusa on, 71, 81; difference necessary for, 75; ignorance and, 71, 74–75, 92–93; politics and, 95; and truth, 67
Krauss, Werner, 26
Kundera, Milan, 195

Language, of literature, 192–93
Law: cultural formation and, 125; exceptionality and, 112–13, 171–72; imperial cultures and, 44–45, 83
Law of compensation, 57
Lee, Mabel, 244*n*25
Lepanto, Battle of (1571), 49
Lerer, Seth, 25, 26
Lethe, 87, 88, 96, 104
Liberal arts, 209, 211, 214
Lieberman, Avigdor, 241*n*36
Lightness, 195–98, 202
Literature: and conspiracy, 130, 132–33; Gao on, 188; "isms" in, 186–87; narrative and coherence in, 129–30; and the state/nation, 16, 177–79, 183–85; and truth/fiction, 172–74
Local, comparative literature and the, 4, 5
Louis IX the Crusader, King of France, 153
Lull, Ramon, 94
Luther, Martin, 77–78
Lu Xun, 191–92

Machiavelli, Niccolò, 228*n*25; *Il principe* (*The Prince*), 62–63, 79
Machtpolitik, 79, 81, 82
Mahmud, Ghaznavid Sultan, 50
Mailer, Norman, *Harlot's Ghost*, 126
Mallarmé, Stephan, *Un coup de dés jamais n'abolira le hasard* (*A Throw of the Dice Will Never Abolish Chance*), 151
Malmqvist, Göran, 178, 180, 182
Malyevich, Kasimir, 67
Mandelbaum, Allen, 190
Mandelstam, Osip, 13, 19–24, 32, 39, 84, 87, 107, 136, 140, 146, 150, 215
Manichaeism, 79, 126
Mansur, Abu Jafur al-, 57
Marburg University, 26, 35
Márquez, Humberto, 46
Marx, Karl, 72–73, 81
Material culture, 132

Maximum, 73–75
McCarthy, Mary, 158, 159
McNulty, Robert, 91–92
Medici, Cosimo de', 73, 79
Medici, Lorenzo de', 79
Medusa, 195–96, 198, 202, 208
Mehmet II, Sultan, 77–78, 79
Melville, Herman, *Billy Budd*, 172–75
Memeplex, 76
Memorialization, 97–98
Memorialization of culture, 89–90, 97
Memory, 12–13, 84–107; Bruno and, 89–90, 93; and coexistence, 104; as compensation, 101; and countermemory, 100–107; culture and, 65, 86–100, 105; forgetting and, 86–87, 94–95; and the future, 93–94, 104; history and, 100; humanity and, 107; industrialization of, 94–95, 101–2; and musealization, 101–3; redemption not necessarily linked with, 55; scholarship and, 105–6; trivialization of, 106
Memos, 6–8, 16–17, 194–95, 206, 209, 212, 217–19
Metanarrative, 214
Methodology, 2–3, 34, 204–19
Métissage, 50
Metrodorus of Scepsis, 94
Mexico, 108–9, 115–16, 234*n*7
Middle voice, 23–24
Mier, Servando Teresa de, 2, 13–14, 108–23, 125, 127, 128, 130, 133, 207, 216; "Carta de despedida a los mexicanos," 116, 120–21; *Memoria político-instructiva*, 114–15
Mimeĩsthai, 23–24, 35
Miniature painting, 47, 49–50, 58–59, 61
Mirror. *See* Speculum
Mitigation, 136–40, 148–51, 156, 218
Mnemosyne, 87–88, 102, 104
Mnemotechnics, 93–95, 97
Modernism, 20–21, 66–67, 129
Modernity: Cusa and, 11–12, 65–67, 69, 228*n*1; forgetting and, 88; Mier and, 13; Nestorian Christianity and, 54; the novel and, 88; and reflection, 214; Turkey and, 28–39
Mongol crusade, 53–55, 61, 153
Mongols, 57
Monroe, James, 109
Monroe Doctrine, 114
Montaigne, Michel de, 9, 17–18; *Essais*, 31–40
Montevideo, Uruguay, 106
Morality: absolutism in, 172–76; war on terror and, 52
More, Thomas, *Utopia*, 74, 94
Moretti, Franco, 9–10
Mufti, Amir R., 26
Multiculturalism, 11, 78, 98
Murakami, Haruki, 130
Murat II, Ottoman Sultan, 47, 212
Murat III, Ottoman Sultan, 47, 49–50
Murat IV, Ottoman Sultan, 57
Musealization, 101–3
Muses, 87, 102, 150
Museums, 101–3
Music, 65–66

Nagasaki, Japan, 213
Nano-technologies, 213
Nation: defining, 180; literature and, 16, 177–79, 183–84; nationality vs., 180; state in relation to, 180–81, 183, 185
National Defense Strategy (U.S.), 162
Nationality, 180, 182
National Socialism, 30, 34–35, 98, 166–67
Nation-state, 185
Naval School of Mechanics, Buenos Aires, 102
Negative theology, 72, 74
Negativity, 65–67
Negotiation, 65, 75. *See also* Diplomacy, Cusa and
Neohistoricism, 216
Nestorian Christianity, 43, 53–54, 153
Nestorius, 53–54
New Criticism, 137

New World Order, 79, 80, 83
Nicholas of Cusa. *See* Cusa, Nicholas of
Nietzsche, Friedrich, 100; *The Birth of Tragedy*, 87–88
Nobel, Alfred, 177
Nobel Prize, 182; in Literature, 177–78, 188
Nomadism, 13–14
Nora, Pierre, 100–101
Nubians, 181
Nussbaum, Martha, 15

Occupation, 3
Old Testament, 29–30, 34–35, 37
Ong, Aihwa, 182–83
Optic sensibility, 136–37, 145. *See also* Visual indirection
Orthomorphosis, 60
Osman I, 46
Ottoman empire, 46–47, 49, 57
Ovid, *Metamorphoses*, 198
Oxford University, 90–91, 107

Painting, criticism of, 137–48
Palestine, 182
Palestinians, 181, 241n36
Pamuk, Orhan, 2, 14, 54, 64, 130, 212, 216; *Benim Adim Kirmizi* (*My Name Is Red*), 47–50, 58–62
Parabasis, 216
Paradox: artistic inspiration drawn from, 139; in the arts, 66; Cusa and, 64, 70, 72, 74, 77, 80; identity and, 66–67; value of, 104
Paranoia, 117, 120, 121, 123, 125–27
Pariah peoples, 164–65, 167
Pascal, Blaise, 70
'Pataphysics, 214–15
Pavic, Milorad, 130
Paz, Octavio, *El laberinto de la soledad* (*The Labyrinth of Solitude*), 123
Peace, perpetual, 78
Pelagianism, 173
Pennsylvania State University, 22, 24
Peripety, 4, 51, 149, 151, 187
Perpetual peace, 78

Perseus, 195–202, 208
Perspective: God's, 61–63; linear, 50, 60–61, 63, 80, 228n25
Philadelphia, Pennsylvania, 114
Philip IV the Fair, King of France, 152–53
Piglia, Ricardo, 117
Pindar, 87
Place, 65, 68
Plan de Iguala, 115
Plato, 93, 96, 124, 196, 217; *Phaedrus*, 97
Pliny, 232n20
Poe, Edgar Allan, 138; "The Purloined Letter," 132
Poetry, history and, 43
Political gravity, 114
Politics: current context for, 76–78, 82–83, 93–95, 101–3, 155, 162, 164–76, 181, 234n7; Herbert and, 152–54
Postcolonial studies, 114
Posthuman, 168
Power: totalitarianism and, 163; truth and, 161
Power of taste, 134–35. *See also* Taste of power
Princeton Institute for Advanced Studies, 26
Pronouns, 188–90, 216
Propaganda, 184
Public sphere/realm, 16, 164–65
Punto Carretas shopping mall, Montevideo, 106
Pynchon, Thomas, 130
Pythagoras, 93

Quadrivium, 210

Reality, truth/fiction and, 161–62
Reality effect, of linear perspective, 60, 63
Realpolitik: absolute law vs., 60; Borges and, 98; and literature, 178–79; Machiavelli and, 63; and memory, 96; and state-nation relation, 185; and totalitarianism, 162; in twentieth-century Europe, 33, 35–37, 39; in twenty-first century, 35, 52–53, 64, 79, 80, 197

Récamier, Jeanne François Julie Adelaide, 110
Recognition, 93
Reconciliation, 103–4
Reformation, 228*m*
Refugee camps, 164
Refugees, 24
Religion: absolutism in, 65; Bruno and, 84–93; and community vs. conspiracy, 112–13; Judeo-Christian concept of humanity's origin, 169–71; and politics, 78–79
Renaissance, 80, 213
Representation, 118
Republic of Letters, 16, 178–80
Revolution, 99
Rhetoric, 33
Rhetoricorum ad C. Herennium libri IV (Anonymous), 94
Righteousness and self-righteousness, 52, 63, 67, 70, 77, 80, 82, 87, 106, 138, 165, 171, 174
Rodríguez, Simón, 109–10
Roma, 181
Romanticism, 116
Rome, 70
Royal Academy (Spain), 116
Rumsfeld, Donald, 241*n*36

Safavids, 57
Said, Edward, 20, 26; *Culture and Imperialism*, 205, 218
Santayana, George, 55, 61
Saussure, Ferdinand de, 76
Saussy, Haun, 6
Schiller, Johann Christoph Friedrich von, 29
Schopenhauer, Arthur, 76
Second Constitutional Congress, Mexico, 108–9
Self-conviction, 52, 59, 65, 77, 104, 127, 138, 155
Self-reflection, 31–40
Self-righteousness. *See* Righteousness and self-righteousness
Seljuks, 57

September 11, 2001 attacks, 51
Sepúlveda, Luis, 130
Serres, Michel, 81–82
Servando, Fray. *See* Mier, Servando Teresa de
Shakespeare, William: *Macbeth*, 79
Shakir, Ibn, 47–48, 50, 54, 59
Shame, 169
Signification, 84–85
Silence, 66–67
Simonides of Ceos, 93, 94
Soberness, 134–36, 155–56
Socrates, 93
Sonnabend, Geoffrey, *Obliscence*, 95
Soueif, Ahda, 241*n*36
Sovereignty, 180–82
Space: and the arts, 66–67; characteristics of, 65–66; and culture, 11, 65, 67–68, 72; Cusa and, 69, 70; place and, 65, 68; virtual, 81–82
Spain, 112
Speculum, 17, 27, 31, 35–36, 196
Spitzer, Leo, 223*n*10
Spivak, Gayatri, 7, 88
Staël, Germaine de, 110
State, 15–16; and literature, 16, 185; nation in relation to, 180–81, 183, 185; sovereignty of, 180–82
Statelessness, 180–82
Stein, Gertrude, 199
Stevens, Wallace, 137–38, 155
Stoicism, 104
Strangeness. *See* Estrangement
Subject, the, 9; affected by action, 23–24; Gao and, 188–90, 193; in relation to nation/state, 180–82
Süleyman the Magnificent, Ottoman Sultan, 57
Surveillance, 52, 81–82
Syllogism, 32–33
Sympnéo, 122
Syncretism, 50
Synístamai, 122–24, 128
Synómnymi, 122
Synomosía, 122, 125, 129
Syntíthemi, 128

Tabucchi, Antonio, 130
Tamerlane, 57
Taste of power, 134–35. *See also* Power of taste
Technologies of recognition, 93
Terror, 156–57, 169–71
Tertium comparationis, 4
Themistocles, 94–95
Theologia negativa (negative theology), 72, 74
Thomas, apostle, 112
Thucydides, 95
Time, 65
Tintoretto, 49
Titian, 49
Toloui Khan, 43
Tonantzín, 112
Torrentius (Jan Simon van der Beeck), *Emblematic Still Life with Flagon, Glass, Jug, and Bridle*, 139–48
Torture, 62, 63, 102, 106, 156–57
Totalitarianism, 161–68, 175. *See also* Absolutism
Tradition, 210–11
Transculturation, 50
Translatio, 211
Translation, 14, 211–12
Treaty of Westphalia (1648), 181
Trivium, 209–14
Truth: Arendt on, 159; Bible and, 34–35; conspiracy theory and, 126; indirection and, 201–2; knowledge and, 67, 76–77; power and, 161; totalitarian states and, 161–62, 168
Turegen, Aylin, 47
Turkey, 28–29, 34
Turkoman Black Sheep, 57
Turkoman White Sheep, 57
Twice-born, 187

Ubiquitous computation (ubicomp), 82
United Nations, 57, 78, 153, 181, 243*n*12
United States: imperial presidency in, 234*n*7; and Latin America, 114; and Mexico, 109; and wars in Iraq and Afghanistan, 46, 52, 55–57, 61–63
University of Padua, 96
Uslar Pietri, Arturo, *La isla de Robinson* (*Robinson's Island*), 110
Utopia, 74

Valéry, Paul, 138
Van der Beeck, Jan Simon. *See* Torrentius
Vanishing points, in history, 44–45. *See also* Perspective: linear
Vargas Llosa, Mario, 161–62; *El hablador* (*The Storyteller*), 102
Venetian painting, 60–61
Venice, 49, 50, 70–71
Vernacular, 212
Veronese, Paolo, 49
Vesta, 122, 124
Victims as victimizers, 159, 176
Virgil, *Aeneid*, 43
Virgin of Guadalupe, 112
Virtual space, 81–82
Visibility, 202–3
Visual indirection, 195–97. *See also* Optic sensibility

Wakefulness, 134–36, 138, 155–56
Weizman, Eyal, 241*n*36
Whitman, Walt, 204, 218
Wilde, Oscar, 100
Wilhelm II, Prussian Emperor, 172
Woolf, Virginia, 223*n*10
World literature, 2, 217
World Trade Center, New York City, 51
Writers: and indirection, 196, 201–2; in relation to nation, 184–85, 193
Writing, and memory, 97

"x," 116
X-Files (television show), 127
Xu Wei, 191–92

Yale University, 24, 26–27
Yates, Frances, 90

Zhu Rongji, 177

Cultural Memory in the Present

Jeffrey Mehlman, *Adventures in the French Trade: Fragments Toward a Life*
Jacob Rogozinski, *The Ego and the Flesh: An Introduction to Egoanalysis*
Marcel Hénaff, *The Price of Truth: Gift, Money, and Philosophy*
Stanley Cavell, *Little Did I Know: Excerpts from Memory*
Paul Patton, *Deleuzian Concepts: Philosophy, Colonialization, Politics*
Michael Fagenblat, *A Covenant of Creatures: Levinas's Philosophy of Judaism*
Stefanos Geroulanos, *An Atheism that Is Not Humanist Emerges in French Thought*
Andrew Herscher, *Violence Taking Place: The Architecture of the Kosovo Conflict*
Hans-Jörg Rheinberger, *On Historicizing Epistemology: An Essay*
Jacob Taubes, *From Cult to Culture*, edited by Charlotte Fonrobert and Amir Engel
Peter Hitchcock, *The Long Space: Transnationalism and Postcolonial Form*
Lambert Wiesing, *Artificial Presence: Philosophical Studies in Image Theory*
Jacob Taubes, *Occidental Eschatology*
Freddie Rokem, *Philosophers and Thespians: Thinking Performance*
Roberto Esposito, *Communitas: The Origin and Destiny of Community*
Vilashini Cooppan, *Worlds Within: National Narratives and Global Connections in Postcolonial Writing*
Josef Früchtl, *The Impertinent Self: A Heroic History of Modernity*
Frank Ankersmit, Ewa Domanska, and Hans Kellner, eds., *Re-Figuring Hayden White*
Michael Rothberg, *Multidirectional Memory: Remembering the Holocaust in the Age of Decolonization*
Jean-François Lyotard, *Enthusiasm: The Kantian Critique of History*
Ernst van Alphen, Mieke Bal, and Carel Smith, eds., *The Rhetoric of Sincerity*
Stéphane Mosès, *The Angel of History: Rosenzweig, Benjamin, Scholem*

Alexandre Lefebvre, *The Image of the Law: Deleuze, Bergson, Spinoza*
Samira Haj, *Reconfiguring Islamic Tradition: Reform, Rationality, and Modernity*
Diane Perpich, *The Ethics of Emmanuel Levinas*
Marcel Detienne, *Comparing the Incomparable*
François Delaporte, *Anatomy of the Passions*
René Girard, *Mimesis and Theory: Essays on Literature and Criticism, 1959-2005*
Richard Baxstrom, *Houses in Motion: The Experience of Place and the Problem of Belief in Urban Malaysia*
Jennifer L. Culbert, *Dead Certainty: The Death Penalty and the Problem of Judgment*
Samantha Frost, *Lessons from a Materialist Thinker: Hobbesian Reflections on Ethics and Politics*
Regina Mara Schwartz, *Sacramental Poetics at the Dawn of Secularism: When God Left the World*
Gil Anidjar, *Semites: Race, Religion, Literature*
Ranjana Khanna, *Algeria Cuts: Women and Representation, 1830 to the Present*
Esther Peeren, *Intersubjectivities and Popular Culture: Bakhtin and Beyond*
Eyal Peretz, *Becoming Visionary: Brian De Palma's Cinematic Education of the Senses*
Diana Sorensen, *A Turbulent Decade Remembered: Scenes from the Latin American Sixties*
Hubert Damisch, *A Childhood Memory by Piero della Francesca*
José van Dijck, *Mediated Memories in the Digital Age*
Dana Hollander, *Exemplarity and Chosenness: Rosenzweig and Derrida on the Nation of Philosophy*
Asja Szafraniec, *Beckett, Derrida, and the Event of Literature*
Sara Guyer, *Romanticism After Auschwitz*
Alison Ross, *The Aesthetic Paths of Philosophy: Presentation in Kant, Heidegger, Lacoue-Labarthe, and Nancy*
Gerhard Richter, *Thought-Images: Frankfurt School Writers' Reflections from Damaged Life*
Bella Brodzki, *Can These Bones Live? Translation, Survival, and Cultural Memory*
Rodolphe Gasché, *The Honor of Thinking: Critique, Theory, Philosophy*
Brigitte Peucker, *The Material Image: Art and the Real in Film*

Natalie Melas, *All the Difference in the World: Postcoloniality and the Ends of Comparison*

Jonathan Culler, *The Literary in Theory*

Michael G. Levine, *The Belated Witness: Literature, Testimony, and the Question of Holocaust Survival*

Jennifer A. Jordan, *Structures of Memory: Understanding German Change in Berlin and Beyond*

Christoph Menke, *Reflections of Equality*

Marlène Zarader, *The Unthought Debt: Heidegger and the Hebraic Heritage*

Jan Assmann, *Religion and Cultural Memory: Ten Studies*

David Scott and Charles Hirschkind, *Powers of the Secular Modern: Talal Asad and His Interlocutors*

Gyanendra Pandey, *Routine Violence: Nations, Fragments, Histories*

James Siegel, *Naming the Witch*

J. M. Bernstein, *Against Voluptuous Bodies: Late Modernism and the Meaning of Painting*

Theodore W. Jennings, Jr., *Reading Derrida / Thinking Paul: On Justice*

Richard Rorty and Eduardo Mendieta, *Take Care of Freedom and Truth Will Take Care of Itself: Interviews with Richard Rorty*

Jacques Derrida, *Paper Machine*

Renaud Barbaras, *Desire and Distance: Introduction to a Phenomenology of Perception*

Jill Bennett, *Empathic Vision: Affect, Trauma, and Contemporary Art*

Ban Wang, *Illuminations from the Past: Trauma, Memory, and History in Modern China*

James Phillips, *Heidegger's Volk: Between National Socialism and Poetry*

Frank Ankersmit, *Sublime Historical Experience*

István Rév, *Retroactive Justice: Prehistory of Post-Communism*

Paola Marrati, *Genesis and Trace: Derrida Reading Husserl and Heidegger*

Krzysztof Ziarek, *The Force of Art*

Marie-José Mondzain, *Image, Icon, Economy: The Byzantine Origins of the Contemporary Imaginary*

Cecilia Sjöholm, *The Antigone Complex: Ethics and the Invention of Feminine Desire*

Jacques Derrida and Elisabeth Roudinesco, *For What Tomorrow . . . : A Dialogue*

Elisabeth Weber, *Questioning Judaism: Interviews by Elisabeth Weber*

Jacques Derrida and Catherine Malabou, *Counterpath: Traveling with Jacques Derrida*

Martin Seel, *Aesthetics of Appearing*

Nanette Salomon, *Shifting Priorities: Gender and Genre in Seventeenth-Century Dutch Painting*

Jacob Taubes, *The Political Theology of Paul*

Jean-Luc Marion, *The Crossing of the Visible*

Eric Michaud, *The Cult of Art in Nazi Germany*

Anne Freadman, *The Machinery of Talk: Charles Peirce and the Sign Hypothesis*

Stanley Cavell, *Emerson's Transcendental Etudes*

Stuart McLean, *The Event and Its Terrors: Ireland, Famine, Modernity*

Beate Rössler, ed., *Privacies: Philosophical Evaluations*

Bernard Faure, *Double Exposure: Cutting Across Buddhist and Western Discourses*

Alessia Ricciardi, *The Ends of Mourning: Psychoanalysis, Literature, Film*

Alain Badiou, *Saint Paul: The Foundation of Universalism*

Gil Anidjar, *The Jew, the Arab: A History of the Enemy*

Jonathan Culler and Kevin Lamb, eds., *Just Being Difficult? Academic Writing in the Public Arena*

Jean-Luc Nancy, *A Finite Thinking*, edited by Simon Sparks

Theodor W. Adorno, *Can One Live after Auschwitz? A Philosophical Reader*, edited by Rolf Tiedemann

Patricia Pisters, *The Matrix of Visual Culture: Working with Deleuze in Film Theory*

Andreas Huyssen, *Present Pasts: Urban Palimpsests and the Politics of Memory*

Talal Asad, *Formations of the Secular: Christianity, Islam, Modernity*

Dorothea von Mücke, *The Rise of the Fantastic Tale*

Marc Redfield, *The Politics of Aesthetics: Nationalism, Gender, Romanticism*

Emmanuel Levinas, *On Escape*

Dan Zahavi, *Husserl's Phenomenology*

Rodolphe Gasché, *The Idea of Form: Rethinking Kant's Aesthetics*

Michael Naas, *Taking on the Tradition: Jacques Derrida and the Legacies of Deconstruction*

Herlinde Pauer-Studer, ed., *Constructions of Practical Reason: Interviews on Moral and Political Philosophy*

Jean-Luc Marion, *Being Given That: Toward a Phenomenology of Givenness*

Theodor W. Adorno and Max Horkheimer, *Dialectic of Enlightenment*

Ian Balfour, *The Rhetoric of Romantic Prophecy*

Martin Stokhof, *World and Life as One: Ethics and Ontology in Wittgenstein's Early Thought*

Gianni Vattimo, *Nietzsche: An Introduction*

Jacques Derrida, *Negotiations: Interventions and Interviews, 1971-1998*, ed. Elizabeth Rottenberg

Brett Levinson, *The Ends of Literature: The Latin American "Boom" in the Neoliberal Marketplace*

Timothy J. Reiss, *Against Autonomy: Cultural Instruments, Mutualities, and the Fictive Imagination*

Hent de Vries and Samuel Weber, eds., *Religion and Media*

Niklas Luhmann, *Theories of Distinction: Re-Describing the Descriptions of Modernity*, ed. and introd. William Rasch

Johannes Fabian, *Anthropology with an Attitude: Critical Essays*

Michel Henry, *I Am the Truth: Toward a Philosophy of Christianity*

Gil Anidjar, *"Our Place in Al-Andalus": Kabbalah, Philosophy, Literature in Arab-Jewish Letters*

Hélène Cixous and Jacques Derrida, *Veils*

F. R. Ankersmit, *Historical Representation*

F. R. Ankersmit, *Political Representation*

Elissa Marder, *Dead Time: Temporal Disorders in the Wake of Modernity (Baudelaire and Flaubert)*

Reinhart Koselleck, *The Practice of Conceptual History: Timing History, Spacing Concepts*

Niklas Luhmann, *The Reality of the Mass Media*

Hubert Damisch, *A Theory of /Cloud/: Toward a History of Painting*

Jean-Luc Nancy, *The Speculative Remark: (One of Hegel's bon mots)*

Jean-François Lyotard, *Soundproof Room: Malraux's Anti-Aesthetics*

Jan Patočka, *Plato and Europe*

Hubert Damisch, *Skyline: The Narcissistic City*

Isabel Hoving, *In Praise of New Travelers: Reading Caribbean Migrant Women Writers*

Richard Rand, ed., *Futures: Of Jacques Derrida*

William Rasch, *Niklas Luhmann's Modernity: The Paradoxes of Differentiation*

Jacques Derrida and Anne Dufourmantelle, *Of Hospitality*

Jean-François Lyotard, *The Confession of Augustine*

Kaja Silverman, *World Spectators*

Samuel Weber, *Institution and Interpretation: Expanded Edition*

Jeffrey S. Librett, *The Rhetoric of Cultural Dialogue: Jews and Germans in the Epoch of Emancipation*

Ulrich Baer, *Remnants of Song: Trauma and the Experience of Modernity in Charles Baudelaire and Paul Celan*

Samuel C. Wheeler III, *Deconstruction as Analytic Philosophy*

David S. Ferris, *Silent Urns: Romanticism, Hellenism, Modernity*

Rodolphe Gasché, *Of Minimal Things: Studies on the Notion of Relation*

Sarah Winter, *Freud and the Institution of Psychoanalytic Knowledge*

Samuel Weber, *The Legend of Freud: Expanded Edition*

Aris Fioretos, ed., *The Solid Letter: Readings of Friedrich Hölderlin*

J. Hillis Miller / Manuel Asensi, *Black Holes / J. Hillis Miller; or, Boustrophedonic Reading*

Miryam Sas, *Fault Lines: Cultural Memory and Japanese Surrealism*

Peter Schwenger, *Fantasm and Fiction: On Textual Envisioning*

Didier Maleuvre, *Museum Memories: History, Technology, Art*

Jacques Derrida, *Monolingualism of the Other; or, The Prosthesis of Origin*

Andrew Baruch Wachtel, *Making a Nation, Breaking a Nation: Literature and Cultural Politics in Yugoslavia*

Niklas Luhmann, *Love as Passion: The Codification of Intimacy*

Mieke Bal, ed., *The Practice of Cultural Analysis: Exposing Interdisciplinary Interpretation*

Jacques Derrida and Gianni Vattimo, eds., *Religion*

The authorized representative in the EU for product safety and compliance is:
Mare Nostrum Group
B.V Doelen 72
4831 GR Breda
The Netherlands

www.ingramcontent.com/pod-product-compliance
Lightning Source LLC
Chambersburg PA
CBHW030336240426
43661CB00052B/1652